WALTER BENJAMIN AND ROMANTICISM

RENEWALS 458-4574
DATE DUE

WALTER BENJAMIN STUDIES SERIES

Series Editors: Andrew Benjamin, Monash University, and Beatrice Hanssen, University of Georgia.

Consultant Board: Stanley Cavell, Sander Gilman, Miriam Hansen, Carol Jacobs, Martin Jay, Gertrud Koch, Peter Osborne, Sigrid Weigel and Anthony Phelan.

A series devoted to the writings of Walter Benjamin – each volume will focus on a theme central to contemporary work on Benjamin. The series aims to set new standards for scholarship on Benjamin for students and researchers in Philosophy, Cultural Studies and Literary Studies.

WALTER BENJAMIN AND ROMANTICISM

Edited by
**BEATRICE HANSSEN AND
ANDREW BENJAMIN**

continuum
NEW YORK • LONDON

Continuum

The Tower Building, 11 York Road, London SE1 7NX

370 Lexington Avenue, New York, NY 10017-6503

First published 2002

British Library Cataloguing-in-Publication Data
A catalogue record for this book is available from the British Library.

ISBN 0-8264-6020-8 (hardback)
     0-8264-6021-6 (paperback)

Typeset by Aarontype Limited, Easton, Bristol
Printed and bound in Great Britain by Biddles Ltd, Guildford and King's Lynn

CONTENTS

Acknowledgements   vi
Abbreviations   vii

Walter Benjamin's Critical Romanticism: An Introduction
BEATRICE HANSSEN and ANDREW BENJAMIN   1

Part I   Walter Benjamin and the Early Romantics   7

 1   Introduction to Walter Benjamin's *The Concept of Art Criticism
     in German Romanticism* PHILIPPE LACOUE-LABARTHE   9
 2   Walter Benjamin's Exposition of the Romantic Theory of
     Reflection WINFRIED MENNINGHAUS   19
 3   The Sober Absolute: On Benjamin and the Early Romantics
     RODOLPHE GASCHÉ   51
 4   *Fortgang* and *Zusammenhang*: Walter Benjamin and the
     Romantic Novel ANTHONY PHELAN   69
 5   'However one calls into the forest ...': Echoes of Translation
     BETTINE MENKE   83
 6   Unfolding: Reading After Romanticism JOSH COHEN   98
 7   The Absolute as Translatability: Working through Walter
     Benjamin on Language ANDREW BENJAMIN   109
 8   Jena Romanticism and Benjamin's Critical Epistemology
     FRED RUSH   123

Part II   Beyond Early Romanticism: Benjamin, Hölderlin, Goethe   137

 9   'Dichtermut' and 'Blödigkeit' – Two Poems by Friedrich
     Hölderlin, Interpreted by Walter Benjamin BEATRICE HANSSEN   139
10   Poetry's Courage PHILIPPE LACOUE-LABARTHE   163
11   Benjamin's Affinity: Goethe, the Romantics and the Pure
     Problem of Criticism DAVID S. FERRIS   180
12   The Artwork as Breach of a Beyond: On the Dialectic of
     Divine and Human Order in Walter Benjamin's 'Goethe's
     Elective Affinities' SIGRID WEIGEL   197

Notes   207
Contributors   243
Index   245

ACKNOWLEDGEMENTS

Philippe Lacoue-Labarthe, 'Introduction to Walter Benjamin's *The Concept of Art Criticism in German Romanticism*' and Rodolphe Gasché, 'The Sober Absolute: On Benjamin and the Early Romantics', are reprinted from *Studies in Romanticism* 31 (Winter 1992), courtesy of the Trustees of Boston University.

Philippe Lacoue-Labarthe, 'Poetry's Courage', is reprinted by courtesy of Stanford University Press.

Winfried Menninghaus, 'Walter Benjamin's Exposition of the Romantic Theory of Reflection' and Bettine Menke, '"However one calls into the forest …": Echoes of Translation', both appear in translation by courtesy of Suhrkamp (Frankfurt a. M.).

ABBREVIATIONS

Note: Abbreviations of works are explained as they occur in each chapter. The following abbreviations of Benjamin's works are used throughout:

GS   *Walter Benjamin: Gesammelte Schriften*, ed. Rolf Tiedemann and Hermann Schweppenhäuser (Frankfurt a. M.: Suhrkamp, 1974–).
SW   Walter Benjamin, *Selected Writings* (2 vols), ed. Marcus Bullock and Michael Jennings (Cambridge, MA/London: Belknap Press/Harvard University Press, 1996–7).

WALTER BENJAMIN'S CRITICAL ROMANTICISM

AN INTRODUCTION

Beatrice Hanssen and Andrew Benjamin

The writings of the Early Romantics (*Frühromantik*)[1] have left a complex philosophical legacy. Perhaps the most insistent question marking that legacy concerns the nature of the constellation that Early Romanticism, particularly the work of Friedrich Schlegel and Novalis, entertains to the present. What, in other words, is the relationship between Early Romanticism and modernity? This question appears important for at least two reasons. First, Early Romanticism ushered in a new philosophy of history and understanding of historical time as prophetic renewal and infinite becoming in the present, whose revolutionary potential, according to its programmatic journal, *Athenaeum*, was to be actualized through unprecedented interpretive and poetic practices. The second reason for rethinking the connection between Early Romanticism and modernity is that integral to the legacy of the former is the centrality of criticism (*Kritik*). Criticism, as conceived by the Romantic movement, did not simply amount to a subject-centred, speculative appropriation of the object under analysis or to the passing of judgment in evaluation. Rather, Romantic criticism demanded an altogether different thinking, indeed 'activation', of the object and hence a different construction of the artwork; it was variously conceived as the fragment, the project, the experiment or as poetry (*Poesie*) – that is, poetry as the progressive, universal project of production and becoming.[2] Moreover, while the post-Kantian Romanticism, inaugurated by Schlegel and Novalis, sought to overcome the negativism of Kant's critical philosophy (*Ath*. fgm. 3), partly by turning to the perceived 'positivism' of Fichte's philosophy of reflection, it still modelled itself on Kant's transcendental method. For, just as critical philosophy brought the producing instance to presentation (*Darstellung*) in presenting the product, so the Jena Romantics aimed to compose not just poetry but a 'poetry of poetry' (*Ath*. fgm. 238), and not just criticism but a 'criticism (*Kritik*) of criticism'. Set up as a collaborative, dialogical critical project, always in process, Early Romanticism understood itself as a comprehensive attempt to think through the nature of criticism, the centrality of the object, and, in the final analysis, the work of art.

Placed within this context, then, it becomes clear just how exceptional Walter Benjamin's early research on Schlegel and Novalis really was, when it was conceived in 1918–19. For, in his critical appraisal of Early Romanticism, Benjamin did not merely seek to record the epistemological presuppositions and aesthetic principles of Romantic criticism. Rather, determined to 'potentiate', that is, to reveal the contemporary potential of their 'idea' of art and criticism, he ultimately hoped to devise a philosophical critique of the artwork with an unabated 'relevance to the present'.[3]

Benjamin's engagement with Early Romanticism forms a vital part of his early philosophical and literary critical project. Having relinquished his original plans to dedicate his dissertation to Kant, he completed his doctoral dissertation in philosophy, titled 'The Concept of Criticism in German Romanticism' (*Der Begriff der Kunstkritik in der deutschen Romantik*), at the University of Bern (1918–19, published 1920).[4] The study defines a crucial stage in his attempt to overcome the *Erlebnis* ideology of the early twentieth century, expressed, for example, in the worship of the poet-hero that marked Stefan George's circle and Friedrich Gundolf's criticism, or in the subjectivism that underpinned Wilhelm Dilthey's *Das Erlebnis und die Dichtung* (*Experience and Poetry*) (1905). For, at the crux of Romantic philosophy stood the *work*, and, fundamentally, the 'criticizability of the work of art' (*SW* 1: 179), not the artist or creator. 'Only since Romanticism', Benjamin wrote to his friend Gershom Scholem in 1918, as he was trying to formulate the first outline of the dissertation topic,

> has the following view become predominant: that a *work* of art in and of itself, and without reference to theory or morality, can be understood in contemplation alone, and that the person contemplating it can do it justice. The relative autonomy of the *work* of art *vis-à-vis* art, or better, its exclusively transcendental dependence on art, has become the prerequisite of Romantic art criticism. I would undertake to prove that, in this regard, Kant's aesthetics constitute the underlying premise of Romantic art criticism.[5]

The resulting dissertation provided an unconventional interpretation of Early Romanticism. Sometimes at the expense of philological rigour, it chemically extracted a Romantic philosophy of art from Schlegel and Novalis's notebooks, lectures, poetry, critical and philosophical fragments. Where the study's first part turned to the movement's theory of knowledge, rooted in Fichtean reflection, which provided the grounding of its art criticism, the second part sought to come to terms with art criticism's potential to disclose the absolute through the artwork's form; Romantic criticism thus bore witness to what Benjamin called 'mystical formalism' (*SW* 1: 123). Steeped himself in a critique of subject philosophy, Benjamin was to find in the Early Romantics a theory of *objective*, 'I-less' reflection, anchored in critical activity and the autonomous work, as well as a concept of critique akin to objective irony. As the reflective, infinite potentiation of the seed of reflection embedded in the individual work, the Romantics' object-centred, 'formalist' criticism successfully surmounted the subjective Idealism of Fichte's *Über den Begriff der Wissenschaftslehre* (*On the Concept of the Science of Knowledge* [1794]), while providing a philosophical antidote to the irrationalism of the prevailing literary climate. Through the reflective interplay between critical activity and the object of criticism, the work of art was brought to completion or fulfilment, meaning that its participation in the Absolute was consummated. Through such 'perfecting, positive criticism' (*SW* 1:154), the artwork was 'romanticized', 'potentiated' (Novalis), or 'absolutized'. No longer the activity of a human or philosophical subject, reflection amounted to an organic process, a continuum, or medium, of immediate reflections, in which reflective centres were connected in infinite systematicity.

What seemed to have struck a responsive chord in Benjamin was the Early Romantics' project to 'philosophize about philosophy', especially their bid to undo modernity's pernicious philosophical problems (such as the object–subject divide or the mediacy–immediacy dichotomy) through the creation of a new mystical terminology. Benjamin was attracted to Schlegel's non-eidetic 'linguistic mysticism', which took the form of the aphorism, the arabesque, the fragment, the *Witz* and critique. Instead of signalling confusion or lack of systematicity, Schlegel's mystical terminology sought 'to grasp the system absolutely' (*SW* 1:138). By transforming reflection into an 'immediate thinking' and an infinite, absolute medium of interconnected immediacies, Schlegel first of all did away with Kant's dichotomy between the mediate (universalizing) concept and immediate (singular) intuition (*Anschauung*). Second, the Early Romantics thus also managed to secure a positive concept of infinitude – unlike Fichte, who rejected infinite reflection as empty regression – which they embraced in a veritable 'cult of the infinite' (*SW* 1:125). But it was Novalis's mystical terminology which would exert a lasting fascination over Benjamin. Using terms such as 'experiment' and 'perception', Novalis's philosophy of nature revealed a theory of knowledge that successfully dissolved the rigid subject–object correlation. In this near-magical process of reflection, humans and natural objects seemed to interpenetrate one another in Democritean fashion.[6] As 'relative unities of reflection' (*SW* 1:146), 'the thing and knowing being [merged] into each other', showing that Novalis's philosophy of nature was closely related to Goethe's 'tender empiria' (*zarte Empirie*) – a style of empiricism that '[conformed] intimately to its object and that, through identification with it, [became] its true and proper theory' (*SW* 1:192n.). As these and similar observations indicate, then, it is not unlikely that Benjamin saw his own encounter with religious experience and a language-based mysticism, influenced by the Cabbala, mirrored in the Early Romantics' theory of criticism and mystical formalism. Tempering the sometimes hubristic pretensions of Schlegel's self-indulgent irony, Benjamin conceived of the romanticized art object as the quasi-mystical disclosure of the Absolute, in which it partook through its sober form.

If Benjamin's entire œuvre, throughout the various stages of his intellectual and ideological development, can be interpreted as a never-ending engagement with the (sober) limits of critique, then his dissertation marks a decisive stage along the way. From his earliest theological work to his materialist theory of cultural analysis – consecrated in the monumental, unfinished *Arcades Project* – Benjamin was concerned with the dialectic between profane modes of reading and the encounter with the Absolute, moving eventually to what the Surrealism essay would call 'profane illumination'. Schlegel and Novalis provided the first principles of a theory that reflected the Absolute in the artwork and the artwork in the Absolute, opening up onto an 'aesthetic Absolute', or, as Lacoue-Labarthe and Nancy have termed it, a 'literary Absolute'.[7] Enthralled by their literary journal, the *Athenaeum*, Benjamin not only invoked its moral superiority to reject an invitation to contribute to Martin Buber's *Der Jude*,[8] but his own planned journal *Angelus Novus* was to claim the 'historical relevance' that the revered Romantic model aptly embodied (*SW* 1: 292). In his 'Announcement of the Journal *Angelus Novus*' (1922), Benjamin proclaimed that, in the contemporary cultural climate, both 'critical discourse and the habit of judgment stand in need of renewal'. If a destructive criticism was to take on the obscurantism of 'literary Expressionism', then 'the task of positive criticism, even more than before and even more than for the Romantics, must be to concentrate on the individual work of art. For the function of great criticism', he added, 'is not, as is often thought, to instruct by means of historical descriptions or to educate through comparisons, but to cognize by immersing itself in the object' (*SW* 1: 293).[9]

As this programmatic announcement indicates, it would take Benjamin some time to acquire a critical distance from the Early Romantic project. Thus, its principle of critical 'potentiation' showed marked affinities to Benjamin's theory that translation, and translatability, ensured the survival of the artwork, *despite* the fact that, in 'The Task of the Translator' (1921, 1923), he characterized Romantic criticism as a 'lesser factor in the continued life of literary works' (*SW* 1: 258).[10] The move from the aesthetic Absolute to a dialectical theory that considered the correlation between secular modernity and the abscondence of the Absolute required a moment of transition, made possible by the *Origin of the German Trauerspiel* (1925, published 1928). It is here, in his *Habilitation* thesis, that Benjamin would start to cast doubt on the merits of a Romantic, reflective criticism that proceeded through 'potentiation' and a (melancholic) immersion in the object. Letting go of the critical task of perfectability, perfection and completion, he now called for critical labour as an act of 'mortification'. Understanding the allegorical Baroque as a more radical cultural period, he dismissed the presuppositions of an aestheticizing era in the thrall of the 'aesthetic symbol', mainstreamed by (a certain) Romanticism; instead, he argued for the retrieval of another temporality, expressed in the dialectical operations of allegory. Aware of the incongruity of the Absolute in a secular age, the *Trauerspiel* book gave up Schlegel's reflective fragment, which, for all its claims to constitutive incompleteness, still functioned within an idealistic framework of organic totality, exemplified in *Ath.* fgm. 206: 'A fragment, like a miniature work of art, has to be entirely isolated from the surrounding world and be complete in itself like a porcupine.'[11] Instead, Benjamin was to dedicate himself to modernity's physiognomy of ruins, to the allegorical narrative of death or the jagged line that separated nature and history from the plenitude of meaning. However, though Benjamin now rejected the criticism of reflective potentiation, he still extolled Novalis for being one of the first thinkers (together with Jean

Paul and Hölderlin) to have understood the essence of allegorical fragmentation.[12] What is more, despite his increasing awareness of the 'untimeliness' of the Romantic project under altered historical circumstances, he never completely abandoned his indebtedness to and admiration of the Early Romantics. Again, the elective affinities he felt to Schlegel and Novalis to a large extent may have been roused by the perceived mysticism of these writers. Much as young Benjamin's early appreciation of Kant hailed the philosopher's mysticism (*SW* 1: 142), so he now chose to highlight the Early Romantics' esoteric side, turning a blind eye to Schlegel's sometimes more profane intentions.

As several passages in the dissertation indicate, Benjamin's understanding of Schlegel and Novalis was in decisive ways mediated through and guided by his study of Hölderlin and Goethe. For Benjamin, Hölderlin's fragment, '*unendlich genau zusammenhängen*' (to 'hang together infinitely [exactly]') (*SW* 1: 126), captured the philosophy of (objective) reflection and the 'continuum of (reflective) form' at the heart of Schlegel and Novalis's philosophy of art criticism. Even before the dissertation, Benjamin's magnificent essay, 'Two Poems by Friedrich Hölderlin "The Poet's Courage" and "Timidity"' (1914–15), performed a critical potentiation as it traced the 'poetized' (*Gedichtete*) through a comparative reading of Hölderlin's two odes, closing with a positive appraisal of the metaphysics of absolute, sober connections realized in 'Timidity'. Moreover, if the dissertation ended with a chapter setting Schlegel and Novalis's category of the idea ('infinity in totality', 'pure form') off from Goethe's conception of art in terms of the 'ideal' and (the Greek) 'prototype' ('unity in plurality', 'pure content'), then Benjamin's magisterial essay, 'Goethe's *Elective Affinities*' (1919–22, published 1924–25), formed the revised sequel to that analysis. Taking the concept of *Kritik* even further, Benjamin now distinguished between the *Sach-* and *Wahrheitsgehalt* (material and truth contents) of Goethe's novel, between commentary and criticism. As he developed a more sustained critique of mere aestheticism, of George and Gundolf, his essay opened up the ethico-theological dimension of Goethe's novel by mooring it in Hölderlin's understanding of the caesura.

Mindful of the complexities that accompany Benjamin's intricate engagement with the Early Romantics, this volume, the inaugural instalment of a new book series, *Walter Benjamin Studies*, for the first time brings together, in comprehensive fashion, representative research that has emerged in this field. The chapters in this volume have been divided into two areas of analysis. Part I discusses Benjamin's intense dialogue with the Early Romantics, notably Schlegel and Novalis, including a history of that engagement and the consequences of it either for the practice of criticism or for a philosophy of language. Part II expands the scope of these questions by treating Benjamin's writings on Goethe and Hölderlin; for, though Hölderlin hardly was a member of the Romantic movement proper, and though Goethe's commentary was full of sceptical appraisals of the Romantics, Benjamin's own encounter with Jena Romanticism almost always transpired in dialogue with these two authors (much, indeed, as the Early

Romantics developed their theory of poetry and criticism in reaction to the magnitude of Goethe's *Wilhelm Meister*).

Taken together, these contributions comprise one of the first sustained attempts to analyse the complexities that marked Benjamin's relationship to Early Romanticism, no less than to Goethe and Hölderlin. Yet, beyond adding to the philological and philosophical understanding of Benjamin's work, this volume hopes to achieve yet another task: that of activating the critical seed sheltered in Benjamin's early work, so as to ask what its translatability – its critical potential and bearings – might be for contemporary concerns with the nature of criticism, historical time, and the object of criticism (the work of art). Inasmuch as contemporary criticism and critical theory do not cease probing the nature of the object of critical activity, such undertakings are still in some way indebted to the large-scale enquiry of *Kritik* initiated by Early Romanticism. How might, then, such contemporary debates be constrained to work through Benjamin's critical heritage, and, crucially, his very own programmatic account of Early Romanticism? Involved in a complex act of translation, these timely responses to Benjamin's Early Romanticism engage with the nature of criticism and therefore with the philosophical and literary-critical dimensions of that engagement.

PART I

WALTER BENJAMIN AND THE
EARLY ROMANTICS

1

INTRODUCTION TO WALTER BENJAMIN'S *THE CONCEPT OF ART CRITICISM IN GERMAN ROMANTICISM**

Philippe Lacoue-Labarthe

The Concept of Art Criticism in German Romanticism is the doctoral dissertation of Walter Benjamin. He defended the thesis successfully in June 1919 (he was then twenty-seven years old) before the faculty of philosophy at the University of Bern; he was awarded *summa cum laude* and the director of his dissertation, Richard Herbertz (who advised Benjamin to continue his work in order to obtain his Habilitation and consequently begin a university career) accepted his essay in the collection he edited for the publisher Francke in Bern. The book was printed in Berlin under the care of the bookseller Arthur Scholem – the father of Gershom, the most intimate friend of Benjamin – and it appeared simultaneously in 1920 in Bern and Berlin under two slightly different titles:[1]

1. Dr Walter Benjamin: *The Concept of Art Criticism in German Romanticism*. Bern: Francke, 1920. (New Bern Essays on Philosophy and its History. Edited by Richard Herbertz. No. 5.)
2. *The Concept of Art Criticism in German Romanticism*. Inaugural dissertation in the Faculty of Philosophy of the University of Bern for the award of the doctorate. Presented by Walter Benjamin in Berlin. Berlin: Arthur Scholem, 1920.

This university success was the last that Benjamin was to know. Constrained, by financial reasons, to leave Berlin (his family home), he tried to present, five years later, his work on the German mourning play as his thesis for the

* Translated by David Ferris. The above essay is a translation of the introduction to the French edition of Walter Benjamin's *The Concept of Art Criticism in German Romanticism* (*Le Concept de critique esthétique dans le romantisme allemand* [Paris: Flammarion, 1986], pp. 7–23). Thanks are due to Philippe Lacoue-Labarthe and Flammarion for permitting this text to be translated and published here. All passages from Benjamin's works and letters have been translated from the original.

Habilitation. But in vain; this book, in particular its form, was judged unacceptable if not also quite 'unreadable'. As a result, Benjamin was separated definitively from a university career.[2]

Properly speaking, the dissertation of 1920 is the sole academic work by Benjamin. In justice, it is true that it was not without difficulty or reticence that Benjamin accepted submission to the discipline (he would not have been able to say, the exigence) of the university. Even though, by vocation, he knew himself to be already engaged on a quite different path, Benjamin yielded to this discipline momentarily; to him all means were good in order to deceive the institution, which is to say, the genre imposed upon him. The dilemma was between writing a dissertation or a book (a work). *The Concept of Art Criticism* is (still) a work of compromise. Despite one or two concessions, this would not be the case for the book on the German tragic drama.

What discouraged Benjamin in this type of writing and what made him disassociate it with the greatest vigour from his personal work was not the 'labour'; on the contrary, it was first and foremost the convention. A letter from November 1918 to his friend Ernst Schoen opens with this unemphatic declaration which possesses, all the same, an infallible justice: 'On every occasion that one makes an allowance for convention, it draws attention to itself, disturbing intimate friends, especially if this convention is perceived as only a convention. So it is with the doctoral exam for which I am preparing.'[3] Since the subject is the university, convention signifies, of course, the scholarly character of the required work. It is in this sense that Benjamin can still write to the same friend on the eve of his defence: 'For now, it is difficult for me to speak to you about my work because it is suspended on account of the exam. Now, I have simply to study in the most scholarly manner because of the exam, the fewer relations I have with the examiners, the higher the demands placed upon me here' (*Briefe* 1:210). Beneath the banality of this statement there is, in reality, something quite different. The hostility of Benjamin to the university was not at all gratuitous, such hostility being itself conventional as was often the case at this time; nor does it arise from the 'singularity' of Benjamin, from his desire for independence or from his stubborn or easily offended character. This hostility was philosophical and, as such, it was on a level with that of Nietzsche and Heidegger: it concerned the essence of knowledge and the very high opinion that Benjamin accorded [things] of the mind and the work of thinking (that is, of art as well). It would be necessary to reread on this point the crucial pages that Benjamin wrote at the age of twenty-two on 'The Life of Students' and which are perhaps among the two or three last great texts on the university bequeathed by the philosophical tradition.[4]

Such a hostility, at the time when Benjamin wrote his thesis, was concentrated on the radical incapacity in which the university found itself, on a state of literary study unable to recognize the proper dignity of language; it is this scorn for language that offended Benjamin most deeply. Again, to the same correspondent, he writes in July 1918:

Today, in my reading for the dissertation, I came across by chance a book by a woman, Luise Zurlinden, *Gedanken Platons in der deutschen Romantik* [Platonic Thought in German Romanticism (Leipzig, 1910)]. The horror that overcomes one when women wish to join in the discussion of these critical matters is indescribable. It is truly a baseness. Moreover, the estimation generally accorded to the Romantics, in particular the Schlegel brothers and above all Wilhelm (who is evidently less important than Friedrich), is indicative of the ignominy which stands as the principle of all literary scholarship. In many periods there has been sterile scholarship, certainly more sterile than in our own time; the shamelessness of scholarly study is however modern. Thus, according to our current experts, translation is considered, on principle, as an inferior kind of production (because, naturally, they do not feel comfortable until they have put everything into headings according to the crudest criteria) and, about Wilhelm Schlegel's achievement as a translator, one dares to speak of an 'identification through feeling'. This tone is customary. (*Briefe* 1: 199)

Here, let us not try to pick up a misogyny that is only too obvious (this was not always the case with Benjamin) even if it is this misogyny that dictates slyly the use of the word shamelessness about modern scholarship. As is the case in Nietzsche, and this is what needs to be retained, the accusation can be summarized as follows: philology is unworthy of its name. These sentences were written by the Benjamin who, several years later in the preface to his translation of Baudelaire's *Tableaux parisiens*, would explain 'the task of the translator'[5] by recalling the essential content of his first philosophical intuitions, at that time unpublished, 'On Language as Such and on the Language of Man'.[6] The task of the translator, he writes in one of those enigmatic and striking phrases of which he had the secret, is 'to buy back in one's own language the pure language exiled in the foreign language' and 'to liberate the language imprisoned in a work by transposing it'. Whatever he failed to make understood by this definition (and it is beyond the present context to attempt to comment on it), it is clear that it rests on a concept of 'pure language'. In fact, it is this concept of pure language that Benjamin always has in mind when he speaks of the dignity of language or about language in its essence. 'Pure language' is language after the manner of the divine word that names and creates the world in Genesis (or after the manner of the highest poetry when it seeks to be equal to the language of Eden, for example, in Hölderlin) in so far as it is not an instrument or a means of communication: pure language is a purely intransitive language.[7] It is such a concept of language (esoteric or mystic according to the words of Benjamin and at bottom very close to the concept Heidegger elaborates in the same years) that underlies his own practice of writing and made him judge intolerable 'the obligation to transparency' that had been placed upon him by the University (or no matter what other institution with a spiritual pretension that failed to institute itself on a radical questioning of the facts or alleged facts regarding language). It is perhaps while explaining his refusal to contribute to a journal (*Der Jude*, directed by Martin Buber) that Benjamin expressed himself with the greatest clarity on this subject. Let me cite this passage at length:

> It is a widespread and dominant opinion, held nearly everywhere as self-evident, that literature can have an influence on both the world of ethics and on human actions by furnishing reasons for those actions. In this respect, language is only a means of *preparing*, more or less suggestively, reasons which, in the depths of the soul, govern the person who acts. It is characteristic of this point of view that a relationship of language to act in which the former would not be a medium for the latter is not taken into account at all. This relation views language as powerless, degraded to pure means; it views writing as a miserable, feeble act whose source does not lie in itself but rather in motives that can be enunciated and expressed ...
>
> Whatever its effect, poetic, prophetic, objective, I can, in general, only understand literature as *magical*, that is, un*media*table. Every salutary, yes, every act of writing which is not catastrophic in its innermost nature has its root in mystery (of a word, of language). Although language may appear to be effective in so many forms, it will not be so through the mediation of its content; rather it will be effective through the purest opening up of its dignity and essence. And, if I disregard other forms of its effectiveness – such as poetry and prophecy – it seems to me, over and over again, that the elimination of the unsayable in language so that language attains the purity of crystal is the form given to us and most accessible to us in order to have an effect within language and, by this means, through language. This elimination of the unsayable seems to me to coincide with an authentically objective, sober style of writing and to indicate the relation between language and act. My concept of a style and a writing at the same time objective and highly political is: to lead to what is refused to the word. Only where this sphere opens itself up in the unspeakable pure power of word-lessness can the magical spark between word and motivated act leap across. There, the unity of both is equally effective. Only the intensive orientation of a word towards the core of its innermost loss of speech penetrates into true effectiveness. I do not believe that the word stands further from the divine than 'effective' human actions, accordingly, it is not in any other way capable of leading to the divine than through itself and its own purity. As a means, it proliferates. (*Briefe* I: 126–7)

This page contains the poetic art of Benjamin. He remained faithful to it in all he wrote even if, in the brief quarter-century which was granted to him for this activity (in his eyes the highest of all because it was identical to thought itself even if in a conversation or a letter), his conception of language was able to, as one says, 'evolve'. The only occasion where it was lacking, if it is necessary, at the very least, to believe his own words, is the dissertation of 1920. Benjamin derived this art principally, but not exclusively, from the Romantics themselves.

In any case, it was in their school that he learnt that criticism belonged by right to literature (to what he persisted in calling *Dichtung*) or, that criticism was, in fact, in its purest demands, the accomplishment of literature. The letter to Martin Buber already cited says this expressly:

> For a journal, the language of poets, of prophets, or even of despots does not enter into consideration nor does song, the psalms or the command. Each of which may in their turn possess a quite different relation to the unsayable and may be the source of a quite different magic. Only that kind of writing which is objective is considered; whether a journal attains to it is, from a human point of view, truly difficult to know, and, to be sure, not many have. However, I think about the *Athenaeum*. (*Briefe* 1: 127)

If, by definition, the 'Dissertation' (the form) imposed on Benjamin turns him away from his own principles of writing, it is not perhaps chance that this dissertation (this book) took as its object the concept of criticism[8] and, more precisely, the Romantic concept of criticism. Nor is it by chance that this dissertation closes and culminates – without taking into account the appendix which possesses a quite different character – in an attempt to define the objectivity (or the sobriety) which is – but not exclusively in critical matters – the keyword, more Hölderlinian than Romantic, of Benjamin's understanding of writing and art.[9] The sole means at Benjamin's disposal to shield this dissertation from its lack of art, from the triviality of academia, was to consecrate it to the doctrine, as he says, where commentary is elevated to the dignity of a work of art. Failing to produce a writing that is itself 'esoteric', such a project was at least able to indicate the necessity of the esoteric that Benjamin referred to as objectivity, as sobriety.

Things, however, were not so simple. What Benjamin complained of constantly was an inability to accede to the esoteric aspect of Romanticism in his work, that is, an inability to accede to what he aspired to under the name of Romantic 'messianism'.

In a letter to Ernst Schoen of 7 April 1919, Benjamin writes:

> Several days ago I completed a draft of my dissertation. It has become what it ought to be: an indication of the true nature of Romanticism which is completely unknown to literary study. However, it is only communicated indirectly since I was unable to approach the core of Romanticism, its messianism (I have only treated its conception of art), still less anything else I consider to be of the highest degree without depriving myself of the required complex and conventional standpoint of scholarship which I distinguish from an authentic standpoint. Yet, from within this work, one might well be able to deduce the state of affairs that I would like to have attained in this work. (*Briefe* 1: 208)

Consequently, the dissertation remains on this side of what he would have needed to say, that is, what he would have needed to touch in order to attain the 'core' of Romanticism, its messianism. Such a messianism is what Benjamin calls the 'historic essence' of Romanticism. In the introduction to the dissertation, the section on the 'Limitations of the Question' is quite clear on this point:

> [This dissertation] does not make the attempt, often undertaken with insufficient means, to exhibit the historical essence of Romanticism; in other words, the questions germane to the philosophy of history remain out of play. Despite this, the statements that follow, especially in regard to the proper system of Friedrich Schlegel's thought and the early Romantic idea of art, contribute materials – but not the point of view – for a definition of this [historical] essence [of Romanticism].

In a note, and only in a note, Benjamin adds that 'this point of view must be sought in the messianism of Romanticism', in 'the revolutionary desire to realize the Kingdom of God', or, as a fragment from the *Athenaeum* puts it, in the desire to found a religion.

The treatment of these subjects was forbidden by the genre of the dissertation: mysticism and scientific (university) requirements were hardly compatible. Mysticism is untreatable. At the very best, Benjamin will maintain the hope that through his 'indirect' clues some 'perspicacious readers' (*Briefe* 1: 202–3) will even be able to recognize this 'objective element'.

But, in taking the point of view that regards messianism as the historical essence of Romanticism, it is not only 'the mode of questioning proper to philosophy, that is set aside (if one understands by 'philosophy of history' a simple area of philosophy defined by scholarship); it is philosophy in its essence. For Benjamin, philosophy is already and will always remain the thinking of history. From this angle, the dissertation bears witness to, in the eyes of Benjamin, an obstacle.

If one follows the genesis of the dissertation project in Benjamin's letters (and in particular the letters addressed to Scholem), everything turns around the name of Kant at the beginning. It is in a kind of repetition (prematurely Heideggerian, this is in 1917), in the 'repetition' and 'continuation' of Kant that the whole philosophical project of Benjamin is to be situated; and besides it is on this point that he felt himself to be in agreement without the least reserve, as far as he was concerned, with the study conducted by Scholem at the same time. The project is still undefined or, more exactly, empty:

> Without to this point having any proof to hand, I hold firm to the belief that, in the sense of philosophy and its doctrine, to which the Kantian system belongs if it does not even constitute it, it can never at any time be a question of shaking up, of overthrowing the Kantian system; on the contrary, it is a question of its granite-like solidity and its universal development. . . . It is solely in the sense of Kant and Plato and, along the way, I believe, by a revision and further development of Kant, that philosophy can become doctrine or, at the very least, be incorporated to it. (*Briefe* 1: 150)

The idea of such a repetition of Kant is so fundamental that Benjamin could even add: 'clear before me, I see the task of preserving what is essential in Kant's thought ...' What this essential consists of Benjamin does not truly know. However, he declares himself persuaded about one thing: 'whoever does not feel in Kant the striving after *the thought of doctrine itself* and whoever, with the greatest respect, does not seize it along with its literalness as a tradendum to be handed down does not know philosophy at all' (*Briefe* 1: 150). Consequently, Kant becomes the general name for the project of philosophy itself: this name entitles the will to philosophize and the support, the sole chance for a support, of tradition in the strong sense of a *tradendum*. It represents the imperative of thought. Moreover, this is not foreign to the 'philosophical style' of Kant – the prime example, in Benjamin, of objective or sober writing. The Kant of Benjamin is a fundamentally Romantic Kant:

> every critique of his philosophical style is ... sheer narrow-mindedness and vulgar gossip. It is absolutely true that in every great scientific creation art must be included (and vice versa) [the whole of Romanticism is here, above all in the 'vice versa' in which is summarized by a stroke everything that Benjamin calls esoteric] and, consequently, it is also my belief that the prose of Kant itself represents the threshold of a great prosaic art. If this were not the case, would the *Critique of Pure Reason* have shaken Kleist to the innermost reaches of his self?[10]

An 'esoteric' or 'messianic' Kant (it is true that the first project envisaged by Benjamin concerned the philosophy of history in Kant – a subject to which Benjamin would never return) in whose name, 'the ultimate metaphysical dignity of an intuition which wishes to be really canonical, will always be made apparent most clearly in its debate with history'. To put this another way, Benjamin adds, 'in the philosophy of history the specific kinship of philosophy with true doctrine will have to be made manifest most clearly; at this point, the subject of the historical development of knowledge that doctrine brings to completion will have to appear' (*Briefe* 1: 151–2).

'Doctrine' is what is sought after at the beginning. Doctrine: the secret core of philosophy, of thinking – and, consequently, the place where thought interrogates its own historical becoming. From this can be explained the first dissertation project, from 1917, about which Benjamin confided to Scholem: 'This winter I will begin to work on Kant and history. However, I do not know if I will find in the historical Kant the necessary positive content for this relation. The development of this study into my doctoral thesis depends on this' (*Briefe* 1: 151).

Without doubt, Benjamin does not exclude that 'the philosophy of Kant may be very undeveloped about this connection'. But, as Benjamin says, again in the same letter to Scholem: 'Considering the silence that dominates his philosophy of history one must believe this (or the contrary)' (*Briefe* 1: 152). The disappointment, however, would be very quick. Barely three months later, Benjamin announces to Scholem that he finds

Kant's reflections [on history] quite unsuitable as a starting point or authentic object of a self-contained study ... In Kant, [these reflections] are less concerned with history than certain historical constellations of ethical interest. And the ethical side of history as a subject of particular consideration is presented inaccessibly. (*Briefe* 1: 161)

This does not mean that Benjamin turns away from Kant. On the contrary, he reaffirms the significance of Kant during the same period ('the necessity of following literally the philosophy of Kant') and, moreover, it is at this moment that he considers for an instant a thesis devoted to the notion of the 'infinite task' in Kant (*Briefe* 1: 158–9 [cf, note 10 above]). However, Benjamin would not return to the first dissertation project.[11]

At this point, another (old) subject of preoccupation resurfaces: the Romantics. In fact, one is witnessing the repetition of an episode of little more than a year earlier: in June 1917, and again to the same Scholem, Benjamin declared that this resurfacing can be seen in the necessity of 'dropping' Kant for lack of time. Consequently, he announced that he was turning back to the Romantics:

I am directing myself first towards early Romanticism, above all, Friedrich Schlegel, then Novalis, August Wilhelm as well as Tieck and later, if possible, Schleiermacher. I start from a group of Friedrich Schlegel's fragments arranged according to their *systematically* fundamental ideas; it is a study I have thought about for a long time. Naturally, it is purely interpretative and whatever objective worth lies in it remains to be seen ... (*Briefe* 1: 137)

Benjamin's goal, from this moment, is very certain: what is to be attained is nothing other than 'doctrine' itself, or 'messianism' – the place where history and religion coincide:

The central issue for Early Romanticism is: religion and history. Its infinite depth and beauty compared to the whole of later Romanticism is that it did not invoke religious and historical facts for the inner bond of these two spheres but rather sought to produce this higher sphere in its own *thought* and life, in which both ought to coincide. From this resulted not religion but an atmosphere in which whatever was without it and whatever pretended to it was reduced to ashes. If Friedrich Schlegel had such a silent disintegration of Christianity in mind, it was not because he questioned its dogmatism but rather because its morality was not Romantic, that is, it was not silent and not alive enough and precisely because it appeared to him to be excited, manly (in the widest sense) and ultimately ahistorical. These words are not to be found in Schlegel, they are an interpretation; one *must* interpret (intelligibly) the Romantics. Friedrich Schlegel breathed in this spiritual fire longer than any other. ... Romanticism is surely the most recent movement which, once again, rescues tradition. Its premature attempt in this period and sphere was aimed at the senseless and orgiastic disclosure of all the secret sources of tradition which ought to have overflowed unswervingly into the whole of humanity. (*Briefe* 1: 138)

Whatever the justness of such a view or 'diagnosis' of tradition (religion),[12] one can see here the 'secret core' of the dissertation. More especially since Kant is not a stranger to this issue: 'In a sense whose depth would first have to be unfolded, Romanticism seeks to achieve with religion what Kant did with the theoretical objects: to exhibit their form. But, does religion have a *form*? In any case, early Romanticism believed there to be something similar in history' (*Briefe* 1: 138).

Given these conditions, everything could be organized around Romanticism; all that was lacking was an angle of attack. In March 1918, Benjamin announces to Scholem that he has 'come upon an idea'. The angle of attack will be the Romantic problematic of the work of art in so far as it clearly presupposes the aesthetics of Kant:

Since Romanticism, the idea first attains dominance that an art-*work* can be considered in and for itself without relation to theory or morality and that it can exist adequately through this consideration. The relative autonomy of an art-*work* over and against art or rather its exclusively transcendental dependence on art became the condition of Romantic art criticism. The task will be to present Kant's aesthetic as being, in this sense, the essential presupposition of Romantic art criticism. (*Briefe* 1: 179–80)

Again, this angle of attack is a last resort. Once more, in the same letter, Benjamin presents the dissertation as an irksome task, that is, as an obstacle to his own philosophical work, to his mathematical apprenticeship, for example, or to the opening of a 'broader debate with Kant and Cohen':

The development of my philosophical thought has reached a cental point. However difficult it will be for me, I must leave it alone in its present state in order to devote my time in complete liberty to it after the completion of the exam. If the completion of the doctorate is blocked by obstacles, I will take it as a sign to pursue my own thinking. (*Briefe* 1: 180)

Of course, obstacles did not fail to rise up. Benjamin confides to Ernst Schoen that the subject 'proves tremendously unyielding'; the sources, in particular, are 'to be found only with difficulty', that is to say, nothing permits the simple establishment of a 'fundamental historical coincidence' of the Romantics with Kant. (*Briefe* 1: 188) (It is this difficulty that Benjamin would skirt around by going back to Fichte in order to disengage the 'philosophical foundations of Romantic aesthetic criticism'.) One must believe, however, that something interested Benjamin sufficiently so that, far from recoiling from this obstacle, he worked unceasingly at 'the core of Romanticism' even going so far as to admit that such a study 'is not a waste of time'. He had the esoteric in sight: 'the relation of truth to history'. Benjamin says as much to Ernst Schoen in November 1918:

> From the Romantic concept of criticism, the modern concept of criticism has arisen; however, for the Romantics, 'criticism' was a quite esoteric concept [of which they had several but none as secret], which was based on mystical presuppositions whatever concerned knowledge and which in whatever concerns art, incorporated the best insights of contemporary and later poets in a new concept of art; this is in many respects *our* concept of art. (*Briefe* 1: 203)

From this, it can probably be explained why Benjamin, in spite of everything, invested so much of himself in the writing of his thesis. At the beginning, it is perfectly discernible, he applies himself with relatively good wishes to the rules of academic discourse; however, things precipitate very quickly and even in the treatment of the Romantic philosophy of art (the second part of the dissertation), Benjamin's own style and tone reappears. This writing is one of the most difficult that modern German has produced in the domain of the essay – brief and incisive, elliptic or, as Adorno says about Hölderlin, paratactic. So much so that even the composition is affected by it and certain sections are not far from realizing what would always remain for Benjamin the ideal or utopia of a book: a book made only from a calculated 'montage' of quotations. This Benjamin knew only too well. At the same time (May 1919) that Benjamin finished his dissertation and complains to Ernst Schoen of having 'to study in the most scholarly manner possible', he admits that 'the composition of this work is very demanding as is, to some extent, its prose' (*Briefe* 1: 210). As if this were not sufficient, Benjamin adds at the last moment – and without letting his adviser know – an afterword or appendix of a dozen pages ('The Aesthetic Theory of the Early Romantics and Goethe') where, in a single stroke, he summarizes what is essential. Again, to Ernst Schoen, he writes: 'I have written an esoteric Afterword for the dissertation, it is for those to whom I would have to present it as *my* work' (*Briefe* 1: 210). When, a little later, Benjamin takes it upon himself to write a summary of his book for *Kantstudien*, it is to this 'esoteric' afterword that Benjamin gives almost exclusive attention. He knew that by this afterword his dissertation became a book, which is to say, a work.

2

WALTER BENJAMIN'S EXPOSITION OF THE ROMANTIC THEORY OF REFLECTION*

Winfried Menninghaus

Walter Benjamin's dissertation is entitled *The Concept of Criticism in German Romanticism*. A more fitting and appropriate title, however, might be: *The Theory of Poetic Reflection in German Romanticism*. For the Romantic concept of reflection represents the nucleus and central focus *of the entire study*, while criticism figures only as *one* of the systematic consequences of this concept of reflection, alongside form, the work, irony, transcendental poetry and the novel – none of which latter is by any means ascribed a subordinate position within Benjamin's exposition. Indeed, it is no exaggeration to state that Benjamin derives all these cardinal concepts from the idea of infinite reflection – or as he himself puts it: 'Through [the theory of reflection], an exposition is undertaken of the [Romantics'] most important concepts of art theory – of irony, of the work and of criticism.'[1]

I THE IMMEDIACY AND INFINITY OF REFLECTION

The first chapter of the dissertation explores 'the Romantic concept of reflection' within Schlegel and Novalis in its 'connect[ion] to its Fichtean counterpart' (*SW* 1:121).[2] The framework for the exposition of Fichte is already outlined in an introductory paragraph by way of an interpretation of two quotations from Schlegel – through which something of profound consequence occurs: Benjamin's first 'exegeses' of Romantic reflection constitute not merely the first in a long series of extremely 'free' treatments of quoted material, but at the same time set the course for significant limitations to and falsifications within his exposition of the concept of reflection. The first quotation, as a forced usage of textual sources, remains relatively harmless and is interesting above all on account of Benjamin's wording, within which the

---

* Translated by Robert J. Kiss.

consciousness of a *mis*use is at once documented and, in seeking to appear objective, blurred:

> Schlegel says once in *Lucinde*: 'Thinking has the peculiarity that, next to itself, it most of all prefers to think about that which it can think without end.' Thus it is at the same time understood [*Dabei ist zugleich verstanden*] that thinking can find an end least of all in reflective thinking about itself. (*SW* 1: 121)

Schlegel speaks of two preferred objects of thinking: thinking about itself and, *alongside this*, thinking 'about that which it can think without end'. As Benjamin's concern lies in infinite self-reflection, an identification of the two 'objects' – such as he could have derived effortlessly from other statements made by the Romantics – is crucial to him here. However, this desired identification can be wrung only with some violence from the sentence he actually quotes – and this is precisely what the flimsy expression 'Thus it is at the same time understood' (by whom? why?) contrives to effect. The shift in linguistic register alone of formulations such as this – which are scarcely encountered outside of Benjamin's dissertation – in itself represents a reliable *index falsi*. Rather than with 'Thus it is at the same time understood', Benjamin introduces his second and more weighty departure from the – *sit venia verbo* – literal meaning (*Wortsinn*) with 'In this way ... thus' ('*Hiermit sind also*'):

> 'The capacity of the activity that returns into itself, the ability to be the "I" of the "I", is thinking. This thinking has no other object than ourselves.' In this way, thinking and reflection are thus identified with each other [*Hiermit sind also Denken und Reflexion gleichgesetzt*]. But this does not occur only to guarantee for thinking that infinity which is given in reflection and which, without closer consideration, may appear to be of questionable value as merely the thinking that thinking does about itself. Rather, the Romantics saw in the reflective nature of thinking a warrant for its intuitive character. (*SW* 1: 121)

As superfluous as is Benjamin's 'thus' ('*also*') on the one hand, as lacking in foundation are the sentences that follow it on the other. Firstly: referring to oneself, for Fichte in particular – but also according to numerous pronouncements by Schlegel and Novalis – is not the privilege of thinking as reflection, but likewise characterizes intellectual intuition. As 'immediate consciousness of ourselves' or our 'actions',[3] this intuition is indeed self-referential, but it does not, however, take the form of logical or transcendental reflection. And *thus* it is premature to infer an identification *per se* of 'thinking and reflection' from Schlegel's assertion of self-referentiality. Secondly, and most importantly: the notion that 'the Romantics saw in the reflective nature of thinking a warrant for its intuitive character' at this point lacks any support whatsoever within the quoted material or in the logic of Benjamin's exposition. Ought Benjamin here to appeal vaguely to that philosophical–historical and systematic function of self-reflection as source and refuge of certainty, and thereby ultimately to the assumption that it is less apt to cast consciousness of the self into doubt – on account of the short distance between or supposed proximity of the poles of reflection – than it is cognition of things 'outside'? Precisely this argument for the dignity of self-reflection is cast asunder by the Romantics, however. Anyway, it is less a concordance with this traditional argument that Benjamin seems to have in mind, and much rather a wish to delimit the Romantic concept of reflection *vis-à-vis* the negative characterization of reflection in terms of indirectness and externality that was propounded contemporaneously in Schelling's writings, and later in Hegel's. But what otherwise frequently constitutes one of Benjamin's strengths – his radical dissolution not only of the paradigmatic hierarchy of 'classical' German idealism but also of the significations of common sense – develops with regard to the Romantic concept of reflection *in the first instance* into a method of misrepresentation. For the reformulation of reflection from a figure of indirect and differential thinking into *the* form of 'direct' and 'intuitive thinking' does *not* belong, in the form claimed by Benjamin, to the Romantics' revolutionary coups in the field of terminology. However, let us turn firstly to a further – closely related – element in Benjamin's introduction of the concept of reflection: the privileging of form as the sole object of Romantic reflection.

Benjamin's first remarks on Fichte relate to *On the Concept of the Science of Knowledge* (*Über den Begriff der Wissenschaftslehre* [1794]), which predates his first *Science of Knowledge* (*Wissenschaftslehre*). Here, Fichte twice employs the term 'reflection' in an analogous sense. First, with regard to *logic*: in this, the empty form of thinking that is indifferent toward all content becomes the theme, the content of abstractive reflection, and thus in turn finds a presentational form, a 'form of form'.[4] By contrast, the science of knowledge – as the doctrine of the 'necessary actions of intelligence' which grounds all particular sciences – addresses forms that are bound 'inseparably' to a content (and vice versa).[5] Yet to the extent that the science of knowledge raises these forms through reflection into consciousness, and thereby incorporates them within 'a new form of knowing or consciousness',[6] here too 'reflection [can be] understood [as] the transformative … activity of reflecting on a form' (*SW* 1: 122). This sense of the 'form of form' is, however, anything but specific: it transcends not only the difference between logic and the science of knowledge, but can be applied with equal skill to practically any kind of (re)presentation (*Darstellung*). Nevertheless, Benjamin believes to have found within it the entire definition of the Fichtean concept of reflection, and from this point on, a correlation of reflection and form asserts itself across all levels of his exposition – leading ultimately to the statement that 'the Romantic theory of the artwork', because and in so far as it amounts to a theory of poetic reflection, is 'the theory of its form' (*SW* 1: 155). This may certainly hold to a large degree – but *despite*, rather than because of the abridged analysis of Fichte's concept of reflection. For in the way that Fichte's early writing defines the combined forms of action of abstraction and reflection, these are ultimately applicable to the most disparate phenomena – and not only to *forms* of thinking: in the *focusing* of reflection *on* something, this something always occupies the position of 'content' that finds a (presentational) 'form' (*eine 'Form'* [*der Darstellung*]) – whether this *content for reflection* is 'in itself' content, form, or both.

The actual stumbling block in this rather insipid discussion of reflection as a form of form lies less in this formulation itself, however, than in Benjamin's interpretation of it: 'What is evidently at stake here', according to Benjamin, 'is an attempt that deviates from Fichte's later grounding via intellectual intuition.' Or, in other words: '[Fichte] defines "reflection" as "reflection of a form", and in this way proves the immediacy of the knowledge given in it' (*SW* 1: 122). Both of the linguistic formulations with which Benjamin seeks to ground these assertions, the 'evidently' and the 'in this way', remain blindspots in the text for which Benjamin fails to offer genuine grounding. For things are in fact otherwise. What Benjamin may be alluding to with the thesis of a 'mutual and reciprocal givenness of reflective thinking and immediate cognition' (*SW* 1: 121) may perhaps, on the basis of his textual sources, be the following: already in *On the Concept of the Science of Knowledge*, Fichte speaks of a supreme proposition that should 'be certain directly' and 'through itself';[7] at the same time, however, reflective abstraction is named as the sole form of cognition – and thus, one might feel drawn to conclude that reflection is the form of immediate cognition. This would be an unjustly rash conclusion, though; for Fichte's meaning – as recorded also in his complete *Science of Knowledge* from the same year – is merely that the necessary and self-certain actions of intelligence are '*sought out*' '*by means of*'[8] or '*through* reflection'.[9] His meaning is not, however, that abstractive reflection itself *is* this direct certainty (which *qua* unconditionality is never provable), nor indeed that this directness *exists in* the execution of abstractive reflection. To the contrary, rather than rashly identifying the goal of cognition and its means – as Benjamin does – Fichte, Schlegel and Novalis alike generally saw there to be an unbridgeable cleft between the two. They did this with reference to a fundamental principle of reflection that Benjamin excises outright – with astounding repercussions – from his exposition, even though it is a central motif of the Romantic theory of knowledge: namely, *reification*.

The 'absolute', the unconditional actions of intelligence, are the exact opposite of 'being any object whatsoever', and *as* delimited objects may never be comprehended. Yet whatever reflection directs itself at immediately becomes an object through the very act of having reflection directed at it. 'Everything, without distinction, on which we reflect … is an object, and consequently falls under the object's laws', Novalis says, before continuing even more significantly: 'in so far as we reflect on it', the non-object also becomes an 'object'.[10] For a philosophy concerned with that which cannot be an object, this casts up the dilemma that 'we wish to represent non-reflection through reflection and pre-cisely on account of this never arrive at non-reflection'.[11] Instead of guaranteeing immediate cognition, reflection produces a reversal in its relation to what is reflected, an '*ordo inversus*'; it guarantees precisely that the absolute 'can never be obtained from within itself'.[12] Schlegel speaks likewise of the 'impossibility of definitely attaining the *highest level* through reflection'.[13] And this is the case especially with regard to self-reflection: where the 'I' reflects itself *as* the 'I', it is already no longer the '*I*', but a 'divided "I"'[14] – divided into subject and object of reflection, into reflecting and reflected poles. As Fichte would later formulate it: reflection, 'by dint of its being, divides itself within itself', and in this way leads to the 'destruction of reality' – bringing with it the danger 'that the entire form of reflection could disintegrate into absolutely nothing'.[15]

This recognition that the act of 'self-grasping' in reflection at the same time is an act of 'self-destruction' led Fichte not, however, to a rejection of reflection, but rather to an 'implementation' of it within the consciousness of its boundaries.[16] Schlegel and Novalis took this second-order reversal of the reversal inherent in reflection incomparably further – so far, indeed, that they came to regard the form of reflection as the most intrinsic (presentational) form of the absolute: the very assumption that underlies Benjamin's theory of the absolute as medium of reflection. This shall be developed later, however. The objective here was simply to highlight that Benjamin's 'deduction' of the immediacy of reflection is too simplistic by far, and that the level it works on – which is unrepresentative of the extent of the problem's consideration within Romantic philosophy – is more apt to draw out contradictory conclusions. It is also not the case that it is only with the *New Exposition of the Science of Knowledge* (*Neue Darstellung der Wissenschaftslehre*) in 1797 that Fichte first departs from viewing reflection as a form of immediate cognition (*SW* 1: 121f.). While it certainly holds that Fichte first employs the term 'intellectual intuition' to designate 'immediate consciousness of ourselves'[17] in 1797 – that is, three years after the first *Science of Knowledge* – he had already spoken in 1794 of the impossibility that the 'I' might, in the reflection 'of its actions, [become] directly ... conscious of itself'.[18]

Therefore, it is by no means simply on the basis of terminological imprecision – as Benjamin insinuates – that the early Fichte never relates the 'expression' 'immediate cognition' to his concept of reflection (*SW* 1: 121). Rather, one might say that the earliest pieces by Fichte occasionally lack clarity in their determination of reflection's boundaries. Incidentally, Benjamin himself revises his equation 'thinking=reflection=immediacy' when he laconically and aptly remarks with regard to the *New Exposition of the Science of Knowledge*: 'The immediate consciousness of thinking is identical with self-consciousness. By virtue of its immediacy, it is called intuition' (*SW* 1: 125). So should something, 'by virtue of its immediacy', now be termed 'intuition', or – as it is referred to prior to and on numerous occasions subsequent to this – 'reflection'? The fact that (self-) 'reflection [is] transfixed' in Fichte's intellectual intuition 'without being annulled' can scarcely hope to mediate this contradiction (*SW* 1: 125). For despite its self-referential character, the principal motive for introducing the concept of 'intellectual intuition' lies precisely in its difference to reflection. And one final observation: at least with relation to Schlegel, it is possible to determine historical reasons, as it were, for Benjamin's all-too-immediate grounding of the immediacy of reflection. For Schlegel thematizes the radical indirectness of reflection relatively seldom, and primarily in texts that have only become accessible subsequent to Benjamin's writing. Novalis's corresponding statements *were* however – at least in part – accessible to Benjamin. For example, a good third of that group of notes on Fichte from 1795/6 in which the interconnection of feeling and reflection is developed,[19] are reproduced in the Ernst Heilborn edition of Novalis that Benjamin used – specifically, the entire section '*Deduktion*' ('*Deduction*'),[20] just without its subsequent commentary and afterword. It remains one of the mysteries of Benjamin's selection of source materials that the motives for a theory of reflection formulated in these accessible sections of Novalis's work are neither mentioned nor quoted in his dissertation. Novalis's most clear-cut statements on the reifying character of reflection are, however, absent from the Heilborn edition – and this applies to the other groups of notes that have become available in their entirety only long after Benjamin too.

More apt and pertinent than Benjamin's exposition of the common ground between Fichte's and the Romantics' concepts of reflection is his exploration of the dividing line between these two: that is, of infinity. Every reflection can itself become the object of further reflection. 'The mechanism of reflection', as Friedrich Schlegel puts it in his *Philosophical Apprentice-Years* (*Philosophische Lehrjahre*) – a work unknown to Benjamin – goes off 'everywhere in all directions into the infinite'.[21] The consequence of this infiniteness is the impossibility of any reflective self-consciousness other than a fragmentary or temporary one. 'Completely and in the strict sense nobody knows himself';[22] or, 'Through no reflection can the "I" be exhausted.'[23] This is because every finite reflection can only *point*, in the mode of incompleteness, to the never-to-be-realized project of complete 'self-penetration' within the infinite context of reflection. The Romantics saw in this the appropriate presentational form – indeed, the appropriate mode of existence – of the inexhaustibility, of the progressive fulfilment of the self. Benjamin highlights this very sharply, but at the same time refrains from grounding or justifying this, and even asserts the impossibility of any such grounding or justification. '[T]hat reflection does not take its course into an empty infinity, but is in itself substantial and filled' is regarded by Benjamin as an 'axiomatic presupposition' of Romantic thinking that is no longer analysable (*SW* 1: 129) – as a 'metaphysical credo' in regard of which the search for a 'reason' is 'totally mistaken' (*SW* 1: 149).

It is difficult to imagine a more crass way for Benjamin to abandon a core element of his exposition to the haphazardness of mere arbitrary acceptance. Only later, however, can there follow a consideration of whether certain 'reasons' may be furnished for this representation of a 'full infinitude' (*SW* 1: 126) of reflection. But Fichte, in any event, arrived at a contradictory evaluation of the inconcludability of reflection – for which Benjamin indeed mentions a reason too. According to Fichte's observation, if one engages oneself thoroughly within the infinite division and doubling into 'thinking I and thought I', into self-consciousness, self-consciousness of self-consciousness, and so on, then one will 'never ... be able to assume real self-consciousness'[24] in the field of theoretical philosophy (provided, of course, that one postulates this 'real self-consciousness' like Fichte, as an identity of subject-objectivity beyond the difference of positing and posited). In this way, the infinity of reflection is seen to constitute a factor that hinders rather than a mode of progressive fulfilment. The concept of 'intellectual intuition' serves precisely as a remedy to this deficiency; and for the same reason, the first *Science of Knowledge* already ascribes the 'source of all self-consciousness' to 'reason', defined as an 'absolute power of abstraction' by dint of which the reciprocal interplay of '[reflected] imagination [is] entirely destroyed, and this destruction ... itself [becomes] intuited'[25] – in order, ultimately, to facilitate a 'complete determination of (in this case, theoretical) reason through itself', i.e. to facilitate a finite and definite '*presentation of the presenting self*' ('*Vorstellung des Vorstellenden*').[26] From here, Benjamin is able to observe succinctly:

> Fichte tries everywhere to exclude the infinitude of the action of the 'I' from the realm of theoretical philosophy and to assign it instead to the domain of practical philosophy, whereas the Romantics seek to make it constitutive precisely for their theoretical philosophy and thus for their philosophy as a whole ... (*SW* 1: 123)

The re-establishment of theoretical philosophy's primacy within Romanticism, as developed by Benjamin with regard to the concept of infinite reflection, has since come to be acknowledged repeatedly as a significant catalyst for the transformative adaptation of Fichtean categories – yet always without reference to Benjamin's paradigmatic groundwork. Nevertheless, it is possible to raise two relativizing observations against Benjamin. First, since there is a primacy of practical over theoretical philosophy in Fichte, then so even for him infinity – as a form of action of the practical 'I' – ultimately retains the upper hand over those attempts to (de)limit it within the subordinated theoretical philosophy. However, this infinite acting of the practical 'I' does not take the form of reflection at all, but rather that of its polar opposite: striving (*das Streben*), or infinite positing. Second, with regard to the containment of reflection through other theoretical modes of action of the 'I', Benjamin arrives at the thesis that 'reflection is not the method of Fichtean philosophy' (*SW* 1: 128). However, this constitutes a blurring of the boundaries of method and content. For Fichte's method, in line with his understanding of the self, is to 'search out' everywhere those necessary modes of action of the human spirit 'by means of reflection'.[27] That by means of these 'series of reflections' other forms of action than reflection itself are uncovered as well, still makes no difference to the method. Even intellectual intuition is introduced by Fichte in the mode of philosophical reflection – despite the fact that intellectual intuition is concerned with the insufficiency of reflection, and although reflection can neither comprise nor even transcend this intuition.

It may be worth pausing at this point in the de- and reconstruction of Benjamin's work. '[T]he moments: immediacy and infinity' (*SW* 1: 125) have been emphasized as defining the Romantic concept of reflection – and this not without neglecting other important facets of its meaning. Although Benjamin's grounding of these 'moments' through source materials is only occasionally satisfactory or sufficient, this deficit can for the most part be remedied.[28] What, however, might have set Benjamin on the course of his conceptual extrapolations in the first place? It is difficult to believe that the reading of Early Romantic writings alone could have done this. For the concept of reflection in these writings does not play anything like the prominent role that it is ascribed virtually without prelude in Benjamin's work – and which has continued to be ascribed to it in a wealth of academic publications ever since. Certainly, the play of reflecting-on-itself long counted as a particularity of Romantic literature, and Schlegel's *Athenaeum Fragments* [hereafter *Ath.* fgms] 116 and 238 on artistic self-mirroring as a commentary on this. However, where such reflecting-on-itself was not simply rejected as unartistic, there was no apparent awareness that the explicit reflection *about* a work *within* that work should amount to anything more than to one extreme and ultimately *marginal* phenomenon of a comprehensive reflective structure – a structure defining both the very essence of the absolute, as well as these artworks, *in their entirety*. There were good reasons for such unawareness, specifically because direct statements about the concept of reflection are extremely scarce within the Romantics' writings. Where these can be found, they by no means refer unambiguously to a systematic leading-role on the part of reflection.

Benjamin also remarks that 'in the Romantics' writings, [source quotations] for certain of their most profound tendencies can scarcely be found'.[29] The reasons underlying the conflict between the ability to claim a 'deep reading' on the one hand and positive philology on the other are not simply systematic and irreducible but also contingent on which editions of a work were available at a given time. Only a fraction of the early texts on philosophy and literary theory of Benjamin's main source, Friedrich Schlegel, were available when he wrote his dissertation. Schlegel's extensive notebooks and study-books – first published in 1957 (*Literary Notebooks*), 1963 and 1971 (*Philosophical Apprentice-Years I and II*), and 1981 and 1991 (*Fragments on Poetry and Literature I and II*) – not only exceed the collections of fragments that were known to Benjamin (*Lyceum*, *Athenaeum* and *Ideen*) manifold in volume, but also constitute a rich source for material pertaining to the elusive central element of Benjamin's study. The position with regard to available texts by Novalis has changed less spectacularly, but is still noteworthy. The Heilborn edition (Berlin, 1901) referred to by Benjamin contains around half of the philosophical fragments and sketches by Novalis that are available today and a good two-thirds of all those texts that are of relevance for Benjamin's study. However, the dissertation scarcely takes advantage of this relatively favourable situation in terms of source material. To the contrary, Novalis's direct statements about the concept of reflection are for the most part neither mentioned nor even considered. Evidently, Benjamin found himself able to integrate these into his conceptualization only in a very partial way. Instead, he succeeded in identifying some representative substitutes for the thematization of reflection within Schlegel's *Athenaeum* and *Lyceum Fragments*. Primarily, though, Benjamin employs the artful tactic of drawing on Schlegel's *Cologne and Paris Lectures, 1804–1806* – referred to after their editor as the *Windischmann Lectures* – as a belated source for the implicit theory of knowledge during the period before 1800. Without seeking to disguise the break between these lectures and the *Athenaeum* period, Benjamin – in an abstraction from the source material's peculiarities – nevertheless perceives there to exist an identical 'component' in their 'basic epistemological positions' (*SW* 1: 120, 131).

In spite of Benjamin's elaborate methodological self-awareness, the quite tangible unavailability of systematic statements on reflection, intuition, etc. does tempt him into a somewhat more than cautious application of the *Windischmann Lectures* to the *Athenaeum* period. But more on this below. First, however, a general observation. Whoever knows the *Windischmann Lectures* only through those passages cited by Benjamin must assume that – in these lectures, at least – reflection is afforded more or less the same esteemed position that Benjamin claims for it retrospectively for the entire early Romantic phase. It is all the more astounding, then, when one discovers the modest degree to which reflection and its theory are evidenced here as well, even in the framework of those chapters dedicated purely to epistemology. For although the entire world is understood here as 'I', and the 'I' essentially as self-referential, reflection is placed only at the bottom end of the epistemological hierarchy. 'Feeling and remembrance' figure much rather as the 'only sources of cognition' and, as cognition's 'triune foundation' (in Christianity), 'hope, love and faith'.[30] In Paul Lerch's dissertation focusing exclusively on the *Windischmann Lectures* – and also known to Benjamin – the general picture is painted in somewhat rough, but generally not unreasonable strokes, with just two paragraphs addressing reflection.[31] And even these set limits, through reference to Schlegel's conceptualization of volition, to the infinity of reflection – a (de)limiting that is analogous to Fichte's, and which Benjamin rather ashamedly acknowledges as 'a weakened compromise solution' (*SW* 1: 132) and 'moderatism' on the part of the later Schlegel (*SW* 1: 149), even though it is from precisely this later Schlegel that Benjamin distils his theory of infinite reflection. All this shows clearly enough just how selectively Benjamin had to proceed even with his widely used 'source writings of the second rank' (*SW* 1: 120) in order to be able to develop his streamlined, tailored theory of reflection from them.

And hence we must return to the question: which dousing rod set Benjamin – in spite of such a bleak outlook on the horizon of source materials – upon the trail of an outstanding systematic significance of the Romantic concept of reflection with its 'two moments', immediacy and infinity? Inspired intuition – is the stereotyped answer put forward by practically all literary theorists, with the power of Benjamin's penetrating theoretical analysis at least having generally won their critical admiration. Another reason – not an alternative, but simply an additional one – lies in the immanence of Benjamin's thinking itself. The 'two moments: immediacy and infinity' (*SW* 1: 125), which from the very beginning govern the theory of reflection as that of a 'medium' of the Absolute, constitute a precise revisiting of the 'fundamental problem' which Benjamin's philosophy of language, as expounded in his 1916 essay 'On Language as Such and on the Language of Man', addresses by way of the term 'magic' – a term that only seemingly points in an opposite direction, and which is likewise borrowed from the Romantics.

> Mediation [*das Mediale*], which is the immediacy of all mental communication, is the fundamental problem of linguistic theory, and if one chooses to call this immediacy magic, then the primary problem of language is its magic. At the same time, the notion of the magic of language points to something else: its infiniteness. This is conditional on its immediacy. (*SW* 1: 64)

Immediacy, infiniteness, medium: this degree of correspondence cannot be coincidental. It is likewise not without cause that the same characteristics are called forth with relation to the term 'reflection' that previously – and also subsequently in Benjamin's writing – are conjured forth with relation to the term 'magic'. For within the conceptual chemistry of the Romantics, both reflection and magic are identical at least in that they are forms of 'totalizing', 'potentiating' and 'romanticizing' – that is, forms with a medial reference to the 'absolute'. What this means is that the pathways of Benjamin's approach to the Romantic theory of reflection have to a great extent been prepared already in his theory of language, which is likewise a Romantic theory. And thus we may account for Benjamin's surprising certainty and also the violence of his penetrating analysis of a thoroughly ungiving selection of textual sources, which characterizes especially the beginning of his dissertation.

2 REFLECTION VERSUS INTELLECTUAL INTUITION

In order to secure the primacy of reflection over other modes of action of the 'I', Benjamin undertakes further delineations of its boundaries. As a consequence of extending infinite reflection to apply to the entire domain of philosophy, he sees the Romantics depotentiating other modes of action of the 'I', or even rejecting these outright: in particular, positing and Fichte's intellectual intuition. Let us consider intellectual intuition first. 'Schlegel's opposition to Fichte', according to Benjamin, 'led him, in the *Windischmann Lectures*, to a frequently energetic polemic against Fichte's concept of intellectual intuition' (*SW* 1: 130). This polemic is the consequence of a criticism of intuition in general. 'Intuition stifles, in fact kills every object, because it cannot take place without the object being thought as a steadfast one – it can be intuited only when it is fixed, held firm.'[32] True cognition by contrast has to free itself completely from the concept of a thing-like object, because only then can it comprise the 'living being' and infinite 'genesis'.[33] The act of intuition reifies what is intuited into a fixed, steadfast object. Precisely this notion of reification was criticized, however, by Fichte, Novalis, the early Schlegel and Schelling also on account of the demarcation of something *as* an object of reflection *through* the form of reflection. And thus Schlegel's criticism of intuition strikes out in part also against that intention which Benjamin pursues with it. Let us consider an example of this. Schlegel observes that: 'We cannot *intuit* ourselves, because in so doing, the "I" always disappears; we can, however, *think* ourselves [*Denken können wir uns aber freilich*].'[34] Now, Benjamin's thesis is this: thinking that should, in place of intuition, be true to the living, non-concretized 'I', is reflection. With regard to the characteristic of reification, though, Schlegel has absolutely every reason *not* to describe this act of thinking-oneself as reflection. Rather than inferring an equivalency of thinking and reflection, as Benjamin does (*SW* 1: 121, 130f), it is at least as plausible to read Schlegel's concept of thinking as a mode of consciousness which is highly versatile and 'alive', thus transcending the reifications both of intuition *and* of reflection. And there exists an outstanding piece of philological evidence to support this too: the terminological history of the formula claimed by Benjamin for his purposes, of 'the ability to be the "I" of the "I"' (*SW* 1: 121). At the beginning of his critical 'Theory of Intuition', Schlegel firstly terms this figure of self-referentiality an 'intuition of intuition', of which there can in turn be a further 'intuition', and so on into the infinite. The relation of these intuitions to one another – but not these intuitions themselves – is defined as that of a 'boundless reflection'.[35] In the subsequent passages, both the structure of boundless reflection and intuition are criticized by Schlegel. Boundless reflection is criticized because, in its infinite self-mirroring, 'the "I" [would in the end] completely lose the object'[36] (incidentally, this accusation of *dissipating every object* through *infinite* reflection is encountered on many more occasions than the other extreme, the accusation of *reification* through each individual *finite* reflection). Intuition is criticized, meanwhile, because it 'stifles' and 'kills' its object through assuming it to be a steadfast one.[37] Only after this double criticism is recapitulated within the concept of thinking does the initial formula again find accreditation: 'the ability to be the "I" of the "I" is thinking'.[38] Thus, a detailed consideration of Schlegel's critique of intuition awakens considerable doubts concerning Benjamin's antithetical inference of an identity of non-intuitive thinking and reflection, and along with this, once again, his untroubled attestation of living 'immediacy' – which Schlegel claims for 'thinking' – for reflection (*SW* 1: 130–31).

Schlegel's critique of (intellectual) intuition, which Benjamin is only too pleased to take up, has still further drawbacks for his conceptualization. It misses the sense of Fichte's concept of intuition, and does not correspond, as Benjamin would have it, to the Romantics' position during the *Athenaeum* period. In the *Science of Knowledge* of 1794 at least, Fichte defines intuition as the exact opposite of fixative reification – that is to say, specifically, he defines it as a 'hovering' synthesis[39] in the productive imagination: 'Intuition as such is not at all something fixed, but rather a hovering of the imagination between contradictory directions.' Any attempt to fix this hovering–living synthesis would 'completely destroy and annul intuition'.[40] This concept of intuition evidently stands at odds with Schlegel's later critique. However, it is of still greater consequence that Benjamin, in referring to the *Windischmann Lectures*, simply suppresses any mention of the early Romantic affirmation of intellectual intuition which fits less well into his conceptualization. It is difficult to believe that he might simply have overlooked, for example, *Ath*. fgm. 76 – 'Intellectual intuition is the categorical imperative of theory'[41] – or any of the numerous references to intellectual intuition within the secondary literature that was known to him.

Yet it is worth proceeding cautiously here. Things are relatively certain only in the case of Novalis. He never rejected intellectual intuition but also never ascribed it anything like the systematic significance that is attributed to it within Fichte and Schelling. Rather than being *the* form of comprehending the absolute, or even being the absolute itself, intellectual intuition figures in Novalis only as a primarily derivative moment in the construction of absolute 'coherence' through the reciprocal interplay of 'feeling' and 'reflection'.[42] The early Friedrich Schlegel by contrast alternates between two positions on intellectual intuition, one of which ultimately asserts itself in the *Windischmann Lectures*. The affirmative one appeals on the one hand to Fichte's contemporaneous reintroduction of intellectual intuition – which does not fall back behind Kantian critique in so far as it is concerned not with 'things in themselves' ('*Dinge an sich*') but solely with consciousness, and not with any being but solely an action of the 'I'.[43] At the same time, such an affirmative position aims beyond this – specifically, at a direct revision of the Kantian restrictions of experience and cognition. Alongside the extremely scant reflections in the *Athenaeum*, it is above all a series of statements that were unknown to Benjamin which point in this direction.

> Intellectual intuition and the categorical imperative are evidently acts of absolute capacity.
>
> Only aesthetics leads us to the *intellectual intuition* of man.
>
> Intellectual intuition is nothing but the consciousness of a prestabilized harmony, of a necessary eternal dualism.
>
> Life is the intellectual intuition of nature.
>
> Intellectual intuition ... is to philosophy as mythology to poetry.[44]

Like these notes from the *Philosophical Apprentice-Years*, Schlegel's first 'completed' system prior to the *Windischmann Lectures* – the *Jena Transcendental Philosophy* [*Jenaer Transzendentalphilosophie*] from 1800–1, which was likewise unavailable to Benjamin – also grants a cardinal philosophical position to intellectual intuition. On the other hand, however, critical statements dating from 1797 onwards can be found in the *Philosophical Apprentice-Years* which do ultimately pass over into the position assumed in the *Windischmann Lectures* and in this respect can offer at least a tendentious grounding to Benjamin's extremely biased selection:

Referring to intellectual intuition, like referring to a sense of the beautiful, does not help.

What one usually terms intellectual intuition ought actually rather to be called the *ideal fact* ... .

Intuition is no source of cognition; for within intellectual intuition ... it is primordial imagination that is rendered into intuition.[45]

To sum up, Benjamin's exclusive fixation on the position 'there is no intellectual intuition for us'[46] is marked too strongly by *his* concerns than that it might still be legitimated through his quasi-archaeological questioning – regardless of the fact that such questioning *in principle* can well support standing at odds with the wording of various particular statements.

3   REFLECTION AND POSITING

With regard to Fichte's concept of positing, Benjamin undertakes another attempt at excluding potential competitors vying to be the paramount act of intelligence. Where the Romantics addressed the concept of positing expressly, things are strikingly similar as with the concept of intellectual intuition. Novalis already finds the word 'positing' ('*Setzen*') to be 'magnificently mean-ingful',[47] and then integrates this form of action – particularly as counter-positing – within his system as well; but it does not possess anything like the fundamental significance that infinite positing has for Fichte. Schlegel on the one hand discerns in positing that which, *alongside* reflection, is 'good in Fichte's form';[48] yet on the other, it simultaneously appears 'fatuous'[49] to him. Of these two tendencies – the 'arbitrary' positing of something as either bad 'empiricism' or high philosophical 'mysticism'[50] – it is, as with the concept of intuition, the negative-critical one that increasingly comes to the fore, on the basis of the very same argument. 'Fichte's *positing* is already realistic, and led him again into *substance*; for what is positing other than STEADFASTLY *constituting*.'[51] Presumably on account of lacking access to practically all of Schlegel's pertinent statements, Benjamin does not even attempt, however, to present his contemplations on positing as being in line with the expressed Romantic theorems. Following a systematic conceptual argument, Benjamin simply highlights two points that are concerned less with positing itself than with its relation to reflection. 'For Fichte', according to Benjamin, 'a self belongs only to the "I" – that is, a reflection exists only and uniquely in correlation with a positing' (*SW* 1: 128). Of that 'which every body is for us', Fichte sees only the 'I' emphasized through the 'principle ... of reflecting on itself' – which for him signifies: the 'I' does not only posit itself, it posits itself *as* positing itself, and moreover as posited *for itself*.[52] Here, reflection is a differential privilege of the 'I' and a backward-loop of the act of positing toward the positing 'I' solicited by a power of counterpositing (a 'check'). The particular being that comes with the positing act of the 'I' and the being-an-'I' that comes with the act of positing oneself are seen thus as a 'special ontological determination'; that is, as a presupposition of reflection. As Benjamin continues, even this 'falls away ... for the Romantics' (*SW* 1: 128). They extend reflection to 'everything' that possesses an 'objective structure' (*SW* 1: 118) of self-referentiality – to literary texts in particular, but ultimately to every spiritual 'entity', and even to the 'idea' of art. A great number of references can be found to support this, even within the texts that were known to Benjamin.

4   POSTERIORITY AND PRIORITY OF REFLECTION, ORIGINATION FROM NOTHING, FEELING

Benjamin's claiming of a sublation of 'being and positing in reflection' (*SW* 1: 128) leads, however, to a wealth of unsolved problems, for it casts up the question of reflection's source. In *re*flecting, reflection *posits* no being, and in re*flecting*, it does not posit any *being*. In this respect one can say that the whole 'being' of infinite reflection consists, as a totality of relation, in the mirrorings of all its parts: that is, as a decentred continuum of centres of reflection. Over and above this, according to Benjamin, this figure of absolute reflection is likewise *the structure of the Absolute itself* (*SW* 1: 132ff.), with the 'methodological absolute' thereby constituting an 'ontological absolute' (*SW* 1: 144). This radical conjunction of epistemology and metaphysics, presented by Benjamin as an axiomatic 'credo', ultimately also grounds the connection between the theory of poetic reflection and the theory of the Absolute. To begin with, a question should be asked regarding this connection that Benjamin expounds only very thetically: can a reflection be thought at all without prior positing, without previous being? The word '*re*flection' itself points already toward something *pre*-existing. Within his initial attempts at a definition, Benjamin holds firmly to the schema of posteriority, of reflection's reproductivity. At first he states that reflection is a 'transformative – and nothing but transformative – activity' (*SW* 1: 122): the modification, therefore, of something preceding. Later on, the 'fulfilment' of the infinite context of reflection is ultimately derived from Benjamin's 'first level of reflection', which constitutes a 'thinking *of* something', of 'matter' (*SW* 1: 127). Only beginning with the second level of reflection, according to Benjamin at this point in his analysis, are we dealing in infinite reflection with a form that arises 'by its own power and self-actively' (*SW* 1: 127). In the context of the Romantic theory of the Absolute, however, this last restriction falls away too. Referring to Novalis's postulation of a 'Fichteanism, without check, without the "not-I" in his sense' and to Schlegel's 'theorem' of a comprehensive ' "*ur*-I" ' (*SW* 1: 132), Benjamin seems to stipulate 'an absolutely neutral origin of reflection' (*SW* 1: 150), an origination 'from nothing' (*SW* 1: 134) – amounting to a complete sublation of the very *re*productivity of reflection. And more still, Benjamin cites Windelband's exposition of Fichtean philosophy.

> Although one usually sees activities as something that presuppose a being, for Fichte all being is only a product of the original deed. Function,

without a being which is functioning, is for him the primary metaphysical principle ... The thinking mind does not 'exist' at the start and then afterward come to self-consciousness through some occasioning causes, whatever they might be; it comes about first through the underivable, inexplicable act of self-consciousness. (*SW* 1: 134)

The notion of an 'idealism that has as it were arisen from nothing' – to follow Schlegel's formulation (*SW* 1: 134) – yields a radical consequence with reference to the activity of reflection. Rather than being merely the *reflection* of something preceding, reflection is conversely even 'logically the first and primary' (*SW* 1: 134), 'absolutely creative' (*SW* 1: 150), 'the originary and constructive factor in art, as in everything spiritual' (*SW* 1: 151). Rather than never being able to comprise the Absolute – as is argued in Fichte and above all in Schelling – the opposite holds here: 'Reflection *constitutes* the Absolute, and it constitutes it as a medium' (*SW* 1: 132, my emphasis). Thus, the concept of reflection has reached a level where Benjamin's first determinations have been left far behind, and even destroyed. Although this (diametrical) shift in the concept takes place over the course of just a few scant pages, Benjamin refrains from drawing attention to this contradiction *as* such. However, a consciousness of these contradictions leads him to dedicate at least one footnote to them – in order to pass these off as contradictions of the object itself. According to this footnote, the Romantic theory of reflection in its totality – and above all in respect of the problem of the origination of reflection and original reflection – leads ultimately 'to purely logical, unresolvable contradictions' in spite of which it is said to be of considerable operational productiveness in the field of art theory (*SW* 1: 191–2, n. 146). A further logical elaboration of this theory might indeed be conceivable, Benjamin goes on, but would presumably 'lead only [yet further] into darkness', rather than illuminate these contradictions.[53] First, however, a few further considerations of deficits in *Benjamin's exposition* of the theory of a constitutive reflection prior to all that is reflected in it.

The scant remarks about a 'Fichteanism without check' and an origination of reflection 'from nothing' leave plenty of space for noting an absence of substance within his conceptual work. At least in part, these remarks fit into that broad history of reception that saw in Romanticism a repeated intensification of Fichte's (itself already miscomprehended) philosophy of the 'I' – that is, a complete dissolution of the 'not-I' within the 'I'. Theodor Haering and Manfred Dick have undertaken far-reaching studies in which they convincingly counter this interpretation.[54] They discern in Novalis a decisive revaluation of the status of the 'not-I' and the objective world *vis-à-vis* the activity of the 'I' – and not simply in isolated remarks such as the question as to whether 'Fichte does not all too arbitrarily place everything into the "I" ',[55] but throughout the entire design of his thought. Only upon first reflection does the formula of a 'Fichteanism, without check, without the "not-I" in his sense' signify the liquidation of the 'not-I'. Upon second reflection, though, it refers to a 'not-I' *in a different sense* to Fichte's – a 'not-I' that does not simply assume the function of a 'check' in the autonomous productivity of the 'I', but rather something of equal value and equal originality.[56] The situation is no different in regard of the formula of origination or that of creation from nothing. For Schlegel, who was most wont of all to employ this trope, '*nothing* and *everything* [were] Romantic categories' in the sense that nothing, in and of itself, already means – *in nuce* – everything: '*Everything* is differentiated from *nothing* simply in that it is *full*.'[57] Under this presupposition, Schlegel can indeed go on to formulate: '*Nothing* must be demonstrated or, that is, *everything* must, depending on how one sees it.'[58] 'Nothing' is therefore not, as Benjamin suggests it be read, the lacking of 'something', but rather the non-present motor of the medium of reflection, and thus is in and of itself the possibility of being everything, the possibility of the unfolding of infinite 'fullness'.[59]

In view of the above, potentials for meaning become discernible within Benjamin's comments on the self-origination of reflection that he himself neither adequately supports nor exhausts. One concept in particular comes into view here, which Benjamin – even though he refers to it only twice and never offers any further explanation of it – deems to mark the 'core' of the theory of poetic reflection. After a reference to Schlegel's *Ath.* fgm. 433 concerning poetic feeling as the capacity for an affection that arises from itself alone, Benjamin ventures a formulation that stands unique in the entire work: 'the point of indifference for reflection, the point at which reflection arises from nothing, is poetic feeling' (*SW* 1: 150). That this sentence receives no clarification cannot be explained away through the fact that Schlegel's statement on poetic feeling likewise stands in radical isolation. For without the prefix 'poetic' (on which a few further reflections drawn from texts that were unavailable to Benjamin shall be furnished later), the concept of feeling, free from every sentimental mis-understanding, is an absolutely fundamental concept of Romantic philosophy. Feeling, for Fichte, rather than being something like the polar opposite of reason or the form of pure inwardness, is 'the basis of all reality'.[60] The feeling of the existence of something – or put negatively, the inhibition of a completely free productivity – denotes the pre-reflective contact of 'I' and 'not-I', out of which all other forms of action emerge: it is only through and in feeling that 'reality becomes possible for the "I", be it the reality of the "I", or of the "not-I"'.[61] Accordingly, the first act of reflection is for Fichte the reflection of feeling – an origin in 'feeling' which in turn does not get lost in the reflection on this reflected feeling (= sensation of feeling [*Empfindung*]), nor in any further reflections, up to and including self-consciousness of the Absolute. Similarly, Novalis too, in his construction of absolute 'coherence' as a reciprocal interplay of 'feeling' and 'reflection', puts forward the formulation, from a strictly epistemological viewpoint: 'The boundaries of feeling are the boundaries of philosophy.'[62] Only at one other point does Benjamin approach this context a second time, without however achieving any significant analytical penetration of it: when he connects criticism – specifically as a reflection and a represen-tation of reflection, and through reference to a remark from Schlegel's *Wilhelm Meister* review – to an 'original reception of the artwork by pure feeling' (*SW* 1: 153).

With his formula locating the point of indifference of reflection in feeling, Benjamin thus touches on the very foundation of the Romantic theory of knowledge. Yet he never pursued this course, and indeed covered over it again. Two reasons for this can be identified in the immanence of his exposition. The first is hypothetical: if the point of indifference of the absolute play of reflections is feeling, then so the claimed priority and constitutivity of reflection is again thrown into question – that is, reflection is once again only the subsequent unfolding of something pre- and non-reflective for the consciousness. This objection can, however, be refuted through reference to the Romantic theory of language and – particularly – the Romantic theory of the self-representation of the Absolute.[63] A second, and philologically provable, reason for Benjamin's trepidation *vis-à-vis* touching on the concept of feeling is that it refers to a moment of the unconscious – to Fichte's theory of primordial consciousless producing, or unconscious representing. It is precisely this moment of the unconscious, however, that Benjamin from the start wishes to keep separate from the Romantic theory of reflection. He understands the Romantic dissolution of reflection from the 'I' that posits being (or rather, his notion of it) as, at the same time, a dissolution from all limitation through pre-reflective being or unconscious action (*SW* 1: 124). The Romantics, according to his thesis, wish to recognize limitation only 'in conscious reflection itself'; they 'shudder at limitation through the unconscious' (*SW* 1: 132). In feeling, however, there is just such limitation or foundation through an unconscious act[64] – and consequently the origination of reflection in feeling would in the end erode Benjamin's theorem of an absolute consciousness as a key feature of Romantic thought. This theorem, which meets with direct contradiction in numerous statements by Novalis in particular, not only hinders Benjamin from undertaking an impartial analysis of the reciprocal grounding of feeling and reflection, but is also responsible for a series of other biases and imbalances within his exposition.

5 REFLECTION AS PROSE VERSUS BEAUTY AND ECSTASY

The strong accentuation of a conscious, rational character of Romantic thinking and writing is not only connected with Benjamin's orientation toward the concept of reflection, to whose sphere of meaning the moment of intensified consciousness as a rule belongs. It evidently also has a polemic function for Benjamin: his study attempts, through the focus of its content as well as its rigid philosophical form, to break as strongly as possible with the depraved conceptualizations of the 'Romantic' which regard it as a formless poetry of the unconscious or of the dark nocturnal regions of experience. In this, Benjamin quite unambiguously has the pronouncements of early Romantic poetology on his side; for time and again, this demands a greatest possible consciousness of artistic production, both in the sense of distanced mastery of its technical – 'artisanal' or even 'factory-like' – mechanism, as well as in the sense of a complete sobriety on the part of art in general.

> The innermost principles of art and science are *mechanical*, and this is new evidence of the Godliness of the mechanical.

> Greatness in music – the very spirit of church music, the fugue – is *mechanical*; it turns like a screw, a lever, or so forth.[65]

Benjamin cites similar pertinent statements by the Romantics (*SW* 1: 175–7), from which he draws a number of questionable conclusions. He almost seamlessly integrates the Romantic idea of prose – regardless of its complex meaning for the Romantic philosophy of form – into the more content-based significance of what is called 'prosaic'. Furthermore, evidently following a conceptualization that maintains a conflict between beauty and conscious reflectedness, he sees, 'in the final analysis, the concept of beauty retreat[ing] from the Romantic philosophy of art altogether' (*SW* 1: 177). Both conclusions fall somewhere between being off the mark and simply wrong: Romantic prose is not purely 'prosaic', and nor does the concept of beauty diminish in significance. Rather, the opposite holds: in the process of constituting aesthetics as an 'objective' discipline (i.e. as a philosophy of art itself rather than of the subjective modes of its perception), the Romantics indeed effect a fundamental turn-around in the concept of beauty – but in this, the significance of beauty is extended only further. The 'objective' beauty of the ancient Greeks on the one hand, and that of Goethe and future literature on the other, were and still are *the* canonic pillars of Schlegel's systematic as well as historico-philosophical aesthetics.

Above all, however, the following is of significance with regard to the theory of poetic reflection: Benjamin does not acknowledge that, for Novalis in particular, the forms of reflection called 'potentiation' or 'romanticizing' have the sense of an augmentation of the conscious and *un*conscious alike (something about which Benjamin could indeed have read in the work of Ricarda Huch)[66] – and so he draws the rash conclusion, through reference to his assumption of absolute consciousness, that 'reflection is the antithesis of ecstasy' (*SW* 1: 104). This conclusion is contradicted not only in a statement by Schlegel that was unknown to Benjamin – 'Poetic reflection is ecstasy'[67] – but can also be contested on systematic grounds. For in a strict epistemological understanding of the word, *Ek-stasis* belongs inalienably within the context of a theory of poetic reflection: on the one hand with regard to the origin of reflection in feeling, to which Benjamin at least alludes; and on the other, with regard to the 'leaps' (*SW* 1: 126) *within* the continuum of reflection – that is, *between* the continuum's levels or decentred 'centres' – which he even stresses. The word ecstasy can, however, be found only relatively seldom within the Romantics' writings. Instead, Schlegel in particular conferred general significance within the philosophy of art upon another term relating to stepping out of oneself, or of a continuum of coherence: *parabasis*. Through reference to this and certain geometric metaphors it will be possible to conceive of the relation of reflection and ecstasy in a way that is at once different to Benjamin and more appropriate to the Romantics.[68]

6   REFLECTION AND IMAGINATION

In Benjamin's dissertation, one of Fichte's and the Romantics' fundamental concepts of thinking can be sought only in vain: that of *imagination*. With polemic intent, Benjamin dissociates the Romantic concept of reflection from the (Fichtean) forms of action of intellectual intuition, positing and unconscious production. But what of reflection's relation to imagination? Here too reasons can be extrapolated from the basic assumptions of Benjamin's study as to why imagination was *not* included in his exposition. To be precise, it would have laid bare scarcely surmountable contradictions. On the one hand, there is no assertion of an analogous verdict or analogous depotentiation on the Romantics' part with regard to imagination, as is claimed *vis-à-vis* intuition and positing. On the other, those very forms of action that are Benjamin's polemic targets do play a pre-eminent role in imagination. For in Fichte, the capacity of productive imagination is essentially '*no reflection*', but rather an unconscious production, and its result an *intuition*.[69] Precisely this circumvention of imagination, however, at the same time precludes insight into some substantial reasons for the Romantics' high estimation of reflection. For just as Novalis transforms the theory of reflection into an objective metaphysics of the Absolute, so something similar applies to imagination – and in such a way that the structures of imagination as hovering between being and not-being, of hovering reflection, and of the Absolute itself are shown to correspond closely to one another. This too is instructive for a theory of poetic reflection that goes beyond Benjamin.

7   THE POLEMIC ABSENCE OF SCHELLING

If one draws together all the above reconstructed definitions, then another gap in Benjamin's text becomes comprehensible: the total absence of Schelling throughout, up to and including the bibliography. In a philosophical work on Romanticism, this absence is sufficiently astounding as to be worthy of consideration *as* an absence. It is known how 'dreadful' and 'repulsive'[70] Benjamin found the conceptual algebra of German Idealism, and one could conclude that this might constitute an initial reason for Benjamin's abstinence *vis-à-vis* Schelling. However, such speculation is wholly unnecessary in regard of his dissertation – since the case here is much rather that almost all its elements stand at odds to Schelling's philosophy. The Romantics depotentiate or even reject intellectual intuition, yet Schelling affords it even greater significance than does Fichte. The Romantics (as Benjamin understands them) deny the unconscious in art and postulate a completely conscious context of reflection. Schelling by contrast conceives of the Absolute as 'something eternally unconscious' in which there 'is no duplicity whatsoever' and which, 'precisely because all consciousness is conditional on duplicity, may never attain consciousness';[71] in his system the role of art consists precisely in the overcoming of this antithesis of conscious *and* unconscious.[72] Above all, though: the Romantics raise reflection, regardless of acknowledging its reifying character, to a mode of self-representation of the Absolute. Schelling by contrast ascribes to reflection – where he does not just describe it as 'mental illness' which by dint of its differential character 'kills' 'identity', and therewith all 'higher being in the bud'[73] – merely a 'negative value', as a 'mere means' that, at least in the form of reversal, approaches the Absolute that reflection is unable to obtain.[74]

From this viewpoint, Schelling's absence appears as a logical function of the dissertation's content, with Benjamin foregoing any explicit discussion of Schelling so as not to compromise his exposition.[75] And in so far as this absence is a form of implicit dissociation, it also gains a polemic quality in the context of the history of Romantic philosophy's reception. In most of the literature on Romanticism cited by Benjamin, Schelling's philosophy is incorporated in a relatively seamless way as a source or commentary on Schlegel's and Novalis's notions of thinking as well. Only in more recent systematic analyses has it become possible to determine either merely a modest significance of Schelling for the Romantics,[76] or else instances of direct opposition between the two.[77] Having said this, the rigid, yet totally tacit opposition to Schelling inherent in Benjamin's argument with regard to crucial philosophical paradigms still stands unique, both within the preceding and subsequent literature (with the rigour of this opposition in part revised through the above critical reconstructions also).

8   THE ABSOLUTE AS RECIPROCITY AND MEDIUM OF REFLECTION

Benjamin arrives at one of his most fortunate terminological coups for the theory of reflection by way of a relation of this latter to the Romantic negation of absolute premiership within the figure of *reciprocity*. Here too, Benjamin relies on an extremely limited basis within his textual sources. He entrusts the supporting of his argument to just a *single* quotation – and it is not coincidental that this quotation comes from that fragment of the *Philosophical Apprentice-Years* which Windischmann published in the appendix to the collection of lectures he edited, and which bears his name. The fragment reads:

> Philosophy must have at its foundation not just a proof assuming the form of reciprocal determination, but also a *concept* subject to *reciprocal interchange*. In every concept as in every proof, one can ask again for a concept or proof of the same. Thus philosophy, like epic poetry, must commence in the middle, and it is impossible to convey and dissect it in such a way that the original and first might immediately and itself be completely grounded and explained. The original and first is a whole, and the way to recognize it is therefore not a straight line but a circle. The

whole of foundational theory must be derived from two ideas, principles, concepts; intuition without any additional matter.[78]

Benjamin limits his interpretation of this fragment to two sentences. He laconically identifies the two 'ideas, principles, concepts' that reciprocally ground one another with the 'two poles of reflection' (*SW* 1:137), and concludes: if the whole of philosophy is a movement *between* these poles, without a firm point *beyond* reflective reciprocity, then so all philosophy is a 'medium'.[79]

At this stage, it is worthwhile drawing attention to certain elements of the significance that these comments will be afforded in greater detail later in this work – in so far as these elements are attested directly in the context of Benjamin's exposition. First, one can locate the quotation from Schlegel within the series of conceptual confrontations with Fichte. The concept of reciprocal determination is indeed drawn from the *Science of Knowledge*, in which latter the idea of *absolute* reciprocity, and of a 'totality' of 'relation' without 'something fixed and stable in itself' is also attested.[80] For Fichte, however, this figure applies only to a certain level of *theoretical* epistemology, and is ultimately relativized through the idea of an absolute 'I' beyond all reciprocity.[81] Schlegel and Novalis by contrast – who repeatedly reject the idea of absolute *premiership* or of an original and first *Absolute*[82] – annul this limitation and expand the figure of reciprocity to the whole sphere of thinking *and* what is thought. The consequences of this are that the Absolute is not something that precedes reciprocity and is itself not subject to it, but rather that it is nothing other than the totality of the poles of reciprocity that are as such *non-absolute* – identical, ultimately, to the reflective interconnection of 'everything real' (*SW* 1:144). And precisely this configuration safeguards reflection from the antecedence and constitutivity that are contradictorily *claimed* throughout Benjamin's other observations. Precisely this configuration bestows upon reflection the priority and constitutivity upon which Benjamin can elsewhere lay only a thetical and highly self-contradictory *claim*. For 'the play of dualism' between the poles of reciprocity, which Schlegel on one occasion refers to directly as the play of 'reflection',[83] posits the Absolute first of all – or better still, *is* the Absolute, as a 'medium' of differential play without a stable foundation. Understood thus, the Romantic theory which defines the Absolute as a medium of reflection is *prima philosophia* by means of negating *prima philosophia*. And in so far as the absolute play of reflections is essentially a movement between their poles – that is, in the 'middle' – this movement again leads on to the question of the 'point of indifference' of creative reflection, to the power of *difference* that in its work, in the structural network of the poles of reflection, is at once realized and disappears *as* such.

9 REFLECTION AND TERMINOLOGY

As the first particular 'fulfilment' (*SW* 1:138) of the medium of reflection, Benjamin presents the form of Romantic philosophy, or to be more precise: its terminology. It is above all characteristic of Friedrich Schlegel's fragments to metaphorize or analogize entire terminological systems and thus, on the one hand, to generate an abundance of near-synonyms, and on the other, to invest particular concepts – by dint of displacing the usual order and referentiality of a multitude of terms – with complex interconnections. As a presupposition for the functioning of these terminological sleights of hand, Benjamin asserts a kind of absolute systematic character of language itself: 'the term, the concept, contained (for Schlegel) the seed of the system; it was, at bottom, nothing other than a preformed system itself' (*SW* 1: 140). Or, in the words of the theory of reflection: 'The presupposition of a continuous, medial coherence, of a reflective medium of concepts, is operative here' (*SW* 1: 140). These lines contain two fundamental assumptions which have become widely accepted ever since de Saussure. First, language does not belatedly describe language-less ideas, but rather both are first constituted *in* the act of articulation, as the partitioning off of *signifier and signified*. There is no signified which is not, *ab ovo*, linguistically structured, and thus always already assuming the position of the signifier; and no signifier whose material structure does not, from and of itself, extend into the stipulation of differences in meaning.[84] According to Benjamin, reflection should as it were be understood no differently, as the mutual and reciprocal production of reflected and reflecting – and even the metaphysical assumption holds here that the differential division in the poles of reflection not only does not run counter to the unpreconceivable Absolute, but that this unpreconceivable Absolute is already located in and of itself in the position of dividing–divided reflection, and thereby experiences its very self-representation in reflection. Second, the *entire* system is contained in every linguistic element, since every sound and every meaning is what it is not on account of some positivity in its substance, but solely on account of its negative and differential relations to all other elements. In just this way every pole of reflection, every level of reflection, every centre of reflection, refers in the medium of reflection as expounded above not to a positive signified outside the reflective 'context', but virtually to all other poles, levels and centres of reflection.

In this way, the Romantic theory of reflective contexts and interconnections 'reflects' the self-referential and differential systematic character of language. The particularity of Romantic terminology with regard to this universal systematic character of language would, then, be the following: in the 'witty [*witzig*]' transpositions with which Romantic *parole* at once confirms and breaks the system of *langue*, the system stands out 'in a flash, like lightning [*blitzartig*]' *as* a system (*SW* 1: 140). For Schlegel, *Witz* (wit) and *Blitz* (lightning) belong inseparably together not 'just' phonetically and metaphorically – and therefore, in the 'mystical' term, even 'with the most extreme truncation of discursive thinking . . . , the maximum systematic range of thought' is attained (*SW* 1: 139). These elaborations on Benjamin demarcate the points of inception that already exist within his own text for an extension of the theory of poetic reflection through linguistic theory.

1 0   THE REFLECTION OF NATURAL OBJECTS

As his second concrete 'fulfilment' – following the terminological form of
Romantic thinking – Benjamin seeks to 'derive' the Romantic 'theory of the
knowledge of objects' out of the theory of the absolute medium of reflection
(*SW* 1: 143–4). He dedicates a first chapter to natural objects and a second to
the work of art. Unlike the second of these chapters, the first is again marked by
a very forced selection of sources, presenting what *can* be read from a few texts
by Novalis as *the* 'early Romantic theory of the knowledge of nature' – although
this finds no parallel in Schlegel, nor coincides with Schelling's philosophy
of nature. Benjamin's 'derivation' obeys the following logic. 'The object, like
'everything real, lies within the medium of reflection' (*SW* 1: 144) – it is,
therefore, only 'relatively' distinct from the subject of cognition. The relation of
the two to one another is not that of a thinking subject to a 'dead' object, but
rather that of 'centres of reflection' in the same medium which can mutually
'incorporate' one another (*SW* 1: 146). For *in* the reflective interconnection of
'everything real', every reflective pole is at the same time a reflected one, and vice
versa. In this respect, there is no mere 'being thought' that is not also a 'thinking',
no 'thinking' that is not also a 'being thought'. This notion of reciprocity
between subject and object of cognition can be found already within Fichte's
theory of reciprocal activity and passivity, in which 'passivity' likewise does not
denote a mere lacking of activity, but an activity with a different direction.
Novalis applied this theory extensively: 'Mere passivity and mere activity are
abstract conditions. Everything is passive only to the extent that it is active, and
vice versa.'[85] The 'self-activity' of the cognizing subject is at once 'a receptivity'
for the object of cognition, and the passive 'perceptibility' of the object of
cognition at once an active 'attentiveness' toward the cognizing subject.[86]

Benjamin interprets this interconnection not only in the general sense of a
reciprocity, however, but in the particular sense of a 'dependence of any
knowledge of an object on self-knowledge by the object' (*SW* 1: 145). Thus, he
interprets the theorem of a self-active, self-thinking object as that of an object
that thinks *of* itself. However, with very few exceptions (*SW* 1: 145–6), this is
possible only by going *against* the grain of Novalis's texts. Precisely what
Benjamin quotes as the 'most paradoxical and at the same time clearest'
reference for his interpretation – Novalis's remarks about passive 'perceptibility'
as active 'attentiveness' (*SW* 1: 145) – simply means for Novalis that within
cognition, the 'passivity' of the object of cognition is at the same time a kind of
'activity' against the object of cognition: not, however, that this activity is
directed *at itself* or that it is *self*-reflection.[87] Benjamin then feels himself
compelled to append a – scarcely convincing – codicil to his interpretation.

> It does not matter whether in this sentence, over and above the
> attentiveness of the object to itself, its attentiveness to the one perceiving
> is also meant; for even when Novalis clearly expresses this thought – 'In all
> predicates in which we see the fossil, it sees us' – that attentiveness to the

one seeing can still be rightly understood only as a symptom of the thing's capacity to see itself. (*SW* 1: 145)

The reader may feel justly astonished: where the wording does not fit with Benjamin's interpretation, 'it does not matter', or 'can still be rightly understood' as 'a symptom' of its diametric opposite! Nevertheless, we can leave it open at this point as to whether or not the Romantic theory of the knowledge of nature that Benjamin constructs is philologically and systematically tenable. For the general theory of the medium of reflection, however, it furnishes two elements that extend beyond its questionable contextualization. The first of these is the tendency to replace the strictly polar 'subject–object correlation' with the interplay of only 'relatively' distinct 'centres of reflection' and an 'immanent connection in the Absolute', as the Absolute understood as the medium of reflection of 'everything real' (*SW* 1: 146). The second – particularly with relation to the figure of reflective criticism – is the Romantic theory of *experiment* as a purposeful evocation of the self-activity of the object of cognition (*SW* 1: 147–8).

11 ART AS MEDIUM OF REFLECTION: BENJAMIN'S PHILOLOGICAL EXPOSITION

Benjamin considered the third of his reconstructed 'fulfilments' of the absolute medium of reflection 'the most fruitful' and 'perhaps ... the only legitimate one': *art* (*SW* 1: 149, 138). According to Benjamin, the 'theory of the medium of reflection' itself would still retain outstanding worth for art even if – seen absolutely – it should prove itself untenable (*SW* 1: 146ff.). As noted previously, Benjamin refrains from providing textual support for this focal point of his exegesis by attributing to it the status of a metaphysical credo: 'It would obviously be totally mistaken to seek in the Romantics a special reason for their considering art as a medium of reflection. For them this interpretation of everything real, thus of art as well, was a metaphysical credo' (*SW* 1: 149). Consequently, Benjamin is not interested in illuminating *why* the Romantics understood art essentially as poetic reflection, but merely *that* they did so. And once again, he must rely for this on an extremely sparse and unwieldy collection of textual sources. For the concept of reflection is encountered in the context of art theory far less often even than within the Romantics' general theory of cognition or metaphysics. And where it is to be found, it often works in favour of the more common understanding which sees in Romantic reflection primarily an unartistic manner of self-*thematization* or of making statements *about* a work of art *within* it – not, however, the integral and constitutive principle of art itself. The term 'poetic reflection' occurs, indeed, just once in all the texts known to Benjamin – and as far as I can ascertain only twice more in those texts that were unknown to him.[88] The need for theoretical construction is therefore all the greater, and Benjamin undertakes this construction across three levels. He takes Schlegel's celebrated statement about poetic reflection as his point of departure; then seeks to prove that the structure of reflection of art is often what is being discussed even where the term itself is not employed; and finally raises the theory of poetic reflection to the status of overriding universality in early Romantic poetology, by deriving from it the incomparably more familiar ideas of irony, transcendental poetry and the novel.

'[O]nly in the famous 116th *Athenaeum Fragment*', according to Benjamin, did the early Schlegel 'characterize ... art as a medium of reflection' with desirable 'clarity' (*SW* 1:150). And yet this fragment supports Benjamin's 'sturdy' claims only in a very partial way, with Schlegel distinguishing three possibilities of a 'progressive universal poetry' within it. According to the first of these, universal poetry can 'lose' itself completely and unconditionally in 'what is (re)presented' (*'das Dargestellte'*), in the object of its representation, whether what is represented is the 'entire surrounding world' or 'poetic individuals of any type'. According to the second, universal poetry can just as radically consist in the poet – he who presents – only being able to find 'expression' for 'himself', for his own 'spirit'. And finally, this progressive universal poetry can *also* 'hover', on the wings of poetic reflection, in the middle, between what is (re)presented and that which (re)presents; can increase the power of this reflection ever more; and can multiply it 'as in an infinite series of mirrors'.[89] Only *one* of three possibilities relates, then, to the model of infinite and medial reflection. And even if – drawing on a tendency of the fragment – one interprets this third way as a synthesis of all three possibilities, this fragment still by no means fits seamlessly into Benjamin's exposition. For both of the next closest ways of reading the fragment stand entirely at odds to this interpretation. These readings arise if, in accordance with the fragment's contextualization and also a remark that Benjamin makes, 'that which (re)presents' is understood as the poet, and 'what is (re)presented' as the objects of his representation.[90] As hovering between the two, reflection would then be either a kind of hiatus *between* author and work – and therefore not that structure of formal self-referentiality which is *immanent* in the work, as Benjamin claims; or else, reflection would hover *within* the work itself, between an author representing himself and the other objects of his representation – in which case it would hardly be that structure of reflection which grounds the entire organization of '*forms*', and which is all that Benjamin is concerned with.

Only the third way of reading this fragment – which is not expressly considered by Benjamin, although his 'employment' of the quotation calls for it – escapes these contradictions. This reading becomes possible if one ascribes to Schlegel's discussion of that which represents and what is represented – despite its relatively unambiguous contextualization – a potential ambiguity extending into Romantic semiology and Novalis's discussion of 'the signifying' and 'the signified'.[91] Within this reading, the reflective to and fro between that which represents and what is represented is, then, *articulation* in Saussure's sense, the language-building force of *différence* that transacts the processes between *signifiant* and *signifié* and thereby first posits these as such. Only when understood in this way does poetic reflection in fact mean the formation of form – since 'what is represented' is not the opposite, but itself a necessary element of linguistic form. And only when read thus does a direct path emerge from what is surely Schlegel's most celebrated fragment to Benjamin's subsequent summarization:

> The pure essence of reflection announces itself to the early Romantics in the purely formal appearance of the work of art. Thus, form is the objective expression of the reflection proper to the work, the reflection that constitutes its essence. Form is the possibility of reflection in the work. It grounds the work *a priori*, therefore, as a principle of existence; it is through its form that the work of art is a living centre of reflection. (*SW* 1:156)

But let us continue to look, first, at Benjamin's 'derivation' of this formulation. Benjamin's second step in 'deriving' this theorem draws on Novalis: 'In many passages Novalis, too, insinuated that the basic structure of art is that of the medium of reflection' (*SW* 1: 150). This assertion is immediately followed by Benjamin's first example of this:

> The sentence, 'Poetry is, indeed, only the more resolute, more active, more productive use of our organs, and perhaps thinking itself would be something not much different – and thinking and poetry therefore are one and the same' ... points in that same direction. (*SW* 1: 150)

That is weak. It is difficult to see how Novalis might 'insinuate' the theory of the medium of reflection through identifying thinking and poetry as 'productive use of our organs'. By contrast, it is easy to see quite how much Benjamin's formulation 'points in that same direction' unintentionally reveals the disparity between the fragment and Benjamin's intention in quoting it. The next example scarcely submits to any greater degree to Benjamin's will:

> Quite clearly, Novalis conceives of art as the medium of reflection *kat' exochen* ... when he says: 'The beginning of the "I" is merely ideal .... The beginning arises later than the "I"; therefore the "I" cannot have begun. We see from this that we are here in the domain of art.' (*SW* 1: 150)

If it is a general weakness on Benjamin's part to seldom provide more than a single line of commentary on quotations; the total absence of any further discussion here concerning these extremely difficult sentences amounts to giving up on comprehensibility. For how should any reader be expected to achieve the following three-part manoeuvre without further assistance: first, to understand why, according to Novalis, 'the beginning arises later than the "I" ' and 'therefore the "I" cannot have begun'; secondly, to infer 'from this' 'that we are here in the domain of art'; and thirdly, to thence be able to interpret all this as compelling evidence for the theory of the medium of reflection? A recourse to the context of the quoted sentences shows, first of all, that Benjamin quite consciously distorts the fragment's semantics in at least one respect – and namely, the one that is central for his argument. For even if Novalis's dismissal of an absolute beginning remains opaque, it is clear enough that Benjamin distorts the conclusion which Novalis draws from this dismissal. By 'art', Novalis here primarily means, specifically, artificiality in the philosophical construction of the 'I' that has no absolute beginning. 'But', Novalis continues, 'this artificial supposition is the basis of a genuine science which always arises from *artificial facts*. The 'I' is to be constructed. The philosopher prepares, creates artificial elements and thus sets about a construction.'[92] Fichte had already explained similarly in his *Science of Knowledge* – which is indeed the doctrine of the 'I' – that the first 'level of reflection' does not deal with pre-existing facts, but with 'facts [of consciousness] that are engendered *artificially*, following the laws of reflection'. And Fichte even speaks, like Novalis, of a 'fact engendered through art'.[93] Therefore, neither Novalis nor Fichte is concerned with art in the sense that Benjamin suggests by way of his abridged quotation, but both are rather concerned with the artificiality of philosophical construction. (At most upon second reflection and following a line of argument different to Benjamin's could the 'metaphor' of art *also* be taken 'literally' here.)

Even though Benjamin's all too direct 'usage' of Novalis's fragment on the artificial construction of the 'I', can barely be justified, the fragment could well be claimed for the *general* theory of the medium of reflection. For what Fichte limits to the first 'level of reflection' – reflection on 'facts that are engendered *artificially*, following the laws of reflection, through the spontaneity of our capacity for reflection' – this construction without something pre-existing, this 'art of invention without data',[94] is related by Novalis within the passage quoted to the entire construction of the 'I', and thereby indeed refers, as Benjamin postulates, to 'an absolutely neutral origin of reflection' as a creative medium. This could have served Benjamin not only to mark the Romantics' difference to Fichte, but also to let the Romantics themselves proclaim their difference *vis-à-vis* Schelling, something that is buried implicitly within the entire design of Benjamin's reading. For Novalis's understanding of the 'I' that does not begin absolutely as an artificial 'product' polemicizes above all against Schelling's conception that consciousness and 'I' both emerged from within the history of nature: 'This is not the *natural history* of the "I" – "I" is no product of nature – no nature – no historical being – but an artistic one – an *art* – a work of art.'[95] What is claimed here for the artificial construction of the 'I' – the figure of construction *in* the medium of representation, the figure of the 'art of invention without data' – was indeed ultimately related to poetry by Novalis. And thus, Benjamin's cursory attempt to attest that Novalis too already regarded art as an absolute medium of reflection, and to show this as the direct content of certain 'tropes' employed by Novalis, *can* still end 'happily', in spite of the initial violence and abridgements that Benjamin enacts: 'Novalis terms poetry … "a self-forming essence".… Thus, reflection is the originary and constructive factor in art, as in everything spiritual' (*SW* 1: 151).

12   THE WORK AS CENTRE OF REFLECTION

The second stratum of Benjamin's effort to define art as medium of reflection renders transparent a connection between reflection's form and other elementary art theoretical terms – a connection at which the Romantics themselves only hinted. The first focus within this reflective grammar of Romantic terminology is on 'a basic concept that could not have been previously introduced into the theory with any definiteness: the concept of the work' (*SW* 1:155). Both in the aesthetics of rationalism and traditional generic poetry, as well as in the first radical negation of these – 'the boundless cult' of subjectivity that expresses itself within 'the theory of *Sturm und Drang*' – the work of art was essentially grounded in *external* principles: through rules on the one hand, and through reference to the work's 'creator' on the other (*SW* 1:154). Schlegel's emphatic concept of the work by contrast enthrones – in an act of radical change that is decisive for the whole of aesthetics – the 'immanent structure' as the sole 'criterion of the artwork', thereby opening the way for the notion of its 'autonomy'. The numerous statements about the work as something constructed-in-itself, complete-in-itself, representing-of-itself or even criticizing-of-itself (*SW* 1:157) correspond, according to Benjamin's observation, in the closest way to the 'theory of art as a medium of reflection and of the work as a centre of reflection' (*SW* 1:155). For the absolute medium of reflection's immanent play is indeed defined precisely through complete self-referentiality and self-supportiveness.

From this grounding in the concept of reflection, there follow two further characteristics of the work of art. The first of these is its 'double nature' of being finite and infinite (*SW* 1:156ff.). In Fichte's and the Romantics' sense, the act of reflection – as 'activity reaching out from within its own confines' versus 'activity returning onto itself' – is an act of restriction, of 'self-limitation'. However, the 'limiting nature' of reflection is counterbalanced by the possibility of – in further reflections – permanently transgressing this 'limiting nature of every finite reflection'. The other pole of the 'double concept of form' given in reflection is therefore the 'self-extension' of the work into an 'infinite series of mirrors', into a virtual infinity (which, on the one hand, extends even beyond the 'inner' infinity of the work and into its continuation in 'criticism', and on the other, refers to the 'idea of art').

A second characteristic of the self-reflective work is the ambiguity of its elements. In the conclusion of Benjamin's derivation of ambiguity from the form of reflection there exists an exact parallel to Jakobson's theory of poetic function as a mode of speech which focuses on its own features: 'Ambiguity is an intrinsic, inalienable characteristic of any self-focused message, briefly a corollary feature of poetry.'[96] The reasons for this essential ambiguity of self-reflective speaking are different, however. For Jakobson, it emerges out of the following consideration: 'By promoting the palpability of signs, the poetic function deepens the fundamental dichotomy of signs and objects.'[97] Attention toward the signs *as* signs effects a kind of loosening of the 'referential function' – not its complete erasure, but the sublation of unambiguity of the 'objective reference'.[98] Benjamin's explanation of the polyvalency of self-reflective structures (of speech) is at once simpler and more formalistic than Jakobson's. According to Benjamin, if one considers just three elements of a structure of reflection, their relation to one another can already 'be conceived and performed in two ways': either as a reflection (of a reflection of a reflection), or as (a reflection of a reflection of) a reflection (*SW* 1: 128ff.). The greater the complexity of the reflection, the lesser the degree of clarity regarding which is the reflecting pole (subject) and which the reflected one (object). The 'dissolution' of this distinction within the 'I'-less medium of infinite reflection ultimately means that any given level of reflection is already – *qua* level of reflection – ambiguous.

13   IRONY, TRANSCENDENTAL POETRY, THE NOVEL

Regardless of the numerous and grave weaknesses of Benjamin's *general* outline, the foremost ideas of Romantic poetology – irony, transcendental poetry and the novel – are devolved upon his *art theoretical* 'fulfilment' of the concept of reflection as if by their own accord. These 'derivations' can be discussed all the more quickly here in that they represent neither objects of criticism nor central foci of the revision being undertaken here.

It was already uncontested long before Benjamin that Romantic *irony* deals in the phenomena of self-reflection. But this reflection was understood largely in terms of being a reflection *on* or *about* something: as the subsequent addition of an explicit self-relativization toward the work 'proper', and as a dissolving of the poetic *sujet*'s subjectivity in a play with itself. Benjamin does not dispute a limited legitimacy of 'irony' in this sense: he terms it 'the subjectivistic irony', which has its 'field of play' above all in 'subject matter' (*SW* 1: 162). 'Under the rubric' of this kind of irony – which is the only one Hegel had in mind in his devastating critique of Romantic irony altogether – 'objections can be raised in principle to the emphasis on the objective moments of [Schlegel's] thinking' (*SW* 1: 161). It is therefore an all the more urgent task for Benjamin to deduce a second sense of 'irony' that rejects 'the notion of a Romantic subjectivism *sans phrase*' (*SW* 1: 163). In reflective form as fundamental structure of the work, Benjamin locates just such *objective* irony. The formal relations of reflection *in* the work, *between* its parts, enact in a general and implicit way that which is only a border phenomenon and exception within material reflecting *on* itself: 'self-extension' – as integration into the relational structure of the absolute medium – through 'self-limitation', through the definition of each individual element *as* a – finite – level of reflection. Irony – as such a schematism of the mediation of conditional and unconditional, and of finite and infinite – within itself enacts the doubleness inherent in the concepts of reflection, of the work and of form. It relativizes 'the determinate form of the individual work' in order to allocate to it an extended fulfilment in the absolute medium of reflection as the idea of art. This 'formal' structure is 'not, like diligence or candour, an intentional demeanour of the author. It cannot be understood in the usual manner as an index of a subjective boundlessness, but must be appreciated as an objective moment in the work itself' (*SW* 1: 165).

The situation with regard to the concept of '*transcendental poetry*' is an analogous one. In philosophy, transcendental, as the focus of knowledge toward itself, already denotes a form of self-reflection. Particularly for Schlegel, the concept of the transcendental 'everywhere lead[s] back to the concept of reflection' (*SW* 1: 169), and most succinctly of all in the 238th *Athenaeum Fragment*, about poetry that – *qua* reflective structure – represents itself. (Benjamin's claim that this celebrated fragment at the same time confuses the concepts 'transcendental' and 'reflection' has quite correctly been countered elsewhere already.)[99] Both from the viewpoint of conceptual analysis, and from a philosophical viewpoint, then, it holds that 'the concept of transcendental poetry points back to the systematic centre from which the Romantic philosophy of art proceeded. It ... presents Romantic poetry as the absolute poetic reflection' (*SW* 1: 169).

Finally to *the novel*. Its enthronement as the highest form of art is, for the Romantics, essentially grounded in the idea of dissolving all generic boundaries, and of mixing all forms within an 'absolute' continuum of discontinuities. Benjamin's discussion of the absolute medium of self-reflecting forms denotes precisely a structure of this kind, and thus he is easily able to understand the novel as the idea of poetic reflection: 'Among all forms of presentation, there is one in which the Romantics find reflective self-limitation and self-extension developed in the most decisive way and at this apex passing into each other without distinction. This highest symbolic form is the novel' (*SW* 1: 172). Through elaborating on this theorem (*SW* 1: 171–2), Benjamin also manages to integrate the 'keystone'[100] of Romantic poetology into the theory of art as a medium of reflection.

14 CRITIQUE (*KRITIK*)

Like 'the objective structure of art ... and ... its formations' (*SW* 1: 118), as well as the semantics of the concepts pertaining to these, Benjamin derives the Romantic concept of critique from the theory of reflection too. As with the fragmentary character of Benjamin's study, there is also a systematic and polemic reason why the concept of critique – despite its serving as the title of the entire work – figures only as *one*, and indeed logically as the last, in a long series of material 'fulfilments' of the medium of reflection. Benjamin formulates this reason in the following, only seemingly tautological, sentence: 'Critique comprises the knowledge of its object' (*SW* 1: 143). The entire innovation of the Romantic concept of critique is contained for Benjamin in this unspectacular sentence – and thereby also a motive as to why the theory of critique is at the same time encountered only as a postscript to the theory of its 'objects'. Specifically, pre-Romantic criticism did *not* comprise an objective and immanent 'knowledge of its object'. In the framework of the subjective aesthetics of reception (*Wirkungsästhetik*) criticism was essentially an expression of taste-based judgements, and in part maintained the avowed impossibility of objective aesthetics. In the framework of normative generic poetics or stylistics, criticism was essentially an assessment of the individual work in relation to rules that remained external to and abstractly pre-existed it. It was not, however, a reconstruction of the work from within itself. Schlegel, countering the 'Kantian ... assertion that no theory of the beautiful is possible',[101] ascribes to criticism its place within an '*objective system* of ... aesthetic sciences';[102] 'explaining [the subjective] effects of the artwork is, however, the province of the psychologist, and does not concern the critic in the least'.[103] Countering normative poetics, Schlegel advocates a knowledge that proceeds from within the self-reflective work's own features: '*Critique* should not evaluate works according to a general ideal, but should search out the *individual* ideal in every work.'[104] Or, as he puts it so exquisitely in the *Wilhelm Meister* review:

> To subject a book, which one can only understand from within itself, to a generic concept compiled and assembled out of customs and beliefs, coincidental experiences, and arbitrary stipulations, is no different to the childish wish to grasp the moon and stars with one's hand and to pack them away in a little box.[105]

As a representation of works based on their own features, critique is not a judgemental 'reflecting *on* a work of art', but rather a consciousness-raising 'unfolding', *in* a new formation, of that 'reflection' which itself already exists in the work as its structural principle (*SW* 1: 151ff.). Both work and critique are therefore 'relative' moments in the same medium of reflection (*SW* 1: 146). This figure of immanent unfolding participates in the doubleness of the Romantic concepts of reflection, form and the work. The reflection of reflection is, on the one hand, the limitation according to its own formal structure of the work that returns into itself, and on the other hand – and precisely in this act of limitation – an extending-out-of-itself on the part of this self-reflective structure into a new, higher level of reflection. In this regard, critique is not only a reconstruction but also an extension of the work: 'The true reader', writes Novalis, 'must be the extended author. He is the higher authority who receives the object already prepared by the lower authority.'[106] Or, in the words of one of Schlegel's notes that was unknown to Benjamin: 'The true critic is an author to the 2nd degree.'[107] How seriously the Romantics took raising the work to a higher degree is demonstrated particularly through Schlegel's numerous statements maintaining that critique can take place only of objects that are still 'not finished',[108] but which are rather aimed at being increased.[109] Indeed, these notes on the consummative function of critique best support Benjamin's assertion of an 'axiomatic presupposition' according to which the infinite intensification of reflection 'does not take its course into an empty infinity, but is in itself substantial and filled' (*SW* 1: 129).

15 CONCLUSION

Benjamin's dissertation is therefore *in toto* a theory of 'I'-less' structures of reflection. Countering the low regard for reflection, as the rule of differential and 'dry' reason, that is generally asserted within German Idealism, Benjamin rather sees the Romantics enthroning reflection as the warrant of immediacy and the full infinity of thinking, and indeed as the (self-representational) form of the Absolute. Within this line of argument, the general exposition of the Romantic theory of reflection – which is the essential innovation of Benjamin's study – relates to its 'application' in a seemingly paradoxical fashion, in that Benjamin's considerable and in part more than marginal violence with regard to the general philosophical grounding of his arguments does not hinder him from undertaking a largely valid 'derivation' of the cardinal concepts of Romantic poetology from the theory of reflection as their centre.

3

THE SOBER ABSOLUTE

ON BENJAMIN AND THE
EARLY ROMANTICS

Rodolphe Gasché

According to Philippe Lacoue-Labarthe and Jean-Luc Nancy in *The Literary Absolute*, Walter Benjamin's dissertation *The Concept of Art Criticism in German Romanticism* has revolutionized traditional studies in German Romanticism. Indeed, Winfried Menninghaus remarks, Benjamin's dissertation is the most frequently cited work in studies on that period of German thought. The reason for the breakthrough effect of Benjamin's dissertation is quite clear: his analysis of the major concepts characteristic of Jena Romanticism – the concepts of art, literature, critique, irony, etc. – is fundamental, in that he shows these concepts to be the cornerstones of a very specific philosophical position distinct from those of the major powerbrokers of the time: Kant and the German Idealists.[1] Even though Benjamin's assessment of the specificity of Romantic thought was made on the basis of the few writings accessible at the time, and, moreover, on a narrow selection of the available material, there is no doubt that his dissertation continues to give us a correct and fruitful view of the Early Romantic philosophical conceptions. Yet it also remains true that the dissertation is thoroughly flawed, not only for philological, but for discursive-argumentative reasons as well. As Menninghaus has forcefully shown in *Unendliche Verdopplung*, Benjamin's work abounds with loose argumentation and makes such free use of citations that they are made on occasion to say the exact opposite of what they say in their original context. Furthermore, the exegeses of some concepts (such as the major one of reflection) are essentially limited and distorted. The semantics of a number of fragments is either consciously perverted or forced in certain directions. Finally, the dissertation makes an extremely selective use of the material, selective to the point of being silent about, perhaps to the point of annihilating, what does not fit his conception. This is especially true for the first part of the dissertation, in which Benjamin lays the general philosophical foundation for his analysis of the chief concepts of Romantic thought. And yet, in spite 'of these numerous and partly more than marginal violences', Benjamin's 'derivation of the cardinal concepts of Romantic poetology from the theory of reflection' remains valid. But even the first part, 'On Reflection', where Benjamin finds 'the trace of a dominating systematic signification of the Romantic concept of reflection with its two "moments" of immediacy and infinity', as Menninghaus notes, demands admiration in spite of all its philological and argumentative difficulties (*Unendliche Verdopplung*, pp. 71, 41). The question thus arises as to what explains this strange paradox of an interpretation that yields correct results despite its poor textual basis and systematic distortion? From where does the surprising confidence that Benjamin demonstrates in his violent penetration of the recalcitrant text material originate? Menninghaus suggests that Benjamin's sagacious analysis of early German Romanticism follows not from any brilliant intuition, but from his own theoretical proximity to the fundamental problems raised by Friedrich Schlegel and Novalis. Menninghaus writes: 'The avenues of Benjamin's access to the Romantic theory of reflection are already preprogrammed by his own largely Romantic theory of language' (*Unendliche Verdopplung*, p. 42). The divining rod with which he approaches the sparse corpus of the Romantics' writings available to him would thus be made up of conceptions and concepts intimately related to the Romantic project itself. At first sight, such a conclusion seems warranted. This thesis of a fundamental affinity of Benjamin's thinking to that of the Romantics seems plausible, not only since a great number of topics that Benjamin deals with throughout his career – from the question of translation to that of the mechanical work of art, not to speak of the notion of critique – are already broached in the dissertation, but also because his own theories on these subjects appear closely related to what in the dissertation he had claimed to be the Romantics' position on these matters. However compelling and fruitful such an affinity thesis may be to account for what Benjamin does in his dissertation, its limits come to light as soon as the specificity and originality of Benjamin's own thinking is to be established. Above all, it is incapable of accounting for Benjamin's repeated, if not systematic criticism of Romantic philosophy. Indeed, *The Concept of Art Criticism in German Romanticism* is anything but a wholesale appropriation or celebration of Romanticism. Its presentation of the main axioms of Romantic thought is not without ambivalence. At times Benjamin shows little sympathy, or even direct hostility toward the Romantics' insights. As we shall see, he accuses the Romantics of obscurity, of failing to clearly differentiate between their concepts, of having become embroiled in unresolvable contradictions, of having developed a metaphysics of limited interest, and finally, and not least, of having committed the philosophically unforgivable crime of confusing and mixing levels of thought – a *metabasis allo eis genos*. In the following, I would like to bring Benjamin's criticism of the Romantics into relief in order to precisely determine his point of departure from Romanticism. The vehicle for this demonstration will be the concept of critique itself.

Benjamin understands his objections to Romanticism as philosophical objections. More generally, he conceives his overall approach to the Romantics as a philosophical one. From the very beginning of the dissertation, the task to write a 'history of the concept of art criticism' (as opposed to a 'history of art criticism itself') is said to be a 'philosophical task or, more precisely, the task of unfolding the problem in a historical perspective' (*GS* 1: 11).[2] The qualification in question is necessary, since Benjamin distinguishes two philosophical tasks: one is concerned with an historical-problematic and the other is systematic. The dissertation is limited to a philosophical enquiry of the first type, but pushes its investigation, as Benjamin notes, to a point where it 'indicates, with complete clarity, a systematic connection' (*GS* 1: 117). In the 'Introduction' to the dissertation, Benjamin gives some indication as to how he wants the terms 'philosophical' or 'historical-problematic', to be understood. After having demarcated such a task from questions concerning the history of philosophy and the philosophy of history, he evokes 'a metaphysical hypothesis', of which he says approvingly that, according to it 'the whole of the history of philosophy in the proper sense is at the same time and ipso facto the unfolding of a single problem' *GS* 1: 12). An analysis of Early Romanticism that focuses on an historical-problematic is, I hold, geared toward exhibiting this one single problem of philosophy in the historical configuration of Romantic thought. Once this philosophical task has been achieved, it would become possible to proceed to a systematic evaluation of the way this one single problem has taken shape in Romanticism and to eventually solve the difficulties that it poses. In order to bring the single problem constitutive of all philosophy as such into view, one must 'determine the entire philosophical scope [*Tragweite*]' of the Romantics' positions, Benjamin remarks (*GS* 1: 77). It is a matter of analysing their concepts – and in particular the concept of critique – 'in keeping with their own most proper philosophical intentions [*nach seinen eigensten philosophischen Intentionen*]' (*GS* 1: 80). In other words, a philosophical analysis, that is, an analysis regarded from an historical-problematic perspective has to focus on what, from a philosophical viewpoint, are the most proper intentions of the Romantics' concepts, as well as on Romanticism's 'positive and negative sides' (*GS* 1: 77). Obviously, an analysis of this kind may have to stretch the meaning of their concepts well beyond what the Romantics themselves intended them to say in order to bring out their philosophical intentions – what they contain in themselves, and what is clear from the very subject matter [*sachlich*] they address.

But since Benjamin undoubtedly accords to the Early Romantics a very special privilege I would like to return to the question of his affinity with them. Romantic criticism's superiority is at least double. First, Romantic criticism is 'the principal overcoming of dogmatic rationalism in aesthetics' (*GS* 1: 71). Indeed,

> 'the Romantics did not grasp form, as did the Enlightenment, as a rule for judging the beauty of art, [or regard] the observance of this rule as a necessary precondition for the pleasing or exalting effect of the work. Form did not count for the Romantics either as itself a rule or as dependent on rules'. (*GS* 1: 76)

But Romanticism does not only repudiate the eighteenth century's celebration of conventional aesthetic rules, it also 'overturned the destructive moments that were present in the theory of *Sturm und Drang*', with its 'boundless cult of productive/creative force as the mere expressive force of the creator' (*GS* 1:71). By finding 'the laws of the Spirit in the artwork itself' (*GS* 1:71), Early Romanticism enjoys the historical privilege of having overturned the major aesthetic ideologies of the time. Early German Romanticism's privileged position is further accentuated by a comparison between it and contemporary criticism. Although contemporary criticism shares with Romantic criticism the overcoming of dogmatism – this overcoming has become 'the painless legacy of modern criticism', and Benjamin notes that the criticism of the nineteenth and twentieth centuries has once again sunk below the Romantic standpoint in that it makes 'the artwork into a mere by-product of subjectivity' (*GS* 1:71). Modern criticism is thus in truth the offspring of *Sturm und Drang* aesthetics. It overlooks the fact that the negation of dogmatism by the Romantics rested on the presupposition of the artwork's immanent and objective laws. This negation, 'along with their [the Romantic presuppositions] liberating achievement, secured [indeed] a basic concept which could not be theoretically introduced previously with any definiteness: the concept of the work' (*GS* 1:71). With this, the Romantics deduced 'from the side of the object of formation, that very autonomy in the domain of art that Kant had lent to the power of judgment in the *Third Critique*' (*GS* 1:72). Compared to contemporary critical thought, which according to Benjamin is 'not determined by any theory, but by a deteriorated *praxis* alone' (*GS* 1:71) – for it, critique is what is most subjective – Romantic theories of art criticism hold a definite advantage. Today the 'state of German philosophy of art around 1800, as exhibited in the theories of Goethe and the Early Romantics, is [still] legitimate', one reads toward the end of the dissertation. Yet, in spite of this unmistakable valorization of Romantic thought, and although from a theoretical viewpoint the Romantic position on art criticism has not been surpassed, this does not mean that Benjamin uncritically promotes a return to their theories. The following statement demonstrates that quite the opposite is true: 'The basic cardinal principle of critical activity since the Romantics, [i.e.] the evaluation of the work by immanent criteria, was obtained on the basis of Romantic theories, theories that in their pure form certainly do not completely satisfy any contemporary thinker' (*GS* 1:72). The philosophical, or historical-problematic presentation of Early Romantic thought will thus have a critical edge. Indeed, if for such an analysis it is a matter of drawing out the Romantic concepts' proper philosophical intentions, a certain ambiguity of Benjamin's approach comes into view: to analyse the Romantic concepts of art criticism according to their own most proper philosophical intentions means to measure them against the one single problem constitutive of philosophy, and to critically radicalize concepts whose own radicality, in the very words of Benjamin, is grounded in 'a certain unclarity [*eine gewisse Unklarheit ist der Grund dieses Radikalismus*]' (*GS* 1:105).

A philosophical investigation of 'critique' is warranted 'because criticism contains a cognitive moment' (*GS* 1:11), Benjamin claims. This generalizing statement acknowledges the fact that the Romantics inherited the concept of critique from Kant. As Benjamin remarks, they raised this concept 'to a higher power, because they referred by the word "criticism" to Kant's total historical achievement and not only to *his* concept of criticism' *GS* 1:. 52). As a result, the epistemological underpinnings of their concept of criticism still have to be made manifest. Although with Romanticism, 'it is a matter of criticism as art criticism, not as an epistemic method and philosophical standpoint' (*GS* 1: 13), their 'higher Criticism' (*GS* 1: 51), as they familiarly called it, 'is thoroughly built upon epistemological presuppositions' (*GS* 1: 11). It therefore becomes indispensable to explicate, isolate and exhibit that theory of knowledge, and this is Benjamin's task in the first part of his dissertation: 'On Reflection'.

Right from the start it becomes clear that, for the Romantics, epistemology and metaphysics are intimately linked. Their philosophy, as presented by Benjamin, comprises a theory of the Absolute as a medium of reflection, and a theory of absolute, or immediate intuiting of this very Absolute.

With the idea of the Absolute as a 'medium of reflection' (I note that it is Benjamin who is responsible for coining the expression), the Romantics laid the groundwork for an entirely original philosophical position in the aftermath not only of Kant, but of Fichte as well. By releasing reflection – and that also means immediate cognition, according to Benjamin – from the restriction to a self-positing I that it had in Fichte, and extending it to mere thinking, or thinking in general, reflection becomes 'the infinite and purely methodical character of thinking', Benjamin writes (*GS* 1: 29). Apart from thus reintroducing infinity into the sphere of theoretical knowledge, a sphere from which it had been excluded by Fichte, the Early Romantics redefined infinity, seeing it no longer, in contradiction to Fichte, as continuous advance, but rather as an infinitude of connectedness. And rather than implying emptiness, the Romantics think of a 'filled infinitude [*erfüllte Unendlichkeit*]' (*GS* 1: 26). But, as Benjamin argues, this immediacy of knowing in reflection is also different from the immediacy of intellectual intuition that Fichte ascribed to the self-knowing and self-positing I. The immediacy characteristic of Romantic thought is *intellectual*; not grounded on thinking's *intuitive* nature, it is purely conceptual. Now, it must be noted that, for the Romantics, thinking is 'proper to everything, for everything is a self' (*GS* 1: 29). Consequently, the medium of reflection is both an infinity of interconnected centres infinitely increasing or potentiating reflection and also the immediate knowledge that these centres have of themselves and others. The Absolute as a medium of reflection is the totality of these thinking centres. This most succinct presentation of the Romantic Absolute must suffice for the moment. A more detailed picture of it will arise when, in a moment, I shall proceed to a discussion of the difficulties that Benjamin has with this conception. First, however, I must briefly address the Romantics' contention that this whole – the Absolute, or the System – can also be absolutely grasped. If there is, indeed, such a thing as an absolute grasping of the whole in a mode of comprehension that is not intuitive, in the sense of *anschaulich*, but intellectual, it is, because the whole, as *the* centre of all centres, 'grasps itself immediately in closed and completed reflection' (*GS* 1: 31). Indeed, if Schlegel can search for 'a non-intuitive intuition [*unauschauliche Intuition*] of the System' (*GS* 1: 47), it is because the Absolute, as the very medium of reflection, cannot escape the logic of reflection. Everything is thinking, and hence thinking must grasp itself reflectively, that is, immediately, as well.

This theory of the reflexive medium and its absolute comprehension does not merit Benjamin's undivided approval. Although his objections appear as marginal and passing remarks, as footnotes, and are never developed or even substantiated, they occur with such frequency and insistence that the task of reading '*The Concept of Art Criticism*' becomes the task of construing their underlying rationale.[3] Of this theory, Benjamin says that it 'has been established with a limited metaphysical interest [*in begrenztem metaphysischen Interesse*]', in other words, it is of limited use or importance to metaphysics. Moreover, any attempt to clarify from a 'pure critico-logical interest' what of this theory the Romantics have left in the dark risks ending in darkness as well. It is a theory, Benjamin concludes (in a footnote), that 'in its totality leads to pure logical, and unresolvable problems' (*GS* 1: 57–8).

Let me try then to elicit from Benjamin's critical remarks throughout the first part of the dissertation the reasons for the preceding devastating appraisal of the Romantics' theoretical presuppositions of their concept of art criticism. I shall do so by first circling back to the question of the unbounding of reflection. With Fichte, the Romantics share the insight that 'the epistemologically authoritative form of thinking' is the 'thinking of thinking'. It is a form of immediate knowing, and 'constitutes for the Early Romantics the basic form of all intuitive cognizing and thus obtains dignity as method; as cognizing of thinking it comprises under itself all other, lower-level cognition ...'. (p. 28). Yet, whereas for Fichte, thinking as the thinking of thinking – or in Benjamin's terminology: second-level reflection directed upon first-level reflection whose subject matter is mere thinking with its correlative thought – achieves completion in the self-positing I, such thinking occurs, according to the Romantics, incessantly, and in everything. 'Accordingly', Benjamin writes, 'the thinking of thinking turns into the thinking of thinking of thinking (and so forth) and with this the third-level of reflection is attained ... The third level of reflection, compared with the second, signifies something in principle new' (p. 30). For Fichte, the thinking of thinking is constituted by 'the Ur-Form, the canonical form, of reflection'. However, for the Romantics this epistemologically authoritative form of thinking is made up by the infinitizing thinking of thinking of thinking that constitutes the medium of reflection. According to the Jena Romantics, this boundless thinking is not only the form of intuitive cognizing par excellence but, in its universality, it comprises all other forms of thinking as well.

Although Benjamin discards the objection that the Romantics' theorem is abstruse by referring to its axiomatic presuppositions (first and foremost to the assumption that, for the Romantics, infinitude is filled and substantial), his discussion of the relation between the Ur-Form of thinking and the Romantic conception of absolute thinking begins to show clear signs of strain. Benjamin holds that 'in face of the Absolute', 'the strict form of reflection' dissolves. This dissolution [*Zersetzung*] manifests itself through a 'peculiar ambiguity' in the third-level reflection. Indeed, the rigorous Ur-Form of second-level reflection, in the third-level reflection, occupies both the position of the object and the subject of thinking. 'The strict form of reflection is thus shaken and assaulted by this ambiguity', Benjamin remarks. He stresses that 'this ambiguity would have to unfold into an ever more complex plurality of meanings at each successive level', and sums the matter up in the following passage.

> On this state of affairs rests the peculiar character of the infinitude of reflection vindicated by the Romantics: this consists in the dissolution of the proper form of reflection in face of the Absolute. Reflection expands without limit or check and the thinking that is given form in reflection turns into formless thinking which directs itself upon the Absolute. (*GS* 1: 30–31)

Two things need to be underlined at this point. Reflection strictly speaking, its strict form, becomes formless. From being characterized by self-limitation and the continual coiling back upon itself that marked Fichte's I, reflection becomes unbounded and thus able to direct itself upon the Absolute. Secondly, the Absolute itself becomes characterized by increasing, and ultimately inextricable and irredeemable ambiguity. As Benjamin argues, in 'a line of thought not thought through by the Romantics with clarity', they, and Schlegel in particular, 'saw immediately and without holding this in need of proof, the whole of the real develop itself in the stages of reflection in its full content, with increasing clarity up to the highest clarity in the Absolute' (*GS* 1: 30). The thesis of a continuity between the two kinds of reflection, the Ur-Form of reflection and absolute reflection, is for Benjamin, the bone of contention. With Benjamin's emphasis on the unbounding of the strict form of reflection, i.e. of the lower form of reflection, and the ambiguity of absolute reflection, a problem, indeed, surfaces. The Absolute, rather than yielding the desired clarity, becomes characterized by increasing ambiguity – and, as we know from essays written before the dissertation, or at the same time, for Benjamin, this is the terrible signature of nature, fate, myth, more generally, of the profane. It is the disastrous consequence of directing the illimited, and hence formless form of the strict kind of reflection upon the Absolute itself. As Benjamin remarks in the footnote to which I have already referred, the logically unresolvable problems with which the theory of the medium of reflection is ridden climax 'in the problem of the Ur-reflection' (p. 58). By contending that there is a steady continuity between lower forms of reflection and absolute reflection, the Absolute loses its distinctness, its univocity, in short everything that separates it from the lower orders.

Yet, what about the Absolute itself? It grasps itself as well in immediate reflection, or cognition, Benjamin notes. He writes:

> Reflection constitutes the Absolute and it constitutes it as medium. Schlegel in his expositions placed the greatest value on the continually uniform connection in the Absolute or in the System, both of which we have to interpret as the connectedness of the real, not in its substance (which is everywhere the same), but in the degrees of its clear unfolding ... (*GS* 1: 37)

For the Romantics, the movement in the medium of reflection is made up by either the potentiation of reflection or its decrease – to quote Novalis with Benjamin, 'by reciprocal elevation and abasement' (*GS* 1: 37). But in the footnote to which I have already made reference several times, Benjamin takes issue with this contention. After having remarked that, in spite of statements to the contrary, cognition for the Romantics can only mean intensification, or potentiation of reflection, he writes:

> 'Reflection can be intensified, but can never be diminished. Only an interruption [*Abbrechen*], never a diminishing of reflective intensification is conceivable. The entirety of the relations of the centres of reflection among one another, not to speak of their relation to the Absolute, can consequently rest only on intensifications of reflections'. (*GS* 1: 57)

For reasons of principle, what Benjamin says here about the intensifying reflections between the centres, or from the centre to the Absolute, is valid for what happens in the Absolute as well. Indeed, Benjamin's critical statement, which gives the Romantics the lie, is an objection [*Einwand*], 'an isolated critical observation', he claims (*GS* 1: 57). What he objects to is not only the illimited potentiation of reflective cognition in the relation of the centres to one another, and in particular to the Absolute, but especially to its use as a model for understanding the way the Absolute comprehends itself. To conceive of the Absolute as grasping itself in a process of a continually increasing reflection is, for Benjamin, an illegitimate projection of forms (or unforms) or movements specific to lower orders onto the Absolute itself.

I have pointed out already that the Romantics believed that 'an absolute immediacy in the grasping of the context of reflection [or the Absolute] is thinkable in the virtual sense' (*GS* 1: 27). Of Schlegel, Benjamin writes, that 'he did not investigate the Absolute systematically, but instead sought to grasp the system absolutely. This was the essence of his mysticism' (*GS* 1: 45). What Benjamin thinks of such a possibility becomes clear when he says that 'the fatal character [*das Verhängnisvolle* (another word linked to the order of fate, *RG*)] of this attempt did not remain hidden' from Schlegel himself (*GS* 1: 45). Indeed, when Benjamin claims that Schlegel characterizes in an unsurpassable way this idea of the absolute comprehension of the system with the question: 'Are not all systems individuals?' (*GS* 1: 46), Schlegel's individual mystic is denounced as mysticism. Just as little as Schlegel neglected or failed (*versäumen* is another significant Benjaminian term) to distinguish mysticism from the mystic, he neglected to pay attention to the difference between the Absolute and individuality. If Schlegel's attempt falls on unsympathetic ears with Benjamin, it is, as we shall see in a moment, because, according to the latter, it rests on an illegitimate mixing of levels of thought.

For Benjamin, such immediate grasping of the Absolute in the case of the Romantics must be clearly demarcated from what takes place with the mystics. Whereas mystics call upon intellectual intuition and ecstatic states, the Romantics are indifferent to intuitability. I read:

Rather he [Schlegel] searches for, to put it in a summary formula, a non-intuitive intuition [*unanschauliche Intuition*] of the system, and he finds it in language. His terminology is the sphere in which his thought moves beyond discursivity and intuitability. For the term, the concept, contains for him the seed of the system; it was, at bottom, nothing other than a preformed System itself. Schlegel's thinking is an *absolutely conceptual*, that is, linguistic thinking. Reflection is an intentional act of the absolute comprehension of the System and the adequate expression for this act is the concept. (*GS* 1: 47)

And yet, although the absolute grasping of the Absolute is thus based on a non-intuitable individuality of the Absolute, an individuality provided by concepts (rather than names) – 'In the Concept alone the individual nature, which Schlegel . . . vindicates for the system, finds its expression' (*GS* 1: 48) – such individuality (of moreover, 'individual concepts') (*GS* 1: 48–9), however intellectual, is still an individuality. And as such, Benjamin seems to suggest it is incommensurate with the Absolute.

Benjamin admits that some, but only some propositions of this, in his eyes, extremely questionable theory of the medium of reflection, have achieved a peculiar fruitfulness in the theory of art.[4] Art is a determination of the medium of reflection, however not a privileged one, as Benjamin sees it, since for the Romantics all things are centres of reflection. Yet, it is argued in the dissertation that the Romantic theory of art in which the medium of reflection is one of forms, 'reaches immediately and with incomparable greater certainty [than in other Romantic determinations of the medium] the metaphysical depth of Romantic thinking' (*GS* 1: 62). Hence, this theory should, while permitting a grasp of the greatness of Romantic thought, also be the privileged place where this thought can be critically examined.

After having recalled that all the laws that generally hold for objective knowledge (which Benjamin had also discussed in his exposition of the Early Romantic theory of the knowledge of nature) hold good in the medium of art as well, the task of art criticism becomes determined as 'knowledge in the reflection medium of art'. Benjamin writes: 'Criticism, therefore, has the same value as observation does in the face of natural objects; they are the same laws that are modified in different objects' (*GS* 1: 65). If observation in the realm of natural objects meant moving or inciting a thing into self-consciousness, then criticism achieves the same goal in the medium of art. 'Thus, criticism is, so to speak, an experiment performed on the art work, through which the latter's reflection is called awake, through which it is brought to consciousness and to knowledge of itself' (*GS* 1: 65). Hence the cognition to which Romantic art criticism gives rise is the work's self-cognition. Criticism in the medium of reflection is not only entirely objective, but for the Romantics, it is also entirely positive: 'the ultimate intention of criticism', Benjamin says, 'is the intensification of the consciousness of the work' (*GS* 1: 67). 'Every critical knowledge of an artistic formation is, as reflection in it, nothing other than a higher, self-actively originated degree of this formation's consciousness. This intensification of consciousness in criticism is infinite in principle; critique is the medium in which the limitedness of the single work refers methodologically to the infinitude of art and in the end is transported [*übergeführt*] into that infinitude, for Art, as it is obvious, is, as medium of reflection, infinite' (*GS* 1: 67). Romantic criticism is predominantly positive, in that through its intensification of the self-consciousness of the work, the art work becomes transported, or converted into Art itself. Compared to this positive transformation, the 'moment of self-negation', that is, the destruction of the work in its limitation, is negligible. By dissolving the single work into the medium of art, Romantic critique renders the finite absolute. It perfects it, as Benjamin's remarks on Schlegel's paradigmatic critique of Goethe's *Wilhelm Meister* indicate:

> the criticism is not meant to do anything other than discover the secret plans of the work itself, [i.e.] execute its concealed intentions. It belongs to the meaning of the work itself, i.e. it is in its reflected form that the criticism should go beyond the work itself, make it absolute. It is clear: for the Romantics criticism is much less the judgement of a work than the method of its completion. (*GS* 1: 69)

Thus, in a letter to Schleiermacher, Benjamin reports, Schlegel refers to his critique of *Wilhelm Meister* as the *Übermeister* (*GS* 1: 67). Criticism, indeed, is 'perfecting, positive' (p. 70), in that it is an *Übersetzung*, a translation of the necessarily incomplete work into its own absolute idea.

For Benjamin this idea of critique as translation hinges on the Romantics' conception of the artwork in terms of form understood as self-limited reflection. As form, the work of art is necessarily a contingent reflection of the medium of reflection. Critique, consequently, must drive these self-limited reflections outside themselves and dissolve the original reflection into a higher reflection. He writes:

> In this labour criticism rests on the germ cells of reflection, the positive formal moments of the work which it resolves into universal formal moments. In this criticism, the relationship of the single work to the idea of art is exhibited and therewith the idea of the single work itself. (*GS* 1: 73)

In short, then, critique in the medium of art is an objective movement in which self-limited reflection, or form, is unbounded through a potentiation of the reflection frozen in the singular work, and through which that work becomes dissolved into the medium of reflection, the continuum of forms, the idea of art itself. While discussing this concept of critique in view of the Romantic theory of assessment, Benjamin introduces a term that shows to what extent critique is anchored in the work itself. Indeed, 'criticizability [*Kritisierbarkeit*]' is an objective characteristic of the artwork, and is the reason why critique as well is

'an objective instance in art' (*GS* 1: 85). This criterion of art – criticizability –
summarizes, as Benjamin puts it, 'the entire art-philosophical work of the Early
Romantics' (*GS* 1: 110). It formulates in most uncertain terms the dependence
of Romantic art criticism on the Romantics' understanding of the work as
formed, that is, limited reflection, and hence the objective need to free reflection
from its contingent limitation as work into the medium of reflection itself.

Critique – a concept which, as Benjamin had noted, is an exemplary instance
of the Romantics' mystical terminology (*GS* 1: 50) – is thus a positive concept:
'to be critical means to elevate thinking so far beyond all restrictive conditions that, so to speak, the knowledge of truth magically leaps from insight into
the falsehood of these restrictions' (*GS* 1: 51). But according to Benjamin, this
generally positive valuation of critique notwithstanding, the Romantics also
'understood how to preserve and apply the unavoidable negative moment of this
concept' (*GS* 1: 51). One would have expected him to refer here to the inevitable
destruction of the work that comes with its elevation into the Absolute, or to
Schlegel's valorization of polemics as the extermination of the mass of bad art,
an extermination required before productive critique can begin.[5] Instead, Benjamin picks out the 'vast discrepancy between the claim and the accomplishment of their theoretical philosophy', in order to suggest that by characterizing
their own theoretical pretentions as critique, the Romantics admitted the very
failure of their enterprise – of critique as a positive procedure, and the attempt
to relate the finite to the infinite, first and foremost. Critique also names,
Benjamin claims, 'the necessary incompleteness of infallibility', 'the inescapable
insufficiency of the Romantics' efforts' to grasp the Absolute absolutely. With
this we can proceed to Benjamin's fundamental objections against what the
Romantics called 'critique'. Yet Benjamin's fascination with Romantic thought
is also a fact. Hence, my task will be double. Apart from establishing what it is
that he finds fault with, I shall try to determine not only the reasons for his
critique, but to outline, however succinctly, his own conception of critique.

In the chapter 'The Idea of Art', Benjamin notes that Romantic art theory
culminates in the definition of the medium of absolute reflection as art, or, more
precisely, as the idea of art. Since 'the organ of artistic reflection is form, the idea
of art is defined as the medium of the reflection of forms. In this medium all the
presentational forms hang together constantly, interpenetrate one another and
are brought into the unity of the absolute art form which is identical with the
idea of art. Thus, the Romantic idea of the unity of art lies in the idea of a
continuum of forms' (*GS* 1: 87). Benjamin's critique of Romantic criticism com-
mences by putting into question the Romantics' philosophical competence to
determine the very nature of this unity of forms, or Absolute, on which their
whole theory of art and art criticism is based. Benjamin concedes that Schlegel's
philosophical efforts 'indicate how much he strove for definiteness [*Bestimmtheit*]'
(*GS* 1: 91–2). Yet, trying 'to give expression to the determinateness and fullness
in which he conceived the idea', he merely came up with the concept of
individuality, Benjamin claims. Undoubtedly, when speaking of the reflection
medium of forms, Schlegel characterizes it as an individual. To conceive of

the unity or continuum of absolute forms, the Absolute, in short, as an individual, is, for Benjamin, to overstretch concepts and 'to grasp at a paradox. Otherwise the notion of expressing the highest universality as individuality was not to be consummated' (*GS* 1: 89). He admits that in having recourse to this paradox, Schlegel aspired 'to secure the concept of the idea of art from the misunderstanding that it is an abstraction from empirical works already present'. This 'valuable and valid motive' is the reason why Schlegel's thought about the individuality of the Absolute is not simply 'an absurdity or even only an error', Benjamin concedes. Yet, what Schlegel did in characterizing the Absolute as an individuality was to 'simply give a false interpretation to a valuable and valid motive'. It was certainly correct, Benjamin continues, to try 'to define this concept [of art] as an Idea in the Platonic sense, as a *proteron te phusei*, as the real basis of all empirical works'.[6] But it was a mistake – indeed a huge mistake, the mistake *par excellence* – to hope to achieve this with the help of 'individuality'. Schegel committed, in Benjamin's eyes, 'the old error of confounding "abstract" and "universal" when he believed he had to make this Idea into an individual' (*GS* 1: 89–90). Only because he confused the universal and the abstract could Schlegel have sought to determine the Absolute as individuality, or work. Even so, for Schlegel, 'individuality' is intellectually and conceptually purified – as is obvious from his reference to 'the invisible work which takes up into itself the visible work' (*GS* 1: 90) – his characterization of the unity of art, the continuum of forms, or art itself as a work, is an infringement upon the rule that forbids mixing genres of thought. Benjamin also calls it a 'mystical thesis' (*GS* 1: 91). To sum up, Benjamin criticizes Schlegel for not having clearly grasped the philosophical nature of the highest universal, and for having contaminated it with concepts that belong to another ontological sphere. Even the sphere of pure concepts is incommensurate with the realm of the idea, or the Absolute. Schlegel is a mystic for Benjamin in that he believes that pure concepts such as 'individuality' or 'the invisible work' could bring the Absolute within reach. Benjamin has no quarrel with the Romantics about the necessity of thinking the Absolute; he only parts company with them when they bring the Absolute into the intellect's range. Made present as an individuality, or a work, the Absolute is stripped of what makes it absolute, i.e., cut off, not only from all sensible but all intellectual presentation as well. As individuality or work, the Absolute has been surrendered to the profane. To present – *darstellen* – the idea of art 'in conceptual concentration' (*GS* 1: 93) is, indeed, a function of the Romantics' theory of reflective intensification. In his discussion of the 'poetry of poetry', another Romantic attempt to present the idea of art itself, Benjamin describes it as 'the comprehensive expression for the reflexive nature of the Absolute'. He adds: 'It is poetry which is conscious of itself, and since, according to early Romantic doctrine, consciousness is only an enhanced spiritual form of that *of* which it is conscious, thus consciousness of poetry is itself poetry. It is poetry of poetry. Higher poetry . . .' (*GS* 1: 96). In short, the Romantic theory according to which the centres of reflection can be elevated to the medium of reflection itself through reflexive intensification condemns the medium of reflection, or the Absolute, to being *only* the enhanced reflection of whatever is reflectively raised to that higher level. By holding that the totality of all works is a work – however invisible or purely intelligible it may be – is to determine the Absolute as a mere potentiation of the singular works that it embraces. Such an understanding of the Absolute (or of consciousness) entails a loss of the force of transcendence and the relativization of difference. Against the backdrop of this Benjaminian critique, another aspect of his suspicions about the concept of reflection comes into view. A reflection that knows only intensification, and not the possibility of diminishing, presupposes and asserts a continuity between the profane and the Absolute that can only make the Absolute tangible as something profane.

Benjamin makes the distinction between the profane and the Absolute in an effort to specify further what the Romantics understood by art criticism and what they saw as its task. The distinction is borrowed from Schlegel himself. 'The organ of transcendental poetry as that very form which survives in the Absolute the downfall of profane forms, Schlegel designates as the symbolic form', Benjamin remarks (*GS* 1: 96). After having denounced the ambiguity of 'symbolic form', and discarded the mythological content of the expression which in that sense 'does not belong to the context' in which the distinction between profane and symbolic form is made, he defines the latter as 'the marking-out [*Ausprägung*] of the pure poetic Absolute in the form itself' (*GS* 1: 97). Symbolic form is exhibition, or presentational form [*Darstellungsform*] purified of and distinguished from the profane forms of exhibition through its reference to the idea of art or the Absolute. Yet, the 'purification' or 'survival' of symbolic or absolute form after the downfall of everything profane is a function of a reflection that elevates itself to the Absolute. 'The "symbolic form" is the formula under which the bearing of reflection for the artwork is comprised', Benjamin notes (*GS* 1: 97). Yet, precisely for that reason, the important distinction between profane and symbolic, or absolute form, becomes blurred. It loses its cutting edge. When Benjamin remarks in a footnote that for the Romantics 'the exhibitional form does not as such have to be profane but can, if entirely pure, participate in the absolute or symbolic form, or finally become it' (*GS* 1: 97–8), it is clear that for him, the latter form is only the reflectively enhanced profane form.

Art criticism, Benjamin suggests, is the reflective movement between the poles of this dulled distinction. He writes: 'Art criticism exhibits this symbolic form in its purity; it disentangles it from all moments alien to its essence, to which it might be bound in the work, and finishes with the dissolution of the work' (*GS* 1: 98). Benjamin could subscribe to this definition of criticism as pursuing the double task of *Ablösung* and *Auflösung* in the perspective of the Absolute. Yet, he is quick to add that 'in the framework of Romantic theories full clarity can never be reached in the distinction of profane and symbolic form, of symbolic form and critique'. Such lack of sharpness 'forces itself upon our inspection', he declares without elaborating. But haven't we seen that for reasons of principle – conceiving the relation between profane form and symbolic form as one of reflection – the Romantics cannot make this distinction as sharp as their own philosophical intention would have it? However, at this juncture,

Benjamin makes an explicit statement that dramatizes, as it were, the gist of what up to this point had mainly been implicit in his objections: 'Only at the price of such unsharp delimitations can all the concepts of the art theory that in the end the Romantics strove for be drawn into the region of the Absolute' (GS 1: 93). In other words, Romantic art criticism is anything but critical: it fails to distinguish, and set apart as trenchantly and vigorously as the concept of criticism calls for. As a consequence, the Absolute – the critical concept *par excellence* – is not only not demarcated from the profane with the necessary rigour, everything profane is drawn into the region of the Absolute, polluting what, in principle, is to be kept pure of all alien ingredients. The very positivity of Romantic critique thus becomes suspicious. But this positivity, and its attendant lack of a discriminating and analytical rigour, is not accidental. Indeed, it stems from the Romantics' metaphysical credo of a continuity between the profane and the Absolute. Criticizability, Benjamin notes, presupposes transition [*Übergang*] from the realm of ideas 'to the single works, such as exist in the medium of art, from the absolute form to the single forms'. It rests on the assumption as well that all singular works can 'vitally coalesce into the unity of the idea itself' (GS 1: 114). Indeed, as Benjamin holds, 'art was that very region in which Romanticism strove to carry through in the purest form the immediate reconciliation of the conditioned with the unconditioned' (GS 1: 114). Criticizability – the very principle that the entire art–philosophical work of the Early Romantics sought to demonstrate – is thus tied up with what impedes criticism, and that against which criticism ought to prevail: transition, continuity, reconciliation between what can be brought together only at the price of paradox, false interpretation, or in other words, a complete surrender of the critical notion of the Absolute to the profane.

However, such radical abandonment of the highest universal to the region of the profane is also an accomplishment of major, and fatal proportion. Benjamin makes this point in the course of his analysis of the Romantic concept of the novel. For the Jena Romantics, the novel is the 'comprehensible manifestation [*fassbare Erscheinung*]' of the continuum of forms, or poetic Absolute. 'It is this, thanks to prose. The idea of poetry has found its individuality, for which Schlegel was seeking, in the form of prose; the Early Romantics knew no deeper and better determination for it than "prose"' (GS 1: 100). But what is 'prose', if it is to be the most proper individuality of the poetic Absolute? In order to conceive of prose's 'unifying function', its role as the 'creative ground' of poetical forms (GS 1: 101), it is necessary that it be understood in all its senses; that is, in an indistinct, and equivocal manner. Prose certainly has the meaning of '*ungebundene Rede*' (GS 1: 109), that is, of a writing style distinguished from poetry by its greater irregularity, variety of rhythm, and its greater proximity to ordinary speech. Benjamin makes it quite clear that 'prose' does not mean 'ornate prose', which – and in this he follows Novalis – 'has nothing to do with art, but a lot with rhetoric' (GS 1: 101). For Benjamin, prose is something transparent and colourless [*farbloser ... Ausdruck*] (GS 1: 101). But in addition to its proper meaning, prose has a figural, improper meaning, namely prosaic, plain, ordinary, sober. Furthermore, this improper meaning cannot properly be distinguished from the proper. But it is this very lack of differentiation, this ambiguity of meaning, that predestines prose to become the comprehensible manifestation of the Absolute. Yet if only 'the purely prosaic [form of prose] fulfils this task' of conferring individuality upon the Absolute, the individuality in question can only be a 'prosaic unity' (*GS* 1: 101). However paradoxical it may seem to conceive of the prosaic, the plain, or the sober as the highest possible manifestation of the idea of art, or of the poetic Absolute, it is 'in truth [a] very profound intuition ... an entirely new basis for the philosophy of art. On this basis rests the entire philosophy of art of Early Romanticism, especially its concept of criticism', Benjamin claims (*GS* 1: 100). It is also a conception 'historically rich in consequences' (*GS* 1: 103). Indeed, Benjamin hints that with it begins a new era of thought, an era that extends into the present. With the Romantics begins the epoch of *absolute sobriety*.

Benjamin points out that the Romantics shared this 'basic philosophical conception' of the prosaic with Hölderlin, although the realm of Hölderlin's thought remained only a 'promised land' for them (*GS* 1: 105). Still, as far as the 'principle of the sobriety [*Nüchternheit*] of art' is concerned, he stands in a philosophical relation to them. 'This principle *is* the essentially quite new and still unpredictably operative basic notion of the Romantic philosophy of art; what is perhaps the greatest epoch in Western philosophy of art is marked out by this notion/principle. The connection this has with the methodical procedure of that philosophy, namely reflection, is obvious. The prosaic, in which reflection as the principle is stamped out in its highest form, is, to be sure, in ordinary use straightaway a metaphorical designation of 'sober' (*GS* 1: 103). Benjamin's demarcation of this conception of art from that of Plato's further shows that the greatest epoch in the Western philosophy of art, an epoch that begins with the Romantics, is characterized by a sobering of the Absolute. The Absolute becomes de-sacralized, de-divinized by reflection – in an intellectual and conceptual process of an intuiting no longer intuitive [*anschaulich*], but soberly rational, down to earth (and hence distinct from the mystics' intellectual intuition of the whole). But not only is reflection sober, the Absolute to which it becomes potentiated – the medium of reflection and the continuum of forms – turns prosaic as well. It is an Absolute only relatively different from the profane forms, one that has been divested of its separating and discriminating force. The sober Absolute is an Absolute that has forfeited its transcendence.

On this principle of Absolute sobriety rests the concept of Romantic criticism. It proceeds on the assumption that the core of the work is 'filled with prosaic spirit' (*GS* 1: 106). Art, for the Romantics, is mechanical, akin to manufacturing, and has its seat entirely in the understanding (*GS* 1: 105). Benjamin writes: 'By means of mechanical reason the work is soberly constituted even still in the infinite – at the limit-value of limited forms' (*GS* 1: 106). The Absolute – what transcends everything profane as the highest universal – that achieves presentation as 'work', is something inherently profane – profanity itself. And the incarnation of such prosaic Spirit in a comprehensible shape is no less profane.

To exhibit this prosaic kernel of all art is the 'final, contentual determination' of criticism, Benjamin argues (*GS* 1:108). 'Criticism is the exhibition of the prosaic core in every work. In his concept, "exhibition" is understood in the chemical sense, as the production of a substance through a determinate process to which other substances are submitted' (*GS* 1:109). The *Darstellung* of the prosaic present in every work – the profane Absolute – is a production on the basis of potentiating reflection. This legitimation of criticism by its prosaic nature, and the prosaic nature of its task, has some distinctive consequences. On several occasions, the dissertation shows that, for the Romantics, critique has no pedagogical aim. Its function is not to assess or judge the work. Romantic critique 'needs no motivation', Benjamin claims (*GS* 1:109). In other words, critique is not a function of a purpose heterogeneous to the work, rather it is exercised for its own sake. 'Criticism is a formation whose origin is, indeed, occasioned by the work, but which persists independently of it. As such it cannot be distinguished in principle from the artwork itself' (*GS* 1:108). It has the same ontological nature as the work of art. Like the work from which it originates, critique is, according to the Romantics, a fact [*Faktum*]. Benjamin quotes Schlegel: 'A so-called *recherche* is an historical experiment. The object and the result of this experiment is a fact. What is meant to be a fact, must have strict individuality ...' (*GS* 1:108). As a fact, then, critique is indistinguishable from the work. Although a potentiation of reflection, critique has no deciding or transcending thrust. This sheer positivity marks critique's departure from what must have been its own most philosophical intention – to separate what cannot be of the same nature. But what of the prosaic Absolute presented by critique? Presented in the individualizing mode of prose, the sober Absolute appears as something absolutely prosaic – itself a fact, only the potentiation of the transitory contingency of the singular work. Benjamin notes: 'By limiting itself in its own form, the artwork makes itself transitory in a contingent shape, but in the shape of the way to passing away, it makes itself eternal through criticism' (*GS* 1:115). Absolutizing the created work, rendering it eternal, criticism presents the Absolute as fact. Yet, in spite of the fact that criticism is indistinguishable from the work, Schlegel, paradoxically yet inevitably, 'valued criticism more highly than the artwork', since the critical activity of absolutizing the work is higher than the creation of art, Benjamin concludes. 'This can be illustrated in an image as the production of blinding brilliancy [*Blendung*] in the work. This brilliancy – the sober light – extinguishes the plurality of the works. It is the Idea' (*GS* 1:119). These final lines of Benjamin's dissertation speak a final critical word about Romantic criticism. The sober light of the prosaic Absolute that criticism exhibits in all works is a blinding light. It is so dazzling that it becomes deceptive. In its brilliancy, all differences fade absolutely. Its spell, the fascination it exerts, is that of the *fact* – of the Absolute become secular.

Benjamin's massive and intransigent criticism of the Romantic conception of art and its concept of criticism thus seems finally to be an outright rejection. And yet, this conception is said to have inaugurated 'perhaps the greatest epoch in Western philosophy of art'. His recognition of and admiration for the

Romantics' achievements is evident, and hence I must return to the question of Benjamin's relation to Early Romanticism, to his debt to the Romantic concept of criticism which he so vehemently criticized. Considering the unyielding, and unrelentingly negative critical gesture that dominates the whole of the dissertation, Benjamin's own concept of criticism arises from motifs that appear only in an understanding of the most extreme implications of Romantic theory. Indeed, the greatness of Romantic thought is linked to its conception of a secular Absolute and of critique as the primarily positive dissolution, and thus the connection of the finite to such an Absolute – in other words, to its total relinquishing of transcendence. From everything we have seen, such a conception of the Absolute, and of the critical relation as a movement in the continuum between the finite and an equally finite infinite, cannot satisfy Benjamin. His critique of the Romantic Absolute, and the Romantics' notion of criticism, is made in the name of the proper philosophical intentions of these very concepts according to which the Absolute has to be distinguished absolutely, and critique must be a movement of rigorous separation, demarcation, scission. Compared to the Romantic concept, his is an *Über*-critique, in the sense in which Schlegel could speak of his critique of *Wilhelm Meister* as the *Übermeister* – an ultra or hypercriticism. Benjamin agrees with the Romantics that all critique must take place in view of the Absolute, but in view of an Absolute that is absolutely transcendent, radically distinguished from everything profane or finite. Between it, and the latter, no continuity is thinkable. Yet, critique is a relating to such an Absolute. It is the movement of transcendence in the realm of the profane, or finite. However, since the Absolute – or rather truth, as Benjamin will call it – is entirely of another order than the profane, all critical relating to it must necessarily lack the certitude of truly transcending the given. Such certitude is not in the power of the critical act. For Benjamin, critique's eventual success in pointing to the Absolute, in enacting a pure separation, or difference, can be guaranteed only by the Absolute itself. Yet even such authentification of the critical relation by the Absolute, were it to occur, would be beyond the cognitive reach of all critique. In contradistinction from the Romantic epistemological optimism which constituted the bedrock of their concept of critique, but whose price was a total sobering of the Absolute – Benjamin's concept of critique is characterized by an essential agnosticism. It is a critique, however, and as such it must take its aim at the Absolute which it severs from itself in absolute purity. Hence, of that Absolute nothing can be known, and least of all that the Absolute has authenticated the critical relation to begin with.

With this both the rationale for Benjamin's critique of the Romantics comes into view as well as his debt to them. He shares with them the insight into the inexorably sober nature of the critical relation. Yet this sobriety, with the extremist implication of a radical loss of transcendence within Early Romanticism, becomes for Benjamin the very sign that the transcending gesture of critique depends on a redemptive justification. Although beyond critique's own reach, such justification is required by what it, as critique, must mean according to its own most proper philosophical intention. If all critique is finite, and if, by itself, it can only reveal a sober Absolute, the pure distinction that it calls for as *krinein* (and the absolutely Other toward which it nevertheless incessantly gestures) requires that critique be suspended in relation to an Absolute whose power would finally fulfill its critical intention. Paradoxically, the universal sobriety in which Romantic thought loses itself turns into the thought of an absolutely 'non-sober' Absolute capable of a *post-factum* endowment of the transcending movement of critique, of conferring actual transcendence upon critique. No finite certitude, no empirical security guarantees that such a conferral has taken place, or shall occur. However, in order to avoid squandering [*versäumen*] the possibility of such a conferral by which the very intentions of critique would become fulfilled, critique must be critical to the utmost – unrelenting and uncompromisingly negative. Of such criticism, Benjamin's dissertation on the Romantic concept of positive critique is a most fulfilling example.

4

FORTGANG AND ZUSAMMENHANG

WALTER BENJAMIN AND THE ROMANTIC NOVEL

Anthony Phelan

Benjamin was in his mid twenties when he began to cast about for a topic on which to write his doctoral dissertation.[1] It is an unkindness among scholars to overtax this early research as the conscious groundwork of his later thought. Although the germs of some ideas and procedures, such as the analysis of temporality and the practice of montage, are clearly present, in scholarly and philological terms Benjamin is often forced to rely on inadequate editions and writes without much concern for the historical or literary context of the work he deals with.[2] Winfried Menninghaus has suggested that the distortions inherent in Benjamin's dissertation have a calculated and strategic role in focusing on significant issues already present in his earliest work, particularly the terms infinity (*Unendlichkeit*) and immediacy (*Unmittelbarkeit*), as they figure in the 1916 language essay.[3] In Benjamin's own orchestration of his argument, however, a certain conception of prose fiction is crucially important as the nexus in which a group of ideas central to his exposition of Romantic theory intersect. Although the concept of *Kritik*, the immanence of criticizability, and a certain seriousness which Benjamin encodes with the term 'sobriety' (as Hölderlin's *Nüchternheit*) have been understood as Benjamin's principal concerns, the possibility of reflection emerges in his exposition of Romantic aesthetics through the mechanisms of prose, understood on the basis of a Romantic conception of the novel – or at least of what Friedrich Schlegel's (not-quite) tautology meant by 'novel': '*Ein Roman ist ein romantisches Buch*' – 'a novel is a Romantic book'.[4] Among the sleights of hand in Benjamin's argument, notoriously, is the move which identifies the prose of the novel with the prosaic as such, and thence with a conception of seriousness as the unornamented. This essay follows the detours Benjamin acknowledges in his text;[5] by considering the foundation of Benjamin's understanding of Romantic reflexivity as the systematic *coherence* designated by the term *Zusammenhang*, and hence as a model of textuality, it will be possible to reinstate the Romantic novel as engendering the structure of reflexivity from which Benjamin's further speculations are derived.

The novel, as understood by the Early German Romantics, particularly Friedrich Schlegel and Friedrich von Hardenberg (Novalis), provides a crucial bridge to their 'basic conception of the idea of art' and to the central role of prose in Benjamin's account of Romantic art criticism (*Kritik*). Because these Romantic theorists and philosophers know 'no deeper or more fitting determination' (*SW* 1: 173) for their idea of *Poesie* than 'prose', they discover with the novel an entirely new foundation for their philosophy of art, and hence for the concept of criticism for the sake of which Benjamin's whole investigation had to be conducted to this point. The announcement of the claim that 'The idea of poetry is prose' thus arrives as the climax of Benjamin's dissertation, before he moves to the last stages of his argument – the introduction of the term *sobriety* as a paraphrase of the prose form provided by the novel – and finally in his esoteric afterword, where he contrasts Goethe's stress on the classical ideal of the *Urbilder,* quintessentially understood as the content pertaining to the Muse(s) ('*das Musische*' ['the museworthy'], *SW* 1: 179) with the Romantic concept of the idea of form.[6]

It is possible in some measure to retrace the steps of the dissertation on its way to the proclamation of the aesthetic significance of prose as demonstrated in the novel. Benjamin cites a novel to provide an initial case of reflexivity at the beginning of the first part of his dissertation in which he will approach Romantic conceptions of reflection through an account of Fichte's *Wissenschafts-lehre.* Friedrich Schlegel's *Lucinde* is quoted to provide a statement of the central claim about thought's relation to itself: 'Thinking has the peculiarity that next to itself, it most of all prefers to think about that which it can think without end' (*SW* 1: 121).[7] Schlegel is next cited in *Athenäumsfragment* (*Ath.* fgm.) 418 where he notes of Tieck's novel *Franz Sternbalds Wanderungen* that 'the Romantic spirit seems to take pleasure in fantasizing about itself' (*SW* 1: 121). These opening citations, following the earlier reference to Novalis's theory of prose (*SW* 1: 119), are the basis for Benjamin's argument that an important distinction needs to be made between the Romantic theory of reflexivity and the structure of Fichte's idealist project. In Fichte, he says, the potentially infinite act of positing is contained or dammed up: 'in the theoretical sphere the activity of positing does not continue to infinity. The special nature of that sphere is constituted by the preclusion [*Eindämmung*] of infinite positing' (*SW* 1: 124): the infinity of self-positing is held, 'arrested' (*SW* 1: 124), and hence limited by the counterposition of the non-I. The Romantic construction of a reflexive structure, their version of this idealist epistemology, does not accept the curtailment of reflection required by Fichte. In Benjamin's paraphrase, Fichte finds in thought itself a disposition of mind (*Geisteshaltung*) in which 'self-consciousness is already immediately present, and does not need to be invoked through a reflection that is in principle endless' (*SW* 1: 125). Sharing the conviction that reflexivity permits unmediated knowledge of the absolute as subjectivity, of the absolute subject, Schlegel and Hardenberg in Benjamin's reading retain the stress on the *form* of reflexivity, which is also central in the earliest version of Fichte's *Wissenschaftslehre* (1794). Here Fichte insists that the proposition fundamental to the structure of a science of knowledge, that is, of a systematic account of the form and content of human knowledge of and being in the world, must be one in which the *form* of the proposition is completely adequate to its content, one in which form and content coincide. This prescription then matches the case of the sentence of identity (A = A). 'It is a question *not* of the cognition of an object through intuition, but of the self-cognition of a method, of something formal – and the absolute subject represents nothing other than this' (*SW* 1: 122). It is this formal consideration, neither held in check by the counterposition of non-I as object of knowledge and understood as representation, nor foreshortened by the elision of the difference between thought and consciousness of thought in a *cogito cogitans*, that opens the reflexive structure to the Romantics' 'cult of the infinite'.

In seeking to account for and render intelligible the Romantics' emphasis on the 'infinitude of reflection' (*SW* 1: 126: '*Unendlichkeit*') as a productive focus for their theory of art, Benjamin is first keen to establish the bad or unproductive sense of some endless sequence of reflection on a preceding reflection which he can derive from Fichte's later arguments in *Versuch einer neuen Darstellung der Wissenschaftslehre* of 1797 [Attempt at a New Presentation].[8] Such a recessive structure can always attribute the awareness of any degree of self-consciousness to some higher instance of self-consciousness, which can itself then become the object of a yet higher instance. And so on. According to Benjamin, Schlegel and Hardenberg do not understand the structure of infinite reflection in terms of such a linearity. He calls such a conception '*eine Unendlichkeit des Fortgangs*', an infinity of 'continuous advance' (*SW* 1: 126). Such an infinity of 'continuous advance' or of *progress* is no more than a view of reflexivity as 'the endless and empty process' (*SW* 1: 125) of a 'thinking of thinking of thinking'. It would not be irrelevant to recognize in Benjamin's term *Fortgang* (advance) a significant parallel to the sense of empty time through which 'history' progresses (*Fortschritt*) in the so-called 'Theses on the Philosophy of History'.[9] The motif of emptiness appears immediately in the context of Benjamin's exposition of *Fortgang* as 'temporally incompletable progress': the successive stages or levels of reflection would require a linear progress through time as well as a metaphysical ascent to higher degrees of reflection. Such a ladder of perfection and the temporality it evokes would be no more than endless.

Benjamin returns to the notion of endless and empty progression in his account of Friedrich Schlegel's claim that Romantic *Poesie* is a 'progressive universal poetry' in *Ath*. fgm. 116. Neither the progress towards greater conformity to artistic rules of the kind imposed by pre-classical canons, nor the search for an ever more complete self-expression associated with the *Sturm und Drang* corresponds to Schlegel's conception. It is not simply an extension of the task of art as 'a vague advance in writing ever-better poetry' (*SW* 1: 168). Such empty infinitude, Benjamin claims, is not *primarily* ('*in erster Linie*', *GS* 1.1: 26) the understanding of reflection elaborated in the work of Friedrich Schlegel and Novalis. Although Benjamin evidently suspects that such a linear understanding might be uncovered in their thought, he characterizes the Romantic infinite with a different term which becomes a repeated motif in the dissertation: *Zusammenhang* (connection).[10]

In the early exposition of Chapter 2 on 'The Meaning of Reflection in the Early Romantics', which Benjamin acknowledges to be schematic ('a schema of [the] Romantic theory of knowledge', *SW* 1:126), the idea of 'continuous advance' or progress as *Fortgang* is contrasted with the alternative, *Zusammenhang*. The term *Zusammenhang* presents a problem for translation. The standard English version here gives 'an infinity of connectedness' for Benjamin's '*Unendlichkeit des Zusammenhangs*'. Before the further detailed elaboration of this idea with reference to Hölderlin is pursued, it is worth pausing to consider the semantics of *Zusammenhang*. It might be translated as 'connection' or 'coherence', and elsewhere in *The Concept of Criticism* it has the concrete meaning of a 'context', but *Zusammenhang* is not really an abstract noun at all: the associated verb *zusammenhängen* means to be joined to or related to something – literally, to hang together. If the successively higher degrees of reflexivity described as a *Fortgang* hang together in a simple sequence, the introduction of the term *Zusammenhang* is evidently designed to introduce a certain complexity which can avoid the linearity of *Fortgang*. At this point, in order to develop this sense of the infinity of connection and coherence as a context, Benjamin has recourse to a phrase taken from Hölderlin's Pindar translations and commentaries. The text 'Das Unendliche' ('The Infinite') yields the phrase '*unendlich (genau) zusammenhängen*' – 'They hang together infinitely (exactly)' (*SW* 1:126).[11] In introducing this preferred formulation from Hölderlin's commentary on 'Das Unendliche', Benjamin repeatedly uses the word *Zusammenhang* and its cognates. First, although he notes that Hölderlin had no direct contact (*Fühlung*) with the Romantics, he nevertheless insists that the poet 'spoke the last and incomparably most profound word in certain complexes of ideas (*Ideenzusammenhänge*)', which the reader is to encounter in the dissertation.[12] This sense of the coherent interconnection of Romantic ideas as a shared project, no doubt very close to the collective philosophizing dubbed by Friedrich Schlegel 'Symphilosophie', appears to suggest that even at the empirical level of personal biographies it is possible for a conceptuality to reflect such coherence in different terms, and in a different form entirely, without immediate contact or any mediated relationship being evident. Later in the dissertation, Hölderlin will be of central importance for the definition of sobriety (*Nüchternheit*) emerging from the claims for the philosophical significance of prose within Romantic aesthetics. Here he can be held within a pattern – the coordinates of the thought of reflection – without recourse to direct forms of causation, such as influence or debate.

Within the scheme of Benjamin's exposition of Romantic epistemology, Hölderlin is cited in order to articulate the notions of infinity, *Zusammenhang*, and the system. Benjamin claims that the phrase that interests him from the Pindar commentary is intended to express '*einen innigen, höchst triftigen Zusammenhang*' (*GS* 1.1:25), rendered in the standard translation as 'an intimate, most thoroughgoing connection' (*SW* 1: 126). The last phrase is more like a version of Hölderlin's other expression in his comments on 'Das Unendliche': '*in durch-gängiger Beziehung*' – which would give 'in universal relation'. While '*innig*' can indeed mean intimate, heartfelt, fervent or deep, and normally appears in the context of emotion (or friendship, or desire), in this passage it has some sense of insistent, 'intense', inward, and interior; '*triftig*', on the other hand, is usually understood as 'valid' or 'apposite', 'appropriate' when used of an argument. This sense is less plausible when qualified by the superlative '*höchst*' – it is not clear anything can be 'extremely' valid. The root in *treffen* – to meet, and hence to hit a mark – suggests that the coherence of which, according to Benjamin, Hölderlin speaks is intense in its interior matches – a coherence of intense and precise correspondences: what holds together is in some sense inwardly apposite, such that the pattern of connections is highly appropriate, proper to itself. In the framework of Romantic thought this same structure is identified as 'a full infinitude of connection' (*SW* 1: 126; '*eine erfüllte Unendlichkeit des Zusam-menhangs*', *GS* 1.1: 26).

The place of the term *Zusammenhang* in Benjamin's exposition should be clear. He has deployed two contrasted conceptions: empty, temporally uncom-pletable progress ('[*leere*] *zeitliche Unabschliessbarkeit des Fortgangs*', *GS* 1.1: 26) as opposed to a fulfilled infinity of systematic coherence ('*erfüllte Unendlichkeit des Zusammenhangs*'). The additional point to be noted here is the stress of '*erfüllt*': the *Zusammenhang* is not simply *full* as a given, but is 'fulfilled' through and in the process of that coherence which constitutes it. In such an infinity, everything coheres, 'hangs together in an infinitely manifold way'. Benjamin describes such coherence as 'systematic' which he offers as a paraphrase for Hölderlin's use of *genau*. *Genau* – exact or precise – stands parenthetically in apposition to the infinity of the proposed coherence in '*unendlich* (*genau*) *zusam-menhängen*' ('hang together infinitely [exactly]'). It is the precision of these relations that makes them intensely and insistently apposite, rendering their systematic nature not merely as a possibility but as the reality of *Zusammenhang*.

Benjamin now needs to explain how the moments of this systematic construction of reflexivity in a fulfilled infinity relate to each other without falling into the empty, temporally uncompletable linearity of *Fortgang*. In a *mediated* way, he suggests, the systematic coherence can be grasped from infinitely many stages of reflection. It is misleading to read this as '*the* infinitely many stages', as if the closure of the totality could be envisaged here.[13] Rather each stage of reflection is to be seen as a mediation. Reflection, as understood by the very early Fichte and by the Romantics, Benjamin is keen to insist, is immediate in itself.[14] The model of reflection that Benjamin seeks to expound in the thought of the Romantics provides a significant counterposition to the opening up of simple linearity in a triple structure derived from Fichte's absolute self-positing I. What is dialectically checked in the unique 'active deed' (*Tathandlung*) of Fichte's derivation, Benjamin suggests, effectively substitutes an ontological ground for the purely formal structures of reflection proper to the Romantics. Instead of being held in an original act of reflection with objective status, on the Romantic view the thinking of thinking is a *formal* principle and therefore has canonical status and authority. Hence a third stage of reflection can be defined as the thinking of thinking of thinking. It is important to recall that Benjamin had claimed that *Zusammenhang* can be 'grasped from the infinitely many stages of reflection' ('*von unendlich vielen Stufen der Reflexion aus*') (*SW* 1: 126; *GS* 1.1: 26). In drawing the comparison with Fichte's ontology, he tackles the same issue: the third stage of Romantic reflection (*Reflexionsstufe*), understood within the organization of reflection, is a 'thinking of thinking of thinking'. This begins to look rather like the linearity of an empty infinity dismissed earlier. Benjamin, however, discerns a crucial divergence from that single trajectory of transcendence. Simple linearity is disrupted by the interposition of parentheses. The '(thinking of thinking) of thinking' paraphrases the subjective action of reflection in relation to its own activity while 'the thinking of (thinking of thinking)' emphasizes the status of thinking as object in the process of reflection. 'And so on', as Benjamin says. That is to say, in Romantic thought the structure of reflection proliferates, opening the enclosed reflexivity of 'thinking of thinking' to ever more plural meanings (*Mehrdeutigkeit, GS* 1.1: 31). This is the reflexive structure of *Zusammenhang*.

Benjamin makes an early attempt at modelling the structure he has in mind when he claims that the mediate grasp of the *Zusammenhang*, or coherence, of reflexivity is possible in terms of its infinitely many stages by tracing a passage, step by step, from any one stage of reflexivity through all other reflections and 'in all directions' ('*nach allen Seiten*') (*GS* 1.1: 26). The empty temporality of '*Fortgang*' is replaced by the fulfilled spatial thought of *Zusammenhang*, realized thus in a sort of multilateral simultaneity. This will raise questions about the dynamics of the space of reflexivity, which will trouble Benjamin from time to time throughout the exposition offered in the dissertation. In seeking to explain the substance of a fulfilled infinity, as projected in Romantic thinking, he adopts an 'auxiliary construction' (*Hilfskonstruktion*) to make possible a logical presentation of a train of thought that, he says, the Romantics themselves had never clearly thought through. The conception according to which 'absolute reflection' would contain a maximum of reality and, at the opposite pole, 'original reflection' only a minimum of reality is evidently derived from Leibniz and the *Monadology*.[15] A similar complaint about the inconsistency and false schematisms of Schlegel's and Novalis's scheme of reflexivity appears in Benjamin's discussion of Romantic epistemology in relation to knowledge of nature. His long footnote (*SW* 1: 191, n. 146; *GS* 1.1: 57, n. 141) points out that the potentiation of reflection cannot correspondingly be depotentiated. While in one sense it is not linear, its direction towards higher levels or degrees cannot be reversed.

Benjamin here is clearly irritated by the unresolved contradictions he uncovers in the Romantic theory of reflection. His 'isolated critical remark' seems to be the occasion, in one of his rare extended notes, for comments directed at the esoteric audience among his contemporaries. Benjamin's uneasiness in regard to the academic conventions of a doctoral dissertation are well known.[16] His recognition that '[o]nly a breaking off, never a lessening, of heightened reflection is thinkable' (*SW* 1: 191) gestures towards an idea of interruption (perhaps, more properly, of abruption – '*Abbrechen*') which, as we shall see, can be related to the dynamics of reflection 'on all sides' ('*nach allen Seiten*'). What is irritating in the prospect of a constantly potentiated reflexivity is its proximity to a notion of consciousness constantly rising to new levels of self-awareness. Instead of such self-transcendence, a different sense of transition is set in play.

The scheme of reflexivity Benjamin is trying to map, in his long note, continues to be cast in terms of an intensification as *heightening* towards the Absolute. In his exposition of Schlegel, at this point, the linear conception of *Fortgang* still has a guiding force, without the complication which is to be introduced by *Zusammenhang*. In the discussion of Romantic epistemology in regard to natural objects, however, a structure of mutuality prevails, and hence a certain element of the lateral within a general context of potentiation and intensification (*Steigerung*). In Romantic epistemology, as Benjamin expounds it, knowledge of objects is always a self-knowledge, even if it is enacted through natural things (*SW* 1: 146; '*Naturdinge*' *GS* 1.1: 57). Human knowing in relation to natural objects is a reflex of the 'self-knowledge of [the] thinking in that [very] being' (*SW* 1: 146, parentheses added to highlight the original sense). This is no naïve claim for sentience in all natural objects, though its apparent model is relatively banal. (Elements of the same reflexive phenomenology survive in Merleau-Ponty's understanding of vision, for example.)[17] Citing Novalis, Benjamin introduces the notion of 'observation' (*Beobachtung*) as the appropriate posture for the attainment of a knowledge of nature, given that the real itself is to be understood as a medium of reflexivity (*Reflexionsmedium*). The intensification of reflection in the observer 'awakens' the reflexivity of the thing observed. Benjamin's term ('*die Selbsterkenntnis ... [kann] wachgerufen werden*' *GS* 1.1: 59) recalls Eichendorff's well-known poem '*Wünschelrute*' (Magic Wand) according to which a song slumbers in all things and when awakened from their dreaming, the whole world begins to sing – if only the magic word can be found. In attempting to (re)construct a dimension of Romantic thought never properly developed by Schlegel and Novalis themselves, it is perhaps significant that Benjamin borrows the term *Hilfskonstruktion* (even though it is less technical and more widely used than 'auxiliary construction') from geometry, given that the scheme of reflexivity he finds in Romantic thought is conceived in spatial terms, or in terms of a spacing; its geometrical sense leaves open the question of how the real enfolded as content in 'the reflections' is to be substantially understood.

It is here that the possible forms of articulation within the *Zusammenhang*, understood both as context and coherence, need to be considered. Three recurrent motifs of Benjamin's construction of Romantic reflexivity are significant: his notion of a *constant Zusammenhang*, marked by the use of the term *stetig*, both adjectivally and adverbially; secondly, the term 'mediality' (*Medialität*), derived by Benjamin from Novalis as a paraphrase of his understanding of the absolute as a medium of reflection; and last, the mechanisms of transition that articulate the dynamics of (the) *Zusammenhang*. These are variously designated in the vocabulary of Schlegel and Novalis as *Übergang* (transition), *übergehen* (pass over) (*GS* 1.1: 17, 22; *SW* 1: 122, 126); *Sprung* (leap), in Schlegel (*GS* 1.1: 22; *SW* 1: 126), '*sich selbst Überspringen*' (overleaping oneself) in Novalis (*GS* 1.1: 66; *SW* 1: 152), in a spontaneous event, associated with the suddenness of the lightning flash ('*blizartig*', *GS* 1.1: 49); and by Benjamin's own term '*Gradnetz*' (*GS* 1.1: 40, 44: system of coordinates), which draws his expository method into close proximity with the Romantic project he seeks to describe.

The almost ubiquitous epithet of the *Zusammenhang* is 'constant', 'permanent'. In justifying the term 'medium of reflection' as a Schlegelian designation for the Absolute, Benjamin notes that Schlegel 'attached the greatest importance to the constantly uniform connection ['*Auf den stetigen gleichförmigen Zusammenhang*' (*GS* 1.1: 37)] in the Absolute or in the system ...' (*SW* 1: 132). The stability of the structure of connection thereby envisaged contrasts with any notion of its instability; and in its derivation from 'stets' meaning 'always', the sense of *stetig* as 'constant' indicates that the *Zusammenhang* is held unchangeably in place, and not subject (within this emphasis) to temporality. In the final, unexamined section of his thesis, Benjamin draws a contrast between the thought of the Romantics in relation to the idea of art, and Goethe's contrary conception of an artistic ideal. There he notes that 'Just as, in contrast to the idea, the inner structure of the ideal is discontinuous [*unstetig*], so, too, the connection [*Zusammenhang*] of this ideal with art is not given in a medium but is designated by a refraction' (*SW* 1: 179, my parentheses). The structural contrast here is between the primordial contents of the *Ur*-phenomena revealed only through the prismatics of tradition, rendered in this passage by the relation to the Greek Muses, on the one hand, and the constant reflexive medium of the Romantic conception on the other, in which the Absolute is held as in a crystal lattice. The constancy and stability of the *Zusammenhang* in Benjamin's account sets it off, once again, as much from a discontinuous sense of tradition and the past as from the developmental sense of connection dismissed as mere *Fortgang*: the *Zusammenhang* is not to be understood as a trajectory, or as in any sense vectorized.

The continuous structure of reflexivity, which Benjamin derives from Romantic epistemology in order to identify it supremely in literature, is a *medium* – as Benjamin says, a 'medium of reflection' (*SW* 1: 132). He recognizes that this term could be ambiguous. Reflection can be understood as itself a medium, for some other thing or process; or the *Reflexionsmedium* may be the medium in which reflection itself occurs. Both are possible and the expression retains both, because reflection is the medium as which the Absolute is given, in, under, and along with particulars (referred to by Benjamin sometimes as 'centres of reflection'); and because the medium for (as it were) reflection is the steady and constant connectivity of *Zusammenhang* (see Benjamin's note: *SW* 1: 189, n. 63; *GS* 1.1: 36, n. 60). The mediality of *Zusammenhang* is explained via a series of quotations from Novalis under the general rubric of Novalis's coinage 'self-penetration' ('*Selbstdurchdringung*'). If Novalis, as quoted here, refers such self-engendered autonomous ('*selbstgesetzmässig*') activity to 'an intelligence' or a '*Geist*' (*SW* 1: 133; *GS* 1.1: 38), Benjamin is quick to find other texts in which a subjectless, self-penetrated chaos is projected as the world rendered immeasurable in the Absolute of reflection. The notion that chaos is the essential ground of all order and system is common in the fragmentary writings of the Jena Romantics. When Benjamin has to take issue with the less rigorous view of Romantic aesthetics offered by other critical expositions, he identifies Novalis's chaos with a passage from Schlegel in which it is expounded as the symbol or 'emblem of the absolute medium', and as 'the scene of a thorough and ordering subjection to the rule' (my translation; 'the scene of pervading governance', *SW* 1: 168; *GS* 1.1: 92: '*Schauplatz ordnender Durchwaltung*') of the principle of autonomy.

In the challenge presented by the Jena Romantics to Fichte's idealism, the central role played by the I for philosophical understanding of consciousness is to be replaced by the mediality of reflection in and as art. The structure of reflexivity without a subject, constructed in Benjamin's montage of material derived from Friedrich Schlegel and Novalis, abandons Fichte's ontological pretensions by universalizing the possibility of self-relation. The phenomenon at the origin of the Romantic thinking of reflection is what Benjamin calls 'bloßes Sich-Selbst-Denken', mere self-thought; and this self-relation as thinking can be attributed to everything: 'for everything is [a] self' (parentheses added: *SW* 1: 128; *GS* 1.1: 29: '*alles ist Selbst*'), paraphrased more clumsily in Part II of the dissertation as the Romantics' 'metaphysical view of the real as a thinking entity [*alles Wirklichen als eines Denkenden*]' – though Benjamin himself notably avoids substantializing the reflexive structure as an entity here. Whatever the occasions of its intimation, in the various determinations of the formal axiom of absolute universal reflexivity – as art, nature or religion – the fundamental structure always retains (in some sense yet to be clarified) its 'character as a medium of thought, as a context of relation established by thinking': '*den Charakter ... eines Zusammenhanges denkender Beziehung*' (*SW* 1: 144; *GS* 1.1: 54). The version by Lachterman, Eiland and Balfour perhaps overclarifies here. More literally this is to be understood as retaining the character of a coherence or connectivity (in the sense we have considered) *of thinking relation*. As in the case of the ambiguous *Reflexionsmedium*, the genitive should not too readily be resolved into agency ('established *by* thinking'): Benjamin's formulation retains the possibilities of thinking *as* the relations within *Zusammenhang* and of such relations being in some way actively possessed of thought, as well as grasped by it. The relations that constitute and are constituted by the *Zusammenhang* are hence always complex and multiple, and not simply causal.

The proper complexity can be rendered accessible by recognizing a comparable form of coherence in the thought of the Romantics themselves, Benjamin argues. They demonstrate patterns of thought having 'systematic tendencies and contexts [*Zusammenhänge*]' that remained obscure to Schlegel and Novalis themselves, but that can be exposed by using the notion of the 'medium of reflection' as a systematic grid to reveal the movement and structure of their thought. In the rather broad discussion of the third chapter of Part I of the dissertation, Benjamin uses the term *Gradnetz* both to describe his own analytical procedure and to indicate the underlying coherence of Schlegel's various literary and philosophical motifs. It seems clear that the increasing tendency in the dissertation to present the thought of the Jena Romantics in a dense sequence of quotations, with relatively little expository matter or commentary, is designed to be a parallel procedure to Schegel's, inviting an intuition of the *Zusammenhang* that is nowhere explicit or reducible to a proposition.[18] In this respect, Benjamin's methods of montage correspond to the Romantic elaboration of the 'medium of reflection' by actively pursuing a philosophical method that 'begins in the middle' and sees in its objects 'a middle term in the medium' (*SW* 1: 137; '*ein Mittleres im Medium*', *GS* 1.1: 43).

Literature is the epistemologically privileged modality of the *Reflexionsmedium* because of its intentionality. In his Cologne lectures, the most Schlegel claims for literature is 'a great similarity of form' to the reflexivity which he there returns to its idealist terminology of the 'I' (*SW* 1: 149). The structural homology is glossed over as a partial identity in Benjamin's account, but the production of the literary work ('*Das Dichten*': *GS* 1.1: 63) as a space of thinking threatens to restore self-consciousness *as subject* to the structure of reflexivity that has been established. This is encountered in two forms: when Schlegel's notion of a self-affect (in *Ath.* fgm. 434) is quoted to explain how self-relation occurs in literature, the readily available self is the author. Novalis has to be cited even to resist Shakespeare, invoked as a focus of reflection by the Schlegel brothers. What must be preserved beyond any subjective locus is 'the integrity and unity of the reflection medium' (*SW* 1: 150). Indeed Novalis, as quoted at this point, avoids even the notion of *Poesie*, preferring the term 'nature' in order to emphasize the impersonality of a subjectless reflexivity.[19] When Benjamin, later in the dissertation, needs to distinguish a Kantian idea of judgement from the Romantic idea of reflection, he comes close to allowing belief in the psychological unity of genres in a single 'complete works' to restore the author as reflexive subject. His *example*, that 'tragedy, for the observer, would continuously cohere [*zusammenhängen*] with the sonnet' (*SW* 1: 165; *GS* 1.1: 87–8), transparently invokes Shakespeare once again. (In fact, groping for an illustration of Schlegel's notion of the invisible, transcendental work of art evoked by the idea of art itself, Benjamin's note (*SW* 1: 195, n. 238; *GS* 1.1: 91, n. 231) acknowledges the parallel between the the idea of art and 'the epitome [*Inbegriff*] of the creations' of a master understood as an oeuvre ('*Gesamtwerk*'). By specifiying such an artist as painter or sculptor ('*eines bildenden Künstlers*') Benjamin seems to want to assert a unity that could not be grasped as any finite textual complex.) At the other pole, as in the case of this observer of a Shakespearean *Gesamtwerk*, stands the reader; but this critical function too must be stripped of its empirical contingency. The true readers, who will be *critics,* are not 'empirical intellects but stages of reflection personified' (*SW* 1: 153).

What is awakened by the observation of the literary work, as *second* nature and parallel to the observation of natural objects, is its reflexive relation to genre and hence to form in general. Benjamin identifies this aspect of Schlegel's critical project in terms of his understanding of the concept of the 'work'. The understanding of or consciousness of a literary text *as a work* relates it to the concept of art itself of which the particular work can hence become a 'centre of reflection'. Ideas of form and genre are freed from the regulative canons of Enlightenment classicism, on the one hand, and from the rule of subjective expressivity that Benjamin identifies with the *Sturm und Drang*. Instead, form can emerge as the inherent self-determination of necessary self-relations. To establish this concept of form, Benjamin cites part of one of the passages of conversation from Schlegel's *Dialogue on Poetry*, just before the 'Letter on the Novel', and confirms the definition of form with *Ath.* fgm. 297, 'A work is formed when it is everywhere sharply delimited [*begrenzt*], but within those limits is limitless' (*SW* 1: 158). In disclosing the activity of the work in any particular work, by which a text is to be understood here, critique encounters the work as a moment in the medium of reflection, that is as a structure of reflexivity.[20] Furthermore, in each work the possibility of form and hence of the presentational forms [*Darstellungsformen*] of art is articulated by the active structure of the text.

This becomes an important factor in Benjamin's account after his not entirely helpful discussion of the fundamental reflexivity of literature (art) as 'transcendental *Poesie*'. He distinguishes between profane form and the symbolic form in which this transcendental *Poesie* is disclosed. Profane form can be characterized as the merely generic. A note (*SW* 1: 197 n. 263; *GS* 1.1: 97, n. 256) comments that presentational form is not of necessity profane, i.e. that, in virtue of their pure exposition, the traditional genres (as Schlegel's essay on Lessing, which Benjamin has just quoted, suggests) can partake of absolute or symbolic form. However, the genre in which the symbolic form is most clearly displayed is the *novel*. Because it is not generically regulated (Benjamin appears to ignore even the requirement of narrative), the formal or ordering principles of the novel must be self-generated and, in virtue of this formality, reflexively autonomous – for any instance of the novel and for the novel as a genre.[21] Schlegel and, for a time, Novalis identified Goethe's second fiction, *Wilhelm Meisters Lehrjahre*, as the canonical example of this unregulated self-generating genre. In explaining the significance of the novel, Benjamin stresses a term that he derives from both Romantic authors when he claims that the novel's 'retarding character is the expression of the reflection proper to it' (*SW* 1: 172, modified; *GS* 1.1: 99: '*sein retardierender Charakter ist der Ausdruck der ihm eigenen Reflexion*').[22] Novalis's description of the novel, as 'a structure articulated in each and every period. Each small piece must be something cut off, delimited, a whole proper to itself' (*SW* 1: 172, modified; *GS* 1.1: 99: '*ein eigenes Ganzes*'), makes it clear that the mode of articulation of the structure of reflexivity as *Zusammenhang* had been modelled on the Romantic account of the novel all along. And it is in this respect that the textual process of the novel, as a delimited but, within these limits, infinite series of delayed or deferred connections, models the workful dynamic of the work, as text. The presence of the sentence, the word, and ultimately the letter – as Novalis claims in the remarkable comment that the true novel is 'a consonant' (*SW* 1: 197, n. 284; *GS* 1.1: 104, n. 277; see *SW* 1: 175) – makes present an immediacy that radiates mediation in all directions, on all sides (*nach allen Seiten*), of the totality of form which is never grasped or formulated aside from this dispersion.

By enacting the deferred canon of its own form in the textual *Zusammenhang* of its (never present) coherence, the novel can sum up and summon up the very possibility of form, and hence opens, in a similarly metonymic and simultaneous way, on to the 'continuum of forms', which is art in the conception of the Early Romantics and of which the novel is the 'comprehensible manifestation' (*Erscheinung*, *SW* 1: 173; *GS* 1.1: 100). This epiphany of the universal reflexivity of literature, and thereby of art, is possible because of the *minimal* formal determination of the form, as prose. It is trivial but nevertheless necessary to note that this does not preclude the possibility of a versified novel – say Vickram Seth's *The Golden Gate* – nor the mixing of forms (prose narrative, including *Märchen*, poetry and song) which typifies the German Romantic novel from Novalis to Eichendorff. Variety of form is exacerbated in Schlegel's own novel, *Lucinde*, in which no one part is formally similar to any other, and only one section ('*Lehrjahre eines Ungeschickten*') really constitutes the narrative sequence that might be deemed proper to a novel. This tendency towards the multifarious can be read in parallel to the function of the prosaic, as resistant to the limitations of genre and as part of the aspiration to the transcendental that is associated with prose, Benjamin claims (see *SW* 1: 174).

The work of prose within the novel – understood as an indication of the structure of reflexivity that subtends art and specifically literature – is, we are to understand, distinct from the activity of plot and the deferrals of action that it requires. However, there remains a degree of ambiguity. Claiming 'retardation' in the Romantic conception of the novel as the pure form of genre without the (Enlightenment) rigour of a canonical standard ('representational form … prevails only in its purity not in its rigour', *SW* 1: 172), Benjamin quotes Schlegel comparing *Wilhelm Meister* to *Hamlet*, the play that centrally preoccupies Goethe's hero. 'Through its retarding nature, the play can seem akin to the novel, which has its essence precisely in that' (*SW* 1: 172): the retardation that is significantly at work in *Hamlet*, of course, is its hero's delay in avenging his father's death. The important consequence is that the play's 'retarding nature' is inextricably bound up with its action as a deferred resolution of its plot.

There is one further sense in which the specifically Romantic form of the novel might easily be confused with the Absolute 'symbolic form' Benjamin wishes to elucidate as the mark and expression ('imprint', *SW* 1: 171; *GS* 1.1: 97: '*Ausprägung*') of the poetic absolute *in* form. He describes this sense as referring to various general terms (*Deckbegriffe*) covering the poetic Absolute of which the most prominent is mythology; Schlegel's use of the category 'arabesque' is cited as such a mythological term. What this seeks to delimit from the central concern of the dissertation with symbolic form is the aesthetic valorization of flamboyance (in Schlegel), on the one hand, or the mystical cult of the book (in Novalis's *Heinrich von Ofterdingen*) on the other.[23] Such mythical figurations of the transcendental in Romanticism would confuse it with a magical power of revelation, as the content of an aesthetic intimation. Schlegel's symbolic form, in the sense that Benjamin wishes to isolate, designates the reach ('*Tragweite*', *GS* 1.1: 97) of reflective structure for the work of literature, rather than the aesthetic celebration of a remote revelatory power.[24] When he cites among the historical consequences of the Early German Romantic determination of the idea of *Poesie* as prose 'the philosophical foundations of later aesthetic schools ... such as the later stages of French Romanticism, German Neo-Romanticism', it becomes clear that he is thinking of Flaubert, the Parnassians and the intellectual circle around Stefan George – the tradition of *l'art pour l'art* from Gautier to the Symbolists (see *SW* 1: 175, 177: *GS* 1.1: 103, 107).[25] In the line of aesthetic myth, therefore, would also stand the Mallarméan 'grand' œuvre', which reconceives Schlegel's original conceptions of the unity of *Poesie*.

Benjamin subsequently quotes Novalis to explain that reflection is consonantal (*SW* 1: 175: 'of a consonating nature'; 'konsonierender Natur', *GS* 1.1: 104), by reference to the fragment mentioned earlier: 'If the novel is of a retarding nature, then in truth it is poetically prosaic, a consonant' (*SW* 1: 197, n. 284; *GS* 1.1: 104, n. 277).[26] This consonantal structuring marks off the vocalic, interrupting its continuity to disclose and articulate movement towards its completion. The logic of incompletion at work in this conception of the novel and/as prose is parallel to that of the fragment. The discontinuity of the (consonantal) break opens up the possibility of critique and hence the reflexivity of the work. The retardation of the action of the novel figures the retardation of prose itself, understood as discontinuous. The reader, as reflection personified, in critique, and negotiating such retardations and deferrals will mark the passage to the next centre of reflection as the transition across a break. Benjamin makes clear in his elaboration of the canonical principle of reflection that 'The forms of consciousness [in Fichte's idealism] in their transition into one another ["*in ihrem Übergang ineinander*"] are the sole object of immediate cognition' (*SW* 1: 122; *GS* 1.1: 21). The prosaic in the novel provides the form in which this essential reaching for the branching contexts of the *Zusammenhang* is epitomized. Stripped down and free of narrative excitement, the pure prose of the novel offers the textual dimensions for a spacing of language, a spacing which 'as a between, holds the Absolute in place. Spacing marks the presence of the Absolute', which can be understood here, too, as opening on to the domain of language as absolute *Poesie*.[27]

This is the model of the prose complex that underlies the conception of *Zusammenhang* in Benjamin's dissertation: the structure of reflexivity it accesses is 'a mediation through immediacies'. Benjamin continues: 'Friedrich Schlegel was acquainted with no other sort, and on occasion he speaks in this sense of a "transition that must always be a leap"' (*SW* 1: 126; *GS* 1.1: 27: '*Übergang, der immer ein Sprung sein muss*'). Prose, but specifically prose as *in the novel*, exhibits the principle of discontinuity, which opens the possibility of a completion that can be intimated as the totality of the work (of prose) but which we are to conceive as finally unbounded by its engagement with the generic and the linguistic. In the remainder of Novalis's formulation of the interruptive nature of reflexivity, Benjamin identifies a further expression of the sobriety of the reflective structure: 'Song sung inwardly: inner world. speech–prose–critique' (*SW* 1: 175; *GS* 1.1: 104: '*Gesang nach innen: Innenwelt. Rede–Prosa–Kritik*'). Reflection here, as 'reflection upon oneself', threatens to resolve again into subjective self-consciousness; instead Novalis dissolves the old distinctions between lyric (as first-person utterance), drama (as third-person utterance) and epic (as the mixed narrative and dramatic genre) to yield a trinity in which, once within the *medium* of language as utterance (*Rede*), the self-relation of interiority is immediately – and hence, as we have seen, as a mediation – *prose* in and as the Absolute of *criticism* (*Kritik*). In Novalis's letter to August Wilhlem Schlegel of 12 January 1798, of which Benjamin makes so much, this is clearly understood literally, as the movements of sentences in their mixtures and free (loose: *locker*) coherences and connectedness (*Zusammenhang*). Such movements of sentences into connectivity set in motion, and even commotion, the projected totality of the text. Through and in its medium '*ein jeder Reiz verbreitet sich … nach allen Seiten*': every stimulus spreads in all directions (see *SW* 1: 174; *GS* 1.1: 101). Such stimulus shares the character of the consonantal interruption, and limpidly reveals the medium through which it, as it were, ripples.

If the understanding of the novel as prose effectively means that the reflexive medium of literature is the *linguistic* Absolute given as the possibility of meaning *tout court*, then the role of the Romantic conception of art evaporates. Yet the paths of Benjamin's exposition reach such a possibility within the framework of a sense of textual totality, given by a conception of the novel. The interruption or hesitancy of each 'period', in Novalis's phrase 'a membered structure' ('*gegliederter Bau*'), holds out the possibility not of some final completion, but of its mediate fulfilment through the movement instigated by the desire for completion it invites. The full subject of a reflexive author or of a reflexive and reconstructing reader (and the two are always close) constantly threatens to return to the textualized complex or grid (*Gradnetz*). In a Romantic understanding of the novel (and in the practice of successive Romantic novelists, Schlegel and Novalis included) the movements of narrative linearity are rendered complex and multiple by circulation and circularity as well as by the action of metonymy ('*nach allen Seiten*') and metaphor, symbol and emblem. Such 'fulfilled' structures give the fundamental model for Benjamin's account of reflexivity in Romantic aesthetics, and resist his philosophical will to strip them of their narrative origins.

5

'HOWEVER ONE CALLS INTO THE FOREST . . .'

ECHOES OF TRANSLATION*

Bettine Menke

Few words have been expended hitherto on the functioning of translation as echo which Benjamin formulates in his 'The Task of the Translator' – yet despite its circumvention within and omission from most previous readings, this is a noteworthy passage. Just as the theme of translation, and of being translated, is essentially a Romantic one, so the echo is a Romantic model, a metapoetic configuration. I wish to demonstrate here, in poetic and acoustic echoes alike, the interaction of the Baroque and the Romantic of which Benjamin's *The Origin of the German Trauerspiel* speaks.[1]

The formulations on which this article shall focus accentuate the disjunction (in and) of translation; the registration of a fissure within this form; a constitutive disjointure which is fundamental to and ought to be retained within translation; a scission; the entry of death within the afterlife. It is here that Benjamin specifies the 'task of the translator', which he differentiates from that of the 'poet' as follows:

> It is the task of the translator to find that intentionality toward the language into which he translates from which the echo of the original is evoked in it ... Unlike a work of literature, translation finds itself not in the interior of the mountain forest of language itself [*im innern Bergwald der Sprache selbst*] but on the outside facing the wooded ridge; and without entering into it, it calls in the original, calls it in at that unique place where the echo in one's own language is capable of rendering the resonance [*Wiederhall*] of the work of a foreign language.[2]

Benjamin here conceptualizes an arrangement of translating under the rubric of the 'echo'. Translation operates from outside the 'mountain forest of language', 'as' remembrance coming 'from the far bank'.[3] It 'calls' from without, 'from the

* Translated by Robert J. Kiss.

outside', into one's 'own' language – into the language it is being translated into – termed the 'language forest', without entering into it: it remains outside that which it faces. It 'calls forth' the original in the foreign language as a re-*call-ing* of the original. Located in the interior, inside of the 'mountain forest of language' ('*im innern Bergwald der Sprache*'), as Benjamin puts it, are meaning and the poet's work, 'because the intention of the latter is never directed toward the language as such, at its totality, but is aimed solely and immediately at specific linguistic relations in which "contents" are given [*bestimmte sprachliche Gehaltszusammenhänge*]'[4] – that is to say, at speaking which means 'something'. The original – i.e. the text that is to be translated – is re*call*ed in translation by way of a turning away, by a diversion not meaning what it says. Translation 'takes place' in place of reproduction or transference, both as a calling forth *and* its reverberation, and *between* the calling forth and the reverberation. The *re*verberation – both off and in the so-called 'own' language ('in its totality') – of that which has been called out differentiates and makes a difference, and thus appears at first glance to contradict the very metaphor of the echo. The German-language proverb that is echoed in Benjamin's formulation[5] highlights this, and the feeling of astonishment that is appropriate here. Athanasius Kircher's rhetorical question as to 'whether one might be able to bring about an echo with a different reverberation of words / to that / which was called out in the first place', and more particularly his rhetorical answer to this, underline such a sense of consternation. For as Kircher notes, it must appear 'as though this is an objectionable statement [*eine widerwärtige Rede*] / with contradictory ideas running through it', since it can scarcely be comprehended

> how this [echoing] voice could be against and contradictory to itself; that one might call out one thing / only to find something else replied in the echo; for the echo is nothing more than a voice or sound that runs or flows, as it were, for and after itself / and can not therefore give back or bring about anything other / than that which flowed or ran in the first instance.[6]

The concern here is directed, then, at that which follows, the otherness of the repetition of this reverberation.

The difference of and in the reverberation revokes the notion of 'intention': the 'counter=voice' ('*Gegen=Stimm*'), as the echo was also termed,[7] can not have become the voice of one's 'own' language, whence it resounds. In Benjamin's concept of speech that is to be echoed, a deferral has already been transacted with regard to the fundamental ordering of the 'own' and the 'alien': one's 'own' voice speaks as an alien one; it becomes the voice, the calling forth of the alien work; it is not the speaking of one's own language or a voice of one's own that rings out from one's 'own' language, but rather a reverberation of one's 'own' voice given to the foreign original.

A sense of consternation is admitted into the topography of translation as echo, such as was engendered in Baroque echo poems[8] and the scenes involving echoes in mourning plays (which latter Benjamin identifies as the playgrounds for these works' intriguers), in which intricate contrivances are instigated with the echo, such as Baroque 'artists of echoes and sound' also knew how to exploit for maximum astonishment. However one calls into the forest, it absolutely *does not* echo back just so – which is the case, contrary to expectation, even with acoustic echoes. In Baroque echo games – *concetti* playing out the division of sound and meaning, of signifier and signified – the focus is on the *joke* (Witz) of repetition, on identity and difference within repetition. If 're=sounding' ('*Wider=Hall*') – as Harsdörffer makes doubly explicit by means of a Latin translation for the German in his *Mathematischen und Philosophischen Erquickstunden* – is indeed that which '*wider (contra) und wieder (iterum)* sends back its sound again', then so re=sounding is defined in the doubling of already doubled repetitions (*Wi(e)derholungen*).[9]

Ovid's Echo – 'the loquacious nymph who is neither able to allow any speaker the last word nor to take up words herself', the 'reverberating one', who is the model for and personification of the echo – 'doubles voices at the end of speech and lets the words that have been heard return'. 'Oh, how often she did wish to near [Narcissus] with flattering words / and to direct tender requests at him – her organ (the tongue) opposes itself / [and] permits her not to begin! Yet what it permits: it / awaits sounds, in order to send back words from these. /' She, or to be more precise her tongue, awaits the sounds in order to *re*-turn these as words with meaning, to implant meanings – that is to say, *different* meanings – in these sounds. 'Echo', as the personification of difference within repetition, makes use of her counterplay in order to create meaning. But this implies: she hears and awaits only 'sounds', instead of the words that were meant, and thus, in her *re*-production has already traversed the words and laid a rupture through them.

This rupture in the words, which is inserted between sounds and meanings and into the chain of letters or grammatical components, momentarily casts out from the concatenation that death which Narcissus would rather embrace than give Echo power of love: it is the incision that ironically makes desire communicable in reverberation, the difference between ' "*emoriar, quam sit tibi copia nostri!*" ' and ' "*sit tibi copia nostri!*" ' given back by Echo.[10] What was rejection becomes an articulation of desire through the breaking of the syntactic construction; the cast out death is not ultimately excluded by the incision through the chain of signifiers and between words and what is meant; but rather, this separation will come to be realized as her death.

Echo is the playing with, the playing out and laying bare of the discrepancy between sound and meaning. Benjamin himself cites the (counter)play of echoes in the Baroque in his 'The Role of Language in *Trauerspiel* and Tragedy': 'The interplay between sound and meaning remains a terrifying phantom for the mourning play.'[11] He situates the echo in these plays' 'deliberately opened-up antitheses', as an example of the Satanic and spectral terror of meaning which – according to allegory – always portends death.

Here meaning is encountered, and will continue to be encountered as the reason for mournfulness. The antithesis of sound and meaning could not but be at its most intense where both can be combined in one [*beide in einem zu geben*], without their actually cohering in the sense of forming an organic unity [*im Sinne des organischen Sprachbaus*]. This task, a deducible one, is accomplished in a scene which stands out as a masterpiece in an otherwise uninteresting Viennese *Haupt- und Staatsaktion*. In *Die Glorreiche Marter Joannes von Nepomuck* the fourteenth scene of the first act shows one of the intriguers (Zytho) acting as an echo to the mythological speeches of his victim (Quido), and answering them with ominous intimations. The conversion of the pure sound of creaturely language into the richly significant irony which re-echoes from the mouth of the intriguer, is highly indicative of the relationship of this character to language. The intriguer is the master of meanings. In the harmless ejaculation of an onomatopoeic natural language they are the obstacle, and so the origin of a mourning for which the intriguer is responsible along with them. When the echo of all things, the proper domain of the free play of sound, is struck as it were by meaning, so it had to be the ultimate revelation of language [*des Sprachlichen*] as that time felt it. And a form was indeed provided for it. 'The echo, which repeats the last two or three syllables of a strophe, often omitting a letter so that it sounds like an answer, a warning, or a prophecy, is something very "pleasing" and very popular'.[12]

Within the echo that repeats, difference and disjunction are always registered as well, as prerequisites for the possibility and location of deceit or deception, whereby deferrals and distortions can intercede, or may already have interceded, in the fissure that marks repetition. However, Benjamin's determination of the echo as a 'free play of sound' goes peculiarly awry, since this latter does not get 'struck (or taken over) as it were by meaning', but rather functions as sound*play* in the reproduction of sounds *only in so far as* it makes these into the setting for *concetti*-esque plays on meaning. This is to be read in the Baroque political play mentioned by Benjamin, in which Zytho's answers enact intriguing plays on words upon Quido's statements and questions, and always portend death:

QUIDO: ich mein den Orth, da meine Seele sicher liegt.
ZYTHO: erliegt –
QUIDO: Wird mir Augusta herz, auch eine gunst erweisen?
ZYTHO: Eisen –
QUIDO: und kombt doch eh noch ist der Abendglantz verschwunden.
ZYTHO: wunden –
QUIDO: ich heg ein keusche Flamm, die nicht in Purpur sticht.
ZYTHO: ersticht.[13]

To let reverberation say something 'different' characterizes the echo as a *trope*. It is a paronomasia or annominatio which, through an 'identity' of or minimal possible difference between signifiers, generates the maximum in differences in

meaning, playing out this difference. That which characterizes paronomasia –
a burgeoning of meanings achieved through the slightest phonetic alteration, or
the production of paradoxes through phonetic alteration – found its poetic
realization as a *concetti*-esque *acudeza* in rhymes (namely, in echo poems). The
'echo' is a form of pun, a play on meaning by means of acoustic deception,
a pseudo-etymological game. It exposes a certain irony of meaning where the
repeated sounds of words themselves seem heavy with meaning: when (Quido's)
'*und solt es kosten auch mein Leben !*' ('and if it costs me my life /') is echoed (by
Zytho) as '– *eben*' ('– precisely'), the latter appears 'pregnant with meaning' and
invokes meaning as spectre (*Wiedergänger*) of the word; the meaning imbued
upon the void of the mechanically repeated (own) words that return as alien
ones is *spectral*. The acoustic echo provides the 'metaphorological model' for an
allusion which in the 'resonance' of its phonic units *ironically* – by embracing
an (always already) 'false' referent[14] – excludes every referent.[15]

Benjamin wrote that 'This game, like other similar ones, which were so
readily taken for foolish trifles, brings us to the heart of the matter [*redet also zur
Sache selber*]'. Thus he implied: it speaks of *language*; what matters here is
language. The echo trope 'speaks' of the relationship between sign and referent
in that it lays bare their relationship as an 'antithesis' – the antithetis of *res* and
verba (in which *verba* first appears as such) applied to sounds and meanings.
The use and exploitation of the multi / contra / valency between sound and
meaning and between identical sounds within echo games' plays on meaning
exposes the cleft between these. This is a *concetti*-esque trope[16] that introduces a
disjunction and tears apart the model of mutual dependency of sound and
meaning, of '*vocabulo significante* and *cosa significata*', and *thereby* organizes
signification in an ingenious – or rather, in a *perceptible* and *artificial* – way.
The 'ingenious signification' of the *concetto* promotes the 'invention of new significations' that are left to appear strange and alarming, thereby rendering 'pure
representation' both a 'pleasure' and a 'source of astonishment'. 'The *ingenio*'s
achievements must be detectable, noticeable' because it is the 'astonishment' at
these ingenious interventions that lays bare the rupture between signifier and
signified and the functioning across and beyond these.[17] Like the mannered
concetto, which Benjamin mentions only in passing as an aspect of allegorical
signification, allegory – through the simultaneous adroitness and artifice of its
own signification, wherein ever more and ever remoter plays on meaning are
produced – lays bare signification itself, the functioning of signification, and
therewith the cleft that is always bridged in signifying, only to at the same time
be cast asunder anew through signification. Allegorical schemata, ever newly
dissociated and dissociating, are at once symptom, expression and thematization
of a crisis in signification presented as a 'crisis of similarity' – just like the
concetti. Allegorically, though, the ever-present rupture – the abyss between sign
and referent – is read as the entering of death within the world, to which its
signification is thereby dedicated.

Since the (rhetorical) echo, in its plays on meaning, exploits and thereby
refers to that difference or discrepancy between sound and meaning or between

repeated ('identical') sounds that can always arise, so the 'principle of the allegorical approach' is enacted in it: as dismemberment.[18] As Benjamin puts it: 'The language of the Baroque is constantly shattered [*erschüttert*] by rebellion on the part of its elements.'[19] Elsewhere (in his 'Commentaries on Poems by Brecht'), Benjamin points out: 'One would do well to ponder the fact that the German word *erschüttern* ('to shatter') conceals in it the word *schütter* ("sparse").' What it comes down to then are the 'holes and gaps'.[20]

As examples of this, not only the rhetoric of the echo may be cited, but also its implementations in reality, such as those presented in Athanasius Kircher's Baroque *Neue Hall= und Thon=Kunst* whose entire presentation is dependent on the rhetorical echo's plays on meaning. Kircher – to whom we shall return later as the chronicler also of an acoustic translation echo – presents the exercise of allowing the echo, in its repetition, to speak 'differently' or to 'reply' through the word *clamore* and its multiply fractured reproduction, according to its graduated partitioning as: **CL/A/M/O/RE**.[21]

> Let us set up for example a four-syllabled echo at the reverberative objects (*Gegen=Stände*) BCDEF / but arranged and divided in such a way / that each of these re=verberates one syllable later and more slowly/ than the previous one. The voice, or the word, shall be the three-syllabled Latin *CLAMORE*. The vocal centre or out-going voice is A, because the reverberative objects are so ordered/ that each reflects back one syllable later, and thus it is clear / that each object will reverberate back a distinct and different word. / At the reverberating object (*Gegen=Stand*) B, *CLAMORE*; *AMORE* at the reverberating object C. *MORE* at the reverberating object D. *ORE* at the reverberating object E, and the terminating *RE* is reverberating at object F. In this way, an ever greater number of different words resounds back from a many-voiced echo.[22]

In the breaking down and playing out of its *re*-productions, **clamore** yields the (Latin) forms: 'the cry', or 'yell', and 'love', 'according to tradition', 'to linguistic usage', 'to stipulation', 'the mouth' – or: 'the voice' or 'face' or 'mask'; 'in the face of' and thereby 'present' – and the 'object'. The exclamation (as object of an exclamation) is dismembered according to the literalness of its letters: **cl-a-m-o-re**. Thus, it is shown not only that the word is pervaded with 'holes and gaps', *shattered*, but also that *literal*ness – exposing the arbitrariness of the metonymic conjoining and division of letters in the construction of meaning – anatomizes whatever might have been meant in the word. The refinement of Kircher's example, which raises it above the level of *mere* example, lies in the fact that all those words which are precipitated from the echo and all those resounding meanings that are cut adrift from it, in turn thematize the echo's formation: the 'yell' or 'cry', and the 'object' (*Gegen=Stand*) on which the sound is broken, and the 'mouth' that figures not only as a 'face' or 'mask' for the 'voice', but at the same time names its phantasmal quality, its being (in the) 'present'. '*Amore*' may seem an exception here, but is motivated by Ovid's tale of Echo, naming that desire which is (dis)articulated and transgressed in reproduction – and in precisely this way has communicated itself. In that its echo speaks of itself and its functioning, Kircher's *clamore* can be seen as a characteristic example of an echo game.[23] Furthermore, it leaves the mouth or face of the voice, as well as the resounding components or objects, and indeed every possible object (*res*) of the echo, to descend into a din (*Getöse*) within which reverberation was already intended, and into an indistinguishability of multiplying and intermingling voices, in which every voice shall be lost: a clamorous zone where points and intervals can be secured neither in space nor in time. The calculated self-referentiality of Kircher's example denies just what it ought to underline: the clear distinguishability of that which resounds back, and the determinability 'that each [object (*Gegen=Stand*)] re=verberates one syllable later and more slowly / than the previous one'. With *clamore*, this calling forth and its reverberations say something different, they speak of a disruptive and indistinguishable cacophony of reverberation, and of the non-sense which language and speech draw in unidentifiable, multiplying, intermingling reverberations.[24]

The rhetorical echo is located at the site of and articulates, to cite Benjamin, 'the antitheses [of sound and meaning] deliberately opened up by the Baroque'; its 'full justification' would be 'yield[ed]' in the synthesis of sound and meaning, the concept of which Benjamin draws from the Early Romantic philosophy of sound and writing (as exemplified by Johann Wilhelm Ritter).[25] Meanings are 'the obstacle, and so the origin of a mourning' 'in the harmless ejaculation [*Erguss*] of an onomatopoeic natural language'[26] – in which imagery we find the invocation of Kant's description of emotion and the sublime.[27] '[L]anguage is frozen in signification.'[28] In its realized discrepancy the echo becomes a resounding (*Widerhall*) – which Benjamin, following a predilection of Romanticism, refers to also as a 'resonance' ('*Resonanz*') – of 'creaturely language', since it functions in the afterlife of the rupture in place of imposed meaning, that is to say, as a 'hindrance'; it becomes the site of mourning, that lament which shall *not* become sound. Thus, the echo fulfils precisely the purpose of the mourning play. The allegorical – i.e. the futile – process of meaning sheds its 'material' and constitutes this for the first time as such: as that which has emanated from language and therefore – within the Baroque – constitutes creaturely language. At the site of hindrance, the 'tense polarity' gives way to an uprising: of 'self-indulgent delight' directed at 'sheer' sound.[29] Where the repetitions of sounds are exploited for tricks of meaning – in other words, where the re-entering of allegorical dissociations prompts sounds to transcend the fixability of meaning – sound becomes the site of disintegration, of 'growing unrestrained', and of the bewildering uprising of contrary, repeating and resonating echoes. This 'bewilderment' of language, commonly termed '*Schwulst*' (bombast),[30] marks – and can therefore be called a 'calculated linguistic gesture' – the obstruction (of 'expression'), that is to say, the rupture that traverses language: 'The chasm between the signifying written figure [*Schriftbild*] and the euphoric language sound compels the gaze to look into the depth at the moment when the fixed massif of the meaning of the word is torn up.'[31]

The echo is revealed in this way – in that, as dissociative praxis, it deals with language – as an exact counter-image to Benjaminian translation. Benjamin cites Rudolf Pannwitz in drawing up a second quasi-topography for the 'task of the translator', which *re*-produces the arrangement of the echo. According to this, translation is an entry: an entering of the translated alien language within the language that is being translated into, wherein this latter, the so-called 'own' language, should not remain self-assured and identical, but rather – as Benjamin cites from Pannwitz – must be allowed 'to be *powerfully affected* by the foreign tongue (language)'.[32] The 'extension' of one's 'own' language through this entry is no continuous development, but rather a shattering that extends (itself) out, a dissociation from and in one's 'own' language. In translating, the relationship between the 'way of meaning' and 'what is meant' – which seem to be con-stituted, respectively, as every specific 'sense' of the work – is ripped open, so that one's 'own' language itself appears alien in the face of all meaning.[33] In this regard, we can quote Pannwitz further: 'it is wonderful how Sophocles' two dramas gain a shattering [*erschütternden*] new sense simply on account of the sublime and profound *miscomprehension* of countless individual words and groups of words'.[34] Translation tears apart the 'way of meaning' and 'that which is meant' – whose relationship in the works is termed the '*Gehaltszusammen-hang*' and the 'sense' – *precisely in that* it draws attention to their mutual depend-ency: because in translation every word, in its literalness, can dissociate 'what is meant', and thereby the sense.

> A literal rendering of the syntax casts the reproduction of meaning entirely to the winds and threatens to lead directly to incomprehensibility. The nineteenth century considered Hölderlin's translations of Sophocles mon-strous examples of such literalness ... Thus, no case for literalness can be based on an interest in retaining the meaning.[35]

De Man engages with Benjamin by means of the rhetorical question: 'Are grammar (word and syntax) on the one hand and meaning (as it culminates in the Satz) on the other hand – are they compatible with each other? Does one lead to the other, does the one support the other?' 'From the moment that a translation is really literal, "wörtlich", word by word, the meaning completely disappears':[36] The dependency of 'what is meant' ('*das Gemeinte*') on the 'way of meaning' ('*Art des Meinens*') reveals itself in translation precisely at the site of their disunity, at that point where the 'way of meaning' turns away from 'what is meant' and becomes noticeable as such – that is to say, as it manifests as a possible disruptive factor for meaning, as a different expression, and as a turning-away of the word from the relation of meaning ('*Gehaltszusammenhang*'), from the relation of the 'way of meaning' to 'what is meant'. The 'interior of the mountain forest of language' ('*den inneren Bergwald der Sprache*') that is not entered here – and which *no* speaker knows, in so far as he wants to say 'some-thing' (and must mean 'something' when and if he speaks) – does not remain, and indeed never was, self-identical and one's 'own'. Within it, it is far more the case that 'meaning something' remains always at the mercy of an uncontrollable, distorting reverberation of the 'way of meaning', or at the mercy of the echo as an acoustical deception, or of literalness as miscomprehension. Just as acoustic deception betrays the sense in the echo, so translation that 'follows' the words is a misunderstanding (of the word for itself) and borders always on a metaleptic transgression, which can produce limitless (non)sense.

The way in which the trope of the echo plays out discrepancy, with which it deals, makes the echo's *different* repetition suited as the figure of translation – and yet it is wholly unsuited to this; for the figure of the echo is a mode of *paronomasia* and, as such, that which translation can never be or remain. Ultimately, paronomasia is the exact *counter*model of translation for which the echo is the model. Paronomasia is an adherence to the literalness of words, which in translation are swept away completely – albeit through the ascription to a 'signified' that is averred to be 'the same'.[37] If translation is elucidated as echo, and thereby as paronomasia, then this is to attribute something utterly contradictory to it. Jakobson asserts that paronomasia is the rule in poetic text, wherein phonemic similarities are taken up as semantic relations, for precisely which reason poetic text is in his opinion untranslatable.[38] Just as translation and echo both make manifest the discrepancy of grammar (the rule of the signifiers) and meaning, so paronomasia exposes the literal word as its own *double*. If translation 'can, [as has been stated] never quite be correct – because precisely the same could be said only by means of the same phonemic and lexical sequence, articulated in the same situation and by the same person',[39] then paronomasia draws attention to the fact that even this '*same* phonemic and lexical sequence' can *never* say 'precisely the *same*' (indeed, this is precluded by the caveat 'articulated in the same situation and by the same person').

The literalness (*Wörtlichkeit*) of translation is that of a *different* lexis and this too distorts, and dis-places the translated word within a miscomprehension, outside the context in which it signified. At the same time, the word (to be translated) is, within translation, (also) always (de)parted from the context, that is the syntax, in which it could 'mean' something; it becomes doubled and disintegrates within that turning (away) through which it directs itself towards an other (the translated) word. What is conveyed in the 'literalness' of translation – i.e. the divergence laid bare by translation, the 'miscomprehension' of 'what is meant' and the 'way of meaning', in which the 'way of meaning' becomes manifest first of all – communicates that which echoes take in and expel as disruption: language as a shattered sequence of elements. The 'literal rendering of the syntax casts the reproduction of meaning entirely to the winds and threatens to lead directly to incomprehensibility'; 'no case for literalness can be based on an interest in retaining the meaning'.[40] Words leave language speechless (*verschlagen die Sprache*); letters disintegrate sense. As de Man puts it succinctly:

> … what is being named here as a disjunction between grammar and meaning, *Wort* und *Satz*, is the materiality of the letter: the independence, or the way in which the letter can disrupt the ostensible stable meaning of a

sentence and introduce in it a slippage by means of which that meaning disappears, evanesces, and by means of which all control over that meaning is lost.[41]

This is what translation transacts. In so far as it speaks dissociatively – in the mode of an exposed dissociation – of language itself, it speaks 'in the mode of trope'[42] of a disjunction on which all speech is founded; it 'speaks' of that which the trope of the echo articulates in an other way – in a troping, a turning away from the scene of referential speech.

The difference in and of reverberation or the 'counter=voice' does not allow the voice that is re-produced to become or remain (the) 'own' voice, but rather grasps dissociatively at the voice itself, allowing the 'voice' to become lost within the literalness of its letters and the clamour of a multiplicity of overlapping reverberations.

In its section on 'The *Art and Effect* of Echoes', Athanasius Kircher's *Neue Hall= und Thon=Kunst* offers not only the exercise of getting the repetition that the echo is to speak 'differently' or to 'answer' pertinently, but also a veritable translation echo. An 'askance or misleading re=verberation' ('*zwerch- oder schlemer Wider-Hall*') should 'artificially' 'be achieved / that answers the voice which has been let out in a completely different tongue (language)'. The means of constructing this 'echo' is somewhat involved:

> Two people are needed for the effect [*Werck*] of such an echo / and the effect [*Werck*] must take the following form: firstly one must choose or determine a space or location where four or five syllables can resound back completely and comprehensibly / and after this one must with all diligence seek out or arrange an object / and namely of a type / that / when the voice of he / who stands in the first position / strikes this reverberating object, / the re=verberation shall reach the hearing of he who stands in the opposite position; yet attention must be paid also / that both persons can indeed hear / but not see one another; ... Following this / as soon as the voice of the first is heard in position A., so the same does resound sideways or askance in position C. [the reverberating rock] and not in A., but in B. / This voice / as soon as it is heard by he who stands in position B. / must he then / reply to / with any word of his choice / and in whichever tongue (language) he wishes, / which answer then resounds in C. / and comes / to the hearing of he / who stands in A.; in which way he himself shall hear something quite different from the echo / than he called out in the first place; ... thus would the one who stands in A. directly and without delay / hear from the echo not that which he called out / but the other's answering voice ...; And thus we also have the knowledge of making a foreign-voiced or differently-answering echo.[43]

Harsdörffer, in his *Mathematischen und Philosophischen Erquickstunden*, summarizes what is new and different between exercises XXV and XXVI, i.e. between 'bringing about an echo with a different reverberation of words / to that / which was called out in the first place' and 'giving in the reverberation a different and non-rhyming answer'. His description emphasizes what is significant here:

> For the latter, two people are required / and it is necessary to look for an echo in a hollow / which repeats four or five syllables / . . . and the article or object is that / the two speak against one another at the same time / with each unable to see but able to hear the other.[44]

In short, the construction of this exercise consists in a doubling of speaker positions and a distracting echo that resounds 'askance and misleadingly' ('*schlems oder zwerchs ausfallend*').

The Baroque 'machines' of Kircher or Harsdörffer count among those that deceive the sight or hearing, and this is precisely what Kircher aims at, as he highlights in the 'Additional Note' to the exercises: 'that / as one can deceive the sight in various ways / so also the hearing'.[45] Deceptions are engineered that undermine the ascription of sounds and noises to their *source*, to the site of their origination, to the 'mouth'. Like the echo games, all those speaking and hearing tubes[46] which Kircher offers in great variety serve this end also: they are intended to permit sound to appear *here* or be withheld *there*, according to the designs of he who is 'master' over sound, its transmission and, therewith, communication. Likewise, Benjamin's intriguers operated by deceiving about the origin or source of the voice. One's own voice as an other, the other as one's own – both sorts of consternation are enacted and may take on menacing traits, as exemplified through the *other* meaning that manifests in re-production, the spectre of one's 'own' words. The spectrality of the intriguer's echo of which Benjamin spoke, appears in the voice's *Doppelgänger*, in that double[47] which distances the voice from itself. One's 'own voice' emanates here (in Kircher's translation echo) from, or out of, a different place and thus transacts (over) the possibility of deception that is intrinsic to every echo and its re-production – one's 'own' is heard as alien, the alien as an / other 'own' (that translates itself). A disjunction is registered in the echo that constitutes both a prerequisite for the possibility of, as well as the site of, deception. At the same time, this points to the possibility of deferment or displacement (*Verschiebung*) that can always intercede in the fissure, and which in this case – in the calculated deception, as in the transmission that translates – indeed should do. It is however questionable as to whether the 'master' might exact absolute control over the transmission of sound, or over meaning – for in the fissure, the voice has always become an other, an alien already. The doubling of speaker positions, that *Doppelgänger*-ism of the voices which is necessary for the translation echo, instigates a division that has, through the difference and differentiation of repetition (always), been admitted into one's 'own voice' already; a division that has, through the 'again [*wieder/iterum*] and against itself [*wider/contra*]' in and of reverberation, always been introduced into the voice and its transmission already. The voice's double, its spectre and *Doppelgänger*, traverses one's own voice – as alien.

The fissure and interval in which deceptions and their machinery take hold function as site and marker of rhetoric, or of the echo as rhetoric of the voice, wherein the voice is displaced within rhetoric. That which Kircher exacts upon the echo as a trick was already included within Benjamin's topography of translation as echo. In his arrangement of calling into and 'the mountain forests of language', the positions of (that which is) the originary and one's own and (the secondary position) of the other are already shifted towards and against one another. Translation's 'voice' – since it is unable to 'mean' anything – speaks in a digression (*parabasis*), always already as an other (calling forth the original, not speaking the language of the original). It does not remain or become a voice – but rather it becomes a disjunctive operation *vis-à-vis* the 'language as a whole' – in reverberation. It speaks as an other and a 'different' voice, from outside, into one's 'own language', awaiting a reverberation from this latter that it 'awakens' and (re)produces, a reverberation whose sole intention can be that dissociation which shall befall the voice and intention. Accordingly, one would need to develop a rhetoric of the voice, which asserted that one's 'own' voice could never remain such in the reverberations of the 'mountain forest of language'.

What kind of echo does Benjamin's text itself (re-)produce of the echo in its topography of translation, however? 'In the trees and bushes' – to quote Harsdörffer – 'there also resides an artful and deceiving reverberation [*ein verschlagener Gegenhall*]':[48] as 'artful and deceiving' as Kircher's translation echo that resounds 'askance or misleadingly'. And Benjamin's echo too is artful and misleading, as an inappropriate metaphor that strays off, and as a 'piece of imagery' that is not completely realizable (for his argument). Benjamin's metaphors for languages in translation – such as translation's echo and the 'image' of fragments, the broken pieces of a smashed vessel that 'must follow each other in the smallest details, but need not resemble each other'[49] – themselves break up, crumble and miss their target, so that translation here experiences a *mise en abyme* – in the functioning of its metaphors. Translation presents the disjunction and withdrawal of that which it facilitates and first allows to appear. Yet it is only in the disrupted imagery that Benjamin's text offers as artful, beguiling and deceiving (*verschlagen(d)e*) metaphors for translation's literal stifling of language (*die Sprache verschlagen*)[50] that 'shattered' language comes to be presented, itself serving to reveal this imagery *as* disruptive metaphors for language's dis-articulation.

As a figure of 'continued life' (living on, forth and away) after death,[51] and as a return of the departed within (acoustic) reminiscence, echo provides translation with a second aspect. According to Ovid, this meant for Echo that: '*vox tantum atque ossa supersunt: vox manet; ossa ferunt lapidis traxisse figuram*'. ('Only the voice and the bones linger still: / the voice remains and it is said that the bones have taken on the form of stone.').[52] 'Echo' provides the model of afterlife as an after-life branded by death, of endurance *as* mortification; while the echo figures as the after-life's discontinuity, which has consequences for (the) remembrance (of texts).

The rhetoric of the voice would have consequences for the Romantic emphasis on the voice which, if it did not exactly unintentionally cover up the 'antitheses deliberately opened up by the Baroque', certainly succeeded in doing so all the more rigorously: these consequences are effective in the afterlife. Echoes – in the Romantic – function as an answer of (or from) nature,[53] as a *voice* of the (dead) past, or as an answer to that question which grows lost amidst the broken monuments, pertaining to the endurance of all great things that have been. Accordingly, in that hallucinatory sharing of a common space of understanding, an end is put to (and a strong hold taken against) all the nonsensical reverberations and the indeterminable and uncontrollable multiplication of 'voices' (in reverberations and their repetitions). In the case of Benjamin's echoes, however, it is to be stressed that the echo is not the *voice* from (beyond) the ruins, but rather that echoes *ruin* words and voices.

With the 'awakening' of reverberation achieved through calling out, Benjamin's topography of translation can be seen to draw one of its defining points from the context of Romantic sound theory. The early Romantic model bestows upon the answer, as a reverberation that is awakened through calling out (to it), a non-hermeneutic question-and-answer relationship that draws avidly on contemporaneous acoustic studies. With regard to such affection, one can turn again to Johann Wilhelm Ritter, to whom Benjamin in his study of the Baroque ascribes an important systematizing role in the context of the aforementioned antithesis of sound and meaning. With reference to a model of sound as oscillation – i.e. as movement that conveys itself (*sich selbst mitteilt*) – which (on the one hand) conceptualizes sound already as *writing* and (on the other) sees it as capable of acting as a matrix of magnetic influences, Ritter expounds:

> It is, as it were, a question to the somnambulist when I mechanically affect the body that is to resound. It [the body] awakens from a deep – as it were, an eternal – sleep; it replies; and in replying, it is not indeed aware of itself, but the life and the organism that have been called forth **in** it are conscious of themselves.[54]

All 'movement through conveyance' (*Mitteilung*) and 'all inner movement also' is 'oscillatory' and, as such, '*sound*'.[55] Acoustical studies' conceptualization of affection through the conveyance of sounds considers sound as 'oscillation' and thus, to quote Chladni, as a literal 'disruption' ('*Erschütterung*') – or more radically still, to quote Ritter, as a 'shattering' ('*Zerschmetterung*'): in this way, the decomposition we met in Benjamin's recalling of the echo (in the form of his topography of translation) is already inscribed here. The 'answer' that is called forth is 'the life' which has been affected by and conveys itself in sound: on the one hand, the 'answer' always comprises only that sound which is *its* life; while on the other, this sound had been affected or called forth as a resonance of an inter-vention' (*Ein-griff*') within the calling-out – that has come from without.[56] The Romantic assertion that it was one's *own* awakened inner voice that answered therefore had a ghostly *Doppelgänger* of its own, in the form of the 'uncanny guest' that was one's 'own' inner voice becoming alien. On the one hand, waking and awakening is – according to the principles of oscillatory sound reverberation, which refers to these as resonance and reverberation – not subject to intentionality (either in that which was called out or in that which is called forth). On the other – and contrary to that which Ritter's concept of a continuity of sounds, oscillations and communications would suggest – the '*coming-from-outside*' and therewith an undermining of one's certainty about the opposition of interior and exterior, or of own and alien, is defining for the conveyance (*Mitteilung*) that trespasses over the borders (between inside and outside). As Benjamin's application of this metaphoricity (of sleep and awakening) for the context of remembrance and forgetting shows, a break or discontinuity is inscribed in remembrance – by dint of the gulf of sleep or forgetting across which remembrance operates – that no remembrance and no metaphor of remembrance can ever hope to bridge.

Sound as such is not simply oscillation, but rather becomes hearable – according to Ritter – only as '*echo*', as a 'breath' that meets resistance and is 'cast back', and in being reverberated becomes present(ed). The '*echo*' that breaks or 'reflects' breath and conveys sound into the realm of the hearable and the manifest traces a *figure*, a 'cipher' with (in addition and at the same time) 'figurative meaning'.[57] What is at stake in terms of resonance and reverberation, then, is that which is absent and has already 'evanesced', yet which in 'lingering on' (*nachklingend*) – that is to say, in a different medium and body of sound, and in a different place and time – conveys itself, and in repetition becomes hearable.[58] In this respect, the echo is a model for memory; as such it binds remembrance to death. – This is the point at which a connection appears between echoes and ruins;[59] what remains of Echo are the voice (*vox manet*) and the bones, which became stones and indicate the sites where echoes are to be heard. The 'eternally' enduring and constantly evanescing voice requires stony monuments in whose place the voice (re)sounds; which become the location of the echo; which become the site of the voice that as personification was a person with a body that decayed; and which become the location of the voice that *as reverberation* is without place, source or mouth – that is to say, 'voice'less. Monuments are put up to Echo and to echoes, and these are the scattered stones that endure. The *ruin* – which Benjamin described as the allegory of allegory – is an emblem of the after-life, of endurance (as 'remainders') which presupposes death and is itself a mode of *mortification*. The ruin is the allegory, that is to say, the 'figure' that is itself broken, the allegory of the works' endurance wherein the relationship between the 'truth content' and 'material content' which determined a work's sense disintegrates (or is disintegrated); only in its mortification does the work gain the form in which it is to be handed down, to live on and live forth.[60] Translation, like 'criticism',[61] is the mortifying (mode of) 'afterlife' of that which remains ruined, dead and disintegrated: the afterlife traverses – and ruins – the 'bodies', and in such a way 'speaks' for that which, in the context of the work and in the closure of its form, had to be excluded (voiceless, mute).[62]

In the – as such, allegorical – ruins there dwell the Saturnian creatures and the brooding of melancholic profundity. From the ruins, the voices of the dead should, for Romantic remembrance, become hearable (again) – as an answer. From the stones put up as monuments to Echo and to echoes, and over these, (E/e)cho's answering voice is now awaited. This is what characterizes the ambivalence of the 'Romantic' echo that appears amidst ruins, and that becomes hearable in resounding from the shattered monuments that have endured as remains. In this Romantic 'reading', the break or the rupture becomes the sign of a supposed former totality which the mourners should once again be able to embrace (in the present), and whose message is to be heard in the 'voice' of the echoes. What reverberated without (making) any sense and, as mechanical repetition, disrupted the unity of sound and meaning in the comprehended word, becomes refigured as an 'answer', and is given back a 'mouth' and face that guarantees sense, because intention underpins anew that which is to be heard. The voices of the past – of that past which answers in the echo – should speak of the continuity of understanding that institutes remembrance.

Nonetheless, this imbuing of a voice in the echoes and as the voice of Echo is but a figure (of speech). The image for this too is Echo, *imago vocis*: this voice *is* a trope, a 'false' (re)production, a postscript that precludes the death, the rupture and the fissure whence the echo emanates. The echo becomes the 'image' for the unobtainable delay and unobtainability of a delaying of all remembrance and all 'speaking' of the remembered – and thus it becomes *the figure of* absence of that which 'speaks', the absence that affects the voice which is *the* figure of presence, that separates the voice from itself, which is precisely a recurrence of itself, a double, and spectre. The entire 'joke' (*Witz*) of the echo consists in the divergence that arises in the fissure, which makes (the figure and translation of) echo possible – just as its whole sense of mourning consists in this.

The echo is, and figures as, a 'making present' that could always be subject already to an artful deceit (*verschlagen und verschlagend*), a deferral, and a distortion. After, and according to, the effects of the machinery and technical constructions of the Baroque and of the rhetorical operations of the echo trope, it will never again be possible to determine and secure the location of the echo's origination. Rather than see the voice as the site where life is given to the dead, the lost past, Benjamin conceived of it in terms of an other endurance of that which had passed: he employed imagery for and in place of the rupture which, as an un-enterable fissure[63] and a diversion, facilitates all translation and will have been entered within all transmissions; he employed imagery as a memorial to that location where the voice becomes lost and where that which has passed becomes posthumously hearable, in the 'space of resonance' ('*Resonanzraum*')[64] that doubles that of the ear, *viz.* in the deferred repetitions (of words) and in the reverberations of multiplied voices and noises.

6

UNFOLDING

READING AFTER ROMANTICISM

Josh Cohen

Invoking a distinctly Romantic language, Benjamin writes in his essay on Kafka of the 'never-ending series of reflections' to which the priest of *The Trial* subjects the parable 'Before the Law'.[1] These reflections come at such a significant moment as to render the novel seemingly 'nothing but the unfolding of the parable'. Benjamin goes on to offer one of his characteristic paired images:

> The word unfolding has a double meaning [*Das Wort 'entfaltet' ist aber doppelsinnig*]. A bud unfolds into a blossom, but the boat which one teaches children to make by folding paper unfolds into a flat sheet of paper. This second kind of unfolding is really appropriate to the parable; it is the reader's pleasure to smooth it out so that he has the meaning in the palm of his hand. Kafka's parables, however, unfold in the first sense, the way a bud turns into a blossom. (*GS* 2.2: 420/*SW* 2: 802)

The relation of Kafka's parables to doctrine is analogous, Benjamin suggests, to the relation of Haggadah to Halakha: that is, the kernel of Judaic legal doctrine (Halakha) is not 'smoothed out' by the Midrashic narratives which interpret it (Haggadah). Rather, the latter unfold the infinite potentialities of meaning concealed in the former.

The twin images of paper boat and flower figure with uncanny precision the two kinds of literary work and their attendant modes of criticism expounded fifteen years earlier in Benjamin's dissertation, *The Concept of Criticism in German Romanticism*.[2] Romantic criticism evaluates art only implicitly, by its choice of objects: for it is only the 'criticizable' work which is worthy of the name of art. As I shall argue throughout this chapter, such a work is defined by just the kind of foldedness figured in the image of the flower in bud. (The 88th of Friedrich Schlegel's 'Ideas' reads : 'There is a beautiful kind of openness that unfolds like a flower to breathe forth its fragrance').[3] For the flower is an image of the criticizable work not only in the sense of a bounded singularity unfolding boundless multiplicity, but also as an exemplar of auto-generation: a flower unfolds itself, just as the Romantic work produces both itself and its reader, who becomes thereby, in Novalis's words 'the extended author'.[4] Criticism traces or, better, is this unfolding, 'less the judgement of a work than its method of consummation' (*GS* 1.1: 69/*SW* 1: 153).

The work that unfolds like the paper boat, in contrast, depositing meaning in the palm of the reader's hand, is uncriticizable because it unfolds only once, freezing the 'never-ending series of reflections' which the true work puts into operation. Inverting the logic of the flower, the boat's multiple folds are reduced to zero. Far from producing itself, its folds are made and unmade externally. The artist who produces the 'paper boat' work has simply concealed unitary sense within the folds which envelop it like so much ornamentation. The critic who unfolds it can only be what Benjamin scathingly refers to as the 'contemporary' critic, for whom 'criticism is compounded of objective knowledge and the evaluation of the work …'(*GS* 1.1: 80/*SW* 1: 161).[5] A. W. Schlegel characterizes this sham criticism devastatingly in *Ath*. fgm. 205: 'They write coldly, superficially, pretentiously, and beyond all measure vapidly … For them correctness is equivalent to virtue. Taste is their idol: a fetish that can only be worshipped joylessly.'[6]

This chapter will mobilize the motif of the fold as a means of focusing the argumentational paths both of Benjamin's Romanticism dissertation and his post-Romantic itineraries. The specific inflection of the unfolding motif is nicely brought out by Gilles Deleuze in the course of his reading of Leibniz as exemplary Baroque philosopher and producer of limitless folds.[7] Deleuze offers an account of the folding–unfolding relation in which, '[u]nfolding is … not the contrary of folding, but follows the fold up to the following fold'.[8] His example of this process – 'the butterfly … folded into the caterpillar that will soon unfold'[9] – is an illuminating variation on Benjamin's blossoming flower.[10] Indeed, Deleuze's description of the complementary movement of folding and unfolding has unmistakable affinities with Benjamin's description of Romantic criticism as a process of infinite refection.[11]

Let us turn, then, to the Romanticism dissertation and trace its conception of reflective criticism. In the dissertation's first part, Benjamin expounds the Romantics' radicalization of Fichtean reflection as the ground for their thinking of criticism. Reflection, we recall, is Fichte's attempt to resolve the Kantian problem of consciousness' representation of itself to itself; it is the process through which thought thinks itself, and, in its next stage, its thinking of itself, engendering a chain of potentially infinite reflections. Fichte curbs this infinity, however, by finding, as Benjamin tells us, 'an attitude of mind in which self-consciousness is already present and does not need to be evoked through a reflection that in principle is endless … In this selfconsciousness … reflection is transfixed, arrested, and stripped of its endlessness, without being annulled' (*GS* 1.1: 25/*SW* 1: 125).

Jena Romanticism, in contrast, explicitly rejects any mechanism which would curb the infinitude of reflection, and instead makes that infinitude its very model of thinking. Thus, if the first level of reflection is thinking of something, and the second the thinking of that thought, it is at the third level that this self-consciousness is intensified to the point of the disintegration of its original form:

The rigorous original form of second-level reflection is assailed and shaken by the ambiguity in third-level reflection. But this ambiguity would have to unfold into an ever more complex plurality. On this state of affairs rests the peculiar character of reflection to which the Romantics laid claim: the dissolution of the proper form of reflection in the face of the absolute. (*GS* 1.1: 31/*SW* 1: 129)

Here, unfolding designates anything but the contrary of folding; rather, it names the ever more ambiguous process of thinking's self-transformation, its perpetual folding, unfolding and re-folding into 'the new shapes' through which, according to *Ath.* fgm. 290, 'the spirit reveals itself endlessly'.[12] Thought's movement, directed 'formlessly' toward the Absolute, dissolves the apparently solid foundations of the lower levels of reflection.

For Novalis and Schlegel, it is this conception of infinite reflection that confers a new, specifically post-Kantian dignity on the meaning of criticism; no longer a 'merely discerning, unproductive state of mind ... To be critical meant to elevate thinking so far beyond all restrictive conditions that the knowledge of truth sprang forth magically ... from the falsehood of these restrictions' (*GS* 1.1: 51/*SW* 1: 142). Folded into the restrictive conditions of false thinking, then, is the 'knowledge of truth' which it is criticism's task to eke out and unfold. The model of this folding of boundless truth into an apparently bounded form is of course the fragment – thus Benjamin's citation of Schlegel's pronouncement that 'every fragment is critical' (*GS* 1.1: 51/*SW* 1: 142). It is the fragment's essential and 'inescapable insufficiency' which prevents it from the artificial completion of criticism's infinite task: 'The word "criticism" affirms that, however highly one estimates the worth of a critical work, it can never furnish the last word on the subject' (*GS* 1.1: 52/*SW* 1: 143). Criticism, in other words, will never furnish the reader's palm with the work's finally unfolded sense. As Lacoue-Labarthe and Nancy argue, the incompletion peculiar to criticism is not a continuous one 'that would provide for the simple progressions of a modern art, but an incompletion of completion [*l'inachèvement de l'achèvement*] that continually renews the necessity for further critical perfection [*parachèvement critique*]'.[13]

Before turning to Romantic criticism's exemplary incarnation as art criticism, Benjamin draws out the key implication of an ever-intensified reflection for the question of knowledge of objects – namely that such knowledge is impossible. In Romanticism, all knowledge becomes self-knowledge, produced by thought thinking itself, in which 'the subject–object correlation is abrogated – there is a subject, if you will, without a correlative object' (*GS* 1.1: 56/*SW* 1: 146), in so far as all objects have been incorporated into the subject's self-knowledge. Or, to employ Lacoue-Labarthe and Nancy's term, there is a 'Subject-Work', that is, the subject as the 'genre' of literature itself, encompassing 'the work and reflection of the work, poetry and criticism, art and philosophy'.[14]

It is, then, only through ever-intensified reflection that other centres of reflection 'can be incorporated into self-knowledge'. This conception of the work as the folding of all reality into itself, famously figured in *Ath.* fgm. 206 in the image of the hedgehog, 'entirely isolated from the surrounding world and complete in itself'[15] – will constitute, as I will come to suggest, one of Benjamin's key points of tension with Romantic criticism.

Part Two of the dissertation sees the process of reflection staged on the terrain of art and its (self-)crticism – art for Schlegel and Novalis being, argues Benjamin, 'the medium of reflection *kat' exochen*' (*GS* 1.1: 64/*SW* 1: 150). It is the task of criticism to bring out the work's reflective character: 'Criticism is, as it were, an experiment on the artwork, one through which the latter's own reflection is awakened, through which it is brought to consciousness and to knowledge of itself' (*GS* 1.1: 65/*SW* 1: 151). Criticism consists not in 'an external reflection on an entity', the unproductive activity figured in the image of the dismantled paper boat, 'but in the unfolding of reflection – that is, for the Romantics, the unfolding of spirit – *in* an entity [*in der Entfaltung der Reflexion* ... in *einem Gebilde*]' (*GS* 1.1: 66/*SW* 1: 151). As such, it is the internal activation of the work's self-knowledge, the release of the infinite futures 'enclosed in the presentational form of the work' (*GS* 1.1: 88/*SW* 1: 165). To take up the terms of Howard Caygill's study, the 'presentational form of the work' is a mere 'surface of inscription' on which the un-Romantic critic – for whom, to recall A. W. Schlegel, 'correctness is equivalent to virtue' (*Ath.* fgm. 205) – fixates, for 'correctness' is a quality of the surface, of the work as it presents itself prior to its unfolding in reflection.[16] Thus, to criticize the work Romantically is to coax from it the 'speculative infinity of configuration' folded into its surface.

As indicated at the outset, the radicality of the Romantic concept of criticism, and perhaps its single most significant consequence for Benjamin's subsequent critical practice, lies in its supersession of criticism as 'the negative court of judgement', that is 'its complete positivity' (*GS* 1.1: 67/*SW* 1: 152): 'Criticism in its central intention is not judgement but, on the one hand, the completion, consummation and systematization of the work and, on the other hand, its resolution in the Absolute' (*GS* 1.1: 78/*SW* 1: 159). This is a peculiarly paradoxical mode of completion, however, whose relation to incompletion is that of unfolding to the folded, consisting in the intensification, rather than diminution, of the work's 'ever more complex plurality' (*GS* 1.1: 53/*SW* 1: 129).

The condition for this mode of criticism is thus the essentially incomplete work elaborated by the oft-quoted *Ath.* fgm. 116. Here, Romantic poetry is the ultimate reflection, incorporating into itself all realities – 'poetry and prose, inspiration and criticism, the poetry of art and the poetry of nature' – which is in fact never actualized:

> The Romantic kind of poetry is still in the state of becoming; that, in fact is its real essence: that it should forever be becoming and never be perfected. It can be exhausted by no theory and only a divinatory criticism would dare try to characterize its ideal.[17]

The invocation of a 'divinatory' criticism here points up the projective character of Romantic criticism, a characteristic which finds its apotheosis in its theory of the novel. And indeed, the contours of this theory can be divined in the folds of *Ath.* fgm. 116, in so far as Romantic poetry's final consummation is to be the novel. As Benjamin elaborates toward the end of the dissertation, Schlegel secretly folds the theory of the novel into the very etymology of the word 'Romantic': 'we are to understand throughout … the essential meaning of the term "Romantic" as "novelistic" [*romangemäss*]' (*GS* 1.1: 99/*SW* 1: 173). Thus, 'if art is the continuum of forms … the novel … is the comprehensible manifestation of this continuum' (*GS* 1.1: 100/*SW* 1: 173), and as such is a promissory note for the book envisioned in the 95th of Schlegel's 'Ideas': the 'eternally developing book' which would constitute the 'single book' of a 'perfect literature'.[18] For Lacoue-Labarthe and Nancy, the Romantic novel would take to the highest power the Subject-Work's 'infinite capacity for self-reference' – 'self-reference' being the translator's rendition of '*repli sur soi*', literally 'folding over on itself' (*AL*, p. 274/*LA*, p. 90).[19] The novel's production of its own theory in self-reflection is the motion of unfolding and refolding revealed in criticism: 'Criticism', writes Benjamin, 'is the presentation of the prosaic kernel in every work' (*GS* 1.1: 109/*SW* 1: 178). This 'prosaic kernel' is the concealed centre of infinite self-knowledge folded into every true artwork – thus it is that '[t]he idea of poetry is prose' (*GS* 1.1: 101/*SW* 1: 173).

I want now to explore the ways in which the conception and practice of criticism unfolded by the dissertation is refolded into two of Benjamin's later essays, namely 'The Task of the Translator' and 'On the Image of Proust'.[20]

The 1923 introduction to his translation of Baudelaire's *Tableaux parisiens* famously begins with an unequivocal rejection of the model of reception as a means to understanding the work of art: 'No poem is intended for the reader, no picture for the beholder, no symphony for the listener' (*GS* 4.1: 9/*SW* 1: 253). As he goes on to elaborate, the condition for reception is communication, which is anathema to the literary work: 'For what does a literary work "say"? What does it communicate? It "tells" very little to those who understand it' (*GS* 4.1: 9/ *SW* 1: 253). The 'communicative' work – surely coterminous with the paper boat of the Kafka essay – 'uncriticizable' in terms of the dissertation, is 'untranslatable' in terms of the later essay. The communicative work exemplifies the 'laughable and astonishing error' castigated by Novalis made by those who believe they '*believe they speak in accordance with things*'.[21] Translation is further impeded the more this erroneous thinking of language insinuates itself into a work:

> The lower the quality and distinction of its language, the greater the extent to which it is information, the less fertile a field it is for translation, until the utter preponderance of content, far from being the lever for a well-formed translation, renders it impossible. (*GS* 4.1: 20/*SW* 1: 262)

What is it that renders 'information' so incommensurable with translation? If not content, what is it that would distinguish the translatable work?

Translation is not an operation performed upon the translatable work, just as criticism doesn't consist in 'any reflecting on an entity'. Translation, in keeping with the logic of Romantic auto-production, should rather issue from its original: 'In them the life of the originals attains its latest, continually renewed and complete unfolding [*erneute späteste und umfassendste Entfaltung*]' (*GS* 4.1: 11/ *SW* 1: 255). To pursue the homology with criticism as the dissertation expounds it, translation is a variant of 'the unfolding of spirit in an entity' (*GS* 1.1: 66/ *SW* 1: 151) and as such 'a special and high form of life'. Thus, the claim that 'all great texts contain their potential (*virtuelle*) translation between the lines' (*GS* 4.1: 21/*SW* 1: 263) is a way of pointing to the 'afterlife' folded into those texts. The unfolding of that afterlife, of its 'translatable' rather than communicative content, is the task of the translator.

The affinity of this task to that of Romanticism is remarked by Benjamin himself: the Romantics, 'more than any others, were gifted with an insight into the life of literary works – an insight for which translation provides the highest testimony' (*GS* 4.1: 15/*SW* 1: 258). If their theoretical writings focused on criticism at the expense of translation, 'their own great translations' nevertheless point to the latter's status as a key medium through which 'the continued life of literary works' could unfold. The dissertation underscores this point in a discussion of the proximity into which Novalis brings criticism and translation, so that each form becomes a different mode of 'a medial, continuous transposition of the work from one language into another' (*GS* 1.1: 66/*SW* 1: 151).[22]

And yet the language which seeks revelation in translation is, crucially, no *particular* language. The translatable essence of a literary work, that which 'presses toward the light' (to take an image from the Kafka essay, *GS* 2.2: 430/ *SW* 2: 810), is what Benjamin terms 'the language of truth':

> the tensionless and even silent depository of the ultimate secrets for which all thought strives … the true language. And this very language, in whose divination and description lies the only perfection for which a philosopher can hope, is concealed in concentrated fashion in translations. (*GS* 4.1: 16/ *SW* 1: 259)

Benjamin cites Mallarmé's figure of '*écrire sans accessoires*' ('writing without implements') as a means of characterizing this language, which would manifest truth without the distortive mediation which insists between human language and its objects. It is 'accessory-less' writing, invisible at the text's irreducibly communicative surface of inscription, which the true translation 'divines' in its folds. Another paired image illuminates this operation: 'Whereas content and language form a certain unity in the original, like a fruit and its skin, the language of the translation envelops its content like a royal robe with ample folds [*wie ein Königsmantel in weiten Falten*]' (*GS* 4.1: 15/*SW* 1: 258). Intimated in these ample folds is precisely the pure 'language of language' – the preoriginal fact of 'language itself', irreducible to any of its particular utterances – concealed in the original. (Though it is worth nothing that when over-ripe, that is, in its afterlife, fruit begins to wrinkle – these wrinkles are the first suspicion of the pure language to be divined in translation.)

In the greatest translations, the royal robe would appear to consist in little more than these 'ample folds' – so overwhelmed is the language of translation by the pure language striving to speak through it. Such translations constitute another, higher form of untranslatablity; if the inferior work is untranslatable because its language adheres too tightly to sense, the greatest translation resists further translation,

> because of the looseness [*Flüchtigkeit*] with which meaning attaches to them. Confirmation of this as well as of every other important aspect is supplied by Hölderlin's translations, particularly those of the two tragedies by Sophocles ... In them, meaning plunges from abyss to abyss until it threatens to become lost in the bottomless depths of language. (*GS* 4.1: 20–21/*SW* 1: 262)

The 'ample folds' of the robe metaphorically displace the abyssal destination of language in translation. Hölderlin's translations, we might say, insinuate *écriture sans* into *écriture avec accessoires*, such that the latter is caught up and suffocated within the former's folds. To attempt to translate Hölderlin's translations would be to strive vainly to render legible the abyssal infinite which completes translation's unfolding and refolding.[23]

The point of departure for a second post-Romantic itinerary is to be found in the Romantic theory of the novel, whose manifestation of the infinitude of reflection, or 'the continuum of forms', can be seen at work in the Proust of Benjamin's great 1929 essay. This infinitude is dramatized by Proust, of course, in his relentless excavations of the forms of memory, and more specifically by his tracing of the incursion of *mémoire involontaire* into purposive memory, or of 'forgetting' into recollection. The mode of recollection proper to night, 'the Penelope work of forgetting' (*GS* 2.1: 311/*SW* 2: 238), is the counterforce to purposive memory, or 'day'. On waking, we grasp 'weakly and loosely, but a few fringes' of the tapestry woven by night, before day 'unravels the web, ornaments of forgetting' (*GS* 2.1: 311/*SW* 2: 238). The tapestry constitutes a further image of auto-production, the subject of which is precisely not 'us' but 'the night' (night, then, as another unfolding of the Romantic dissolution of the subject–object relation) – Lacoue-Labarthe and Nancy's Subject-Work – into whose space Proust seeks to be absorbed: 'This is why Proust finally turned his days into nights, devoting all his hours to undisturbed work in his darkened room with artificial illumination, so that none of those intricate arabesques might escape him' (*GS* 2.1: 311/*SW* 2: 238).

The image of Proust, then, yields far more than a belletristic biographical illustration; into it is folded the ungraspable time of night put to work in his writing. The Proustian text is the incursion of the infinite 'remembered event' into the day of recollection, the finite 'experienced event'. Hence Benjamin's question: 'Can we say that all lives, works and deeds that matter were never anything but the undisturbed unfolding [*die unbeirrte Entfaltung*] of the most banal, most fleeting, most sentimental, weakest hour of the one to whom they pertain?' (*GS* 2.1: 312/*SW* 2: 239). One's 'most banal hour' is a repository of experience inaccessible to the wakeful, purposive consciousness of day, whose concealed depths writing struggles to draw into the light. The quest for the recovery of this experience from the folds of banality is the 'blind, senseless, obsessive quest for happiness' (*GS* 2.1: 312/*SW* 2: 239).

Read through the Romantics, this quest for happiness is nothing but the infinite movement of the novel itself, its essential incompletion, 'forever becoming and never perfected'. When Schlegel writes in *Ath*. fgm. 297, that '[a] work is cultivated when it is everywhere sharply delimited, but within those limits limitless and inexhaustible,'[24] he might be divining the Proustian text, especially as read by Benjamin. Discussing Proustian eternity, Benjamin remarks: 'The eternity which Proust opens to view is intertwined time, not boundless time [*die verschränkte, nicht die grenzenlose Zeit*]' (*GS* 2.1: 320/*SW* 2: 244) – in other words, a limitless time within limits. His universe of intertwining, the world of *correspondances* first understood by the Romantics, embraced by Baudelaire but 'revealed in our lived life' only in Proust, expands the horizon of the visible by folding into it that which eludes purposive seeing. Benjamin illuminates this operation beautifully:

> He is filled with the insight that none of us has the time to live the true drama of the life that we are destined for. This is what ages us – this and nothing else. The wrinkles and creases in our faces [*die Runzeln und Falten im Gesicht*] are the registration of the great passions, vices, insights that called on us; but we, the masters, were not home. (*GS* 2.1: 322/*SW* 2: 246, emphasis mine)

The wrinkles or folds of aged skin (my earlier image of wrinkled fruit seems apposite here – Proust's novel, after all, unfolds the afterlife of youth) are markers of the absence of self to self – of the infinity of experience which must elude the quotidian surface of wakefulness.

Proust's novel perpetually re-enacts the failure of writing to recover the infinity of experience, an experience that Carol Jacobs reads as the other key to the figure of foldedness in the essay, the figure of the rolled-up stocking.[25] The stocking is a symbol of the 'dream world in which everything happens not in identical but in similar guise – opaquely similar to one another' (*GS* 2.1: 313/*SW* 2: 240).[26] Children see in the rolled-up stocking both a 'bag' and a 'present', both a form and its contents – 'And just as children do not tire of quickly changing the bag and its contents into a third thing – namely, a stocking – Proust could not get his fill of employing the dummy, his self, at one stroke in order to keep garnering that third thing, the image which satisfied his curiosity – indeed assuaged his homesickness' (*GS* 2.1: 313/*SW* 2: 240). For Jacobs, the play of plenitude and emptiness which fascinates the child mimes Proust's grasp for the hidden contents of self, a grasp which always and necessarily results in the *voiding* of self, 'the desire ... to transform the dummy over and over again into an empty image'.[27] The Proustian image thus becomes a marker of the irreducible discrepancy between life and literature, of the 'opaque similarity' that governs the dream world. Yet where Jacobs identifies in this image only its own emptiness, a token of the voided contents of self, Benjamin's language points repeatedly to an absolute plenitude of experience whose ungraspability is attested to by 'the fragile, precious reality of the image' (*GS* 2.1: 314/*SW* 2: 241). Thus, the empty-ing of the stocking perpetually unfolds Proust's struggle to assuage his 'home-sickness ... for the world distorted in the state of resemblance, a world in which the true surrealist face of experience breaks through' (*GS* 2.1: 313/*SW* 2: 240). To claim that the image is a token of this 'true surrealist face of experience' is not to draw Proust (or Benjamin) into the mimetological, figural model of language Jacobs rightly sees dissolve in this essay; for if Proust is unassuageably homesick, it is precisely because 'true experience' must always remain absolutely other to the 'homely' space of figural language.

Where, then, might we see the itineraries of Romantic and Benjaminian criticism diverge? In this concluding section, I want to locate this divergence in the thinking of veiling which emerges with Benjamin's introduction of the concept of 'constellation' in the 'Epistemo-Critical Prologue' to the *Trauerspiel* study.[28] In the Prologue, he draws on the same motif of the unveiling of the goddess at Saïs employed by Novalis in the *Disciples at Saïs*. Lacoue-Labarthe and Nancy characterize the unequivocal argument of the latter text as being, 'that religion is a matter of the unveiling of truth (in other words of the sub-ject [*AL*, p. 202/*LA*, p. 76])',[29] citing from the second of the 'Paralipomena' the following sentence: 'Someone arrived there – who lifted the veil of the god-dess, at Saïs. – But what did he see? He saw – wonder of wonders – himself' (*AL*, p. 202/*LA*, p. 139). For Romanticism, then, truth consists in the unveiling of the truth of self; in this respect, the artwork's self-reflection can be understood in terms of unveiling, an ever-intensified revelation of the Subject-Work.

Benjamin's use of the same motif in the Prologue to elaborate the relation between truth and the veil is an instructive contrast:

> Truth is an intentionless state of being made up of ideas. The proper approach to it is not therefore one of intention and knowledge, but rather a total immersion and absorption in it. Truth is the death of intention. This, indeed, is just what could be meant by the story of the veiled image of Saïs, the unveiling of which was fatal for whomsoever thought to learn the truth. (*GS* 1.1: 216/*OGTD*, p. 36)

How does this passage stand in relation to Romanticism? Certainly, Romantic reflection presides similarly over 'the death of intention', if intention is under-stood through the prism of subject–object relations. And yet we should recall that the dissolution of the object of knowledge in Romanticism takes place by

way of the incorporation by beings of 'other beings, other centres of reflection, more and more into their own self-knowledge' (*GS* 1.1: 56/*SW* 1: 146).
Reflection, in other words, is that process of unveiling which enables the self to
see 'wonder of wonders – himself', and as such retains a residue of intentionality, displaced from the subject to the work itself. It is this process, I
suggest, which is being implicitly critiqued in the above-cited passage from the
Prologue, and, a clearer contrast still, in the meditation on beauty toward the
end of the 1922 Goethe essay:

> For the beautiful is neither the veil nor the veiled object but rather the
> object in its veil. Unveiled, however, it would prove to be infinitely
> inconspicuous [*unscheinbar*] ... Thus, in the face of everything beautiful,
> the idea of unveiling becomes that of the impossibility of unveiling. It is
> the idea of art criticism. The task of art criticism is not to lift the veil but
> rather, through the precise knowledge of it as a veil, to raise itself for the
> first time to the true view of the beautiful.[30]

Art criticism here, then, is defined explicitly against the Romantic model of
the unveiling of the truth of the subject. This difference is brought out with
exemplary lucidity at the end of Blanchot's essay on the *Athenaeum*. Blanchot
enumerates a number of difficulties with Jena Romanticism's project, com-
pacted in Schlegel's above-cited comparison of the fragment, or 'miniature work
of art' to a hedgehog, 'isolated from the surrounding world and complete in
itself' (*Ath.* fgm. 206). This comparison, argues Blanchot, 'leads the fragment
back toward the aphorism, that is to say, the closure of a perfect sentence'.[31]
This closure is then read as the inevitable result, firstly of 'considering the
fragment as a text that is concentrated, having its centre in itself rather than in
the field that other fragments constitute along with it'.[32]

Is this not precisely Benjamin's criticism of 'the older generation of the
Romantics' in the 'Prologue'? 'In their speculations truth assumed the character
of a reflective consciousness in place of its linguistic character' (*GS* 1.1: 214/
OGTD, p. 38). Criticism unfolds the 'linguistic character' of truth out of works
not, as he puts it in his 1923 letter to Florens Christian Rang, 'the intensification of consciousness in them' – and Benjamin adds in a pointed parenthesis,
'(*Romantisch!*)' – but by 'the representation of an idea'.[33] To represent an idea in
criticism is to situate it in its proper constellation. As the Prologue puts it, 'Ideas
are to objects as constellations [*Sternbilder*] are to stars' (*GS* 1.1: 214/*OGTD*,
p. 38). Ideas, that is, enable the representation of the artwork not to itself, as in
Romanticism, but in its relation to its counterparts. This distinction anticipates
precisely that made by Blanchot in charging Schlegel with 'neglecting the interval
(wait or pause) that separates the fragments ...'.[34]

The distinction between the 'intensification of consciousness' and the unfolding of truth's 'linguistic essence' in artworks hinges above all, as Rodolphe
Gasché has argued convincingly, on Romanticism's and Benjamin's divergent
understandings of the artwork's relation to the Absolute.[35] The intensification

of consciousness in the work leads inexorably to its absorption in the Schlegelian 'invisible work'. Gasché comments: 'By holding that the totality of all works is a work – however invisible or fragmentary it may be – is [sic] to determine the Absolute as a mere potentiation of the singular work it embraces. Such an understanding of the Absloute (or of consciousness) entails a loss of the force of transcendence and the relativization of difference.'[36] Benjamin, then, refuses a stubborn idealist residue in Romanticism that projects the artwork as the space in which truth comes to full self-consciousness in the work.

This refusal is registered in his shift of focus from Romantic symbol to Baroque, and, later, Baudelairean and Kafkan allegory, a shift we can now read as a rejection of the view that the artwork unfolds solely within itself – for allegory is distinguished by its essential failure to find meaning fulfilled in itself. To the essential incompleteness of the Romantic work, ascending towards its resolution in the Absolute, Benjamin counterposits the arbitrary incompleteness of the allegorical work, doomed to necessary irresolution, 'to pile up fragments ceaselessly, without any strict idea of a goal' (GS 1.1: 354/OGTD, p. 178). Returning to the flower with which I opened this chapter, we might say that where the symbol contains the plurality of petals within the unity of the blossom, allegory begins with the blossom's withering, with the formless scattering of its petals.

Ultimately, however, this tendency toward the 'untidy', 'disordered' character of allegory, as Benjamin himself contends in the 'Allegory and *Trauerspiel*' chapter, may be part of the inner tendency of Romanticism itself: 'a genuine history of the Romantic style could do no better than to show . . . that even the fragment, and even irony are variants of the allegorical. In short: the technique of Romanticism leads in many ways into the realm of emblematics and allegory' (GS 1.1: 354/OGTD, p. 188). Allegory, then, would be Romantic incompletion raised – or unfolded – to the next power. It is criticism's insistently Romantic task to trace the ever-shifting itineraries of that unfolding.

7

THE ABSOLUTE AS TRANSLATABILITY

WORKING THROUGH WALTER BENJAMIN ON LANGUAGE

Andrew Benjamin

Translation does not open the way towards language. Language as a concern is already implicated in the activity of translation. Any act of translation works with a series of presuppositions that are inherently linguistic in nature. Even if the commonality of objects could be assumed, such an assumption in regard to language is more demanding. If there is something in common and thus something which is shared between all natural languages, then once the pursuit of that commonality is restricted to the field of language, the question of that which is essential to language as such cannot be avoided. Even though what is meant by 'sharing' or the 'common' is yet to be clarified, their possibility is the question of that which is essential to language. Translatability is not the privileged place from which to consider language, as though there were some distance between language and translation. Rather, once translatability is allowed to be the address of that which is essential to translation, then a concern with translation will have already opened up the question of language itself.

That a word, or a sentence, or a work written in one language can be translated into another is a commonplace. The history of translation, coupled with reflections on the act and possibility of translation, all attest to the relatively uneventful nature of the activity. However, it is not sufficient to restrict a treatment of translatability to the history of the continuity of translation, or even the discontinuities that such a history has to incorporate. History can only ever confirm that translations are possible and that translatability is a question to which reference continues to be made. History cannot answer the question concerning the nature of translatability itself.

If it is possible to take up translatability independently of the recourse to history, then the question that emerges is how is the movement of translation – translatability – to be understood? In order to pursue translatability, two terms will structure the response. In the first place there is the *necessity* for translation.

Secondly there is the *possibility*. The mediating figure allowing this response to take place will be the writings of Walter Benjamin, in particular his early and unpublished paper on language, 'Über Sprache überhaupt und über die Sprache des Menschen', though allusion will also be made to his famous introduction to his own translation of Baudelaire's 'Tableaux parisiens', i.e. 'Die Aufgabe des Übersetzers'.[1] Consequently, rather than generate what would amount to an abstract discussion of 'necessity' and 'possibility', these terms are to be pursued via their refraction through Benjamin's engagement with language and translation.[2]

Benjamin's work can be taken as setting the scene for any understanding of translatability. This is not due to his work harbouring an inner truth concerning translation *per se*. Rather it is located in the link he sets up between translatability (*Übersetzbarkeit*) and the field of language. 'Translatability is an essential quality of certain works, which is not to say that it is essential that they be translated; it means rather that a specific significance inherent in the original manifests itself in its translatability' (*SW* 1: 254/*GS* 4.1: 10). The significance of this formulation is clear. Translation, and hence the work's translatability, reveal a special quality at work in the original. What is it that inheres in the original? The quality is not reducible to the work's meaning, nor can it be identified with the work's historical or cultural importance. That quality, quite straightforwardly, is the work's translatability. While this appears to be no more than a simple tautology – translation reveals the original's translatability – it nonetheless remains the case that the fact that a work can be translated already indicates something distinct about the activity of language. The original's language occasions translation; the target language presents the translation. The linguistic nature of translation – the reality of translation as sanctioned by language – enables words to be distinguished from numbers. It allows language to be distinguished from sign systems that depend upon differing forms of universality. Indeed, it is the very absence of universality that occasions the necessity for translations, and yet it is also the presence of an essential quality in language that allows for translation. There are two preconditions at work here. The first is the necessary absence of universality that generates the need to translate, while the second is the necessary retention of a form of universality in any account of translation's possibility. What is problematic is not the appearance of paradox arising from the affirmed presence and absence of the universal, but the work of the universal and thus the conception of universality within this treatment of translatability. As will emerge, this universal does in the end take the form of a linguistic Absolute.

The formulation 'linguistic Absolute' is not found in Benjamin's writings. And yet, it is not being simply adduced. It refers to a conception of universality having two fundamental characteristics. The first is that as a universal it neither causes nor subsumes particulars. What this means is that it neither gives identity through a causal relation where the universal is that which gives the particular its quality, nor does it subsume particulars such that their identity – their correct and thus actual identity – occurs as a consequence of that subsumption. What this means is that there is a conception of universality, though it is not one that plays a constituting role in regards to the identity of particulars. This opens up the second fundamental characteristic: the absence of a causal relation between universality and particularity does not entail the absence of universality. It is possible to refer to Kant's conception of the 'aesthetic idea' or even his formulation, also in the *Critique of Judgement*, of the 'indeterminate concept' to see how it is possible to retain a productive sense of universality without holding to a determinate, thus causal, relation between universal and particular. While it could be concluded that the absence of such relations renders the retention of the universal or the Absolute otiose, such a conclusion would miss the force of their presence. Indeed, Benjamin's text is of great significance precisely because it can be read as arguing that particularity – in being particular – already recalls its relation to the universal ('language as such'). In other words, independently of questions concerning causality, there is an already present relation between the universal and the particular. Integral to Benjamin's project is the work of that relation. To write, therefore, of the linguistic Absolute acknowledges Benjamin's relation to Early Romanticism, though more significantly in this context it allows for the terminological presence of universality.

In order not to let the problem of the universal fall from view, assessing this complex set-up will be undertaken here by pursuing the interconnection between translation's necessity and its possibility in greater detail. From the beginning, the necessity for translation is evidenced in the inescapable need for translation. Allowing for this need is already to acknowledge the plurality of languages. The ineliminability of this plurality complicates the question of universality since what has to be at work within translation, and thus in any account of translatability, is a conception of the universal that allows for this precise form of plurality. Possibility appears to be at odds with necessity since possibility must hold to the universal within particularity. And yet, it is precisely because this is not the case, and that such a possibility is itself occasioned by the universal, that it demands a rethinking of universality. In sum, therefore, necessity refers both to the specificity of languages – of the always already plural presence of languages – and then to what amounts to the inescapable obligation of moving from one to the other within acts of translation. Rather than a simple addition, possibility is already at work within the realization of that which is marked out by translation's necessity.

Translation's necessity arises, initially, because of the absence of a universal correspondence between words and things. Necessity is the ineliminable consequence of the proliferation of languages. In the first place, necessity is presented by the impossibility of pure naming. Pure naming – Adamic naming – is addressed, implicitly and explicitly, by Benjamin in both of the texts mentioned above. Part of the argument of 'On Language as Such and on the Language of Man' is that the only way in which it is possible to think the proliferation of natural languages is in relation to the paradisiac language. The argument in that text must be traced in order to open up the nature of the necessity within translation. The text sets in play a specific form of movement. For Benjamin there is not just the once and final move from Paradise to the Fall; there is also the movement at work in the actuality of the Fall. (The Fall therefore defines the present condition of language.) The consequence of its occurrence is that it is then continually recalled, by there having to be a continual working through of that which the reality of Paradise was taken to have occasioned, namely the insistence of 'pure language'. Within such a movement translation becomes the most emphatic expression of this workful recall. There is, however, a potential conflict here. Translatability occurs, it can be argued, because the Fall brings with it the proliferation of languages. Equally, however, it brings universality into play precisely because translation continually has to work through – work through by recalling – that which went with the Fall, namely 'the Paradisiac state that knew only one language'. The point of contestation here is not the proliferation of languages as such, but how the proliferation is to be understood. As has already been intimated, the philosophical question is the relationship between the particular and the universal. If each natural language is a particular, what then is the universal? This question sets in play what will emerge as the force of Benjamin's argument. Equally, however, it also marks the major point of contestation within the formulation of that argument. While every translation is constrained to recall 'Paradise', the point of contestation is the extent to which that recall demands an explication in terms of loss, and thus has to be structured by the interpretive hold of mourning and melancholia. Rather than demanding an explanation in terms of loss, it is always possible that 'recall' here may do no more than mark the ineliminability of the linguistic Absolute, i.e. the already present universal.

In Benjamin's text, translation arises in the context of his commentary on the first chapter of Genesis. In order to understand both the commentary and the investigation of language taking place within it, it is essential to observe his *caveat lector*. His concern is neither with biblical interpretation nor in working with the Bible as the locus of 'revealed truth'. Rather, the biblical text, as well as Benjamin's own reflections, have the same concern with language. In both what is presupposed is, in Benjamin's own formulation, 'language as an ultimate reality, perceptible only in its manifestation, inexplicable and mystical'. The emergence of translation in this context is neither arbitrary nor merely adduced. Translation returns any consideration of language to that which is essential to language. Translation is precisely what allows for a relationship between languages to be established. (Perhaps, it is the only real relationship.) It is in terms of that relationship and what could be described as its pre-existent quality, that it is possible to have any understanding of the relationship between human language and what he calls 'language as such'. Benjamin presents the pre-existent interrelatedness in a formulation that contains an ineliminable reference to God. (As will be seen, this particular form of reference to God needs to be interpreted as signalling the absent possibility of that complete translation to which all translations necessarily refer. God is inexpressible except in the form of his pure expression; he is identical with his being expressed.) 'Translation attains its full meaning in the realization that every evolved language (with the exception of the word of God) can be considered as translation of all the others' (*SW* 1: 69–70/ *GS* 2.1: 151). While the description pertains to translation, what in fact is being described is translatability. The claim concerns how it is possible to move from one language not simply to the next but to all languages, and therefore to any other language. Each move re-enacts the primordial relation that already holds between all languages. Translatability cannot be approached therefore outside the recognition of this ineliminable primordiality.

Benjamin's commentary is complex and demanding. The background to the discussion of Genesis is provided by 'expressibility' and 'communicability'. The latter provides language's universality. What language communicates is that which is inherently communicable, namely the mental as opposed to the material existence of things. The argument for this position leads to an important discussion of the name precisely because the name is the pure enactment of this essential quality. Benjamin writes: 'in name appears the essential law of language, according to which to express oneself and to address everything amounts to the same. Language – and in it a mental entity [*ein geistiges Wesen*] – only expresses itself purely where it speaks the name, that is, in its universal naming' (*SW* 1: 65/ *GS* 2.1: 145). The return to Genesis occurs, as has already been noted, because of its own rehearsal of this conception of 'the essential law of language'.

God's role is decisive. 'God spoke – and there was.' However, the significance of God's creativity is in the relations that, as act, it envisages. Creativity in God cannot be separated from knowledge. For Benjamin the biblical words that accompany creation – 'And he saw that is was good' – construct a tight relationship between the following: knowledge (God's cognition); God's knowing that what was, was good; the word that created it; the name deployed in the act of creation. In Benjamin's formulation the name is 'inwardly identical with the creative word'. The human, however, was located outside this relationship, though created in its image. The human was not created by word: God did not name the human as such. The human's relation to language therefore is importantly different. Benjamin interprets the text as suggesting that with human language there is a distancing of the relationship between God and language. In the case of the latter, language could not be separated from God's creativity. With the human, however, creativity is replaced by knowledge. That is why human activity is marked by a particular form of the interrelationship between naming and knowing. The relationship between knowing and naming defines both the difference between the human and God, though at the same time it defines the possibility of the human's relation to God: 'God made things knowable in their names. Man, however, names them according to knowledge.' The human does not create. God creates. However, each time naming occurs – naming dictated by knowledge – the human acts not as God, but in God's image. As Benjamin points out, this occurs at its greatest acuity when the human names its own kind. The giving of the proper name brings creation and knowledge into their most intense encounter, and yet even within it they are not identical. The impossibility of identity gives rise to a spacing. Spacing, as a between, holds the Absolute in place. Spacing marks the presence of the Absolute here understood as the domain of language as such – because, as a between, it is opened up by the distinction between the human and God.

There is another important point of connection between the human and God that needs to be noted. It concerns the place and understanding of language after the Fall. However, in order to understand such a repositioning of human language and then to situate a concern with translation within it, it is essential to take up an early reference to 'magic'. In a complex and difficult passage Benjamin argues that 'all language communicates itself *in* itself; it is in the purest sense the "medium" of communication. Mediation which is the immediacy of all mental communication, is the fundamental problem of linguistic theory, and if one chooses to call this immediacy magic, then the primary problem of language is its magic. At the same time the notion of magic points to something else: to its infiniteness [*auf ihre Unendlichkeit*]' (*SW* 1: 64/*GS* 2.1: 142–3). The infinite nature of language resides in the absence of any possible limit to what can be expressed. Language is – is what it is – in its being expressed and its expression precludes limits. They are precluded because the continuity of expression is the continual opening up of the infinite in language. Here finitude is distanced because of the consequence of the distinction that Benjamin draws a number of times in the text between that which is said 'in' language and that which is said 'through' it. And yet the question that arises here concerns how this connection between 'magic' and the infinite is to be understood. The answer lies in naming. More exactly, it lies in the distinction between the position that he is developing in the text and what he refers to as 'the bourgeois conception of language'. The latter is that conception of language in which the word is taken as the means and medium of communication, where the word refers to a factual object and its locus of address is defined by the intersubjective. What is precluded from this set-up is what is occasioned by the distinction between 'in' and 'through'. In broad terms the distinction has to be read as given by the founding distinction between human language and 'language as such'. It signals therefore the internal structure in which the ineliminability of universality – what has here been called the linguistic Absolute – figures. The 'bourgeois conception of language', in insisting on language as the neutral medium of communication in which the work of language is no more than the act of referring or the conveying of information, is constrained to preclude from any consideration the question of what occurs in the separation of language and world, and hence in the domain of language itself. Language as having its own work opens up, almost by definition, the question of language itself.

If taken literally, the force of the claim that language communicates itself has to be true. It is clear that the the use of any name does not communicate the thing named. All that is communicated is the thing as named and therefore the thing's 'linguistic being'. Once accepted as a point of departure, then the task of having to explain the nature and consequences of the distinction cannot be avoided. The magical quality of language in addition to its infinite nature has to be understood as part of that task. The site of the opening up of the infinite resides initially within naming gestures towards that which is always at stake in naming, i.e. language's relation to God. Once language is conceived as that which communicates itself, then in the absence of an addressee language works to address itself to God. Benjamin formulates this position thus: 'in naming, the mental being of man communicates itself to God'. And yet, what does a claim like this mean? It cannot be the result of a simple either/or. Either it is the case that language has the quality attributed to it by its 'bourgeois' conception, or 'it communicates itself to God'. Moreover, if the *caveat lector* is followed and the claim demands an interpretation in which the ostensibly theological residues are not present in a determining sense, then how is 'God' to be understood?

Magic becomes the term used in this context to account for paradox set by the non-mutually exclusive relation between the material and the immaterial. Moreover, it is magic that works to break the hold of the subject over language's possibility and thus over that which works within it. Finally, it attests to the necessity that language be approached, and has to be approached, in terms of its manifestations, even though it is precisely the manifestations that obscure whatever it is that is proper to language. In this context language becomes 'inexplicable' and 'mystical'. While it will be necessary to come back to these terms, they need to be understood at this initial stage as signalling the abeyance of that conception of language in which use and thus language's manifest work are taken to be identical with language itself. What remains outside the hold of its manifestation is this 'itself' quality of language. (Any discussion of this quality is already a discussion of translation's possibility and therefore of translatability, precisely because it addresses that which is proper to language where propriety cannot be reduced either to an abstraction or the multitude of natural languages.) The attempt to elucidate this quality is the reason for the commentary on the creation stories in Genesis.

Translation is introduced into the commentary in the attempt to differentiate the 'mystical' from its identification with that position in which the word is understood as 'the essence of the thing'. A concern with translation emerges as the consequence of a specific argument. There is a twofold move in which the interconnection between the finite and the infinite of language, and the link between the human and God, are reworked. And yet, it is through the word that the human is necessarily linked to the world of things. Not only does this undo the possibility of an arbitrary relation between word and thing, it achieves that end by redefining that which is proper to the being of being human. If, as Benjamin argues, 'the absolute relation of name to knowledge exists only in God', then not only does the question of the nature of human language arise, what must also be questioned is the very possibility of being able to pose that question other than in relation to God. However, this is not a straightforwardly theological argument. What is being staged here is a claim about the relationship between particularity (the plurality of languages) and the universal, or Absolute. What this means is that the reference to God has to be read as a reference to the simultaneity of creating, being and naming. This is the position that will emerge from Benjamin's engagement with Genesis 1–2. Nonetheless, it is worth noting even at this stage that God comes to name, and thus be the name for, that simultaneity. It is descriptive of the set-up prior to the Fall. Theology, for Benjamin, provides the language in which the Absolute's necessity can be both posited and identified.[3]

What is at stake is the extent to which any engagement with particularity is, in virtue of its being an engagement, that act that already presupposes the effective nature of the Absolute. Responding to this problem, and it is the problem of translation *par excellence*, necessitates tracing the detail of the closing sections of Benjamin's text. The pivotal moment is the Fall. The Fall becomes the moment staging the presence of the Absolute in terms that are, in the end, proper to it: namely, the necessary impossibility of the Absolute's actualization. With the Fall there is a retention of the Absolute. Never present as itself, it is only ever present within – perhaps also as – the symbol of the non-communicable.[4] Moreover, the Fall has its own topology. Fundamental to it is the spacing that it sets in place. The significance of this spacing, as has been indicated, is that it holds the Absolute in place. It is held by the spacing that it constructs and which constitutes it as non-communicable. Its communication – understood as the immediacy of its presence – would entail the elimination of spacing and thus the refusal of the plurality of languages.

Prior to the Fall, the language of man was such that it cognized and knew all. Benjamin quotes from Hamann that all that the human enacted was the 'living word' and that 'God was the word'. God created and all that he created was good. The apples whose function it was to yield a 'knowledge of good and evil' fell outside the smooth coextensivity between word, creation and knowledge. This is the reason for their content being 'nameless' ('*namenlos*'). In eating the apples the world of the 'nameless' is opened up. Knowledge enters from outside. The intimacy of word and knowledge is forever broken. Rather than the already present word there is now the necessity to name. Hence, there will have to be in every subsequent use of language an addition. No longer is the word identical with the purity of its expression; there is an irreparable cleavage between word and expression. After the Fall the word has to name; it has to encounter the world of things. This accounts for why in this context Benjamin writes that 'the word must communicate *something* other than itself'. The addition, the 'something' is for Benjamin 'the fall of language-mind'. What this means is the presence of another relation. The word understood as 'externally communicating' (*äusserlich Mitteilendes*) emerges as a 'parody' of the word of God: it is a parody of the expressly immediate enacted by the mediate. In the enactment there remains the mark of a no longer present immediacy.[5] Further, it is a parody of the relations between creation and word defined by the 'Adamite language-mind'. What this means is that rather than the Fall being a complete break, it is an interruption in which what was lost was the coextensivity between naming, knowledge and creation. Rather than chaos, what arises is a parodic version of that relation. This opens up a new relation of identity between the word – imbued with the knowledge of the Fall – and the 'externally communicating word'. The basis of this relation is the decision: i.e. a form of finitude.

Benjamin presents three consequences for language that are a direct result of the Fall. The first is the emergence of language as governed by utility, and therefore on the level of its constitutive elements, and more generally as a system, language becomes the work of signs. The second is the necessity for the decision: this is described in the text as the 'magic of judgment'. The third is that the break with pure expression and the introduction of utility provides the basis for abstraction. The first and second of these consequences are of central importance here. They allow for a staging of language as it occurs after the Fall. Moreover, they indicate why the plurality of languages, in Benjamin's sense of the term, refers to that which makes such a plurality possible – namely the Fall – and thus what allows for communication between them: i.e. translatability understood as the unstated presence of the Absolute within particulars. In other words, the Fall understood as the move from the Absolute yields a conception of particularity, and thus a world of particulars, that opens up two paths. The first is to take particularity as an end itself. As such it would be governed by utility and the work of signs. Or, secondly, there is the possibility of understanding particularity as a conception of singularity in which universality – the Absolute – is always already present. While the nature of that presence demands separate attention the existence of these two paths is of central importance. Both are possible. Benjamin's conception both of language and translation is the attempt to stage the second. In pursuing the second it then becomes possible to give an account of language's utility and thus of systems of signs without either being taken as commensurate with language itself.

The introduction of utility occurs once it is no longer possible to deploy 'the eternal purity of the name'. The human is constrained to name and thus to occasion an act – one with its own potential infinite and thus its own distinct magic – which identifies and places. In so doing, it reaffirms both the impossibility of pure naming within the plural possibilities of any one act of naming. Both pertain and hold true at the same time. Utility is not mere utility. It has been conditioned by an opening – the Fall – that introduces a distinction turning human language into a possibility that is dependent upon the impossibility of its being able to maintain the paradisiac continuity between naming, creating and knowing. This introduces the second consequence: the necessity for the decision. In this context, Benjamin's point is a difficult one. The complexity of the actual passage cannot be avoided: 'from the Fall, in exchange for the immediacy of name [*Unmittelbarkeit des Namens*] damaged by it, a new immediacy arises, the magic of judgement which no longer rests blissfully in itself' (*SW* 1: 153/ *GS* 2.1: 71–2). Judgement is that which emerges with knowledge of good and evil. In creating the world, the Fall occasions an internal setting in which the connection between knowledge and name is irreparably broken. With the advent of knowledge the name abandons pure interiority. Its infinite – its magic – in no longer being internal becomes external. Now, it is magic that occasions the plurality of languages. There is an identity – a type of identity – between the word that 'knows good and evil' and what he describes as the 'externally communicating word'. Whatever it is that is proper to the knowledge of things, pertains to names, 'good and evil' and 'babble', in the precise sense that it demands clarification and purification. The knowledge of things falls outside the arbitrary such that after the Fall naming recalls – a recalling that announces a form of mourning – the continuity of naming, knowledge and creating. Benjamin summarizes his argument concerning the Fall as a foundational event within the history of language in the following terms:

> After the Fall, which, in making language mediate laid the foundation for its multiplicity, it could only be a step to linguistic confusion. Since humans had injured the purity of the name, the turning away from contemplation of things in which their language passes into man needed only to be completed in order to deprive humans of their common foundation of an already shaken language mind. (*SW* 1: 72/*GS* 2.1: 154; mod. trans.)

Fundamental to Benjamin's position, therefore, is that the necessity for translation arises with the Fall once the Fall is understood as a linguistic event. Moreover, translation's possibility lies in the constancy of its recall of that which occasioned its necessity. This amounts to the claim that for Benjamin while 'translatability' is 'the essential quality of certain works', that quality is not there as an addition and thus as a supplement to the work. As had been intimated, translatability becomes translation's possibility in so far as translation – the act – is always the enactment of its necessity: the necessity to translate between the plurality of natural languages given their ubiquity. There are two aspects of this description that have to be pursued.

The first harbours the strength of Benjamin's position. It pertains to the retention of a conception of a linguistic Absolute. The second, which it can be argued is formally not essential to Benjamin's position, concerns the retention of a structure of mourning and melancholia to account for the effects of the loss of the paradisiac language. While for Benjamin, in terms of the detail of his own formulation, mourning and melancholia play an important role, it is in the formulation of their inescapability that such a positioning emerges as mere appearance. Benjamin argues the following in relation to the interplay of mourning and naming:

> ... how much more melancholy it is to be named not from the one blessed, paradisiacal language of names, but from the hundred languages of man, in which name has already withered, yet which according to God's pronouncement, have knowledge of things. Things have no proper names except in God. For in his creative word God called them into being, calling them by their proper names. In the language of men, they are, however, overnamed. [*In der Sprache der Menschen aber sind sie überbenannt.*] (*SW* 1: 73/*GS* 2.1: 155)

The plurality of natural languages abounds with names, ones for the same object. Every time man names, he names the distance from God and thus marks that which has been lost. The object of loss was the simultaneity of creating and being. The use of names by man is for Benjamin, as has been noted, a simple parody of this initial setting. And yet there is another interpretation of what is actually going on in a passage such as this. Its significance as an interpretation, despite its departure from the letter of Benjamin's formulation, stems from the fact that not only does it reinforce the strength of Benjamin's treatment of language, it goes directly to the heart of a concern with translatability.

The plurality of languages emerges with the Fall. Plurality is announced by an actualization of the impossibility of the uninterrupted continuity of naming, knowing and being. With this plurality finitude comes into play. Finitude has a twofold determination. In the first place it is marked by the decision and, in the second, it has the infinite as its condition of possibility. Understood in the terms set by this twofold determination, finitude breaks the insistent hold of a transcendent conception of language on the one hand and the reduction of language to simple referentiality on the other. Given this particular conception of finitude and its relation to the infinite, a question arises: why should the impossibility of allowing the infinite actual presence necessitate either mourning, melancholia, or any other form of recourse to a problematic of loss? The impossibility of pure presence could have been an original state of affairs. In fact, it is possible to rewrite Benjamin's position in different terms: ones not bound and stayed by such a problematic. It will be in terms of this rewriting that it becomes possible to address translatability in a more sustained way.

For Benjamin 'loss' is inescapable. However, what was it that was lost? While it is possible to identify in the text an answer to this question – indeed an answer has already been adduced – the question of loss remains. How is the initial interconnection of naming, knowing and being to be understood? This question – and here it is vital to follow the spirit of Benjamin's analysis – has to be understood as emerging within a study of language and not theology. There are two elements at work here. Firstly, loss entails the impossibility of any full presentation of the continuity of naming and being. Secondly, loss entails the impossibility of posing the question of 'language as such' independently of its relation to the workful presence of natural languages. The move from Paradise to linguistic plurality is a version of secularization. In this context Benjamin's own work, and with it his concerns with 'translatability' as opposed to the fact of translation, allows for an interpretation of the Fall that is no longer determined by loss. Equally, it is possible to argue that what the text of Genesis allows to figure, and thus what is given in the Paradise of language, is a conception of the Absolute. Its being given, actuality can only occur in Paradise; its having been actualized is the description of Paradise. The departure from Paradise – again understood as an event within the history of language – is a departure that retains the initial set-up. However, it is retained in terms of the necessary impossibility of its actualization. Now, while that can be approached in terms of a generalized problematic of loss, it need not be. What was 'lost' also functions, as Benjamin indicates, as the ostensible condition of possibility for the movement between languages: the movement of translation. Loss, therefore, even though it can figure in an account of translatability, is not a necessary component.

What has the force of necessity, however, is the claim that finitude, and thus particularity, have their ground in the ineliminable presence of the infinite. What resists actualization is that ground, and therefore any conception of the finite will be marked not by loss but by the incomplete.

Translation between languages is a necessity because of the need or desire to communicate. What makes that possible is a condition that is proper to language. That condition is the fact of translatability. (It figures in the distinction between that which occurs 'in' as opposed to 'through' language.) Any one language is therefore both itself – the concrete determinations of a natural language that are the object of study by linguistics – as well as having a quality that is in excess of those pragmatic concerns but which is proper to language. This element – which persists within any one natural language – is not a transcendent condition. It is not a Platonic idea since it is not the cause of the particular's identity.[6] As such, what is precluded is the path that leads from translatability to the question of language itself. The question – What is language? – cannot be drawn out either from the activity of translation, or even from a concern with translatability. Benjamin's works lead to the particular as that which evidences, in the particular's actualization, and thus in the process of translation, the reality and thus the presence of translatability. This occurs without that presence being able to sustain a realm of questions that would have force independently of their place within the complex domain of particulars: i.e. the domain of translations.

Translatability while at work within communication is itself communicated by acts of translation. This restriction means that there has to be the silent word and thus the realm of pure language. Pure language remains unvoiced because its presence is no longer a possibility. And yet 'pure language' remains. Once again what emerges as the insistent question is not 'pure language', but the nature of its presence. Following Benjamin, it can be argued that this presence is best defined in terms of that which is recalled in any one translation. Once freed from the problematic of loss, what is recalled is that which makes translation possible. Possibility is the condition of language itself. Translatability is not just the 'essential condition' of certain works, it is the infinite of language: the linguistic Absolute.

The difficulty of this as a conclusion demands that the question be posed again: What is the linguistic Absolute and why is it to be identified with translatability? Answering this twofold question provides a way of formulating the inherent complexity in the term 'translatability'. While it is possible to view translatability as no more than an abstraction, it would then only ever be given after the event of translation and thus could not be deployed in any account of translation's possibility. Benjamin's text on language is of great importance because it allows for the introduction of a realm which, while not present – an absence which in the context of Benjamin's own text is the consequence of the Fall – is both translation's possibility and that which any one translation will recall in its effectuation as a translation. It is not a transcendental condition. It is summoned within the particular translation, rather than being present in terms of a formal causal structure. In being both summoned, yet not present, it marks the necessarily incomplete nature of any translation. Natural languages 'over-name'. However, the incomplete is not defined in relation to a once-completed translation that has now vanished, nor is the incomplete to be incorporated into a teleological development leading to completion and thus the final translation. While this may be a potential at work in Benjamin's writings, it is, nevertheless, one that can be resisted by distancing the hold of a problematic of loss and thus viewing the Absolute in terms of a presence that precludes actualization. The incomplete, once freed from the hold of loss, does not necessitate there having been an original purity that is no longer effectively present. Finitude does not entail that the infinite was once actual; it simply depends upon the retained presence of the infinite as that which is recalled within finitude.

In general terms the incomplete refers to a particular formulation of the ontological in which there is the presence of a complex origin: an original set-up that can be designated as anoriginally complex. The presence of a founding state of dislocation precludes there being any one after-effect – the act of translation – that would instantiate the founding plural event and allow it to be represented as such. Here the plurality can be situated between the act of translation and that which is summoned. Any translation announces this founding state: one which in being irreducible precludes a further reduction to the world of things and the world of words. The incomplete translation refers in the first instance to there being a relation between words and things and thus to there being a relation between knowing, naming and being. These relations are contentless. They are pure relationality itself. As pure relationality all translations refer to them even though they are not their particular instances. The move from the original to the translation takes place in reference to these relations. As pure relationality, as the spirit of translation, and thus as the incorporation into language of knowing and being – bringing with it a fundamental redefinition of language – these relations delimit the absent presence form of the linguistic Absolute.

Finally, as has already been argued, the linguistic Absolute stands opposed on the one hand to the Platonic idea, in which identity is given and secured via participation, and on the other to its separation – in terms of them becoming a separate object of philosophical questioning. The linguistic Absolute has to be understood in terms of that which allows for its occasion. 'To occasion' involves a twofold movement. It is both to happen and to allow to happen. The question that pertains to an occasion is whether that which allows for it can be approached, understood or represented independently of the occasion itself. With regard to the linguistic Absolute – understood as the term standing for the propriety of language – the answer must, in every instance, be in the negative. The happening of translation – its occasion – is only explicable in terms of the distinction between necessity and possibility. Once possibility is introduced, then the reality of translation – the continuity of its taking place – opens up that which occasions but which cannot be identified either with or within the actual work of particulars. The contentless relations of knowing, naming and being need never have been seamless in order to account for particularity. They figure as pure relationality.

The linguistic Absolute is only ever announced in its being recalled. Its most intense form occurs within the practice of translation, because in the movement between two natural languages something other than the specificity of each is present. In the move from one to the other there is the summoning of the contentless relations that continue to be re-enacted with endless variety within translations. The endless, however, always ends in a particular translation. This is the decision: the result of judgement's inescapability. The endless – the infinite – can only be expressed in terms of the impossibility of its expression. Translatability becomes not just a possible predicate of language, but once language is held apart from any reduction to the field of linguistics, then it is translatability that announces the presence of that which cannot be presented in its own terms. Translatability becomes the essential quality of language as it announces the infinite of language. Formulating this complex set-up in a precise manner is best done in terms of the structural presence of what has been identified here as the linguistic Absolute. Universality is maintained, while the site of investigation and analysis is the insistent presence of particulars. Particulars occasion – while being the occasion of – the universal.

8

JENA ROMANTICISM AND BENJAMIN'S CRITICAL EPISTEMOLOGY

Fred Rush

'We are digging the Tunnel of Babel'
(Kafka, *Nachgelassene Fragmente*)

Among much else, Walter Benjamin and Theodor Adorno shared their academic failures. Both submitted *Habilitationsschriften* at the Frankfurt University under the supervision of the unorthodox Kantian Hans Cornelius, and both were unsuccessful in gaining the degree. Adorno's rejected thesis dealt with the unpromising topic of whether Kant's faculty psychology could find a place within it for a Freudian theory of the unconscious.[1] Benjamin's work was a study of the still more unlikely subject of the function of allegory in German Baroque drama, *Origin of the German Trauerspiel*. In a way the result was even less auspicious than Adorno's. Benjamin's thesis committee suggested he withdraw his candidacy, and the book with it, in order to spare himself the disgrace of rejection. He followed their advice.

In the development of Adorno's thought, the Kant–Freud thesis is unremarkable. Adorno seems to have come to see its failure as deserved and never returned to the project. The same is not true for Benjamin. Although he seems to have taken his disappointment finally in his stride, Benjamin always maintained that the book was central to his thought. Moreover, the ideas contained in it exerted an enormous effect on the young Adorno. For, in the *Trauerspiel* study Benjamin introduces or refines several concepts crucial to the development of early critical theory, among them the ideas of a constellation of concepts, the importance of fragmentary philosophical expression, and a highly idiosyncratic view of the nature of language.

In this chapter I present a view of Benjamin that stresses the unity of his early thought, here understood as the period culminating in the *Trauerspiel* study. In particular I emphasize the importance of Romanticism, and Benjamin's work in it, for the epistemological theory contained in the Preface to the *Trauerspiel* book. One feature of the Romantic tradition that Benjamin critically appropriates that I stress involves extending a Kantian way of thinking about the organization of art into more general epistemic contexts. I then use this under-standing of the influence of the Romantics on Benjamin to throw into relief the role of 'the Absolute' in his thought. In addition to the *Trauerspiel* study, I con-centrate on two other works from the period prior to Benjamin's turn to Marx: the short essay 'On Language as Such and on the Language of Man' (1916) and his PhD dissertation *The Concept of Criticism in German Romanticism* (1919).

1

As is well known, Benjamin's views, and especially those from the early period, exerted an immense influence on what was to become the early Frankfurt School.[2] But, unlike many other thinkers who formed critical theory, Benjamin was all but untouched by Hegel, whose cast of mind he found 'repellent'.[3] Remaining outside the agenda that Hegel set, Benjamin could develop a highly original alternative account of the structure of art and knowledge, that could be used as an antidote to classical, totalizing Hegelian and Marxist ways of thinking about these matters. Of course Benjamin did not conjure his account out of thin air. It has historical antecedents in the Romanticism of the so-called Jena circle that drew its philosophical sustenance from the very thinker whose views Hegel displaced: Kant.

Very important for Romanticism, and in turn for Benjamin, are Kant's views concerning the structure and content of artworks. And these views are situated in the more general context of his views on the production of art, that is, his theory of genius. For Kant, genius is the faculty for originating what he calls 'aesthetic ideas'.[4] Like rational ideas, aesthetic ideas strive to represent a totality that is beyond sensory experience. But, unlike rational ideas, aesthetic ideas are particularized and embodied in sensory form.[5] An aesthetic idea is a manifold of intuition that is not exhaustible by any determinate subsumption of it under concepts – aesthetic ideas illustrate concepts, but do not mandate how a manifold is to be construed as falling under particular concepts. Aesthetic ideas are present in the structure of the work by virtue of what Kant calls 'aesthetic attributes'. To take Kant's example: the poet expresses the idea of grandeur by means of the verbal or visual image of the eagle of Jupiter. What is sensuously present in the work is not the concept 'grandeur', but rather certain attributes with which grandeur is associated.[6] It might seem reasonable to allow that different attributes might express the same aesthetic idea (grandeur might be expressed differently), and that the same sensuous marks that constitute an attribute might express different aesthetic ideas (Jupiter's eagle might be expressive of something other than grandeur). Yet the truth of this depends on how strong Kant takes the unity of aesthetic idea and attributes to be. There is good reason to believe that he thought them inseparable and the unity to be analogous to organic unity. Thus, 'grandeur' does not capture or name the aesthetic idea, rather more something along the lines of '*this* grandeur as expressed in these attributes' is in order.[7] Moreover, attributes *indeterminately* express ideas. They present any number of ways that the manifold that makes up the attribute might be construed. Because aesthetic attributes express their idea indefinitely, interpretations concerning how the idea is expressed, or even the content of the idea itself, will be unending.

Kant's view is a very sophisticated variant of the eighteenth-century idea that an aesthetic object is a multiplicity in unity in which the competing components of a plurality of elements and the unity of the work are in balance.[8] Kant's doctrine of the harmony of the faculties fundamentally reorients aesthetic theory, on the formal side, by substituting an analysis of subjective for objective harmony. But Kant's views on the way ideas are related to the content of the work are no less revolutionary. On standard empiricist accounts, artworks cause ideas to be related to one another solely by virtue of forces of attraction between them. For Kant, however, the work is much more than a prop for imaginative association. Ideas are structural components of the work itself, their presence made possible by their attributes. As such, they introduce into the very structure of the work an open interpretive texture that results ultimately from the indeterminacy of conception relative to the work's sensuous nature.

2

Important as this development is in the history of the ontology of art, Kant does not think that the structure of the artwork affords a general metaphysical and epistemological model. But this is precisely the value of Kant's aesthetics for the Jena Romantics, so crucial to Benjamin's development.[9] The most important representatives of this branch of Kant reception are Friedrich von Hardenberg (Novalis) and Friedrich Schlegel. From the resources of Kant's philosophy they developed a powerful series of countermeasures to the reductive foundationalism characteristic of the great philosophical systems of classical German Idealism.[10] A centrepiece of Jena thought is the argument, which Novalis first advances in notebooks written on Fichte's philosophy in 1795–96 known collectively as the *Fichte-Studien*, that the ultimate ground of subjectivity is beyond reflective experience. If this is true, then foundationalism in the theory of subjectivity is a phantasm, since any foundation would have to be reflectively accessible in order to provide the sort of warrant that foundations must. In extreme summary, Novalis arrives at the conclusion that cognitive contact with the ultimate foundation from which the distinction between subject and object issues is not possible, by showing that Fichte's conception of such a ground is incoherent. The ground is supposed to be accessible through, and constituted by, an act of what Fichte calls 'intellectual intuition' (*intellektuelle Anschauung*). But Fichte smuggles into this notion of intellectual intuition, which is supposed to be an immediate, pre-reflective awareness of the I of itself, the illicit dualistic idea of knowing self-relation. The sort of pre-reflective, conscious immediacy Fichte desires is impossible.[11] The inability to have cognitive access to the ultimate ground for subjectivity does not make Novalis sceptical of the existence of the ground, any more than it made Kant sceptical of it. Nor does Novalis give in to the temptation to craft a special form of non-reflective yet conceptual thought that might penetrate to this Absolute, as did Hegel.[12] Instead he allows for the sublimity of the Absolute, insisting that the idea of the inexpressible (*das Unsagbare*), or the ineffable, has an ineliminable role to play in the account of the possibility of experience. We cannot help but strive for the unconditioned, though all we can hope to discover is that which it conditions.[13]

Taking to heart the substance of Kant's view that art suggests various conceptual determinations without settling upon any one, Schlegel suggests that art can pick up where philosophy runs up against its reflective limitations. Building upon Novalis's reflections on the Absolute, Schlegel holds art to be a paradigm case of deep knowledge. But it is a mistake, Novalis and Schlegel think, to expect that art can provide what Fichte's notion of intellectual intuition was unable to do: a direct, yet non-reflective cognitive access to the Absolute.[14] Art can display its elusiveness, and does so by virtue of its elliptical manner. Its content is indeterminate, which means that it can support in principle any number of interpretations of its meaning. To the extent that the work presents a specifiable content, it is only to, at the same time, indicate that it cannot be exhaustive. To put the point in a way important for Benjamin, art presents a fragile harmony – a unified structure in which the elements have as much plurality as is consistent with unity. Structured in this way, art indicates our inability to grasp final content in the very act of trying to do so. And this parallels our situation as inherently reflective beings in relationship to a fundamental nature that we can never finally grasp.

Although all art has this character of indeterminacy or 'infinity' that reflects our inability to represent the Absolute, not all art does so self-consciously. This is the importance of irony for Schlegel, for ironic works point to their provisional nature in just this way, reflecting a completely general and philosophical stance or orientation toward the world. The ironic work makes explicit what is implicitly the truth of all art works. It shows this unapproachability of the Absolute by establishing an equilibrium between affirmation and distance from its content. An artwork affirms itself in that it presents a perspective upon the Absolute. But the work registers *within its perspective* the fact that, *qua* a perspective, it is partial, or a 'fragment'.[15] It is but one of many attempts to express the Absolute. Irony thus involves an acute awareness of one's own perspective as a perspective.[16]

We are now in a position to assess the Kantian heritage of Romantic irony. To do this we must connect up the ideas of indeterminacy of the artwork and multiple interpretation with that of the relation of reflection to the Absolute. The key is to recall that the work is indeterminate for Kant precisely because it is attempting to express an ideal content, that is, one that transcends any attempt to render it completely and exhaustively. This suggests to the Romantics a model for *showing*, but not saying, the ever-elusive nature of what transcends all experience. This is not precisely Kant's point of course. It is an important lesson to take from Kant's aesthetics that the artwork's conceptual underdetermination and reliance upon an idea for its basis allows for particularity of its elements (and thus 'beauty') to 'shine through' it, but he does not think that art has self-consciously to show this fact. Regardless of the precise debt to Kant, what this appropriation of his thought allows is a complete inversion of the Hegelian narrative according to which art must give way to the superior apparatus of philosophy. It is rather art's task to lead, and to do so by its native means: irony, fragment and poetry.

3

The Concept of Criticism in German Romanticism concentrates primarily on the Jena circle's views on literary interpretation and criticism, and does not directly discuss the more epistemological and metaphysical themes I have just stressed as important for Novalis and Schlegel. Nor could it have had, since Novalis's *Fichte-Studien*, which is the epistemological linchpin to Jena Romanticism, was not available until 1928 – well after Benjamin's dissertation. But it is not true that Benjamin's interest in the Jena theory of criticism is limited to its importance for critical practice. He finds in this critical theory a general model of interpretation that he considers significant for more explicitly epistemological themes.

What interests Benjamin about Jena critical practice is the role of critical interpretation in 'constituting' or 'completing' the artwork and the consequent shift away from issues of critical judgement to those of critical comprehension (*GS* 1.1: 69/*SW* 1: 153–4). This critical function stems from three elements of the Jena view on the Absolute that we have been considering. One of these is the inherently perspectival nature of the work and its ironic status. The second element is something we have not yet stressed, and that is the demand – stated in different ways by the Jena circle (i.e. that there must be a 'philosophy of philosophy' or a 'poetry of poetry') – that philosophy be *reflexive* (*GS* 1.1: 85/ *SW* 1: 164). And they contribute to the uniquely Jena version of a third idea crucial for Benjamin, one that we have seen present in Kant's analysis of artistic content. That is the thought that the truth or content of the work is immersed in its particulars. I will come back to this third line of influence in Section 5.

That (true) interpretations constitute artworks is certainly a central feature of Jena literary theory. The work's perspectival nature solicits further interpretation because the work exhibits its perspective as part of its structure. To understand a work is to regard it as able to be supplemented by interpretation just because it is incomplete. In fact, this is a weaker version of the claim that the Jena writers typically make: art is not just incomplete, it cannot be completed – it is a never-ending dialogue or dialectic. For, any interpretation must also be 'poetry' according to Schlegel, so interpretation itself will be partial and will solicit supplementation, and so on.[17] Benjamin exploits this understanding of the relation between interpretation and work. This comes out most clearly in his view on philosophical fragments and their connection with irony.[18]

For Schlegel the concept of a fragment has a (roughly) Leibnizian basis. The most important aspect of this heritage is an analogy of fragments to monads, resulting in the views that all fragments are holistically connected with one another and that the relations between fragments are analysed as a property of a system composed of nothing but its self-affecting constituents. Both Leibniz and the Romantics treat the relationship of part to whole in an organic way.[19] Thus, they think that the only adequate analysis of the parts of a system, and of their relationship with one another, must make appeal to their nature *as parts* – that is, to properties they have only in virtue of their functions in the system. For Leibniz, who raised synecdoche to the level of a metaphysical principle, monads are self-sufficient perspectival substances that are extrinsically unrelated to anything else. Belonging together in a single world is a product of correlated perceptive states of the individual monads. The systematic property of pre-established harmony is what the relation of monads to one another consists in. Because the correlation consists entirely in synchronized independent and internal changes of monads, this systematic property is not one that compromises the substantial integrity of the monad. Monads are together, not because they are joined in synthetic unity but in such a way that their differences persist. Romantic fragments are perspectival, as are monads. All finite monads, which is to say all monads but God, can consciously represent in only a partial way their inherent interconnection with all other monads, in proportion to their apperceptive capacities. Humans, as finite substances, have limited apperception, and this means that a large part of the connection of things is only registered subconsciously and only available consciously in terms of indistinct feeling. In the same way, Schlegel urges that individual fragments may more or less explicitly represent their relation to other possible fragments, but that a large part of this interrelation is connotative or affective.[20] Both individual fragments and collections of them are then but perspectives on a non-perspectival whole that can only be cognitively approached, yet never reached. What the concept of irony adds to this picture is that systems of fragments are 'truer' because they recognize this incompleteness structurally.

The second element of Romantic critical theory that Benjamin emphasizes is the demand for reflexivity (*GS* 1.1: 26–40/*SW* 1: 126–35). The Jena Romantics inherit from Fichte the idea that knowledge, even representation, is only possible if based ultimately in self-relation. Novalis and Schlegel have different ways of expressing this point. For Novalis, it is bound up with the role that feeling (*Gefühl*) plays in his account of the Absolute and its connection with what he calls the *ordo inversus* and the philosophical procedure he terms 'Romanticiz-ing'.[21] Because we only can represent by means of concepts, representation of an Absolute that is not accessible through conceptual thought carries a con-ceptual imprint. In truth, the Absolute can only be felt, and that feeling can only have the epistemic status of belief or faith (*Glauben*). The inverse order consists in the reversal of priority in favour of reflection that results from thinking about the category of the non-reflective reflectively. This results in what is problem-atic with Fichte – the idea that being self-aware exhausts our nature. Feeling is a useful category for Novalis because it reverses the reversal. For Schlegel, reflexivity is bound up with irony. Irony is reflexive in character or, perhaps more precisely, is a product of reflexivity. For, irony is the correct cognitive attitude towards one's perspective on the world, once one asks what ultimate foundation that perspective has. Since the Jena group tends to distinguish perspectives in terms of representation, there exists a very strong connection between the requirement of reflexivity and reflection. For, if we reflect on reflection, we come to realize that our nature as beings for whom knowledge consists in representation determines us never to have knowledge of the Absolute. If we are maximally reflective (that is reflexively so), we discover that the only way we can show the Absolute is by displaying to ourselves the limitations of reflection.

Regardless of the doctrines in the Jena concept of criticism Benjamin finds important, and later exploits for his own theoretical purposes, it is impossible to miss that he is sometimes critical of the Romantics. His objections are very compressed, centring on the 'conceptuality' of Romantic criticism (*GS* 1. 1, 218, *OT* 38; cf *GS* 1.1, 47–8, *SW* 1, 140–1). In light of what we have said about Jena Romanticism, it is possible to reconstruct the objection as follows. Novalis and Schlegel were both concerned, in their own ways, to forward non-foundational theories of *subjectivity*. The Absolute functions in these accounts as an origin for subjectivity which must be posited without our ever being able to have access to it in a cognitively significant way. This means that the Absolute is a non-accessible origin for being a subject, and its non-accessibility is supposed to block the Fichtean move to find in this basis of subjectivity a ground for a systematic theory. What bothers Benjamin is not the concept of the Absolute *per se*; indeed, the Absolute is a central concept for him. The problem is rather a claimed lingering and impermissible place for the concept of immediacy in the Jena picture that follows upon the characteristic way that the Jena writers are still in the thrall of the project of developing an account of subjectivity.

Now, it might seem that the suspect idea is feeling. While there is admittedly a difference between this role of feeling for Novalis and the role of intellectual intuition in Fichte (i.e. the latter sort of immediacy is supposed to provide immediate access to a ground for cognition, the former not), the argument might go, the fact that one can be in a relationship with the Absolute that is immediate *at all* is suspect. This is not Benjamin's criticism, however. Benjamin claims that, although the Romantics follow Fichte in rejecting a reflective ground for cognition, they still view the value of art to be intimately tied to reflection – art for both Novalis and Schlegel is an endless and indeterminate process of reflective articulation of the Absolute. There are two connected problems with this, both having to do with Romantic perspectivism. The idea that the Romantics may indulge in is that, though we can never get all the way there, artworks *qua* perspectives on the Absolute tend to have a cumulative and progressively inclusive character. If one thinks of the Absolute as throwing up a plethora of appearances or, less metaphysically, as supporting infinite proliferative representation, then a certain picture comes into view. One might think that the more perspectives one invents and inhabits, the more adequate to the Absolute one is, if only for the reason that occupying more perspectives gives one a better view of its elusiveness. Benjamin is quite correct to point out that especially Schlegel is apt to talk about an ideal total artwork which is the (impossible) sum of all works as what *would be, were* art ever adequate to the Absolute. Attention to the subjunctive here is important, for in it lies the ideal role that the concept of a *Gesamtkunstwerk* plays in Jena Romanticism. What Benjamin objects to is the idea that entertaining or inhabiting multiple perspectives *converge* upon the Absolute, even if a point of absolute convergence is only ideal. It is the idea of increasing degrees of immediacy that offends. For Benjamin, the profane world of finitude is of an entirely other order from the Absolute, so an 'infinite *approach*' of the profane to the Absolute is an impossibility. Moreover, Benjamin rejects the notion that wilfully multiplying perspectives will yield new views on the Absolute, for reasons we shall discuss later. 'The New' is not an intrinsic good for Benjamin, especially not in connection with accounting for how one most accurately expresses the relation between humankind and the Absolute. The guiding thread running through these two criticisms – of the idea of nearing the Absolute through inhabiting many perspectives and of the notion that inventing new perspectives helps along in this convergence – is that reflection threatens to become a species of profane and 'fallen' intellectual commerce for Benjamin. To immerse oneself in its sheer variety is not to take into full account its fallen status.

4

Before turning to the importance of the critique of Romanticism for the epistemological centrepieces of Benjamin's early thought – the conceptions of Ideas and constellations – it is necessary to provide one more piece of background. We must develop a general understanding of Benjamin's philosophy of language.[22]

A major influence on Benjamin's theory of language is J. G. Hamann, whom Benjamin quotes with approval in a 1916 essay 'On Language as Such and on the Language of Man' (*GS* 2.1: 147/*SW* 1: 67). Hamann was a leading voice of the German counter-Enlightenment who developed an account of the philosophical importance of language in a series of highly idiosyncratic and hermetic writings.[23] Along with Herder, Hamann pressed the complaint that Kant had ignored the constitutive role of language in thought. But it is less this attempted 'linguistic turn' and more the substance of Hamann's views on the nature of language that is appealing to Benjamin. Both Benjamin and Hamann are attracted to the idea that human language is but a fractured remnant of a primordial, divinely ordained language that consisted exclusively of rigorous proper names – that is, names that refer uniquely and non-arbitrarily to one and only one thing (*GS* 2.1: 143/*SW* 1: 64–5).

According to Hamann, God created things in nature through divine word, so language inheres in the very nature of things. Hamann thought that every thing was a word, though things that could not express themselves in language were mute ones (cf. *GS* 2.1: 142, 149–52/*SW* 1: 63–4, 69–71). It is given to humankind to be able to utter words and name the things – by naming the things (calling them) Adam achieves a world with them (calls them forth). But this naming was not a matter of linguistic autonomy; the names are given to humankind divinely by the very creator who created things by words. After the Fall, human language descends into multiplicity; different languages develop just because humans no longer enjoy access to the divine names for things (GS 2.1: 154–5/SW 1: 72–3). The differentiae of languages consist in their arbitrary and multiple names for things and, even more, in their reliance on general abstracting terms – concepts. Conceptual thought attempts to plumb the nature of things by treating each thing, not as the particular, intrinsically significant thing that it is, but by construing it as alien and as instrumentally significant in virtue of the properties it shares with other things. To be a discursive being is just to have fallen from grace. Our connection to this first state is not entirely sundered, however. Both Benjamin and Hamann believe that profane language (as well as profane history) bears traces of 'pure' language prior to the Fall, dispersed throughout the several languages. This is why Benjamin rates translation more 'original' than the original of which it is a translation. For, if profane words bear subliminal traces of pure language that gave rise to them through the disintegration of the language into the multiplicity that makes languages differ and thus profane, translating words from one language into another captures more penumbral meaning in virtue of (slightly) reintegrating language as a whole. Translation is recovery of meaning accomplished by reuniting the trace elements of meaning that words share with one another.[24]

What Hamann and Benjamin propose is, to be sure, a conception of the fundamental nature of language that is squarely at odds with the majority view that treats discursivity as unproblematic and even fundamental. But it is important to see that the central claim that the descriptive properties of language are not fundamental does not rely upon the religious narrative being true.[25] One way to bring this view into closer connection with contemporary thought is to consider it in light of the question of the cognitive status of metaphor. From the point of view of beings consigned to discursivity, metaphor is as close as we can come to aboriginal naming. Figurative language does not reduce the meaning of a thing to one determined by a concept (or one range of concepts), as is prerequisite to literal meaning, and thus is 'truer'. Poetic language turns out to be more denominative and literal than its 'literal' counterpart. Conversely, what we ordinarily think of as literal language, and as possessing superior means 'to get things right', is reconceived as arrested poetry. So, to summarize, the controlling idea seems to be that original, absolutely specific meanings are at present dispersed amongst the connotative ranges of general terms. And, to the extent that poetry emphasizes this range, it 'redeems' or recovers the original meaning.[26]

Benjamin's views on language gain an extra dimension when considered in light of his understanding of mimesis. Although he does not fully develop his views on mimesis. until the 1930s, they are consistent with the essay on language, with several short pieces written during the early period on the nature of similarity,[27] and with the idea of an 'originary perception' (Urvernehmen)

developed in the Preface to the *Trauerspiel* book (*GS* 1.1: 216/*OT*, p. 36).[28]
He postulates that the capacity to see resemblances between things is the product
of an impulse to act like something else. This impulse is prior to representational
capacities, a behaviour that attempts to cope with nature by acting like it. Rather
than mastery through fungible linguistic signs, or even expressive language, this
control involves a palpable sense of accommodation of voice to the nature of the
thing. Resemblances between things 'seen' in this manner tend to respect their
inherent natures, and do not involve articulated preconceptions that efficiently
organize things for human use by means of general descriptions. Benjamin claims
that this mimetic capacity is logically and historically prior to language, having
'migrated into' (*hineingewandert*) it very early in the form of naming
(*GS* 2.1: 209). Benjamin here stresses the ultimate mimetic character of onoma-
topoeia. Language is not essentially communicative or descriptive, rather it is an
attempt to take on the character of nature and intervene in it through sonic and
phonetic action. But even this primordial onomatopoetic language is at a remove
from true divine naming, Benjamin argues, since its components *qua* linguistic
elements must have some autonomy as signs.

5

Kant and the Jena Romantics agree that there are things, or aspects of them, that
transcend all possible conception, although their conception of what is
transcendent and how much one can say about them are different. They also
agree that the possibility of experience (i.e. what can be known) is coextensive
with intuition that can be brought under concepts. We can have no experience of
cognitive import of conception-transcending things, or of their conception-
transcending aspects. That is, Kant and the Jena Romantics deny that we can have
a special non-conceptual access of cognitive import to conception-transcending
things, or their conception-transcending aspects. Although one may have
reservations about the messianic utopian element in Benjamin's thought, there
are strong arguments for viewing him along lines similar to the Romantics on this
issue. The charge of non-discursive archaism – appropriate to Klages, the George
circle and possibly to Heidegger – is misplaced here.[29]

When one turns to the 'Epistemo-Critical Preface' to the *Trauerspiel* study,[30]
the text in which Benjamin most thoroughly presents the epistemological and
metaphysical underpinning to his aesthetic views, and the positive account of the
Absolute that he thinks improves upon its Romantic counterpart, one encounters
an unstable blend of Plato, Leibniz and the very Romanticism in question. The
key to reconstructing and assessing Benjamin's views in the Preface is his conception of an Idea. He generally wants to avoid two ways of thinking of Ideas,
both of which mistake them for concepts and then give different accounts of the
nature of Ideas according to their rival views on what concepts are. On the one
hand, Benjamin does not think that Ideas are atemporal 'super-concepts', nor
that we have special non-sensible access to Ideas first and then turn to an
understanding of the structure of the world led by the knowledge we have

gleaned from them. On the other hand, Benjamin rejects the view that Ideas are most general concepts arrived at by an empirical process of abstraction. This would rob Ideas of their essential reality as non-mental entities. He states that Ideas are 'real' entities, that they inhabit a 'completely intelligible world', are 'not given' in the empirical one (*GS* 1.1: 216/*OT*, p. 36), and even that they are 'pre-given' (*GS* 1.1: 210/*OT*, p. 30). Yet, Ideas appear only through their particulars, where 'appearing through' seems to require something along the lines of the neo-Platonic doctrine of the 'participation' of universals in particulars, where an Idea is thought of as something like a force that interpenetrates its particulars, imbuing them with ideality (*GS* 1.1: 214–15/*OT*, pp. 34–5). The only access to ideality is through the phenomena, and the phenomena are only what they are as experienced by virtue of their ideality.

Constellations (*Sternbilder/Konstellationen*) are connections of particulars in Ideas, and the difficulty in explicating the relation of Idea to particulars is especially pressing when explaining the nature of constellations because it is just here that one naturally averts to relation of general representation to particular in order to understand the relevant sense of 'in'. This is the move that Benjamin wants to avoid at all costs. To this end, he writes that constellations are 'truthful' groupings of phenomena without the hegemony introduced by conceptual determination. Ideas do not subsume particulars under them in order that we have knowledge of the particular through the subsumption, and thus constellations are not subsumed collections of particulars. Thus does Benjamin write that 'the phenomena are not annexed to or incorporated into (*einverleibt*) Ideas', nor are they contained in them. Ideas are their virtual arrangement (*virtuelle Anordnung*) or their 'objective interpretation'(*GS* 1.1: 214/*OT*, p. 34). In fact, Benjamin makes a stronger claim that Ideas have nothing at all to do with knowledge (*GS* 1.1: 214/*OT*, p. 34). In saying this, I take him to be issuing at least two caveats over and above the one just mentioned. First, Ideas do not order bits into bodies of knowledge – Ideas are not 'theoretical', nor are they 'theories'. Second, Ideas are not regulative desiderata that guide theory construction. Given this cluster of claims involving conception and knowledge, a good starting-point in clarifying what a constellation is and its relation to an Idea might be to specify more precisely the sense in which Ideas and constellations are 'non-conceptual' and why that might be a good thing.[31]

As we saw in the discussion of Benjamin's views on language, he believes that the relation of the particular to the universal in conceptual experience is one in which the former is subordinated to the latter.[32] He thinks that this way of orienting oneself in the world arises from an alienating separation of subject and object, in compensation for which the subject attempts to control the world. There are passages that seem to view conceptual thought *as such* as instrumental, pernicious and levelling (see, e.g. *GS* 1.1: 215/*OT*, p. 35). In this vein Benjamin often stresses a very literal understanding of *Begriff*, which emphasizes the root meaning of grasping or seizing hold of (*GS* 1.1: 209/*OT*, p. 29: '*Erkenntnis ist ein Haben*'). But does *any* deployment of concepts prejudice particularity? In a minimal sense it does, for deploying any concept does select out features of a thing for special attention, if only for now, at the expense of other features. And it is true that the selected features are meaningful because they are shared with other (potential) instances of the concept in question. But the threat to particularity does not seem very great, because it is a poor inference indeed from the favouring of some shared properties of a thing for some purposes to a reduction of the thing to those properties. Hanging meaningfulness *for the most part* on shared properties may even lend some credence to the hyperbolic claim one finds especially in Adorno that they are thereby treated as 'the same' or even 'identical'.[33] But this does not license an assimilation of predication to 'identity thinking'. Danger of 'identification' would seem to arise only in proportion to the number and weighted cultural significance of the shared predicates, and not as a result of sheer predication. After all, things can be 'the same' in a variety of ways and also be very different in others, and one does not necessarily hide the other from view.

The view that conception involves prejudice and reductive conceptual dominance becomes more plausible if one distinguishes certain forms of highly articulated and systematic conceptual thought that are *particularly* controlling from concept use in general. In this vein, one might hold that certain forms of conceptual thought are pernicious because they overdevelop the fundamental nature of generalizing or abstracting representation in ways that are severely reductive and instrumental, say theories of purportedly universal scope. The way such reductive thought would enter implicitly in ordinary discourse would involve something like the notion of ideology. I would suggest that much of Benjamin's denunciation of concepts, systems of them and systematicity in general could be interpreted in this light. It should be noted, for instance, that Benjamin's attitude towards systematic thought is actually more complex than it is often taken to be. True, he does say that conceptual schemes are 'spiders' webs'(*GS* 1.1: 207/*OT*, p. 28) and that philosophical systems take a mathematical model when they should not (*GS* 1.1: 208/*OT*, pp. 28–9). But he also says that systems themselves are not the problem, so long as they are determined by the 'world of Ideas' and not by concepts (*GS* 1.1: 214/*OT*, pp. 33–4). A constellation might even be considered a 'system', so long as one varied enough the criteria for systematicity. And, while Benjamin is wary of the reductive tendency of conceptual thought, he prizes the conceptual ability to differentiate things, that is, to analyse complex structures into elements (*GS* 1.1: 213–14/*OT*, pp. 32–4). Only by virtue of this can we break down ordinary reductive ways of thinking of things. This already involves specific cognitive commitments, for analysis only isolates elements in terms of characteristics deemed salient, and thus selects out or ignores other characteristics of things. Further, the assembling (*Einsammlung*) of elements into constellations involves concepts as well. In fact, Benjamin does not think that the analysis into elements and their assembling into a constellation are two discrete stages of the process of construction – they occur simultaneously (*GS* 1.1: 214/*OT*, p. 34). Concepts are necessary for treating the particulars as more than particular, and, therefore, constellations are best thought of not as 'non-conceptual' but rather as 'ways' of using concepts.

Even though there is conceptual labour involved in constructing a constellation, the connections in which it consists are not supposed to be exhaustive arrangements of the phenomena. The controlling idea seems to be to allow for as much particularity as is possible, given that the only way that we have to order things is in terms of comparison and attention to their affinities.[34] Whereas theories result from and deploy explanation (an inherently nomological form of enquiry that fixes meaning in terms of covering laws) and are thus concept- and not thing-guided, constellations result from interpretation. Benjamin will allow in all sorts of interpretative regimens well beyond the orthodox in order to tease out hidden affinities smoothed over by approaches to the phenomena that are overly systematic and to show how constellations resist conceptual reduction. Structurally, constellations consist of elements that can be in extreme tension (even to the point of contradiction). Such elements serve to mark out the extremities of the Idea in question – that is, its boundaries.

Let us draw together the strands of the analysis. Constellations come about through interpretation of the particulars, and this in turn allows the Ideas immanent in the complex to come partly into view. This is the special sense in which Benjamin says that constellations 'represent' Ideas. Pertinent here is a notion of *re-presentation* (*Wiedervergegenwärtigung*) – that is, making something present again, not 'representation' as deployed in standard representational theories of cognition (*GS* 1.1: 214/*OT*, p. 34). Ideas are (Benjaminian) names, dispersed in profane language and thought. Benjamin also calls Ideas monads (*GS* 1.1: 228/*OT*, pp. 47–8), and it is probable that he uses the term 'phenomena' throughout the Preface in Leibniz's sense to designate epiphenomenal individuals. Like monads, Ideas contain within each of them the totality of the world, but only obscurely and from a point of view (*GS* 1.1: 208/*OT*, p. 28). Incompleteness or elusiveness comes about on two levels. One can never exhaustively interpret an Idea. This is because we are limited discursively. If one could have non-profane (i.e. non-conceptual, synoptic) access to an eternal Idea, one could achieve a view of its mirroring of the structure of the Absolute that would be fully explicit. But, even so, the Idea would still only show the totality of the Absolute from its point of view. On both levels, as it is and must be, the divine interconnection of things is occluded.

6

When focusing on Benjamin's interpretation of Romantics at the conclusion of Section 3, I offered a characterization of the difference between the Jena conception of the Absolute and its importance for Benjamin. To recapitulate: according to Benjamin the Jena conception is potentially suspect because the way the Absolute has an influence in things is cashed out in terms of an equally suspect theory of reflection. While the Romantic refrain that the Absolute is elusive certainly sounds in Benjamin, it does so in an entirely different register. Elusiveness for the Romantics is defined in terms of evading conceptual or representational access. And, on at least one strand of thought in Romanticism, representations can compound to make the ever-elusive Absolute less so. Benjamin thinks that this idea of progressive reflective purchase on the Absolute, through art or otherwise, gets the transcendent nature of the Absolute wrong. Romanticism has grave difficulty accounting for how the Absolute can constrain its interpretations. This goes hand in hand with its prediliction for novelty for its own sake. For Benjamin this reverses the precedence of nature over reflection as a potentially fallen mode of understanding. If it is correct to characterize Jena Romanticism as a 'progressive' account of the Absolute in which inventing new perspectives and coining neologisms play a key role in insight, Benjamin's view might be called 'retrogressive'. It is 'retrogressive' in the sense that Benjamin thinks that Ideas *qua* monads are all there *already* and what we need to do is excavate the names they urge us to recover through what Benjamin, adapting a line of thought present in Klages, calls 'Platonic unforgetting' (anamnesis). By 'retrogressing' one does not attempt to reconstitute the work, of course; rather one allows the work to show that it is and always was but a ruin, and that it must be so for all time. Works are saved *as* ruins, not *from* them. What is needed then is precisely *not* new ways of representing the Absolute proliferated for the sake of their novelty. In fact, proliferation of perspectives is dangerous for Benjamin, it carries us away from the essential hermeneutic task and increases profanity.

There are many important questions still to ask about Benjamin's account of names and Ideas. Amongst other things, one might still question its nostalgic component, utopianism, or the role that the concept of a return plays in the theory. Also perplexing is the issue of how much of this account of Ideas is taken over into Benjamin's later thought and under what guise. Whatever the answers turn out to be, a large part of any assessment of such issues will involve seeing them as part of Benjamin's complex reaction to Jena Romanticism and its transmission of Kant's philosophy.

PART II

BEYOND EARLY ROMANTICISM

BENJAMIN, HÖLDERLIN, GOETHE

9

'DICHTERMUT' AND 'BLÖDIGKEIT'

TWO POEMS BY FRIEDRICH HÖLDERLIN, INTERPRETED BY WALTER BENJAMIN[1]

Beatrice Hanssen

1

The figure of inversion has played a prominent role in twentieth-century critical attempts to read the text of modernity as a correction of Idealism and to release the subversive, modernist potential of Early Romanticism (*Frühromantik*). In a notable, jointly authored essay, published in 1977, Manfred Frank and Gerhard Kurz returned to Novalis's notion of *ordo inversus* to suggest that inversion was the trope (Gr. *trepō*, to turn, reverse) *par excellence*, paradigmatic of modern poetics.[2] They held that inversion, a figure of reflection (*Reflexionsfigur*) found in the writings of Hölderlin and Kleist, as well as Kafka, served as a corrective to the model of transparent self-consciousness that Fichte put forth in his *Über den Begriff der Wissenschaftslehre* (*On the Concept of the Science of Knowledge*) (1794).[3] If all thinking involved an act of positing (*thesis*) and proceeded according to the principle of contradiction (*Gegensatz*), Fichte argued, then self-consciousness itself was a thinking of thinking in which the subject of thinking of, *and* agent recognized itself to be the ground positing, the real – an agent that Fichte called the *absolute I*. Inversion, however, as Frank and Kurz maintained, offered a profound critique of such hubristic Idealism. Reflecting on the very limits of reflection, inversion unmasked this figure's alleged autonomy, together with the self-positing of the subject, as mere figments of the imagination. Upsetting the balance between thetic I and the object of reflective positing, inversion revealed how reflection, in truth, was dependent on the incontrovertible facticity of the real.[4]

Some years before Frank and Kurz, an eminent member of the Frankfurt School, Theodor Adorno, addressed the inherently subversive operation of a figure closely related to inversion, namely parataxis. Following the ineluctable logic of negative dialectics, Adorno's essay 'Parataxis' (1964) demonstrated how the paratactical constructions typical of Hölderlin's later poetry radically disrupted the thetic, identificatory logic that ruled German Idealism, culminating in Hegel's speculative philosophy.[5]

Traditionally, parataxis has been considered a grammatical device of coordination, concatenation, and serialization that does not make use of coordinating or subordinating conjunctions. While parataxis, as a rule, does not necessarily produce logical disjunction, Adorno applied the term to the frequent *non sequiturs* and reversals of predicative logic common in Hölderlin's late hymnal work. Drawing on the Hölderlin fragments collected under the rubric 'Reflexion', Adorno reinterpreted parataxis as a 'constitutive dissociation', as an anti-Idealistic linguistic strategy that undermined the hierarchical, even synthetic, function of discursive language.[6] More than just a stylistic 'micro-technique', parataxis in reality was to be seen on a grander scale, as it exemplified the disintegration of coercive, thetic logic. This much was clear, Adorno suggested, from one of Hölderlin's theoretical fragments on inversion:

> One has inversions of words in the period. Yet the inversion of the periods itself, then, must prove greater and more effective. The logical position of the periods where the ground (the grounding period) is followed by becoming, becoming by the goal [*Zweck*], the goal by the purpose, and where the subclauses are always attached at the end of the main clauses to which they refer – is certainly only very seldom of use to the poet.[7]

Just as the mechanism of inversion could upset the hierarchical relation between ground and becoming, main clause and subclause, so parataxis, Adorno contended, derailed the teleological drift, or *Zweck*, of speculative thought. Only by exposing the multiple effects generated by this poetry's paratactical structure, Adorno went on to argue, could the critic–interpreter grasp the 'poetized' (*Gedichtete*) of Hölderlin's late poems.

In using the term *Gedichtete*, Adorno in fact appropriated a concept that his friend Walter Benjamin had introduced in his Hölderlin essay, 'Zwei Gedichte von Friedrich Hölderlin – "Dichtermut" und "Blödigkeit"' ('Two Poems by Friedrich Hölderlin: "The Poet's Courage" and "Timidity"') (1914–15). With this term, Adorno not only sought to qualify the strangeness, otherness, and sublime darkness that distinguished Hölderlin's late lyrical work, but also its truth content; the latter eluded traditional methods of literary analysis (such as philology or the genetic critical method), no less than Heidegger's ahistorical, anti-philological interpretations, which were oblivious of aesthetic form. Only an immanent analysis that followed the 'de-limiting' force of the object under study could fathom how this poetry's strangeness transcended subjective intentions, stemming as it did 'from something objective, the demise of its basic content in expression, the eloquence of something that has no language'.[8]

Underscoring the radical implications of Hölderlin's late style, Adorno at the same time was mindful of the possible Idealistic pitfalls that might accompany

Hölderlin's syntactical turn against syntax. For, in a first moment of analysis, parataxis, it could be argued, threatened to reinstate the stronghold of a thetical I, entangled in a series of self-propelling revolutions. To capture the discrepancy between appearance, or the surface layer of Hölderlin's poetry, and an innately critical, subversive force, hiding from view, Adorno again resorted to Benjamin's work, this time to terms introduced in the latter's 1922 Goethe essay, namely *Sachgehalt* ('material content') and *Wahrheitsgehalt* ('truth content'). For the (Idealistic) threat of infinite regress, Adorno noted, existed at the level of this poetry's mythical *Sachgehalt* – a term that not only referred to the 'material content' but also to the realm of aesthetic appearance as semblance (*Schein*). In reality, a deeper meaning, or *Wahrheitsgehalt*, lay concealed underneath the mythical surface. Indeed, Hölderlin's late poetry put so much pressure on the syntactical period that, in sacrificing the coherence of standard syntax, it simultaneously relinquished the position of the Idealistic, self-reflective subject and, with it, its particular mode of producing meaning. At the same time that parataxis undermined the 'use value' of ordinary language, it also ran counter to the poetical ideal of ever attaining a revealed language of plenitude. It is precisely in the abscondence of such revealed language, and the ensuing hiatuses and metaphysical barrenness it left behind, that Adorno located Hölderlin's authentic modernity.

As Adorno read Hölderlin's metaphysical writings against the grain, his radical interpretation at first glance seemed to depart from the poet's philosophical principles. For, in his fragment 'Urtheil und Seyn' ('Judgement and Being'), Hölderlin unmistakably qualified absolute Being as prereflective or anterior to the *Ur-teilung* (primordial division) of reflection, and hence as anterior to the division of subject and object in judgement (*Urteil*). To be sure, Adorno acknowledged that reflection, for Hölderlin, counted as the traumatic falling away from the *parousia* of Being. Yet, precisely in the pursuit of reflection in its most rigorous sense, Hölderlin's poetry wrested itself free from the trappings of Idealism: 'The healing of what the Romantic–mythologizing thesis conceives reflection to be guilty of is to occur, according to the Hölderlinian antithesis, through reflection in the strict sense, through the assimilation of what has been oppressed into consciousness through remembrance.'[9] To be seen as an act of remembrance, poetic self-reflection restored repressed nature to consciousness without, however, reinstating the fulcrum of a cohesive subject. Here it is vital to add that the *Gedichtete*, in the final analysis, was realized in and through the dialectical constellation of form and content. For, as an anti-Idealistic principle, parataxis not only manifested itself at the level of form but was doubled, as it were, at the level of content. If at the formal level Hölderlin's late poetry undermined the hierarchical, subject-ing logic of Idealism, then at the level of content it offered a philosophical *anamnesis* of nature, a figure suppressed in Hegel's philosophy of spirit. *Anamnesis* here no longer alluded to the interiorizing gesture of a self-reflective subject, nor was it related to the Platonic contemplation of the *eidos*. Rather, this radically different mode of recollection consisted of a reflection to the second power in which reflection pondered its own negativity and finitude. No longer the ruse of a self-doubling Idealistic subject, this self-reflection ultimately was that of the *logos*, or language, which, folding back onto itself, dialectically redeemed itself.

In the Hölderlinian figure of the *Genius*, this self-critical movement reached its pinnacle, attesting to this poetry's unmistakable departure from the infinitely potent, self-positing subject of Idealism. As he made peace with his imminent death and finitude, recognizing his affinity to nature's transience, the genius in the end expelled the mythical, sacrificial manifestations of death that still lingered in the final stanza of the hymn 'Patmos'. For, ultimately, Hölderlin's figure of the genius managed to escape dangerous entanglement in myth through the force of an altogether different style of reflection and its organon, language.[10] To illustrate how Hölderlin's late poetry surrendered to the force of language, Adorno resorted to an intricate, revealing wordplay involving the multiple connotations of *Fug* and *fügen*. Thus, in the late ode 'Blödigkeit' ('Timidity'), Adorno observed, Hölderlin celebrated the *Genius* for the obedience (*Fügsamkeit*) and docile passivity with which he relinquished the hubristic stance of the spirit.[11] Hölderlin's admiration of these sober, modest virtues found its formal correlate in his poetic technique of paratactical serialization (*fügen*),[12] in which the poet could be seen to obey – in German *sich fügen* – language's higher, liberating authority. As Adorno hastened to add, it was no one else than Benjamin who had first called attention to the salvational passivity that permeated Hölderlin's late poetry.

2

From the very start of his intellectual career, Adorno proved to be one of Benjamin's most avid readers and commentators, always ready to wrest the critical potential or kernel from under what others considered to be the mythical layer of Benjamin's work.[13] While in his early Frankfurt lectures Adorno adopted Benjamin's theory of natural history, laid out in the latter's *Origin of the German Trauerspiel* (1925, 1928), in his unfinished *magnum opus*, the *Aesthetic Theory*, he addressed the melancholic, allegorical status of the modern artwork along decidedly Benjaminian lines. It is hardly surprising, therefore, that in 'Parataxis' Adorno drew upon Benjamin's early Hölderlin essay to substantiate his unravelling of Hölderlin's *Gedichtete*. In the same way that he considered parataxis to be a figure through which Hölderlin's poetry could be salvaged from the reductive, recuperative metaphysics of Heidegger's *Seinsphilosophie*, so Adorno keenly stressed the subversive logic of Benjamin's essay. Indeed, much like Adorno's essay, Benjamin's 1914–15 interpretation of the two odes from *Nachtgesänge* (Night Songs) demonstrated the anti-Fichtean tenor of Hölderlin's mature poetry, albeit implicitly. Furthermore, the theory of Idealistic and Romantic reflection, it must be added, very much formed the heart of Benjamin's earliest intellectual work. Thus, in many ways, the Hölderlin essay can count as a prelude to his 1919 dissertation, devoted to the concept of art criticism (*Kunstkritik*) in Early Romanticism.[14] Most importantly, Benjamin there showed how Schlegel's and Novalis's conceptions of objective irony and reflection ventured beyond the subjectivism of Fichtean Idealism.

Still, Benjamin's philosophical intentions can hardly be assimilated to the logic of negative dialectics, which Adorno all too eagerly projected back onto his friend's Hölderlin essay. While it is true that Benjamin, like Hölderlin, ended up celebrating the poet's passivity and obedience (*Fügsamkeit*), he did so through a remarkable and potentially troubling existential reading of the merit of death. Most crucially, however, Benjamin did not so much seek to identify the disruptive, disjunctive operations of Hölderlin's serial, linguistic technique (Adorno), but tried to grasp the harmony of *absolute connectedness* that permeated his poetic universe. To bring the differences between both positions to the fore, this chapter will, in a first moment of analysis, linger on the intricacies that mark the seemingly mythical layer (or *Sachgehalt*) of Benjamin's Hölderlin interpretation, before subjecting its critical potential to closer scrutiny.

To read Benjamin's essay in its own right, it is first of all necessary to recognize that Hölderlin remained a focal point throughout much of Benjamin's writerly career. Already as a high-school student, Benjamin had given a presentation on Hölderlin, which may well have provided the first outline of the 1914–15 essay.[15] The essay itself testified to the climate of Hölderlin revivalism that was propagated by Stefan George's circle, and gave rise to the first historical-critical Hölderlin edition started by Norbert von Hellingrath. Upon learning about von Hellingrath's untimely death at the front, Benjamin noted how much he regretted no longer being be able to send him a copy of his Hölderlin study, for which von Hellingrath's 1910 edition of Hölderlin's Pindar translations had served as 'the external motivation'.[16] Moreover, the essay itself was also an epitaph or memorial to another poet and casualty of the First World War, Fritz Heinle, who, together with his girlfriend, had committed suicide at the war's outbreak. In focusing on the Hölderlinian figure of the poet's finitude, Benjamin also clearly mourned and worked through the death of his lost friend and poet.[17]

Though the 1914–15 essay would remain the only long study Benjamin was to dedicate to the poet, Hölderlin's presence can be sensed in many of his early letters, while Hölderlinian *topoi*, such as the caesura, *das reine Wort* (the pure word), *Nüchternheit* (sobriety) or *die Wahrheit der Lage* (the truth of the situation), persisted throughout his so-called German period, as evidenced by the 1919 dissertation, *Der Begriff der Kunstkritik in der deutschen Romantik* (*The Concept of Criticism in German Romanticism*), the 1921 translation essay, 'The Task of the Translator', and the 1922 Goethe interpretation, 'Goethe's Elective Affinities'. In 'The Task of the Translator', for example, Hölderlin's Sophocles translations were said to exemplify not just the translation's openness to the foreign, adverse as they were to the purely national; they also bore witness to the 'enormous danger inherent in all translations: the gates of a language thus expanded and modified may slam shut and enclose the translator in silence'.[18]

Given this intricate web of connections and cross-references, the reading I propose of Benjamin's Hölderlin essay will be framed by two supplementary analyses: first, a discussion of the thematics at the core of his 1919 dissertation, notably the Early Romantics' concept of objective reflection, which, despite visible differences, resonated with Hölderlinian poetic figures; second, a short interpretation of Benjamin's Goethe essay, which serves to illustrate how he dramatically revised, even rethought his earlier Hölderlin analysis. For though the essay on Goethe's novel *Elective Affinities* returned to Hölderlin, it also advanced a staunch critique of the absolute connections and metaphysics of death that still ruled the earlier Hölderlin interpretation.

3

If in an initial stage of his doctoral studies Benjamin planned to dedicate his dissertation to Kant, eventually, under the guidance of Richard Herbertz, he would focus on the Early Romantics' concept of art criticism (*Kunstkritik*).[19] Yet, his interest in Kant remained quite lively, as indeed it would throughout his life. In a letter of June 1917 addressed to his friend Gershom Scholem, Benjamin argued that the Early Romantics' endeavour to lay bare the form of religion, i.e. history, resembled Kant's transcendental project of uncovering form in the field of theoretical philosophy.[20] Benjamin's interest concerned the Early Romantics' 'mystical formalism' (*SW* 1: 123), also called 'undogmatic', 'free', or 'liberal formalism' (*SW* 1: 158) – all terms meant to capture the innovative concept of form that they introduced into the philosophy of art. Individual presentational form (*Dartstellungsform*) was the organ through which the work of art participated in the Absolute, to be conceived of as an immanent medium of reflection and a continuum of forms. Art criticism, in turn, was an act (*Tätigkeit*) of reflection, which, in activating the potential or reflective seed embedded in the work's form, helped to unfold the work in the medium of absolute reflection that was art. By adopting the structure of reflection as their basic epistemological concept, Schlegel and Novalis proved indebted to Fichte's philosophical system, albeit that they introduced notable revisions. For, according to Fichte's *Wissenschaftslehre*, reflection amounted to a 'thinking of thinking', in which thinking (*Form*) became the matter (*Stoff*) of a thinking to the second, and third, power. However, the Early Romantics departed from Fichte's system in so far as this mode of thinking (a form of form) was no longer carried out by an I, be it an absolute I or an empirical one, but by a 'self', which could include artefacts and natural objects. Art criticism amounted to 'I-less' reflection (*Ichfreie Reflexion*). As the interplay between several poles of reflection, criticism 'potentiated' (Novalis), 'romanticized', or 'poetized' the artwork, that is, helped 'to transform the individual work into the absolute work of art' by assimilating it to the Absolute (*SW* 1: 163). The Absolute, in turn, was to be conceived of as an objective medium of reflection, a system of multiple, multifarious connections (*Zusammenhänge*) encompassing lower orders of reflection, such as the singular work of art. Individual form functioned as a *Grenzwert* (limit-value); for, as the work's a priori, its *Daseinsprinzip*, discrete form was the principle through which the work was transported into the absolute medium of forms. While acknowledging irony's conceptual difference from reflection, Benjamin called attention to Schlegel's theory of objective irony or irony of form – a positive, redemptive mode of irony clearly distinct from the violent, nihilistic force of mere subjective irony. Rather than annihilating the work of art, it '[drew] the work nearer to indestructibility' (*SW* 1: 164), unveiling it to be a mystery. Relating this numinous revelation of absolute form in the artwork to the Platonic conception of the *eidos*, Benjamin described the process by using a 'double concept of form':

> The particular form of the individual work, which we might call the presentational form, is sacrificed to ironic dissolution. Above it, however, irony flings open a heaven of eternal form, the idea of forms (which we might call the absolute form), and proves the survival of the work, which draws its indestructible subsistence from that sphere, after the empirical form, the expression of its isolated reflection, has been consumed by the absolute form. The ironization of the presentational form is, as it were, the storm blast that raises the curtain on the transcendental order of art, disclosing this order and in it the immediate existence of the work as a mystery. The work is not, as Herder regarded it, essentially a revelation and a mystery of creative genius, which one could well call a mystery of substance; it is a mystery of order, the revelation of its absolute dependence on the idea of art, its eternal, indestructible sublation in that idea. (*SW* 1: 164–5)[21]

Benjamin's analysis of objective irony did not prove to be concerned with the radical disjunctive force that more recent critical studies, such as Lacoue-Labarthe and Nancy's *The Literary Absolute* or de Man's 'Rhetoric of Temporality', have ascribed to the work of irony. Nor did his treatment of irony reveal affinities to the grammar of logical disjunction and allegorical fragmentation for which his *Trauerspiel* study later rightly would become famous. Put differently, irony, as discussed in the dissertation, did not incur the empty infinitude of a reflective mirror gallery, nor did it seem to be caught up in the entrapments of a permanent *parabasis*. As becomes clear, Benjamin did not seek to show how the possible derailment of reflection eventually ran counter to the search for the Absolute that infused the Early Romantics' critical project. Quite the contrary, he proved more interested in discussing how Fichte and the Early Romantics respectively had proposed to halt the threat of infinite regress lurking in reflection (or the thinking of thinking of thinking, *ad infinitum*). Fichte's *Wissenschaftslehre* introduced the concept of *intellektuelle Anschauung* (intellectual intuition), while the Early Romantics averted the danger by means of what Benjamin called *mediate immediacy* in absolute reflection. Infinity for the Romantics no longer meant empty progression or regression but a network of fulfilled, infinite connections and reflections, an interplay among isolated reflections and the Absolute, the very medium of reflection. Indeed, as the above passage on irony demonstrated, ironization itself was to be considered a reflective process of infinite potentiation, a critical act in and through which the work of art was brought to completion or perfection. In dissolving the work's presentational form, irony lifted the veil that covered the transcendental order of art, revealing the work to partake of a mystery of absolute order. Infinitude, in other words, hardly related to the empty infinity of mathematics or the endless progression characteristic of numerical serialization, but was more of the order of the intricate, ornamental patterns that adorned the Alhambra. This much can be gauged from a short essay that Benjamin wrote in 1916, called 'On the Middle Ages' ('Über das Mittelalter', *GS* 2.1: 132–3). Admiring the consummate harmony and immanence of Oriental ornamentation, Benjamin maintained that the Early Romantics' formalism could hardly be of the order of the Gothic ornament; for had not Schlegel disqualified the latter as magical schematism and empty, purely decorative form, devoid of absolute content? Gothic style stood for a diminished, miniature world – *die verkleinerte Welt*[22] – while Oriental ornamentation partook more fully of the Absolute. About the Oriental world of thought, Benjamin said: 'Its innermost difference from the spirit of the Middle Ages consists in the fact that it has the absolute present as its powerful content, out of which it develops the language of its forms' (*GS* 2.1: 132). Just as the Oriental ornament was consummated in and by the Absolute, so Schlegel's idea of a progressive, universal poetry (*Universalpoesie*), Benjamin implied, held out the promise of an infinite process of completion or fulfilment (*Erfüllung*). Certainly, in fragment 116 of the *Athenaeum*, Schlegel had proclaimed that the task of universal poetry could never be completed. Benjamin, for his part, did not brush over these passages. Yet, he refused to read this endless expanse of infinitude as the reign of a syncopating, empty, mechanical time. Instead, the distance between the present and the as yet inaccessible future for him unmistakably carried messianic overtones – messianism being the very 'heart of Romanticism'[23] – for it pointed to the however distant, yet possible return of plenitude. In other words, in this early phase, infinitude did not yet elicit the logic of disjunction that Benjamin later, in the prologue to the *Trauerspiel* book, as if still contemplating the Alhambra, would capture in the figure of fragmentary, allegorical mosaic.

As he brought his account of Romantic art criticism as reflection to conclusion, Benjamin called upon a kindred spirit, 'whose relationship to the Romantic school, within the history of ideas, remains unclear if his particular philosophical identity with this school is not considered', namely, Hölderlin. Indeed, though Hölderlin's poetry could hardly be conflated with the Early Romantics' poetics, at crucial moments in Benjamin's analysis Hölderlinian themes functioned as interpretive hinges. To capture the 'full infinitude of interconnection' (*Zusammenhang*) that characterized the mediate immediacy of Romantic reflection, he invoked a phrase taken from a fragment that accompanied Hölderlin's Pindar translations: '*unendlich (genau) zusammenhängen*' (to 'hang together infinitely [exactly]') (*SW* 1: 126). More profound still were the philosophical affinities between Romantic art theory, notably, its conception of prose as 'the idea of poetry', and Hölderlin's 'principle of the sobriety of art' (*Satz von der Nüchternheit der Kunst*). If absolute reflection itself transpired as the dialectic between the particular and the general, between the movements of 'self-limitation' and 'self-extension', then this interplay was laid down nowhere more clearly than in the Early Romantics' theory of prose (*SW* 1: 172). 'In ordinary usage', Benjamin explained, 'the prosaic – that in which reflection as the principle of art appears uppermost – is, to be sure, a familiar metaphorical designation of the sober' (*SW* 1: 175). Setting up a convergence between prose, the prosaic, and sobriety (or temperance), he called upon a poetic *topos* vital to Hölderlin's work as a whole. For the word not only played a pivotal role in the poem 'Half of Life' ('Die Hälfte des Lebens'), where it appeared as 'hallowed-sober water' (*ins heilignüchterne Wasser*); the term also emerged in Hölderlin's fragments on reflection, where it functioned as the necessary limit preventing a perilous state of ecstatic self-loss, as is clear from the following excerpt.[24]

That is the measure of enthusiasm which is given to every individual, that the one keeps the presence of mind to the necessary degree in the greater, the other one only in smaller fire. Where temperance [*Nüchternheit*] forsakes you, there are the boundaries of your enthusiasm. The great poet is never abandoned by himself; he may elevate himself as far above himself as he wishes. One can fall upward just as well as downward. The latter is prevented by the flexible spirit, the former by the gravity that lies in the temperate presence of mind. However, feeling is probably the best temperance [*Nüchternheit*] and presence of mind for the poet, if it is authentic, warm, clear and strong. It is the spirit's bridle and spur. It impels the spirit with warmth, [and] it defines its boundary with tenderness, authenticity and restrains it so that it does not go astray; and thus it is at once understanding and will.[25]

As poetic feeling, sobriety was a gravitational force, akin to the (Socratic) virtue of *sophrosune*, the temperate counterweight to boundless enthusiasm. Furthermore, in one of Hölderlin's letters to Casimir Ulrich Böhlendorff, dated 4 December 1801, 'Junonian sobriety' (*Junonische Nüchternheit*) stood for a mode of control (*Bändigung*) that was typical of Hesperian presentational form (*Darstellungsform*) and thus counterpoised to the Oriental 'holy pathos', at the root of Greek art. But, as Hölderlin imparted to his correspondent, Homer, whose work expressed the Apollonian realm of 'the fire from heaven' (*das Feuer vom Himmel*), by the same token was deft enough also to incorporate Occidental sobriety into his art. The critic Peter Szondi has provided one of the most authoritative interpretations of this letter to Böhlendorff. As he explained, the interplay between Occidental sobriety and Greek pathos did not merely transcend customary classicist attempts to catalogue the respective characteristics of antiquity and modernity; for Hölderlin, the interplay established a necessary, constitutive tension (*Spannung*), which he already had announced in his earlier theory of the *Wechsel der Töne* (Alternation of Tones), and which he henceforth regarded to be the artistic ideal to be realized in poetry.[26] However accurate this reading might be, Szondi nonetheless seemed to interpret this interplay primarily as a subjective aesthetic principle, as the poet's *Geschick*, to be actualized in each and every poem through the poet's craft, or *technē*.[27] Benjamin, by contrast, went beyond these purely subjective conditions, establishing that this alternation between sobriety and ecstasy constituted the very essence (*Wesensbestimmung*) of *objective* reflection. As the antidote to Platonic *mania*, sobriety was the law that ruled the structure of reflection, conceived of as a dialectic between sober self-limitation and ecstatic self-extension: 'As a thoughtful and collected posture, reflection is the antithesis of ecstasy, the mania of Plato' (*SW* 1: 175). Objective reflection, furthermore, needed to be understood by means of the notion of *technē* that Hölderlin developed in his 'Annotations to Oedipus' (*Anmerkungen zum Oedipus*), that is, as the 'lawful calculus' (*gesetzlicher Kalkül*), the '*mechanē* of the ancients', or the 'craftsmanlike' art lacking in modern poetry. The 'manner of this making, then', Benjamin determined, 'is reflection' (*SW* 1: 177). In contrast to aesthetic theories that either interpreted form as the expression (*Ausdruck*) of beauty or advocated the lawlessness of the ecstatic, creative *Genie* concept of the Storm and Stress movement (*Sturm und Drang*), Benjamin defined Romantic reflection as a sober, prosaic mechanics of *technē* or form. Objective irony or irony of form was its structure. Tying together these observations about objective irony, reflection, and the law of sobriety, Benjamin concluded that

> the Romantics were thinking of 'made' works, works filled with prosaic spirit, when they formulated the thesis of the indestructibility of genuine art objects. What dissolves in the ray of irony is the illusion alone; but the core of the work remains indestructible, because this core consists not in ecstasy, which can be disintegrated, but in the unassailable, sober prosaic form. By means of mechanical reason, moreover, the work is soberly constituted within the infinite – at the limit-value of limited forms. (*SW* 1: 176)

If the artwork harboured an indestructible yet veiled core, then the task of genuine reflective art criticism was to activate objective irony; by peeling away the work's outward layer, its final 'consummation' could be fully achieved. Essentially, this meant that the work's external form needed to be shed so as to reveal the eternal, prosaic, sober kernel by means of which it partook of absolute form, or the idea. Only in this way, Benjamin wrote in conclusion, could the sober, numinous splendour of the idea, its 'sober light', be revealed (*SW* 1: 185).

4

Completed four years before the dissertation, Benjamin's Hölderlin essay did not yet explicitly pursue the dialectic of reflection that would form the basis of the dissertation. Yet, as if anticipating the later work, the essay already carried out the critical imperative of bringing the work of art to completion, and it unambiguously pointed to Hölderlin's poetic virtue of sobriety. For through immanent formal analysis, the essay set out to reveal how his late poetry exhibited the law of divine sobriety.

Couched in language that at times was strongly marked by neo-Kantianism, the essay was more than just a commentary on two of Hölderlin's late odes, 'The Poet's Courage [*Dichtermut*]' (from around 1800) and 'Timidity [*Blödigkeit*]' (1802), published as part of the *Night Songs (Nachtgesänge)* (1805).[28] In his difficult methodological introduction (*SW* 1: 18–21), Benjamin defined new interpretive principles that were to serve as the foundation and justification of his aesthetic commentary. The programme of the essay was to reveal the a priori of the poems in question, more precisely, what Benjamin called their *inner form*, or the poetized (*Gedichtete*).[29] As the *sine qua non* of the ideal work of art, the poetized was simultaneously the precondition of the poems and the task (*Aufgabe*) that needed to be realized in the artwork no less than in the critic's commentary. Ultimately, as Benjamin hoped, this absolute task of ascertaining the poetized, while a 'purely methodical, ideal goal', might one day prove applicable to a theory of the lyric and of literature in general. Alluding to the terminology of scientific foundation typical of the prevailing neo-Kantian climate, he conjectured that, in a distant future, (aesthetic) judgement, 'even if unprovable, can nonetheless be justified' (*SW* 1: 21).

Before we consider what Benjamin might have meant by the 'poetized', it is crucial to note that he in all likelihood borrowed the term – together with the related concepts of 'inner form' and *Gehalt* – from Goethe's writings on aesthetics. Benjamin probably came across the term in a letter that Goethe sent to Karl Friedrich, Graf von Reinhard.[30] Complaining about the public's response to his 1809 novel *Die Wahlverwandschaften* (*Elective Affinities*), Goethe ended by prophesying that his readers would eventually be forced to accept the novel's *Gedichtete*, much as they habitually were obliged to accept certain historical facts (*das Geschehene*), such as the execution of an old monarch. As for 'inner form', this term was a translation of the Greek *endon eidos*, a central concept in Plotin's *Enneads*, whence it travelled via Shaftesbury and Herder to Goethe and the Early Romantics. As an aesthetic category, the term *endon eidos* was still very much at the heart of discussions among some of Benjamin's contemporaries, and appeared, for example, in Norbert von Hellingrath's dissertation on Hölderlin's Pindar translations or in Elisabeth Rotten's study of Plato and Goethe.[31] Inner form easily became a key term in organic conceptions of literature and the arts, in that it offered an antidote to Aristotelian empirical form, thus speaking to the critic's desire to overcome the dualism between outward form and spirit. In his early writings, particularly his comments on Mercier's 'Du Théâtre ou nouvel essai sur l'art dramatique', Goethe likened inner form to the mysterious stone of the alchemist, for it possessed the same magical power to weld together 'vessel [*Gefäss*] and matter, fire and cooling bath'.[32]

Yet, where Goethe in his letter to Karl Friedrich used the poetized in a non-technical sense, meaning 'fable', Benjamin converted the expression into a veritable *terminus technicus*, turning it into nothing less than a 'category of aesthetic investigation' (*SW* 1: 19). In his methodological introduction, the poetized attained a host of different specifications. First, as the 'particular and unique sphere in which the task and precondition of the poem lie', it was 'the intellectual-perceptual [*geistig-anschaulich*] structure of the world to which the poem bears witness' (*SW* 1: 18). To understand what Benjamin meant by these ostensibly enigmatic phrases, one must follow the various discrete levels of his analysis. At the epistemological level, the poetized was a structure that joined the intuitive (*anschaulich*) to the spiritual, or intellectual (*geistig*), thereby overcoming the division between the different human faculties. At the poetic level proper, the poetized was to be thought of as a non-mimetic structure, as the grid of the world, or, better, of a syncretic *kosmos* (Greek for 'order'), in which the semantic, phonetic, aesthetic, and ethical realms were all attuned to one another. As such, the poetized was inherently an ideal sphere – as expressed in the term *Aufgabe* (task) – a sphere to be realized in and by every poem. In this respect, Benjamin seemed to lean on the Aristotelian model of *dunamis* and *energeia*, in so far as he distinguished between virtual, inner form, on the one hand, and the one actualized in the individual poem, on the other; hence his use of the phrase '*besondere Gestalt*' ('particular configuration') (*SW* 1: 19). Above all, the poetized opened up onto the realm of truth, *die Wahrheit der Lage*, 'the truth of the poem', which was to be materialized by obeying the law of *poiēsis*, or *Gestaltung* (giving form or shape).

To explicate this artistic task of poetic *Gestaltung*, Benjamin introduced a quotation by Novalis taken from the latter's notes on the Sistine Madonna. The quotation itself is not insignificant when seen in the larger context of Benjamin's early work, for not only did it appear in the Hölderlin essay; it also returned in the dissertation and the epistemo-critical prologue of the *Trauerspiel* study. The *Gedichtete*, Benjamin noted, was not purely the product yielded by the work of *poiēsis* (*Gestaltung*) but also signified the poetical imperative that lay at the origin or genesis of poetic truth as such. The poetized was the sphere in which the

> peculiar domain containing the truth of the poem shall be opened up. This 'truth', which the most serious artists so insistently claim for their creations, shall be understood as the objectivitiy of their production, as the fulfilment of the artistic task in each case. 'Every work of art has in and of itself an a priori ideal, a necessity for being in the world' (Novalis). In its general character, the poetized is the synthetic unity of the intellectual and perceptual orders. This unity gains its particular configuration as the inner form of the particular creation. (*SW* 1: 19)

In turning to this process of creative genesis and formation, Benjamin adopted a tone and style very similar to that of a lecture by the neo-Kantian Paul Natorp, entitled 'Kant und die Marburger Schule' (Kant and the Marburg School). Discussing the logos, or reason, as the original law of human creation, Natorp transferred the act of formation (*Gestaltung*) from the divine register of

Genesis to the human act of creation, that is to say, to acts of radical determination (*Bestimmung*) that brought unification in the chaotic manifold:

> 'In the beginning was the act', the creative act of object formation [*Objektgestaltung*], in which man alone constructs himself in this act, deeply and completely impresses the character of his spirit upon his world – or better yet, an entire world of such worlds, which he can all call his own. But the creative ground of all such acts of object formation is the law and, in the end, the arche-law, which one still, understandably enough, calls the law of the logos, the ratio, reason.[33]

Where for Natorp this creative arche-ground, in the final analysis, was reason, for Benjamin it was essentially a poetic law, Hölderlin's '*Leben im Gesange*' (life in poetic song).

At a second level of specification, the poetized took on the meaning of a limit-concept (*Grenzbegriff*), a demarcating sphere between two concepts, those of the poem and of life. The poetized was a transitional, mediating sphere that realized the passage or transition between two functional unities: the 'idea of the task', or life, and the 'idea of the solution', or the poem. As a balance between two extremes, the poetized held together form and life, preventing the poem from sliding into either direction, that is, either towards dead, mechanical form ('a concoction [*Machwerk*] alien to art and nature') or towards pure nature ('an endearing, artless natural product') (*SW* 1: 20). Overcoming the traditional form–content dualism, the poetized stood for the virtual, synthetic unification of matter and form, 'the potential existence of those determinations that are effectively [*aktuell*] present in the poem' (*SW* 1: 19).

In this context, the term 'life' acquired ulterior meaning. For, as Benjamin proceeded to argue, 'one could say that life is, in general, the poetized of the poems. Yet the more the poet tries to convert without transformation the unity of life into a unity of art, the plainer it is that he is a bungler' (*SW* 1: 20). This passage only makes sense once one recognizes that Benjamin's organicist conception of life was part of a long philosophical tradition and, centrally, that it brought into play decidedly Hölderlinian connotations. The vitalistic metaphysical unity he had in mind was the one to be found in Hölderlin's *Hyperion*, which evoked the tragic unification of disparate, opposing forces; in the essay 'About Religion' ('Über Religion'), which opposed '*das höhere Geschick*' and '*das höhere Leben*' to *Not*; and, finally, in 'Das Werden im Vergehen', which was structured on the principle of '*das harmonisch Entgegengesetzte*'. Following this Idealistic strand of interpretation, Benjamin suggested that the term 'life' needed to be conceived of in terms of the category of myth. Myth, here, was no longer the opposite of the higher verity of philosophy. Only later would this more common conception of myth, derived from Plato, emerge in Benjamin's work, namely in the Goethe essay, where he would use it to separate the fallen realm of mere cognition and knowledge from truth. In the Hölderlin essay, by contrast, the category of myth signalled a world of absolute connections and relations (*Beziehungen*), an intensity of multiple coherences presided over by the Law of Identity (*Identitätsgesetz*).[34] Determined by multiple connections between the intuitive and the intellectual, between the perceptual and the province of ideas, the poetized stood for absolute synthetic unity, governed by the rule of identity. This law, Benjamin underscored, not only applied on an epistemological level but also exemplified the kind of mythical world to which the poem bore witness:

> The law according to which all apparent elements of sensation and ideas come to light as the embodiments of essential, in principle infinite functions is called the Law of Identity. This term describes the synthetic unity of functions. It may be recognized in each particular configuration it takes as an a priori of the poem. The disclosure of the pure poetized, the absolute task, must remain – after all that has been said – a purely methodological, ideal goal. The pure poetized would otherwise cease to be a limit-concept: it would be life or poem. (*SW* 1: 20–1)

It now becomes obvious why Benjamin called the task of ascertaining the poetized absolute and ideal. By this he did not mean to imply that it resembled the 'empty kind of infinity' ('*leere Art der Unendlichkeit*'), which a fragmentary text from 1917 would link to the Kantian concept of the infinite task (*unendliche Aufgabe*) (*GS* 6: 51). Rather, the ideality of the pure poetized was such that it escaped the grasp of finite cognition. As far as the method of aesthetic commentary was concerned, this meant that no one element of the poetized was to be considered separately or in isolation, unless an infinite series of other functional unities were brought into play – a phenomenon that Benjamin captured, as we shall see, by means of the term series (*Reihe*).

Having laid out these methodological principles, Benjamin now turned to a comparative reading of 'Dichtermut' and 'Blödigkeit', which painstakingly traced the Law of Identity, showing how, though an organic unity was lacking in the poem's original version, it was magisterially realized in the final one. Pursuing the 'power of transformation' (*SW* 1: 24) through which the poetic law of identity was eventually realized, Benjamin demonstrated how the flaws of the original poem – still hampered by a 'considerable indeterminacy of the perceptual' and an 'incoherence of detail' (*SW* 1: 22) – were to make way for the instauration of a poetic cosmos in which the rule of identity revealed itself at all possible levels of analysis.

If the first version, 'The Poet's Courage', was marked by 'a considerable indeterminacy of the perceptual and an incoherence of detail' (*SW* 1: 22), then its formlessness was generated by a fundamental 'indeterminacy of the shaping principle' (*SW* 1: 23). Rather than being firmly moored in myth, the poem exuded the Greek world of mythology. Thus, it treated its subject, 'a destiny – the death of the poet', not immanently but by analogy, through the image of the setting sun (*SW* 1: 23). By comparison, 'Timidity' fulfilled the poetic law of *Gestaltung*. At an epistemological level this meant that the law of identity required the joining of matter to form, intuition to idea, of that which was determined (*bestimmt*) to that which determines (*bestimmend*). At a linguistic level, the last poem exemplified how the logic of analogy and comparison between the poet and the sun god Apollo had been replaced by an *Ausgleichung* (evening out) of the Hölderlinian orders of gods, poets, and people, thus establishing an absolute balance (*Gleichgewicht*) from which the third element, the *tertium comparationis*, had disappeared. Poets, gods and mortals now mutually determined and were determined by each other. Illuminating in this respect was Benjamin's image of the two scales that 'are left in their opposing positions, yet lifted off the scale beam' (*SW* 1: 25). This image epitomized the change from a logic of comparison to a harmonic differentiation in unity, an absolute poetic equilibrium. Stated differently, mythology was replaced by myth. Inasmuch as 'Timidity' surmounted the lures of a world ruled by Apollo and the Greek fates, it departed from classical mythology, and from the torso-like, allegorical nature of classicist works, eulogized in Winckelmann's Apollo of Belvedere and materialized in Goethe's Weimar aesthetics.

'Timidity' decidedly shied away from such adulation of Greek form, opening up onto an Oriental tapestry, an interweaving or interlacing of different fates, which found their centre in the poet's courage as he sacrificed himself for the community in death. In 'The Poet's Courage', Benjamin charged, beauty, worshipped through the figure of Apollo, still functioned as a cover-up for the impending threat of death (the German term Benjamin used was *eingekleidet*, GS, 2.1: 122). Only because the poet showed a readiness to accept his fate (*Schicksal*) could his poetic world essentially reveal itself to be a *good* world, and the poetic task emerge as an ethical one (*GS* 2.1: 117). By the same token, the poem now bid farewell to the preponderance of mere life, idyllic nature (Schiller), and a false, so-called natural affinity between poet and people. The transition from the field of pure necessity to the realm of bounded freedom was symbolized by the step of the poet's *Genius* on the carpet of truth (*die Wahrheit der Lage*) and by the wilfulness, even arbitrariness (*Willkür*), of its Oriental ornamentation.[35] At the level of metaphysical truth, aesthetic form was the organ in and through which truth made its appearance, a constellation grasped in the image of 'the truth of the situation [*Lage*]'. Benjamin captured this constellation by means of the term *Bilddissonanz* (*GS* 2.1: 117; dissonance of the image, *SW* 1: 29). A synaesthesia that merged seeing (*Bild*) and hearing (*Dissonanz*), *Bilddissonanz* also referred to Hölderlin's treatment of dissonance in 'Über die Verfahrungsweise des poetischen Geistes'.[36] The icon of the carpet served as a connecting bridge that facilitated the passage from the perceptual, and the minimal difference of apparent dissonance, to unification in harmonious truth.

The principle that ensured the passage, the translation, among the various layers of the perceptual and the intellectual, or spiritual, was none other than the law of poetry, the plastic law of *Gestaltung*. Though this poetic law was such that the poetized eventually could only be intuited, thus defying analytical differentiation, Benjamin nonetheless sought to unravel the *Gestaltzusammenhang* of the poem's last version. The word *Gestalt* here must be understood in all its possible different meanings, that is, as discrete figure or shape; as plastic aesthetic form; and, no doubt, as absolute, ulterior form (*eidos*). In the complex architectonic universe that the poem 'Timidity' disclosed, each figure received a more pronounced identity to the degree to which it proved bounded and interlocked in connecting chains (*Reihen*). As a result, the different situations or positions (*Lage*) of the people, poet, and the gods were rearranged (*verlagert*) into a new order, ruled by the law of poetry: 'In the context of poetic destiny, all figures acquire identity; for here they are sublated within a single vision [*Anschauung*], and though they may seem governed only by their own whim, they do finally fall back into the boundedness (*Gesetztheit*) of the poem' (*SW* 1: 25–6). This law, Benjamin contended, yielded the poem's *Gesetztheit* – a word that condensed the meanings *gesetztes Wesen*, law (*Gesetz*), and sobriety (*Besonnenheit* or *Nüchternheit*).

Preceding all forms of individuation, as well as what Dilthey called 'worldviews' or *Weltanschauungen*, this law formed the origin and ground of the poetic cosmos. In essence an awesome, terrific force, this principle of poetic *Gestaltung* necessarily brought about an objectification (*Versachlichung, Vergegenständlichung*) (*GS* 2.1: 119) of the people, the poet, and the gods. In formulating this mechanism of objectification, Benjamin may well have had in mind the operation of 'formalization' that befell Antigone and Kreon, as Hölderlin maintained in his annotations to Sophocles's tragedy. But the movement Benjamin described also resembled the one found in Hölderlin's 'Über die Verfahrungsweise des poetischen Geistes', in which the spirit submitted to a law of exteriorization (*Entäusserung*).[37] That is, the people were subjected to a movement of spatialization, turned into an '*extension* of space' (*SW* 1: 26), within which the gait (*Gang*) of the genius and the fate of the poet could take their course. The people were to become the signs, symbols, and extensions of historical space (*das Geschehen*), while this expanse in turn was punctuated by the poet's (temporally marked) interventions. As such, there thus existed a mutual interdependence of time and space, as signalled by the homomymic words *Lage* (location, situation), *Gelegenheit* (opportunity), *gelegen* (situated or opportune), and *verlagern* (shift, move, rearrange). Indeed, time itself was spatialized (*die Plastik der Zeit*) in the concept *Augenblick*, the moment of decision, rife with opportunity waiting to be seized by the poet. These multitudinous interactions found their sensuous fulfilment (*sinnliche Erfülltheit, GS* 2.1: 120) or resonance in an auditory register, through an additional series of homonyms: *Schicksal* (fate), *Geschick* (fate, fortune or skill), *geschickt* (past participle of *schicken*, to send; or the adjective skilful) and *schicklich* (seemly, fitting). Indeed, in this cosmos of euphony, the words *geschickt* and *bestimmt* acquired special resonance. *Geschick* should not only be translated as 'sent', that is, as the carrier of a temporal, teleological meaning, for in it the meanings of 'skilful' and, by implication, 'fate' equally resounded:

The poet appears among the living, determining and determined. As in the participle *geschickt* [sent], a temporal determination completes the spatial order in the event – namely, of being-found-fitting. This identity of orders is once more repeated in the determination of purpose or destination: 'for/ to someone to some end'. As if, through the order of art, the act of animating had to become doubly clear, everything else is left uncertain and the isolation within great extension is hinted at in the phrase 'for/to some-one to some end'. Now it is astonishing how, at this site, where the people [*Volk*] is in fact characterized in the most abstract way, an almost wholly new figuration of the most concrete life arises from the interior of this line. Just as what is skilful will emerge as the innermost essence of the poet (as his limit with respect to existence), just as what is skilful appears here before those who are alive as that which has been sent, so that identity arises in one form: determining and determined, centre and extension. The activity of the poet finds itself determined with respect to those who are alive; the living, however, determine themselves in their concrete existence – 'to/for someone to some end' – with respect to the essence of the poet. The poet exists as sign and script of the infinite extension of its destiny. This destiny itself, as will become clear later, is poetry. (*SW* 1: 27–8)

The word *bestimmt* here can be taken in the sense of 'to be determined', to have an identity, but also in a teleological and ethical sense, as 'to be determined for'. As such, the poet and the people reciprocally established and limited each other. This proliferation of meanings through phonetic proximity is especially evident in the phrase *die Wahrheit der Lage*, in so far as *Lage* not only brought into play a spatial abode but also the decidedly *existential* terms of situation or ability (*Möglichkeit*), present, for example, in the German expression *in der Lage sein* (to be in the position to do something). In its namesake *Gelegenheit* (opportunity, situatedness), which in the later Goethe essay would be contrasted with *Erlebnis* and unambiguously functioned as an ethical concept, time and space were once again fused. As near rhymes, all these homophonic words were the sensuous manifestation of the poem's verse 'Be rhymed for joy' ('*Sei zur Freude gereimt*'). Rhyme, Benjamin suggested, was thus a principle that ensured not substantial but functional identity. When held against Adorno's essay 'Para-taxis', then, it becomes evident that Benjamin's interpretation of these rhyming chains or series, attesting to 'the infinite possibilities of rhyme', were hardly meant to evoke the mechanics of disruptive concatenation; rather, a world of multiple, harmonious correspondences was disclosed.

If the people, objectified in the spatial *extension* of history, formed a first level of existence, then at the second, metaphysical level resided the gods, who were closest to the realm of pure ideas and to the plasticity, or inwardness, of time. Here, the principle of *Gestaltung* announced itself in the fact that the gods, like the people, were to become elements of the poet's fate. In this respect, Benjamin's analysis implied, the poem 'Timidity' also advanced a covert, yet pronounced criticism of Fichte's brand of Idealism, notably of the absolute I that believed it could constitute itself as well as the world in *auto-poesis*. For, in Hölderlin's universe, such *Selbstgestaltung* (formation of the self) and

Selbstsetzung (positing of the self) were acts of hubris that eventually brought on a negative reversal, or a lapse into dead form:[38]

> The structuring, the inwardly plastic principle, is so intensified that the fate of the dead form breaks over the god, so that – to remain within the image – the plastic dimension is turned inside out, and now the god becomes wholly an object. The temporal form is broken from the inside out as something animated. The heavenly one is *brought*. Here before us is the ultimate expression of identity: the Greek god has entirely fallen prey to his own principle, the form. The highest sacrilege is understood as hubris, which, attainable only by a god, transforms him into a dead form. To give oneself form – that is the definition of 'hubris'. The god ceases to determine the cosmos of the poem, whose essence – with art – freely elects for itself that which is objective: it brings the god, since gods have already turned into the concretized being of the world in thought. (*SW* 1: 32)

By thus interpreting the ascendance of the gods as a dialectical reversal into dead form – for eventually they too were 'brought' – Benjamin shrewdly inverted the logic of the Greek word *theos*, whose etymological meaning is that of thesis, or positing.[39]

Finally, the principle of objectification (*Vergegenständlichung*) was such that the poet, too, in the final analysis, was subjected to a movement of dephenomenalization. Rather than referring to an instance of *Selbstgestaltung*, a Promethean act of self-begetting, the lines 'Doch selber / Bringen schickliche Hände wir' ('Yet we ourselves / Bring suitable hands') inscribed the predicament of the poet's eventual objectification. By giving himself over to death, the poet was to become the 'principle of form [*Gestalt*]' (*SW* 1: 35) and thus a boundary or frontier to life. The poet, Benjamin wrote, 'brings his hands – and the heavenly ones. The intrusive caesura of this passage produces the distance that the poet ought to have from all form and the world, as its unity' (*SW* 1: 35).

As becomes evident from Benjamin's subsequent reference to the 22nd letter of Schiller's *On the Aesthetic Education of Man* (*Über die ästhetische Erziehung des Menschen*, *SW* 1: 35), the poet's death did not simply evoke his inescapable transience. Schiller's letter called for the dissolution of the work's 'material reference through the form', so that death, or the decline of matter, also enacted the identity of form and formlessness. In reality, this meant that ultimately – or so Benjamin suggested – the task of engendering life was to be realized through death. In 'Timidity', courage no longer stood for an individual asset or quality, as was still the case in 'The Poet's Courage'; now it meant humble, passive submission to death, the latter being the spiritual principle that held together the poet's cosmos. In the liminal situation of death,[40] at the ultimate point of indifference, that is, as a dead hero, the poet redeemed the world, offering atonement and a *Versachlichung* of the horrific forces that beset the body (*SW* 1: 34). Defined as a relation to the world, the resolute acknowledgement of death now became the gravitational centre of these manifold poetic relations:

The world of the dead hero is a new mythical one, steeped in danger; this is the world of the second version of the poem. In it an intellectual principle has become completely dominant: the heroic poet becomes one with the world. The poet does not have to fear death; he is a hero because he lives the centre of all relations. The principle of the poetized as such is the supreme sovereignty of relationship, shaped in this particular poem as courage – as the innermost identity of the poet with the world, whose emanation is all the identities of the perceptual and the intellectual in this poem. (*SW* 1: 34)

This intellectual principle of heroic identification with the world thus in the end constituted the point of 'comparativeness' (*Vergleichbarkeit*) (*SW* 1: 33) between 'The Poet's Courage' and 'Timidity': in point of fact, it was the concrete manifestation of the poems' *Gedichtete*.

But heroic, poetic death also drew upon a thematics that went beyond the confines of Hölderlin's poetry, as it resonated with the Idealistic philosophy of tragedy, analysed by Adorno, Szondi and Lacoue-Labarthe.[41] In essence, the poet's death, at the crux of 'Timidity', testified to the cathartic, sacrificial structure celebrated in Schelling's *Briefe über Dogmatismus und Kritizismus*, Hölderlin's fragment 'Die Bedeutung der Tragödien', or in his annotations to the Sophocles translations. Nowhere is this allusion to tragic death clearer than in Benjamin's deployment of the term 'caesura' (*Zäsur*), which referred to the disruptive prosodical effect of 'Timidity's' final verse lines, gesturing to the poet's hands. Not by accident, the term caesura appeared prominently in Hölderlin's 'Annotations to *Oedipus*', where, as 'the counter-rhythmic interruption' or intervention of the 'pure word' (*das reine Wort*), it provided the necessary counterbalance to ecstatic, tragical *mania*, to tragical *transport*, which itself was empty and 'aorgic', the most unrestricted (*ungebundenste*). Invoking the genre of tragedy, Benjamin thus ventured beyond the boundaries of the lyrical poem, much as Hölderlin had resorted to the mechanics of poetic meter (*Silbenmaß*) to define the nature of tragical equilibrium (*Gleichgewicht*).

Besides staging the poet's death, or self-erasure, as the incursion of a tragical caesura, 'Timidity', Benjamin went on to argue, also attested to an 'Oriental, mystical principle' that formed the very counterweight to Greek plasticity:

In death is the highest infinite form and formlessness, temporal plasticity and spatial existence, idea and sensuousness. And in this world every function of life is destiny, whereas in the first version, in the traditional way, destiny determined life. That is the Oriental, mystical principle, overcoming limits, which in this poem again and again so manifestly sublates the Greek shaping principle that creates an intellectual cosmos from pure relations to intuition, sensuous existence, and in which the intellectual is only the expression of the function that strives towards identity. (*SW* 1: 34)

Again, the passage clearly drew upon Hölderlin's poetic and philosophical convictions. For, without a doubt, Benjamin meant to allude to Hölderlin's famous letter to Friedrich Wilmans, dated 28 September 1803, in which the poet, commenting on his Sophocles translations, promised to bring out the Oriental element in Greek art. This Oriental (and for Benjamin essentially mystical) principle equally related to the predominance of the figure of Dionysus in Hölderlin's poetry – a predilection echoed later by Nietzsche, whose *Birth of Tragedy* pitted the Dionysian element against the *principium individuationis* of Apollonian illusion (*Schein*). Years later, in the *Trauerspiel* study, Benjamin would criticize Nietzsche for his lack of philosophical sobriety, for turning humans into a mere appearance (*Erscheinung*), thus depriving his aesthetic philosophy of tragedy of an ethical and historical dimension.

What to infer, then, from the emergence of such an Oriental principle at the end of the Hölderlin essay? Clear parallels can be drawn to the final section of the dissertation, which, as we saw, likewise was to end with the figure of Hölderlin. In concluding his comparative interpretation of 'The Poet's Courage' and 'Timidity', Benjamin suggested that the eccentric realm of death, the erasure of matter, the dominance of form, the interruption of the caesura, initiated the transportation into a higher, sacred realm, which extended beyond mere Greek form, namely, the realm of the *mysterium*. The poet's sacrifice in death marked the sudden emergence of the mystical, pure word that lay lodged at the heart of Hölderlin's poetic universe: 'sacred sobriety' (*heilige Nüchtern-heit*). At the height of the poet's self-loss, through the intervention of ecstatic death, sacred sobriety manifested itself. As if further to compound this paradox, Benjamin closed the essay with a reference to Hölderlin's poem 'Autumn' ('Der Herbst'), stemming from the period of Hölderlin's fall into madness, or *geistige Umnachtung*: 'Myths, which take leave of the earth, / ... They return to mankind' (*SW* 1: 36). Ending with the poet's lapse into insanity, Benjamin resorted to a familiar theme in Hölderlin scholarship. True to the verse from the hymn 'Patmos', 'Wo aber Gefahr ist, wächst / das Rettende auch' ('But where danger threatens / That which saves from it also grows'),[42] Benjamin indicated that the moment of catastrophe would overturn, revealing the possibility of imminent salvation. In the night of insanity, Hölderlin retained a mode of sobriety or 'sacred memory' ('*das heilige Gedächtnis*'),[43] to quote from the second stanza of 'Bread and Wine'. For even if the poem 'Autumn' spoke of the flight of myths (*Sagen*), it also at once announced a categorical return to earth. However fated the poet's plight might seem to be, ultimately his vicarious suffering in death might well redeem the world.

5

How exactly one is to interpret the status of poetic death with which Benjamin ended his Hölderlin interpretation can be thrown into sharper relief through the *Wahlverwandschaften* essay, which offered an answer to, even a reflection of sorts on, the critical categories employed in the Hölderlin essay.[44] As an earlier draft of the *Wahlverwandschaften* essay indicated, the text was obviously conceived on the basis of a tripartite, dialectical outline, whose three sections originally had the following captions: 'The Mythical as Thesis', 'Redemption as Antithesis', 'Hope as Synthesis' (*GS* 1.3: 835–7). In many ways, the essay thus anticipated the *Trauerspiel* book, more specifically its endeavour to turn to the philosophy of history and to go beyond the dualistic, anti-dialectical schematism of the neo-Kantians. In its dialectical interplay between commentary and criticism, knowledge (*Erkenntnis*) and truth, the beautiful and the sublime, and finally, the *Schein* (*videtur*) of the *Sachgehalt* and the *Schein* (*lucet*) of the *Wahrheitsgehalt*, the essay evidently complicated the *dunamis–energeia* model of the Hölderlin essay, without, however, completely severing its links to that text. In the first section of the Goethe essay, Benjamin reintroduced the term *Gedichtete*, yet this time seemingly to define 'the mythical material layer of the work' (*SW* 1: 314). Mythical here no longer signified a world of absolute connections founded on the poetic law of shaping (*Gestaltung*), but rather meant the surfacing of a natural world, ruled by fate; fate, in turn, no longer denoted the interweaving of textual and ethical threads but was the sign of a pre-ethical world, dominated by guilt and by what the essay 'Fate and Character' called parasitical time: the eternal return of the same.

As in his Hölderlin interpretation, the theory of tragedy still guided Benjamin's understanding of *Elective Affinities*. For, if the silence, or 'speechless rigidity', of the tragical hero *ex negativo* conveyed the sublimity of tragedy, then this same mode of silence also marked the main female character of the novel, Ottilie. To atone for the natural, mythical forces that emerged as the moral institution of marriage eroded, Ottilie was to undergo the tragic ritual of death. Going beyond the narrative of the novel, Benjamin discerned elements of this same mythical fate in the 'sobriquet' that Jean Paul gave to Goethe – the Olympian – a title for 'the dark, deeply self-absorbed, mythical nature that, in speechless rigidity [*sprachlose Starre*], indwells Goethe's artistry' (*SW* 1: 314). The force of the mythical could also be gleaned from Goethe's biography, notably from his peculiar hankering after silence and secrecy and his urge to destroy all earlier drafts of the novel. From this panoply of elements, Benjamin drew the following conclusion:

> If the existence of the material contents is in this way concealed, then the essence of those contents conceals itself. All mythic meaning strives for secrecy. Therefore, Goethe, sure of himself, could say precisely of this work that the poetized [*das Gedichtete*], like the event [*das Geschehene*], asserts its rights. Such rights are here indeed owed, in the sarcastic sense of the word, not to the poetic work but rather to the poetized – to the mythic material lawyer of the work. (*SW* 1: 314)

However, in keeping with a dialectical movement that transpired in the novel, cryptic silence and mythical secrecy eventually were elevated to the level of eschatological hope and the manifestation of divine, apocalyptic secrecy. A redemptive kernel lay concealed at the core of the mythical novel in the form of the novella about the 'Marvellous Young Neighbours'. Emitting a divine, redemptive spark of light, the novella announced the transition from the false shimmering of mere aestheticism to the realm of ethics and truth. In a Kierkegaardian turn, Benjamin favoured the figure of the individual (*der Einzelne*, GS 1.1:184) and the 'moral uniqueness of responsibility' (*SW* 1:322), which he opposed to his older conception of the hero, the scapegoat, or vicarious sufferer, of the community. Now, Benjamin held, 'in the moral domain, all representation [*Stellvertretung*] is of a mythic nature, from the patriotic "one for all" [*Einer für alle*] to the sacrificial death of the Redeemer' (ibid.). No doubt, Benjamin here targetted the Hölderlinian figure of the poet ('*Einer für alle*'), no less than the Christian figure of the saviour. Above all, his polemic was directed at Friedrich Gundolf's psycho-biographical study of Goethe[45] and Stefan George's celebration of the poet as demi-god, creator, and arche-ground (*Halbgott, Schöpfer, Urgrund*). Much as in the Hölderlin essay, hubris was uncovered to be the delusion that one could give shape to oneself, be self-productive, be one's own ground: 'But the life of a man, even that of a creative artist, is never that of the creator. It cannot be interpreted any more than the life of the hero, who gives form to himself' (*SW* 1:324). In this context, Benjamin reintroduced the Hölderlinian images of the *Genius* and *die Wahrheit der Lage*. If the poet was to live up to the classical vocation, he needed to seize the *Gelegenheit* (opportunity or occasion), a condition radically antagonistic to Dilthey's vitalistic conception of (poetic) *Erlebnis* (lived experience). Such an act of seizing opportunity meant tearing oneself loose from the mythical web through ethical decisions, *Entscheidungen*, which opened up onto the realm of truth. Again, in contrast to the novel's framing narrative, which dealt with the amorous quadrangle between Eduard and Charlotte, the Captain and Ottilie, the novella offered a 'purer promise' (*SW* 1:329), bringing light to the Hades-like twilight of the novel (*SW* 1:331) and promising the day of decision in the near-fatal leap of the marvellous children. In this new moral world, mythical silence and Ottilie's inability to take decisions had been substituted by the moral power of the word, or the voice of conscience: 'For if the moral world shows itself anywhere illuminated by the spirit of language, it is in the decision. No moral decisions can enter into life without verbal form and, strictly speaking, without thus becoming an object of communication' (*SW* 1:336).

In the third and concluding section of the essay – originally entitled 'Hope' – Benjamin returned to the figure of the caesura. Advancing extensive reflections on the nature of the beautiful and the sublime, he called upon this Hölderlinian figure to capture the interactions between these two realms. Now joined to the notion of *Entscheidung*, the caesura was laden with ethical, tragical and theological meaning. As such, it revealed how all artistic creation was essentially grounded in an ethico-theological dimension. For the caesura now announced the near-apocalyptic, violent incursion of the 'expressionless' in the realm of beauty, whose seemingly smooth surface was ruptured by the intervention of the mysterious, sublime word that defied pronunciation. Linking these observations to Hölderlin's poetics, Benjamin noted: 'The "occidental Junonian sobriety" – which Hölderlin ... conceived as the almost unattainable goal of all German artistic practice – is only another name for that caesura, in which, along with harmony, every expression simultaneously comes to a standstill, in order to give free reign to an expressionless power inside all artistic media' (*SW* 1: 341). Foundational to the metaphysics of artistic creation, the intervention of this constrictive word lent form to mere chaos. And while the interrupting pure word could not 'separate semblance from essence in art', Benjamin admitted, it 'prevented them from mingling', thus shattering the aesthetic illusion of a false, errant, absolute totality (*SW* 1: 340). Anticipating the *Trauerspiel* study's critique of aesthetic symbols, the Goethe essay already provided the outlines for Benjamin's later theory of aesthetic fragmentation: 'Only the expressionless [*das Ausdruckslose*] completes the work, by shattering it into a thing of shards, into a fragment of the true world, into the torso of a symbol' (ibid.). Finally, the Hölderlinian caesura also symbolized the epiphany to which all good textual criticism eventually should lead. Endowed with weak apocalyptic power, true criticism (*Kritik*) needed to rekindle the living flame of truth in the dead ashes of mere textual commentary (*Kommentar*).

When read against the Hölderlin essay, the figure of the caesura may at first seem merely to reiterate the main interpretive movement of that text, adding just a variation on a well-known theme. For does the caesura not, in essence, again announce the sudden, unexpected manifestation of the sober, sacred ground that holds all different strata of meaning – ethical, aesthetic, theological – in balance? Yet nothing could be more misleading than to assume that the Goethe essay merely established a syncretic cosmos, presided over by the metaphysics of absolute connections. As if to revise his youthful work, Benjamin took leave of the organic language of myth and fate, as well as of the *endon eidos* model that grounded his understanding of 'Dichtermut' and 'Blödigkeit'. But, more significant still, the interpretation as a whole led to the intervention of a wholly different disruptive element when, in the final lines of the Goethe essay, suddenly, a new conception of irony – the counter-image of the one invoked in the dissertation – made its appearance. Wrapping up his account of the tragic love between Ottilie and Eduard, Benjamin singled out a line from the novel's narrative: 'Hope shot across the sky, above their head, like a falling star' (*SW* 1: 354–5). What needed to be extrapolated from this image of the falling star, Benjamin speculated, was a 'most paradoxical, most fleeting hope', which 'finally emerges from the shining of reconciliation [*Schein der Versöhnung*]'. At a narrative level, such hope no doubt pointed to the possible reconciliation and immortality in death that awaited the tragic lovers. But in true Benjaminian style, the passage was also charged with larger aesthetic and philosophical claims. For if these final lines spoke of the dialectical *Schein der Versöhnung*, then, evidently, they also conjured up the entire dialectical apparatus of sublation and reconciliation on whose outcome these lines simultaneously cast doubt. Indeed, the term *Schein* itself was more than duplicitous in so far as it could mean either the 'illumination' or the mere 'semblance' of reconciliation (*SW* 1: 355). It appeared, then, that the negative potentiality of reflective irony now played its diabolical game in the double meaning of *Schein*. To be sure, as the Goethe essay as a whole patently showed, Benjamin still firmly believed in the divine, hallowed nature of aesthetic beauty and in the teleology of a divinely ordained history. For, as he maintained, human history in the long run amounted to a history of necessary veiling, whose cover would not be lifted to reveal its hallowed secret until the very last, until the apocalyptic end of time.

Yet, what demands attention here is that Benjamin, however haltingly, at once took leave of the harmonious, self-enclosed formalism that underpinned the intricate Hölderlin essay. Despite its seemingly closed-off structure, a fissure, a rift rippled the deceptively smooth surface of Benjamin's Goethe interpretation. Opening up onto a larger vista, the duplicitous passage about the *Schein der Versöhnung* seemed rife with a meaning whose significance Benjamin would not fathom until he turned to the Janus-faced figure of allegory in the *Trauerspiel* study. For it was there, in the historico-philosophical analysis of the sober, torso-like, allegorical structure of the artwork that Benjamin – while never truly giving up the (albeit tangential) encounter with the Absolute – decisively questioned the metaphysics of absolute connection that infused the Hölderlin essay.

10

POETRY'S COURAGE*

Philippe Lacoue-Labarthe

For Maurice Matet, since it is a question of courage.

That, after a brief period of fanatical activism in 1933–4, Heidegger's entire political preaching is to be sought in the discourse which he conducts on poetry – and on Hölderlin in particular – is not something we have invented. Heidegger says it himself.

At a transitional point in the course, *Hölderlin's Hymns 'Germania' and 'The Rhine'*, given in the winter semester of 1934–5 – the first, or very nearly the first, course he taught after his resignation from the Rectorship – one reads, as a reminder of the 'task of the course' (*die Aufgabe der Vorlesung*), the following, which is perfectly clear:

> The goal of this course remains to recreate finally in our historical Dasein a space and a place for what poetry is. That can happen only when we bring ourselves into the sphere of power [*Machtbereich*] of a true poetry and open ourselves to its effectivity. Why is Hölderlin's poetry chosen for this? This choice is no random selection from the poems available. It is a historical decision. Let us name three of its essential grounds: (1) Hölderlin is the poet of poets and of poetry; (2) From which it follows that Hölderlin is the poet of the Germans; (3) Since Hölderlin is this in a concealed and difficult way, poet of poets as poet of the Germans, he has not yet become a power in the history of our people. Since he is not yet that power, he must become so. To contribute to this is 'politics' in the highest and more proper sense, so much so that whoever effects anything here has no need to talk of the 'political'.[1]

(I note in parenthesis: you will have recognized here the 'unscrambled' transmission of the message that the Rome lecture of a couple of years later – 'Hölderlin and the Essence of Poetry' – will go to great lengths to encode, at once very skilfully and very crudely, notably through the suppression of the signifier 'the Germans'. It is as though, far from home yet still on 'allied' soil, Heidegger had

* Translated by Simon Sparks.

obscurely prepared his future reception, his French reception in particular. And you will not be unaware of the consequences, including those for French poetry, that Henry Corbin's translation of this lecture has had since 1938.[2] But that is another question.)

That such a claim for a ' "politics" in the highest and most proper sense' (the word *politics*, we should note, is, even here, always in quotation marks), takes, beyond its manifest 'nationalism', the exact form of the theological–political, is something Heidegger of course never mentioned – he would have challenged it most firmly. No one, with very few exceptions, has really noticed this. Yet it is no less clear.

I will take only one example, the one offered most immediately. It comes from the 'Preliminary Remark' to the same course – perhaps (largely) written after the fact, though this is neither entirely certain nor of any great interest – soberly entitled: 'Hölderlin'. I quote:

> He must still stay long hidden, particularly now when 'interest' in him is beginning to stir and 'literary history' is in search of new 'theme'. One writes now on 'Hölderlin and his gods'. That is the most extreme misinterpretation, through which all possibility of action is forbidden to this poet, who still comes from the future of the Germans, under the pretext of finally doing him 'justice'. As if his work needed justice, especially from the poor judges who are today in circulation. One handles Hölderlin 'historically' and fails to recognize this one essential thing, that his work, which is still without time and space, has already overcome [*überwunden*] our historicizing activity and founded [*gegründet*] the commencement of another history, the history which begins with the struggle [*Kampf*] where the fleeing or the coming of the god will be decided.[3]

(Allow me a second parenthetical remark here. Whenever this note may have been written – it sanctions, in any event, in a highly charged vocabulary, the careful and deliberate publication of a course from 1934 with which it is in perfect harmony – one thing is clear: up until the testamentary interview granted in 1966 to the editors of *Der Spiegel*, Heidegger will change practically nothing of the discourse which he will have started to conduct from the moment of his 'withdrawal' from National Socialism. For the record, I recall the declaration of 1966: 'Only a god can save us now. The only possibility that remains for us is to prepare, through thinking and poetry, a readiness for the appearance of the god or for the absence of the god in our decline; in the face of the absent god, we founder.'[4] Let us pass over the very dated pathos of the decline; or, if you prefer, the haunting fear of nihilism. All the same, in a proposition of this sort the theological–political – as one can call it without exaggeration – finds itself confirmed. The theological–political is particularly tenacious in Heidegger, and we must understand that if 'real National Socialism' was, in his eyes, nothing but 'politics', this was because it lacked not only an authentic sense of the *polis* (thought as the *Da* of *Sein*), but also a theology, and that is to say, as we have already seen, a notion of the essence of art and of the unique opportunity to have 'grounded the beginning of an other history'.)

I will not enter here into a consideration of the complex and cunning relations that Heidegger maintains with theology, a word which he never challenges. I take *theology* in its simplest sense: discourse on the divine. In order that things be totally clear, I will cite the passage that is probably the most explicit in this regard, the one where, in the 'Letter on "Humanism"' (1946), seeking to define an 'ethics' before the ethical, that is to say, an 'ethics' which responds or corresponds to what is no longer even called 'ontology' – for this occasion, lacking anything better, I will call it an arche-ethics – Heidegger draws on the Hölderlinian motifs of the homeland (*die Heimat*) or of 'German' (*das Deutsche*). Here is the passage – and do not forget that, at that time, this discourse also counts as a clearing of his name:

> 'German' is not spoken to the world in order that the world might be recuperated through the German essence, but is spoken to the Germans in order that, from out of the destiny that links them to other peoples, they might become world-historical along with them ... The homeland of this historical dwelling is the proximity to being.
>
> In such proximity, if at all, it must be decided whether and how the god and the gods refuse themselves and the night remains, whether and how the holy day dawns, whether and how in this emergence of the holy an appearance of the god and the gods can begin anew. But the holy, which alone is the essential space of divinity, which in turn alone grants the dimension for the god and the gods, comes to appearance only when Being itself, beforehand and after long preparation, has shown itself and has been experienced in its truth. Only thus does the overcoming [*Überwindung*] of homelessness begin from being, in which not only men but the very essence of man lose their way.[5]

In 1934 Heidegger spoke to his students of the task of his teaching. There was an injunction in that. Such a task was already none other than the 'task of thinking' in so far as, at the 'end of philosophy', it chimes with the task it takes to have been that of poetry – Hölderlin's task: to prepare for the coming of (or announce the turning away from) god and the gods. We are face to face with a nihilism even more radical than that expressed in Nietzsche's 'God is dead', which supported – this needs to be borne in mind – the entire engagement of the Rectoral Address. The task of thinking, the task of poetry: this sort of arche-ethics would have ruled Heidegger's theological–political preaching.

If this basic hypothesis is right, I would like, in consequence, to put forward a few propositions – in the rather terse form of a simple reminder. There are five of them:

1. The theological–political is supported, quite obviously, by a theologico-poetics (once again, lacking anything better, I risk this phrase). Hölderlin's 'preaching' authorizes Heidegger's own 'political' preaching of the 1930s (and

beyond), but only on the condition that we understand: that, on the one hand, this entire 'preaching' (i.e. Hölderlin's – and I doubt that, in the end, it was one) thus has no authority since it both lacks authority and is authorized by nothing and no one (it is not a god who, as in the *incipit* of ancient poetry, dictates the poem; rather, it is the 'failure of the god' that 'helps' the poem, that, at the limit of the possible, renders it possible); and that, on the other hand, this authority is an authority only because it is, at the same time, the madness (the protective night of the gods) which has sanctioned the impossible possibility of the poem, a poem which has still not been heard (which is why, moreover, the Germans remain indebted to Hölderlin).

The ancient theological–political, as is confirmed by the *Introduction to Metaphysics* (1935), stems from Homer, under the orders of the Muse, giving 'Greece its gods'.[6] The modern theological–political suspends the poem of the annunciation – the gospel – of the coming or withdrawal of the god.

2. In the expression 'theological–political', the political is what concerns the national, or, in Hölderlin's more precise locution, the '*nationell*'.[7] It is, in other words, what concerns the people. Although in the 'Letter on "Humanism"' Heidegger credits Marx with having experienced the essential homelessness of modern man through the concept of alienation (this insight needs to be born in mind: Marx is not so far removed from Hölderlin: the organized delocation of the masses by 'industry' is a fact, and it is a matter, in both Marx and Hölderlin, of an *alienation*), he challenges – and will always have challenged – internationalism, like nationalism, as a figure of unreserved subjecthood. By which one should understand their doctrines and, *a fortiori*, their ideologies. Just before the passage from the 'Letter on "Humanism"' which I recalled a moment ago – and after having remarked that Nietzsche, who had himself experienced this homelessness, 'was unable to find any other way out' of it because he remained prisoner to the 'reversal of metaphysics' – Heidegger says:

> When, however, Hölderlin composes 'Homecoming', he is concerned that his 'countrymen' access their essence within it. He in no way seeks this essence in an egoism of his people. He sees it, rather, in terms of belonging to the destiny of the West. But even the West is not thought regionally as the Occident in contrast to the Orient, nor merely as Europe, but as world-historical [*weltgeschichtlich*] from out of nearness to the origin.[8]

Be that as it may, during the 1930s this problematic of *Heimatlosigkeit* (of 'uprootedness', as it was willingly called in the international of the conservative revolution) forced one to substitute for the Kantian question (in an indissociably *Aufklärer* and metaphysical style) 'What is man?' the question 'Who is man?', a question which invariably finds its truth in the question: 'Who are we?', which means, no less invariably, 'Who are we, we Germans?'. One possible response is, for example: 'The philosophical people *par excellence*' or the 'people of thinkers and of poets'.[9]

3. The theological–political is, in turn, supported by an appeal or a call to myth. I have already tried to show this elsewhere, and so I will not insist upon it here.[10] This remark holds for the entire great (German) metaphysical tradition since its Romantic inception, with the Schlegels certainly, but above all with Schelling – a friend of Hölderlin, as we know. Heidegger's apprehension of poetry is overdetermined by speculative Romanticism. Which is why, more-over, poetry (*Dichtung*) is defined in its essence as language, *die Sprache* – or, what amounts to the same thing, language is defined as the original poetry (*Urdichtung*) of a people – and why it is in turn defined in its essence as *die Sage*: *ho muthos* [myth]. Not like *Heldensaga*, heroic legend, as Heidegger will say in the 1950s, but like the *muthein* [to speak/narrate], which, in its indistinct difference from *legein* (the gathering, as language, of the 'there is'), is alone capable of pronouncing divine places and names. In any case, *Dichtung*, like *logos* in its Aristotelian–phenomenological definition, is apophantic: *dichten*, by way of the high-German *thîton* and the Latin *dictare*, is *deiknumi*: to show, to designate, to make appear. Every sign (*Zeichen*) is a showing (*Zeigen*), which is to say, a naming (*Nennen*), on whose basis alone there is being. These corre-lations are well known. That Heidegger could, with regard to language, refer to von Humboldt is not unimportant.[11]

4. Politics, in the sense in which Heidegger understood it without ever wanting to hear it spoken of (always those quotation marks . . .), was nonetheless organically linked in the 1930s to National Socialism, to fascism, with all the compromises that one knows or can easily imagine. Despite his denials, his half-confessions, or his lies, Heidegger was never really able to defend against this. If one can thus speak of a *politics* of Heidegger during these years – and I main-tain that there is one, inscribed, explicitly or not, well beyond the 'ordinary' compromise, in the texts themselves – then I would willingly say that this politics stems from what I will call (once more for lack of anything better) an arche-fascism. Such an arche-fascism has nothing to do with the hyper-fascism with which Breton, around 1934, prided himself on having reproached Bataille. On the other hand, it has everything to do with the terrible sentence, all the more authoritatively pronounced for its timidity, passed by Benjamin when, at a meet-ing of the College of Sociology where Bataille was speaking about the sacred, he whispered in Klossowski's ear: 'In the end, you are working for the fascists.'[12] The logic of the *arche*, as Benjamin was well aware, is absolutely formidable. And in this context it is clear that, in reality, Heidegger's discourse against 'real fascism' had no other ambition than to set free the *truth* of fascism.

5. Bound up, under these conditions, with the theological–poetical, the theological–political assigns to poetry a mission, in the most banal sense that this word has taken on since the Romantics. This mission is, as we have seen, a *struggle*. Now, if such a struggle is, in Heidegger's eyes, an absolute necessity, it is because there is danger. When, in the Rome lecture of 1936, he condenses his 1934 course to the thread of five *Leitmotive* lifted from the Hölderlinian corpus, Heidegger retains a prose fragment, opposed to the declaration regarding the 'innocence' of poetry, in which language (*die Sprache*) is said to be 'the most

dangerous of all goods' ('*der Güter Gefährlichstes*' [*SA* 2.1: 147]). He proposes this commentary, which, for its part, needs no commentary:

> But in what way is language the 'most dangerous of all goods'? It is the danger of all dangers because language initially creates the possibility of a danger. Danger is a threat to Being by beings. But it is first by virtue of language as such that man is exposed to the manifest, which, as beings, attacks and bombards him in his Dasein, and, as non-beings, betrays and disappoints him in his Dasein. Language first creates the manifest realm of the threat and the errancy of being, and thus the possibility of the loss of Being, that is – danger.[13]

And a few lines further on he adds, still with respect to language:

> In language the most pure and the most concealed, as well as the confused and the common, can come to be expressed [*kann ... zu Wort kommen*]. Indeed, the essential word [*das wesentliche Wort*], which has to be understood and so become common property of all, must make itself common. Accordingly, in another fragment Hölderlin writes: 'You spoke to the divinity, but you have all forgotten that the first-born are never for mortals, that they belong to the gods. More common, more everyday must the fruit become; then it becomes the possession of mortals.'[14]

Heidegger glosses this as follows: 'The pure and the common both form in the same way a said.'[15] *Ein Gesagtes, eine Sage*: a myth.

One can easily deduce at least three things from this text. First, in the face of danger itself, danger in its essence (a threat that weighs on Being), an arche-ethical quality is assumed and required of poetry: namely, courage. This is, moreover, probably the only arche-ethical quality that one can detect in the Heideggerian discourse of the 1930s. What I here try to call the arche-ethical consists purely and simply in the experience of courage. Since, second, every 'ontological' danger is also and necessarily a historial danger – and the historial is, if you like, the political without quotation marks – a responsibility is given to poetry, as to the thought which responds to it. One could call this responsibility transcendental in so far as upon it alone depends the possibility of a people's history. (This, one could show, in a certain way amounts to saying that courage lies in the decision.) The entire question in the commentary on Hölderlin is one of knowing whether or not the Germans are capable of entering into history and of opening a history, of becoming Germans, just as the Greeks, with the unprecedented courage to which tragedy attests, became Greeks. Finally, the obvious consequence of this is that the poet is defined as a *hero*, in the sense given to this word in Section 74 of *Being and Time*, where Heidegger says that historial Dasein (the people) must choose its heroes in the tradition. In direct lineage from the Nietzschean interpretation of history and from ancient agonistics, the poet is more than a model, an example. Or, according to the terminology of the moderns, as present in Heidegger as in Nietzsche, he is a figure: a *Gestalt*. Heidegger, who will violently refuse any figure stemming from Nietzschean-ism – from Zarathustra to Rilke's Angel and even, certainly much more belatedly, to Jünger's Worker – will nonetheless accept, and more than accept, the figure of the hero of poetry, of the demigod, the mediator or intercessor between the gods and men, immortals and mortals: the one who, says Hölderlin (or at least a certain Hölderlin), seizes the signs of the divine at the pinnacle of danger – under the immediate threat of being struck by lightning – in order to transmit them to the people in a veiled form. (The second part of the course of 1934, devoted to the hymn 'Germanien', develops this motif at length. But it runs throughout Heidegger.)

I resigned myself to this reminder only to introduce my real topic for this paper. Here, then, is its outline, and it goes without saying that it is only an outline. As you will see in a moment, a much fuller analysis would be necessary in order to do justice to the question I would like to raise.

It so happens that exactly twenty years before the beginning of Heidegger's commentary, Hölderlin and, in Hölderlin, the same motif of courage, were the occasion for an opposite, so to speak, interpretative gesture. But one not entirely opposite, which is, I believe, of tremendous consequence.

I allude here to Benjamin's famous essay, written in the winter of 1914–15, entitled 'Two Poems by Friedrich Hölderlin'.[16] As you know, this text remained unpublished until 1955, when Adorno and Scholem issued the first collection of Benjamin's scattered essays. Obviously, Heidegger could not have known it. Yet my intention is not to 'compare' the two interpretations. That would be of only very limited interest. In turning to this text, it is much more a matter of taking the measure of an epoch (from which we are far from being free) and of the philosophical questioning which underpins it: our politics, and not only our politics, still depend on it.

The text, to which a brief introduction is needed here, is a study of two versions of a single poem – which is, in reality, made up of three versions, though Benjamin deliberately neglects the intermediary one – the second (and last) of which, most certainly dating from after his trip to France, attests to the work of 'rewriting' – or rather *internal translation* – to which Hölderlin relent-lessly devoted his so-called 'final years'. The first version, you will not be surprised to learn, carries the title 'Dichtermut', 'The Poet's Courage', according to the old meaning of *Mut* in German. The second version is entitled 'Blödigkeit', a diffi-cult word which is usually translated as 'timidity' or 'awkwardness'.[17] The motif of the poem is the same in both versions. It is the motif of the vocation or the mission of the poet, a vocation or mission which requires – let us hang onto the word – the arche-ethical quality of courage. We are already on the same ground upon which Heidegger will situate himself.

It is not uninteresting to note, moreover, that Benjamin's essay responds to what he too defines as a task: *eine Aufgabe*. The task, this time, is not that of a teaching. Rather, it is that of critique, or of what Benjamin a little pompously calls 'the aesthetics of poetic art'.[18] And this task is organized by the search in the poem for what Benjamin names with a word that Heidegger will systematically employ: *das Gedichtete* – a word which neither invent (it is attested in Goethe) and which, as a concept, signals in both Heidegger and Benjamin toward the essence (or the Idea) of poetry. (The word is supposed to be untranslatable because *dichten* is untranslatable. Working on a suggestion by Beda Allemann, Maurice de Gandillac bases his French translation on the Latin etymon *dictare* and suggests 'dictamen', in what he calls the 'old' sense [though Rousseau and several others still take the term in this way] of 'that which dictates conscience'. An ethical sense, then. Faced with this difficulty, most of Heidegger's English translators elect 'poetized'. That is perfectly acceptable, but 'hesitation' reveals all the more forcefully, if we can hold these two suggestions together, the connection that unites the problematic of poetry and that of ethics.)[19]

The question – the question which dictates, if I can put it like this, the task of critique – is thus the following: how are we to gain *access* to the *Gedichtete*, dictamen, or poetized? This is a question of method, as Benjamin will not cease to say, Benjamin, who will never trouble to distinguish himself from the vocabulary of philosophy, just as Heidegger will obstinately make use of it, first of all against all post-Cartesian metaphysics, at least up to Hegel, by reducing *methodos* to *odos*: *Weg, Wegmarken, Holzwege, Unterwegs zur Sprache*, etc. Despite the similarity of the 'approaches' in many regards, the problematic of access (which is a sort of breaking in) is not that of wayfaring. Benjamin speaks neither in terms of essence nor even – although he will do so a bit later – of origin. The language he uses is the Kantian or post-Kantian one of the a priori. The principal reference which underpins his long 'methodological' introduction is a fragment from Novalis saying: 'Every work of art has in itself an a priori ideal, a necessity for being.'[20] If there is an aesthetics here (an 'aesthetics of poetic art'), it is, in a somewhat unexpected sense, transcendental. The dictamen, which is above all not the cause of the poem or that which would allow it to be 'interpreted', and which in itself is in no way 'poetic' (no more so than is the essence of *Dichtung* in Heidegger), is purely and simply the *condition of possibility* of the poem. Its prerequisite, says Benjamin.

In order to establish this, Benjamin founds his argument on two concepts.

First, the concept, borrowed from Goethe, of 'inner form' (*innere Form*) or 'content' (*Gehalt*) – a word to which, as one knows, Benjamin will remain faithful throughout his critical enterprise, as is evidenced, for example, by the opposition between *Sachgehalt* [material content] and *Wahrheitsghalt* [truth content] in the great essay on the *Elective Affinities*, a much later jewel.[21] Here is how he introduces this concept, and one will see once more that it is again, and not by chance, a question of task:

> The inner form, what Goethe described as content, will be shown in these poems. The poetic task, as the prerequisite of an assessment of the poem, is to be ascertained. The assessment cannot follow how the poet has solved his task; rather, the seriousness and greatness of the task determine the

assessment, for the task is derived from the poem. It is to be understood as the prerequisite of the poem, as the spiritual–intuitive structure of the world to which the poem testifies. This task, this prerequisite, will here be understood as the ultimate ground open to analysis. Nothing will be ascertained about the process of lyric production, nothing about the person or world-view of the creator, but about the particular and unique sphere in which the task and the prerequisite of the poem lie.[22]

The poem's prerequisite (its condition of possibility) is thus the task, singular each time, of the poem – that is to say, for it amounts to the same thing, that to which the poem, each time, testifies. One will see in a moment that such a testimony is always a testimony to truth or, to the extent that it is singular and always singular, the attestation of a truth. Exactly twenty years later, Heidegger will also speak of testimony: in the Rome lecture which comes out of the winter semester course – I will stay with this single example – he will note that, when Hölderlin speaks of language as the 'most dangerous of all goods' (one which consequently threatens truth itself), he also defines it as the gift made to man in order that he can 'testify [*zeugen*] to what he is' (*SA* 2.1: 147). It is here of little moment that Heidegger modifies the proposition and moves from *what* (*was*) man is to *who* (*wer*) he is, according to the political–ontological aim with which we are familiar. What *is* essential is that, in Heidegger as in Benjamin, whatever the difference in their interpretation of truth, poetry is defined as 'telling truth' or as 'speaking in the name of truth'. If you like, poetry is the *martyr* of truth. (No doubt this is why – but I will come back to this – as soon as poetry is thus understood, the destiny of poets actually becomes, through a sort of metonymic sliding, that of martyrs.)

Task, testimony: in their unity (the task *is* testimony) these two thus constitute the poem's prerequisite, or its a priori, what one might call its 'authorization' (an authorization very much prior to the authority of the poet, and doubly so in so far as, authorizing the poem, it makes the poet possible). Nonetheless, before access to the complete definition of *dictamen* can be entirely cleared, a second concept is missing. This concept – we have already heard the word in passing – is 'figure' (*Gestalt*), which brings with it, in an absolutely necessary way, the concept of 'myth'. Here is how Benjamin introduces it: challenging all examination of the creative process and the creating subject, he devotes critique to the sole consideration of 'the particular and unique sphere in which the task and the prerequisite of the poem lie'; and he adds:

This sphere is at once the product [*Erzeugnis*] and object of the investigation. It can itself no longer be compared with the poem, but is the sole thing in the analysis that can be established. This sphere, which for every poetry has a special configuration, is described as the dictamen. In this sphere the characteristic realm containing the truth of the poem will be developed. This 'truth' which the most serious artists so insistently claim for their creations, will be understood as the objectivity of their production, as the fulfilment of the artistic task in each case ... In its general form, the dictamen is the synthetic unity of the spiritual and intuitive orders. This unity gains its particular figure as the inner form of the particular creation.[23]

The dictamen is thus *Gestalt*, figure (I stick to this translation for reasons of economy). More precisely, for each poem the figure is the mode of the presentation *and* articulation of its inner form or its content. But why is it a matter of a figure? Why this word – and this concept – of *Gestalt*?

There are, it seems to me, two reasons for this.

The first is the one just advanced by Benjamin: in general, he says, the dictamen is the 'synthetic unity of the spiritual and intuitive orders'. This vocabulary is clearly derived from Kant's, along the lines of the derivations carried out by Jena Romanticism ('spirit' for 'understanding', for example). Understood correctly, this proposition simply amounts to saying that the dictamen is the *transcendental schema* of the poem. The *Dichten*, the 'poetizing', is referred to the transcendental imagination, that 'art concealed in the depths of the human soul'.[24] Or else, and this is a category I willingly use in recalling the opening Heidegger attempts to draw between *Kant and the Problem of Metaphysics* and the lecture series 'The Origin of the Work of Art', to an originary *techne* which founds a world because it is the archaic or principial configuration (*Gestaltung*) of the world. In Benjamin's language: the dictamen is a 'limit-concept', a limit between the poem itself and that to which it testifies, that to which it attests in its truth ('life', says Benjamin), being the condition of both, of one *as* the other. It guarantees the 'transition' between two 'functional unities', that of the poem (prior to the distinction between form and matter) and that of life (prior to the distinction between task and solution). It is simplest here to quote:

> Through this relation to the intuitive and spiritual functional unity of the poem, the dictamen shows itself as a limit determination as regards the poem. At the same time, it is but a limit concept as regards another functional unity, since a limit concept is not possible except as the limit between two concepts. The other functional unity is now the idea of the task, corresponding to the idea of the solution which the poem is. (Task and solution are separable only *in abstracto*.) For the creator, this idea of the task is always life. In it lies the other extreme functional unity. The dictamen thus turns out to be the transition from the functional unity of life to that of the poem. In it, life determines itself through the poem, the task through the solution. The ground lies not in the individual life mood of the artist, but in a life correlation determined by art.[25]

The dictamen, as *Gestalt*, is a figure of existence. Or, what amounts to the same thing, life (existence) – in so far as the task of the poem is to testify to it – is itself, in its truth, poetic. A poem can say, in truth, that we live (exist) in truth. Which is to say poetically. ('Full of worth, but poetically, man dwells on this earth'; 'Voll Verdienst, doch dichterisch, wohnet der Mensch auf dieser Erde' [*SA* 2.1: 372]), says Hölderlin in a line upon which Heidegger will later comment at length.)[26] Poetry is our destiny. Our dictamen, in fact.

Whence the second reason, I think, that Benjamin advances in order to justify the word – the concept – of *Gestalt* (a highly 'charged' word – concept – at the time he uses it, from a philosophical point of view [less Hegelianism than Nietzscheanism] as well as from a political one: it will be one of the key words of the 'conservative revolution' then beginning to dawn). Benjamin remains cautious. He is speaking, he says, only in 'general' terms.[27] Be that as it may: *Gestalt* refers to myth; or, if you prefer, every figure (but we could just as much say every model, or every example) is potentially mythic, not in an abstract or remote sense of myth, but in the sense that life (existence) itself is – I borrow the formulation of 1936 from Thomas Mann – 'life in myth', which is to say, 'quotation'.[28] Here is what Benjamin says:

> The categories in which this sphere, the transitional sphere of both functional unities, is ascertainable are not yet preformed [*vorgebildet*], and perhaps their closest correlation is to the concept of myth. Precisely the weakest results of art refer to themselves through the immediate feeling of life, whereas the strongest, with respect to their truth, do so through a sphere akin to the mythic: the dictamen. Life is in general the dictamen of poems [*das Gedichtete der Gedichte*].[29]

The mythic, thus understood, is above all not the mythological, that is to say the stereotyped organization (or correlation) of mythemes, the weakening of their reciprocal tensions. The mythic – which *is* the dictamen or which the dictamen *is* – is existence itself in its configuration or its figurability. Which is why a poem is ultimately a gesture of existence – a gesture with a view to existence. The poem, let us respect Benjamin's vocabulary, is a figure of life. Which amounts to saying that life is poetic. Essentially. Not because it is 'poetizable' (this would be mystification *par excellence*: mythology), but because the dictamen of poems, which is never this or that particular poem from which, nonetheless, it is indissociable, *dictates* life.

Here, the dictamen is *courage*. This is perhaps the dictamen of every dictation, the poetized of every poem. Of literature in general. Benjamin, in any case, thought that:

> The law according to which all apparent elements of sensibility and of Ideas show themselves as the epitomes of essential, in principle infinite functions, will be called the law of identity. It describes the synthetic unity of functions. In each of its particular figures it is recognized as an a priori of the poem . . . Until the applicability of this method to the aesthetics of the lyric as such, and perhaps of further realms, has been examined, additional exposition has to be ruled out. Only once this has taken place can the a priori of the individual poem, or that of the poem in general, or even that of other poetic types or of poetry in general, clearly come to light.[30]

Here, then, the dictamen is – let us for the moment hang onto this cautious localization – courage: 'The Poet's Courage'.

It is not my intention to reconstitute Benjamin's demonstration. I will simply and somewhat dryly give its principle. This principle is relatively simple, while the demonstration is, on the contrary, very complex.

From the outset, remarks Benjamin, 'The Poet's Courage' is a mythological *topos*. And it is treated as such by Hölderlin in the first version of the poem. It is the *topos* of the properly heroic poet, the intercessor or mediator between the gods and men (other more or less contemporaneous poems speak of the poet as a demigod, precisely the motif which will hold Heidegger's attention), who consequently braves the greatest risks in order to complete his task or mission. In Benjamin's judgement, since critique is a matter of judgement, the simple repetition of the *topos* alone explains the weakness of the first version of the poem: neither does the relation of man to the divine (or of the poet to the god that he invokes as his model) escape convention, nor is the essence of fate (that is to say, the inscription of death in existence) truly grasped. The poem is powerless to give figure to a world:

> Hölderlin's object in the first version of his poem is a fate: the death of the poet. He sings the praises of the sources of the courage to die this death. This death is the centre from which the world of poetic dying must arise. Existence in this world would be the courage of the poet. But here only the most vigilant suspicion can feel a glimmer of this structure of laws from a world of the poet. Timidly at first the voice rises to sing a cosmos, whose own decline is signified by the death of the poet. But the myth is formed out of mythology. The sun god is the ancestor of the poet, and his death is the fate through which the death of the poet, at first only mirrored, becomes real ... The poem lives in the Greek world, animated by a beauty in line with the Greek and governed by the mythology of the Greeks. The particular principle of Greek figuration is not, however, fully unfolded.

> *Denn, seitdem der Gesang sterblichen Lippen sich*
> *Friedenatmend entwand, frommend in Leid und Glück*
> *Unsre Weise der Menschen*
> *Herz erfreute ...*

> For ever since the song from mortal lips escaped
> Breathing peace, availed of sorrow and happiness,
> Our melody has filled with joy
> The hearts of men ...

These words only feebly contain the reverence that filled Pindar – and the late Hölderlin with him – before the figure of the poetic. Nor, considered thus, do the 'bards of the people', 'pleasing to all', serve to lay an intuitive world ground for this poem. The figure of the dying sun god testifies most clearly to an uncontrolled quality in all its elements. Idyllic nature still plays its particular role against the figure of the god. Beauty, in other words, has not yet become a completed figure.[31]

In the second version, on the other hand, the mythologeme of the setting sun, of the decline, of the twilight, etc., is abandoned. And with it, that of the hero mediator and the bards of the people. Benjamin's intuition here is that, by undoing the mythological, the second version paradoxically reinforces the mythical through which it seeks, as we have seen, to think the dictamen. The dictamen appears in its truth – the essence of courage attained – only with the collapse of the mythological, only at the precise point of its failure. Here, Benjamin speaks of the 'deposition [*Umsetzung*] of the mythological'.[32] Much later, still concerning Hölderlin and now directed against the Heideggerian commentary, Adorno will speak of 'demythologization'.[33] Obviously, such a failure of the mythological does not happen without a certain failure of the theological. In any case, not without a certain dissociation of the theological–political. I will come back to this.

The deposition of the mythological is a deliberate gesture: it moves toward a conquest of objectivity and of the concrete – that is to say, technically, if you like, toward a sort of literalization, toward a prosaicness, toward a phrasing which would conceal itself from the phrasing of eloquence and of antique *pathos*. Toward the abandonment of the stereotypes of sacralization. Let me give a single example, that of the revision of the first two lines – upon which, moreover, Benjamin is relatively uninsistent. The first version says:

Sind denn dir nicht verwandt alle Lebendigen?
Nährt zum Dienste denn nicht selber die Parze dich?
(*SA* 2.1:62)

Are not all the living akin to you?
Does not the Parca herself nourish you to serve her ends?

This is indeed the traditional *topos* of death: the Parca, absolute servitude before death, the community of all mortals ('all the living'). In the second version, however, one reads, in an unchanged rhythm:

Sind denn dir nicht bekannt viele Lebendigen?
Geht auf Wahrem dein Fuss nicht, wie auf Teppichen?
(*SA* 2.1:66)

Are not many of the living known to you?
Does not your foot stride upon the true, as upon carpets?

'Many of the living' is substituted for 'all the living', 'known' for 'akin': this is a first step toward objectification, an initial renunciation of the abstraction of 'mortals', an initial determination of the 'living' (those who are 'known').

Which immediately leads, in the second line, to the simultaneous abandonment of the nominal reference to the Parca and to the literalization of the mythologeme: from the threads of the 'many' fates is woven something like a carpet of the dead, which is the truth of being mortal. Or of death not in its truth, but as truth itself. And it is because the second version attains this truth that the dictamen of courage can suddenly appear in all its force. At the end of his demonstration, Benjamin has no difficulty stating this new determination of courage – the most accurate there is, so long as we undertake to read Hölderlin through to the end:

> The dictamen of the first version knows courage only really as a quality. Man and death stand opposed, both motionless, having no intuitable world in common. Certainly, the discovery of a deep relation to death in the poet, in his divine–natural existence, had already been attempted, but only indirectly through the mediation of the god to whom death mythologically belonged and to whom the poet – again mythologically – drew closer ... The duality of man and death can only be based on a casual feeling of life. This duality ceases to exist as soon as the dictamen pulls itself into a more profound connection and shapes [*gestaltet*] for itself a spiritual principle – courage – from life. Courage is self-abandon to the danger that threatens the world. In it lies concealed a particular paradox, which for the first time allows the structure of the dictamen of both versions to be fully understood: danger exists for the courageous, and yet he does not respect it. He would be cowardly if he respected it, and if it did not exist for him he would not be courageous. This odd relation is resolved in that it is not the courageous himself who is threatened by danger, but the world. Courage is the life feeling of the man who abandons himself to danger, so that in his death he broadens it into a danger for the world and at the same time overcomes it.[34]

And a bit further on:

> The world of the dead hero is a new mythic one, steeped in danger: this is the world of the second version of the poem. In it a spiritual principle has become thoroughly sovereign: the becoming-one of the heroic poet with the world. The poet has no need to fear death; he is a hero because he lives in the centre of all relations. The principle of the dictamen as such is the supreme sovereignty of relation.[35]

The spiritual principle (the word is repeated twice), the sovereignty of relation: the dictamen of courage attests to the congruence – or the 'fit': 'But we ourselves / Bring fitting hands' ('*Doch selber / Bringen schickliche Hände wir*'), reads the end of the second version (*SA* 2.1: 66) – between (poetic) heroism and the danger of the world. This is the point where the mythological, even the theological, fails, if both consist in the separation of 'elements' and the refusal of 'relation'. Commenting *in fine* on the third stanza of the last version in order to note the 'sublation of the order of mortals and the heavenly ones',[36] Benjamin insists:

> It is to be supposed that the words 'a lonely deer' describes man, and this accords very well with the title of this poem. 'Timidity' has now become the authentic stance of the poet. Transposed into the centre of life, nothing remains for him but the motionless existence, the complete passivity that is the essence of the courageous; nothing but to give himself over entirely to relation.[37]

As to the failing of the mythological (of the theological): I think one could speak even more precisely of a 'deconstruction' in the sense that Heidegger had begun to give this term, though he – unlike Benjamin, who did not have the concept at his disposal – failed to see the extent to which it is at work in Hölderlin's last poems. That is to say, the extent to which it unworks them. In no uncertain manner, Benjamin finds the reason for this 'deconstruction' in the principle of *sobriety* as it is developed by Hölderlin in the 'Remarks' which accompany the translations of Sophocles, namely, as the guiding principle of modern poetry. As that which dictates, if you like, the task proper to it. At the end of his essay, he writes this, whose political – and more than political – import you will appreciate:

> In the course of this investigation, the word *sobriety*, which might often have served as a characteristic, has deliberately been avoided. Only now must Hölderlin's phrase 'sacredly sober' be named, its understanding having now been determined. It has been remarked that these words contain the tendency of his later creations. They arise from the inner certainty with which these creations stand in his own spiritual life, in which sobriety is now allowed, is commanded, because it is sacred in itself, standing beyond all elevation to the sublime. Is this life still that of the Greek? This is no more the case than that the life of any pure work of art as such could be that of a people, no more too than what we find in the dictamen could be the life of an individual and nothing else.[38]

And in order that things be entirely clear, I will cite this – the very last passage:

> The contemplation of the dictamen, however, leads not to myth but – in the greatest creations – only to mythic attachments, which in the work of art are formed into a unique unmythological and unmythic figure that cannot be better conceived by us.
>
> If there was a word with which to grasp the relation between that inner life, from which the later version of the poem arose, and myth, it would be Hölderlin's, from a period even later than that of this poem, 'The legends which grow distant from the earth ... / Return to mankind.'[39]

Put differently, there is no way of hanging anything theological–political on this failing theological–poetical. The poem or the hymn has no historial mission. Sobriety, we know, is what Benjamin, a few years later in his thesis on Jena Romanticism, will identify with prose. He will say, in speculative terms borrowed from Fichte: 'The Idea of poetry is prose.'[40] And for this very reason he will make Hölderlin the secret – decentred – centre of Romanticism. One could thus risk saying, somewhat tersely: sobriety is the courage of poetry. Or else: the courage of poetry is prose. Which does not, of course, exclude versification.

Poetry's courage: this can be understood or accentuated in two different ways.

Either it is a matter of a subjective genitive: in which case courage is the courage of poetry for itself, the courage of poetry for poetry (let us call this its stubbornness), and, in the discovery of the poetized or of the dictamen, it is a matter of something like the arche-ethical of poetizing as such. The poem is the arche-ethical act. We are here on the level of what the Romantics called 'reflection', and even, up to a certain point, on the – Heideggerian – level of the 'poetry of poetry'. The regime is that of a pure intransitiveness. According to Benjamin's reading, poetry's courage means: the courage to leave the mythological, to break with it and to deconstruct it. It is the courage to invent poetry, to configure the poem as the testimony which it is. Thus the destiny of poetry, after what Jean-Christophe Bailly has called the 'end of the Hymn',[41] would in fact be prose as the 'true-saying' of the poem about the poem.

Or else it is a matter of an objective genitive: courage is the courage poetry must have in its transitive (prophetic or angelic) function, through which it would confront a danger of the world and announce a task to be completed. The ethical act would then be less the poem itself than what the poem dictates as task. And perhaps one would no longer be on the level of the arche-ethical if, unlike the ethical, the arche-ethical is an ethics that does not know what the good is (I propose this distinction in the wake of Lacan's discourse in *The Ethics of Psychoanalysis*,[42] but also in the wake of that conducted by Heidegger in the 'Letter on "Humanism"'). Or if, one could put it thus, the obligation of the arche-ethical – perhaps impossible to meet, but that is its incommensurable responsibility – is to tear itself away from the (mimetic) ethics of the example, the most ancient and ruinous ethics we know: namely, the cult of the hero, the metonymic sliding from the *martyrdom* of poetry to the poet as *martyr*. Recall: (1) Hölderlin is the poet of the poet and of poetry; (2) Hölderlin is the poet of the poet in so far as he is the poet of the Germans. From one proposition to the other, 'the poet of poetry' has been forgotten. A whole politics is decided there.

One must not jump to the conclusion that this difference in inflection or accentuation traces the dividing line between Benjamin and Heidegger, even if, on the ideological and political (which is also to say philosophical) register things could not be more clear nor the difference more cut-and-dried. In reality, in both Benjamin and Heidegger – although assuredly not in the same way – intransitiveness and transitiveness ceaselessly trespass upon one another. It is a matter, each time, of that to which poetry testifies in attesting as such, that is to say, in attesting in its relation to the true, in its *telling truth*. Is this the – modern – vocation of martyrdom? Courage itself? Yes, but only according to its failure. Yes, on the condition that we finally accept what is being testified to, the 'lack of God', as Hölderlin put it, or – what amounts to the same thing – our *a-theistic* condition.

Let this be understood as homage to Benjamin. The most humble and grateful possible.

Whenever philosophy addresses itself to poetry, it takes on a responsibility – and, moreover it demands that it do so: it responds, it says, to the responsibility with which poetry believes itself to be authorized.

Heidegger, a notable example, responds to Hölderlin in order to respond from him. It is a matter, he thinks, of courage as such, which is the courage of History.

This project, as I will show elsewhere, is theological–political. Formidable in that it reinforces and tries to *verify* fascism. I would want to cut in here, in a way which would no longer simply be that of an opposition, with a theological–poetical project. Such a project is Benjamin's: he would have the immense merit of recognizing the theological in the figure of its failure and of turning poetry – whence we came – toward prose, where we are.

BENJAMIN'S AFFINITY

GOETHE, THE ROMANTICS AND THE PURE PROBLEM OF CRITICISM

David S. Ferris

In the abstract Benjamin wrote to describe his dissertation on the Romantics he draws attention to this study as an examination of the Romantics' concept of criticism from the perspective of a 'metahistorical problem'.[1] The introduction to the dissertation also insists on this perspective. In that introduction Benjamin speaks of this work as 'the contribution to the investigation of an historical problematic [*zu einer problemgeschichtlichen Untersuchung*] which would have to present the concept of criticism in its transformations [*Wandlungen*]'.[2] In both these remarks, Benjamin specifies that his enquiry into the concept of criticism does not simply raise a critical problem. Rather, critical problems are both the occasion of an historical problematic and the means of its access.

Why an enquiry into the concept of criticism does more than raise a problem specific to criticism is discernible from Benjamin's observation that the recognition of a critical problematic goes hand in hand with a presentation of the transformations experienced by the concept of criticism. Since the concept of criticism is subject to such transformations, it remains unable to transcend the conditions under which it operates; its capacity for transformation being a sign of this inability. For this reason, Benjamin is entirely correct to state that his investigation of the concept of criticism in the Romantics cannot be restricted to the Romantics alone. The Romantics are, as Benjamin points out, but one moment in the development of criticism. Consequently, to examine the Romantics is not to privilege one moment over another. Instead, it is to recognize within the Romantics a problematic that affects not just a particular moment or epoch in history but the history to which all such moments or epochs belong. In this respect, such a problematic is metahistorical. The Romantics afford Benjamin the opportunity to broach such an historical problematic.

Why Benjamin chooses the Romantic concept of criticism, rather than another historical moment, is clarified partly in a letter to Ernst Schoen from

November 1918 composed while Benjamin is writing the dissertation. In this letter, he insists on a genetic relation between the Romantic concept of criticism and the modern concept of criticism: the latter 'has arisen' (*hervorgegangen*) from the former.[3] On the strength of this remark, Benjamin's interest in accessing an historical problematic through Romanticism is also aimed at delineating the extent to which the criticism of an era is defined by its response to a problematic. History, in this sense, is understood as the medium in which a problematic is given existence and expression. Without this history no such thing as a modern criticism 'arising' from a Romantic concept of criticism could be conceived; however, this does not mean that modern criticism is simply just another moment in a history that records the changing predilections of critical practice – as if the appearance of a representational art in the nineteenth century and then the appearance of a non-representational, conceptual art within modernism were discrete, exclusive moments. Instead, what is at stake is the initiation of a theoretical and philosophical critical project within Romanticism, a project that determines the modern era of criticism as the response to a problematic whose persistence grants it historical as well as critical status. For Benjamin, Romanticism therefore marks the point when criticism overcomes its shortcomings as a descriptive praxis and is transformed into the privileged medium for the theory of art. Thus, to enquire into the Romantic concept of criticism is to enquire into a problematic that affects not just a particular moment or epoch in history but the history to which all such moments or epochs belong (in the sense that a particular epoch defines itself as an epoch through its criticism, which means, in effect, through its theory of art). By enquiring into such a problematic, Benjamin's interest is also an interest in the possibility of critique, in particular, for Benjamin, the possibility of a philosophically grounded criticism. Such an interest is what this chapter will treat under the title of Benjamin's affinity.

If criticism is a response to an historical problematic, what then is such a problematic? In the abstract to the dissertation, Benjamin offers the following question as a summary of the problematic approached by the dissertation: 'concerning the theory of art does the concept of its idea or does the concept of its ideal possess some knowledge of value?' (*GS* 1.2: 707). Between the concept of the idea of art and the concept of its ideal, Benjamin poses the problem of the theory of art. The problem broached by this question is outlined in more detail in the Afterword to the dissertation when Benjamin takes up the relation of the Romantics to Goethe – not in order to provide yet another tracing of literary history but in order to define, from a philosophical point of view, the historical problem that constitutes the understanding of art, in short, its criticism.

Benjamin's 'Afterword' to the dissertation begins by firmly opposing Goethe to the Romantics. Benjamin's interest in this opposition arises from the extent to which it can 'widen our knowledge of the history of the concept of art criticism' (*GS* 1.1: 110; *SW* 1: 178). The emphasis is on the history of such a concept and does not presume to favour the concept of art of either Goethe or the Romantics. Their relation is the chosen field of enquiry, however, this is not just any relation but one that Benjamin will describe as exhibiting a 'critical stage' in the history of the concept of art criticism. Benjamin then goes on to state that 'what comes immediately to light' in this opposition is 'the problem-historical relation between the Romantics' concept of criticism and Goethe's concept' (*GS* 1.1: 110/*SW* 1: 178). Through an appositional phrase this relation is immediately defined as 'the pure problem of the criticism of art'. Thus, the problem that belongs to the criticism of art is what is at stake, but this problem, as Benjamin insists, also possesses a historical dimension. In what way can it then be a *pure* problem? What, in its purity, can claim to be 'a problem of the criticism of art' and, at the same time, be historical? The task set by this question is not one of providing an appropriate mediating account of what is presented as an opposition between criticism and history on the one hand, and between the idea and ideal (or Goethe and the Romantics) on the other. Rather, the issue lies in precisely how this purity is understood.

Already, in the Afterword to the dissertation, Benjamin draws attention to this purity and, in particular, the extent to which it poses the critical question the dissertation moves towards. Benjamin states: 'The question of the relation between the Goethean and Romantic theories of art thus coincides with the question of the relation between pure content and pure (and, as such, rigorous [*strengen*]) form' (*GS* 1.1: 117/*SW* 1: 183). To understand why Benjamin casts the relation of Goethe and the Romantics in terms of pure content and pure form, recognition of the immediate context of this remark is required. The preceding remark is introduced by the following sentences: 'The Romantics define the relation of the artworks to art as infinity in totality – which means that the infinity of art is fulfilled in the totality of works. Goethe defines it as unity in plurality – which means that the unity of art is found again and again in the plurality of works. This infinity is that of pure form; this unity is that of pure content' (*GS* 1.1: 117/*SW* 1: 183). For works or art to have a relation to art – if they are to found art as their concept – two modes of relation are envisaged by Benjamin: infinity and unity. Both of these modes aim at an all-encompassing definition of art as the necessary condition of defining the relation of artworks to art. In the case of the Romantics, such a definition depends on the ability of the totality of artworks to exhibit the infinity of art. This ability, according to Benjamin's analysis of the Romantics, is located in a notion of form that serves as the limitation or restriction of the individual work of art. Such a form is defined as 'the objective expression of the reflection proper to the work' (*GS* 1.1: 73/*SW* 1: 156). So defined, the work of art, through its form, is, first and foremost, a 'living centre of reflection' (ibid.). How this initial centre accedes to an infinity is described by Benjamin in the following words: 'In the medium of reflection, in art, new centres of reflection are continually forming. Each time, according to their spiritual seed, they embrace, as they reflect, larger or smaller contexts. The infinitude of art attains to reflection first of all only in such a centre ... that is, it attains to self-comprehension and therewith to comprehension generally' (ibid.). The infinity of the Romantics' understanding of art is an infinity of reflection, which, as Benjamin points out, is achieved for the Romantics through the action of a criticism (as well as an irony) that 'dissolves the original reflection in one higher, and so continues' (ibid.). This activity produces what Benjamin describes as 'universally formal moments' (ibid.). Yet, such moments, even though 'they represent the relation of the individual work to the idea of art' they do not, in Benjamin's regard, provide an adequate account of the content of art. By defining the content of art as religion, Schlegel, according to Benjamin, has 'covered up and obscured' (ibid.) his idea of form. As a result, Benjamin adds, Schlegel could 'grasp the work of art from the side of its content only in an unclear way' (ibid.). Benjamin concludes: 'his idea of form actually gains nothing' (ibid.). It is this understanding of form as the basis of an infinite medium of reflection that Benjamin describes in the Afterword to the dissertation as an understanding of art predicated on 'pure form' albeit an understanding that is limited by its purity, by its inability to define adequately a content.

This shortcoming of the Romantics is matched by a shortcoming in Goethe's theory of art. As can already deduced from the remark in which Benjamin first characterizes the Romantics' theory of art and the theory of Goethe in terms of pure form and pure content. In Benjamin's remarks on Goethe in the Afterword, pure content is discussed in terms of the ideal through which Goethe articulated his theory of art (as opposed to the idea of art in the Romantics). Benjamin emphasizes that no common ground exists between this ideal and notion of the idea of art developed by the Romantics from their concept of pure form. Benjamin states: 'The Romantics do not acknowledge an *ideal* of art' (*GS* 1.1: 111/*SW* 1: 179). Yet, this does not mean such an ideal is to be disregarded, and Benjamin underlines this when he recalls that the Romantics had already approximated such an ideal in the 'semblance' (*Schein*) provided by religion and morals (ibid.). This semblance is precisely what Benjamin refers to when he describes the lack of clarity exhibited by Schlegel when he sought to define the content of art. The issue Benjamin takes up here is the question of what the Romantics did not think through in all rigour – precisely the question Benjamin hints at when he first characterizes the opposition of the Romantics and Goethe as an opposition between pure content and what he qualifies as 'pure (and as such rigorous) form' (*GS* 1.1: 117/*SW* 1: 183). Benjamin's criticism of Schlegel's lack of rigour is recurrent in the dissertation. However, it is not a criticism of the whole Romantic project, rather, it is a criticism of an unjustified end. Religion, used as a sign of the content of art, provides one example of this unjustified end. Yet another occurs when Benjamin criticizes what he calls the 'false interpretation [Schlegel] gave to a valuable and valid motive', namely, 'to secure the concept of the idea of art from the misunderstanding of those who wanted to see it as an abstraction from empirical artworks' (*GS* 1.1: 89–90/*SW* 1: 167). To secure this idea of art from being reduced to an abstraction from the empirical, Schlegel sought to define the ground of the idea of art in terms of an individuality so that what was universal would also have an individual existence. It is this move that Benjamin criticizes as a false interpretation (leaving open the possibility of an interpretation that would not be false).[4] At this point, Benjamin's remarks on the ideal of Goethe as an expression of pure content take on significance since they provide the example of an attempt to resolve one side of the critical problem: the definition of the content of art.

Beyond the appearance of content in the Romantics, Goethe represents the extreme example of what the Romantics did not achieve: a justified account of content. For Goethe, the ideal is the content that all artworks strive to express. However, the only way artworks can express this ideal (and still preserve its ideal character) is by a fracture or breaking (*Brechung*). Benjamin compares the Romantics' idea of art to Goethe's ideal as follows: 'Just as, in contrast to the idea, the inner structure of the ideal is discontinuous, so, too, the connection of this ideal of art is not given in a medium but is designated by a fracture' (*GS* 1.1: 111/*SW* 1: 179). Because the work of art can never contain the ideal it designates (and still have an ideal to designate), the ideal exists, not as something created but as nature (*GS* 1.1: 112/*SW* 1: 180). As a result, Benjamin concludes, Goethe's task in art was to 'grasp the idea of nature and thereby make it serviceable for the archetype of art (for pure content)' (ibid.). As pure content, the ideal demands that the artwork exist in a fractured state. In this state, the art work protects the ideal from what Benjamin characterizes as 'a ruinous materialist misunderstanding' (ibid.). But, at the same time, this need to protect the ideal poses the question of how a content can be present in the form of an artwork – precisely the same question, albeit inverted, that emerges from Benjamin's discussion of Schlegel's attempts to provide a content for his theory of art (*GS* 1.1: 73–4/*SW* 1: 156). Where the Romantics discover the idea of the artwork in its individuality and therefore do not have to provide an account of this individuality, Goethe's ideal must do quite the opposite. Goethe's ideal, as an ideal, is inimical to individuality, yet, it can have no significance for art if the relation of individual artworks to this ideal cannot be accounted for. In this case, Goethe must distinguish individuality from an ideal that threatens to make the former irrelevant. To do so, Benjamin argues, Goethe can only conceive of an individuality that must be torso-like (only on this condition can individual works exist otherwise they would all lay claim to being the ideal): 'In relation to the ideal, the single work remains, as it were, a torso. It is an individuated endeavour to represent the archetype, only as a prototype can it last with others of its sort, but they can never vitally coalesce into the unity of the ideal itself' (*GS* 1.1: 114/*SW* 1: 181). In Goethe, such an individuality then poses the question how the content of art is recognized, since unlike the Romantic theory of art, Goethe's theory requires that there be no relation between individual works and the content they strive to express (if there were such a relation, no ideal would be conceivable).

Benjamin takes up the issue of how, for Goethe, the individual artwork relates to its pure content by remarking first of all that an individual work can only 'resemble' (*gleichen*) the ideal or archetype 'in a more or less high degree' (*GS* 1.1: 111/*SW* 1: 180). By subsequently placing the word 'resembling' within quotation marks in his own text, Benjamin already signals the equivocal status this word will have as a means of describing the relation of the artwork to its pure content. Benjamin points out that such 'resembling' is not to be understood as providing an equivalent or even an imitation of the ideal. Instead, resemblance is understood by Benjamin as signifying the 'relation of what is perceptible in the highest degree to what in principle is only intuitable' (ibid.). Resemblance is thus used to describe a relation between two categorically different modes of understanding (the ideal and the individual work) even though there must be an unbridgeable fracture between these two modes. The recognition of resemblance is therefore also the recognition of the failure that perception must experience as an understanding of the ideal. Goethe's ideal of art, according to Benjamin's reading, is therefore a 'necessary perceptibility [*Wahrnehmbarkeit*]' but a perceptibility that can 'never appear purely in the artwork itself' (*GS* 1.1: 112/*SW* 1: 180). The ideal demands perceptibility without ever being equivalent to the object in which it is perceived (the art-work). The consequence of this demand is that the essential problem confronted by the artwork in Goethe is a problem of presentation since whatever is presented in the artwork, 'the correlate of the content', cannot, as Benjamin notes, be compared to the pure content that demands expression in the artwork.[5] In this respect, Benjamin sees clearly that any notion of representation must be refused by this theory of art since representation assumes that what is presented is identical with the content, the ideal or archetype. What is presented by the individual artwork must then remain contingent when compared to the ideal. Otherwise it would supplant the ideal from which it derives its significance. The lack of relation to the source of its significance is the essential demand of a theory of art based upon a pure content. As a result, form can only be an incidental element of the artwork. It becomes in Goethe, as Benjamin observes, a matter of style. In a theory of art based on pure content, form simply loses its meaning, it becomes, in Benjamin's words, 'representation of a typifying sort' (*GS* 1.1: 118/*SW* 1: 184).

By retracing Benjamin's analysis of form in the Romantics and content in Goethe, his purpose in opposing Goethe and the Romantics becomes clearer. Both in their purity represent irreconcilable tendencies, but both in their theory of the work of art fail to articulate 'the pure problem of the criticism of art' (*GS* 1.1: 101/*SW* 1: 178) that prompts their theoretical undertakings in the first place. As we have seen in the case of the Romantics' notion of form, a purity of form indicates a failure to adequately take into consideration the content of the artwork. Similarly, when Benjamin considers Goethe's theory of art, purity indicates a failure to consider the formal element pursued by the Romantics. But, when Benjamin indicates how such a failure occurs in Goethe, an indication of what constitutes the pure problem for both Goethe and the Romantics is given: 'The concept of the archetype loses its meaning for the problem of form as soon as it is supposed to be thought of as its solution (*GS* 1.1: 118/*SW* 1: 184). In addition to interpreting the consequence of Goethe's concept of pure content, this remark also comments on the pure form of the Romantics. At the point where a concept, in its purity, is thought to provide a solution, it is no longer meaningful for the problem it attempts to solve. Given this situation, Benjamin points out that, in Goethe, the solution can only be mythical, can only 'circum-scribe the problem of art in its total scope' (ibid.). What remains to be thought is what Benjamin refers to as 'presentational form':

> In the final analysis, Goethe's concept of style also relates a myth. And the objection to it can arise on the basis of the lack of distinction prevailing in it between form of presentation [*Darstellungsform*] and absolute form. For the question of the presentational form still must be distinguished from the problem of form previously examined, namely, that of absolute form. (Ibid.)

To the extent that Goethe understood the form of presentation as a fractured expression of the ideal, it persists (through this fracturing) as a measure of the beauty associated with the ideal. In its fractured state, the work of art is a measure of the ideal it cannot be but only resemble. The form in which the work of art is presented is therefore contingent. As Benjamin insists, to consider this contingency of form in Goethe in terms of an absolute form is to relate a myth. In other words, any question of an absolute form is to be thought from the perspective of what Benjamin names 'presentational form'. This latter form is not to be overlooked. Benjamin's discussion of Goethe's theory of art thus brings him to a question that also has repercussions for the absolute form pursued by the Romantics. To ignore the question posed by this 'presentational form', as Benjamin points out, is in fact to refuse the problem posed by the very idea of an absolute form – the same idea that the Romantics pursued even as they gave a wrong interpretation to it. Benjamin states: 'Goethe's theory of art leaves unresolved not only the problem of absolute form but also that of criticism' (*GS* 1.1: 119/*SW* 1: 184). Through Goethe, Benjamin recovers the essential problem that also afflicted the Romantic theory of art. The problem of absolute form now appears in the guise of 'presentational form'. By associating this problem of absolute form with the persistence of the problem of criticism brings the dissertation's Afterword to its closest point of articulating the 'pure problem of criticism'.

To articulate such a point, Benjamin must reinstate the possibility of criticism into a theory of art that had in fact rendered criticism insignificant. As Benjamin points out, such insignificance is a direct result of Goethe's theory since it requires that 'the pure contents as such are not to be found in any work' (*GS* 1.1: 112/*SW* 1: 184). Because the work does not contain what the work ex-presses, its ideal, then criticism of the artwork is irrelevant. Its function as an indication of the ideal is a given. This is why, in the case of Goethe, Benjamin can conclude, 'criticism of an artwork is neither possible nor necessary' (ibid.). This critique of Goethe signals the extent to which Benjamin recognizes the necessary persistence of criticism within the theory of art. The price Goethe pays for a theory of art based on pure content is to refuse to recognize this persistence. This alone can explain Benjamin's interest in the Romantics whose valuation of criticism was pursued to such an extent that the activity of criticism became more important than the work of art. In effect, this valuation of criticism was the price the Romantics had to pay for a theory of art based on pure form since it was only through the activity of criticism that form could be absolutized.[6] Benjamin's critique of the Romantics on this score, when added to his critique of their lack of clarity on the content of art as well as his critique of the false interpretation they gave to the individuality of the work of art, indicate the extent to which it is only in such purity that the historical problem of criticism, its pure problem, can appear. Since this clarity leads to yet another incidence of purity, in this instance, the purity of the problem Benjamin identifies as being at the very basis of criticism (and by association, absolute form), the task arising from Benjamin's discussion of both Goethe and the Romantics is the task of thinking a concept in its purity.

In a note to the passage from the Afterword in which Benjamin opposes the Romantics' infinity of pure form unity to Goethe's unity of pure content, this notion of the purity of absolute form is referred to:

> There is, of course, an equivocation here in the meaning of the term 'pure'. In the first place, it designates the methodological dignity of a concept (as in 'pure reason'), but it can also have a substantively positive and, so to speak, morally tinged significance. Both of these meanings figure above in the concept of 'pure content' as exemplified in the Muses, whereas absolute form is to be conceived as 'pure' only in the methodological sense. For its concrete determination – which corresponds to the purity of the content – is presumably rigour. And this the Romantics have not brought out in their theory of the novel, in which the entirely pure – but not rigorous – form was raised to the absolute. Here, too is a sphere of thought in which Hölderlin surpassed them. (*GS* 1.1: 117, n.315/*SW* 1: 200, n.323)

Where Goethe's pure content would assume both moral and methodological significance, the problem of absolute form that remains for Benjamin can be pure only in a methodological sense. Rather than be enforced by a moral significance, it is to rely upon rigour (*streng*). This is the point where Benjamin distinguishes the critical project formulated in the *Kunstkritik* essay from the Romantics who approached the problem of absolute form but who sought to resolve it in a way that lacked rigour. To retain rigour here, as the last line of Benjamin's dissertation points out, is to avoid extinguishing the plurality of works, to avoid extinguishing the very basis of Goethe's theory of art but without resorting to a theory of pure content as a means of preserving that plurality. The turn towards Goethe at the conclusion to Benjamin's essay on the Romantics is therefore no backward step towards a figure whose theory of art the Romantics were compelled to refuse in order to formulate their own theory of art. Rather, their theories of art are the inevitable example of the historical problem that lies at the basis of criticism for Benjamin. This is why, in the end, neither the Romantics nor Goethe can be privileged over one another. Benjamin concludes: 'Even today the problematic of German philosophy of art around 1800, as exhibited in the theories of Goethe and the early Romantics is legitimate. The Romantics did not resolve or even pose this question any more than Goethe did. They work together to introduce this question to historical thought. Only systematic thought can resolve it' (*GS* 1.1: 118/*SW* 1: 183).

The question of criticism broached by Benjamin's dissertation on the Romantics is not seen as directly resulting from either the Romantics or Goethe. Even though they may 'work together' to introduce this question to 'the history of thought' the nature of this problem remains obscured by the tendency to give a mistaken account of absolute form (as myth in Goethe, as religion in Schlegel). The significance of Benjamin's reading of both Goethe and Schlegel is its ability to account for this tendency in terms of an unresolved problem which Benjamin names 'the pure problem of criticism'. Yet, criticism, even as a pure problem, admits resolution at this point in the development of his thought. Here, Benjamin entrusts the possibility of resolving such a problem to systematic thought. The question posed here concerns the extent to which systematic thought can fulfil the promise ascribed to rigour in Benjamin's footnote on the equivocalness of the word 'pure'. If, according to that footnote, a concrete determination of pure form is to be achieved, then that determination, in Benjamin's understanding, would also be a determination of pure content. Rigour in the form of systematic thought is granted the ability to achieve such a solution. However, and Benjamin does not discuss this, there remains the question of what kind of criticism is possible once the pure problem that produced the theories of the Romantics and Goethe is resolved. For Benjamin, as his critique of Goethe's understanding of pure content makes clear, the activity of criticism is not to be sacrificed within any theory of art, but as Goethe's theory also indicates, a theory of the content of art runs the risk of making criticism of the artwork irrelevant since the work is either art (and therefore sustains the theory) or it is not art (and therefore can be ignored because it has no relation to the theory). The issue for Benjamin is to account for a concept of criticism within a theory of art but without the failure to account for the content of art exhibited by the Romantics.

Benjamin cites Hölderlin as the example of one who surpassed the Romantics in rigorous thought, yet, apart from an essay predating the dissertation by almost five years ('Two Poems by Friedrich Hölderlin' [written 1914–15]), what the name of Hölderlin stands for in the dissertation remains relatively undeveloped except for the notion of sobriety Benjamin had turned to at the end of the earlier essay.[7] Instead, the primary extension of what Benjamin sketches out at the end of the dissertation occurs in the subsequent essay, 'Goethe's *Elective Affinities*', written immediately after the dissertation (1919–22) but not published until 1924–5.[8] In particular, one passage from the beginning of the third section of this essay takes up the question of systematic thought and its relation to art. This is precisely the question posed by the Afterword to the dissertation and precisely the question that leads to the invocation of Hölderlin as the source of a more rigorous solution than the one offered by the Romantics.[9] The passage begins:

The shock taken at every criticism of art that supposedly stands too close to the work, by those who do not find in that critique an image of their egotistical dreaming, testifies to so much ignorance about the essence of art that a period for which the rigorously determined origin of art is becoming ever more alive [*lebendig*] does not owe this complaint a refutation. (*GS* 1.1: 172/*SW* 1: 333)

The language with which this passage opens takes up the call for a rigorous and systematically worked-out solution to the problem of criticism. In this case, what is in the process of being worked out (and which Benjamin associates with the modern age) is a 'rigorously determined origin of art'. This origin, so determined, holds forth the promise of a criticism whose proximity to the art it criticizes would refuse any illusion that art is intended for the 'egotistical dreaming' of its readers. Determining the origin of art then becomes a solution to the problem of criticism since art becomes known in terms of its own specific existence thereby defining for criticism the object of its enquiry (and rendering irrelevant at the same time a critical praxis that avoids the question of what art is by always viewing it as the medium for the specular representation of a subject).

The 'rigorously determined origin of art' admits no direct approach in Benjamin. As the following sentences indicate, the only possible approach is by means of analogy:

Let us suppose that one makes the acquaintance of a person who is handsome and attractive but impenetrable, because he carries a secret with him. It would be reprehensible to want to pry. Still, it would surely be permissible to enquire whether he has any siblings and whether their nature could not perhaps explain somewhat the enigmatic character of the stranger. In just this way criticism seeks to discover siblings of the work of art. (*GS* 1.1: 172/*SW* 1: 333)

By analogy to this passage, art is a secret, an enigma for criticism. As this enigma, the problem of criticism is what criticism cannot help but take as its object: art. In this respect, criticism not only discovers the purity of its problem in the very object that is intended to validate its existence, but also, it legislates this problem for itself through its own existence. Without criticism, art cannot be a problem, and, without art, criticism cannot have a problem, that is, a problem of essentially methodological rather than moral origin (as Benjamin's note to the adjective 'pure' cited above indicates). This explains why criticism can never solve its own problem, since the problem in question is constituted by a criticism that can only recognize itself through its failure to provide an adequate account of art. In the case of the Romantics and Goethe, this mani-fested itself in the purity of their accounts of form and content as their theory of art attempted to overcome the 'pure problem of criticism' by means of the very purity that prompted this attempt. Because these attempts lead to a situation in which criticism is either rendered irrelevant (Goethe) or overvalued (the Romantics), Benjamin poses the question of a criticism that takes up the problem of its own constitution. In the above passage from his essay on Goethe's *Elective Affinities*, Benjamin recognizes this problem when criticism is set the task of discovering the siblings of the work of art. The problem is such that it is only through what has an affinity to the work of art that the problem of art can be approached.[10] For Benjamin, such an affinity is possessed by philosophy: 'All genuine works have their siblings in the realm of philosophy. It is, after all, precisely these figures [*Gestalten*] in which the ideal of philosophy's problem appears' (*GS* 1.1: 172/*SW* 1: 333).

The affinity between the artwork and philosophy is not one of straightforward analogy. The realm of philosophy is not simply a sibling (singular) for the artwork, it is what contains siblings to a genuine work of art. How Benjamin understands this analogy is introduced in the subsequent sentence when he describes these siblings as figures 'in which the ideal of philosophy's problem appears'. The artwork, and, it is to be presumed, its rigorously determined origin, is located in what Benjamin refers to as not just the problem of philosophy but the ideal of this problem. The language used here recalls Benjamin's characterization of the historical problem of criticism in the dissertation as the relation of the idea of art presented by the Romantics and the ideal of art presented by Goethe. That the problem of art should now be found in the ideal of the problem of philosophy would suggest a repeat of the relation between the ideal and the plurality of artworks in Goethe. Yet, where Goethe's ideal, as presented in the Afterword to the dissertation would provide an answer to the question posed by a plurality of artworks (namely, what is the purpose of this plurality: to indicate the ideal unity), Benjamin would appear to disassociate the ideal of philosophy from any such answer. Benjamin writes:

> The whole of philosophy, its system, is of a higher power than can be demanded by the concept of all its problems taken together precisely because the unity in the solution of all these problems is not ascertainable by questioning. If the unity in the solution of all these problems were ascertainable by questioning, then with respect to the question which asks about [this unity], a new question would immediately arise on which the unity of its answer together with that of all the others would be based. From this it follows that there is no question which encompasses the unity of philosophy in its questioning. (*GS* 1.1: 172–3/*SW* 1: 333–4)

The systematicity of philosophy (and here it is to be recalled that Benjamin states at the end of the dissertation that only 'systematic thought' can resolve the problem of the philosophy of art) resists the questions posed by the methodology of philosophical enquiry. Benjamin's argument in support of this statement emphasizes the logical impossibility of a unity being constituted by a plurality. Yet, if this argument is not to fall back within the Goethean model (and therefore deny the validity of criticism), Benjamin must still be able to determine this ideal as meaningful but without the one-sidedness of Goethe's pure content. It must also determine the form of art. To approach this ideal (which is to be the ideal of a problem) Benjamin uses the very question he has just denied. He adopts the form of this question by referring to the concept of a non-existent question: 'The concept of this non-existent question which asks after the unity of philosophy indicates within philosophy the ideal of the problem' (ibid.). The ideal of the problem is indicated by the failure of a question to exist. At the same time, this failure is understood to ask about the unity of philosophy. This unasked, non-existent question asks after a unity it can never 'encompass' (*umspannen*) but, in so doing, it is for Benjamin an indication of the ideal of philosophy. Not only is this a question that fails to become a question by failing to exist as a question but it is through the recognition of this failure that the possibility of an ideal of philosophy attains existence. Since this necessary failure of the question becomes the essential sign of the ideal of philosophy, it is also such a failure that would permit the recognition of the pure problem of criticism through its sibling, art. In each recognition, however, there remains this figurative, ghostlike question that must never achieve individual existence if philosophy is to have the ideal of a problem and, from this, allow the pure problem of criticism to appear.

An immediate consequence of Benjamin's formal indication of the ideal of a problem at the highest level of philosophy is that this ideal does not allow itself under any circumstance to be questioned.[11] What then constitutes a question that is not a question and which is so necessary to Benjamin's understanding of the way in which philosophy has an affinity to art? Benjamin's response to this is to offer what the ideal of the problem in philosophy has the greatest affinity with:

> If, however, the system cannot also in any sense be questioned, there are creations [*Gebilde*] that without being questions have the deepest affinity [*Affinität*] with the ideal of the problem. These are works of art. The work of art does not compete with philosophy itself, it simply enters into the most precise relation to philosophy through its affinity [*Verwandtschaft*] with the ideal of the problem. (*GS* 1.1: 172/*SW* 1: 334)

Art, which finds its siblings in the realm of philosophy, and these siblings which indicate the ideal of the problem in philosophy, now finds itself to be the sibling of its sibling since it is now art that gives expression to the question philosophy cannot ask if the ideal of its problem is to be recognized. But, even though art exists as the medium posing the hypothetical question in which the ideal of the problem is indicated, Benjamin insists that art does not compete with philosophy. Instead of competing, it is said to possess a relation to philosophy. This relation is defined by Benjamin in terms of the affinity (now *Verwandtschaft* rather than *Affinität*) that is at the centre of the work by Goethe that forms the subject of Benjamin's essay: *Die Wahlverwandtschaften*. That Benjamin should describe such a relation in terms of the concept that forms the main subject of Goethe's text indicates that more is at stake in Benjamin's choice of texts than the place of the *Die Wahlverwandtschaften* in German scholarship of the time.[12]

The movement of Benjamin's argument in this passage exhibits a necessary circularity as it progresses from art to siblings, from these siblings to the ideal of the problem of philosophy, from the ideal of the problem back to art as the example of the non-existent question through which the ideal of the problem is indicated within the realm of philosophy. At stake in this argument is the status of the artwork as what makes manifest the ideal of the problem of philosophy, that is, at stake is art as a form of presentation whose content is an ideal but not an ideal that denies criticism. Here, art, as a form that poses the problem of its content, makes such a problem manifest. As such, artworks belong to that multiplicity in which Benjamin recognizes the appearance of the ideal:

> And truly, according to a lawfulness [*Gesetzlichkeit*] which generally speaking is grounded in the essence of the ideal, this ideal can only present itself in a multiplicity. However, it is not in a multiplicity of problems that the ideal of the problem appears. Rather, it lies hidden in the multiplicity of works and its promotion (*Förderung*) is the business of criticism. In the work of art, criticism allows the ideal of the problem to appear [*in Erscheinung ... treten*] in one of its appearances [*Erscheinungen*]. (*GS* 1.1: 172–3/*SW* 1: 334)

'Ideal'. 'Multiplicity of works'. These terms mark strongly an affinity with Goethe's theory of art. At the same time, Benjamin insists on a difference in the relation of these terms: where Goethe posited an ideal that made criticism irrelevant, Benjamin will recognize an ideal that demands, calls out for criticism as the source of its appearance. The task of this criticism is therefore not the production of a medium of reflection as it was for the Romantics, rather, such criticism is to bring forth in the artwork the truth-content that remains in the closest affinity to the highest problem of philosophy: 'What it finally exhibits in every appearance is the virtual formulability [*die virtuelle Formulierbarkeit*] of its truth-content as the highest philosophical problem; that before which it pauses [*innehält*] out of reverence for the work and out of respect for the truth is this formulation itself' (ibid.). That Benjamin's theory of art is a theory of appearance is clearly stated here. As appearance, art protects the truth-content in which its significance is decided, since, as a mode of appearance, art can only exhibit the possibility of formulating such a content. For Benjamin, it is the task of criticism to bring art to this moment. In this respect, the active role given to criticism by the Romantics is fulfilled but without, in Benjamin's eyes, the false interpretation or obscurity of Schlegel's theory of art as pure form. Art thus becomes the form which poses the problem of the formulation of its truth-content but in so doing achieves the closest affinity with the ideal of such a problem in philosophy. The posing of such a problem – the formulation of the truth-content – is the truth-content of the artwork. This truth is, in its most essential form, the inability to realize this formulation, as Benjamin indicates in a sentence that determines the sole condition under which such realization would be conceivable: 'That formulability [*Formulierbarkeit*] could indeed be realized [*einlösen*] only if the system were able to be questioned [*erfragbar*] and should thereby transform [*verwandeln*] itself from an appearance of the ideal into the existence [*Bestand*] of the ideal, an existence that is never given' (ibid.). As Benjamin's description of the limitation of questioning in philosophy already stated, no question is able to encompass the unity of philosophy and thereby realize such unity. The problem is ideal in this respect, since it is by definition resistant to appearance in art and to questioning in the system of philosophy.

What maintains this ideal while distinguishing it from Goethe's theory of art is the pausing or leaving off (*innehalten*) that Benjamin emphasizes: the pausing that criticism is brought to as it faces the formulation of the truth-content of art. Within the essay, 'Goethes Wahlverwandtschaften', Benjamin will articulate this pausing as well as what causes it by invoking what he terms the 'expressionless'. Just as philosophy is only really truly completed by the ideal of its problem, so the work of art is completed by the expressionless: 'Only the expressionless completes the work, by shattering it into a thing of shards, into a fragment of the true world into the torso of a symbol' (*GS* 1.1: 181/*SW* 1: 340). At the limit of appearance there is what defines appearance as appearance, since this is what it can never express: the expressionless. The finitude of such appearance presents the artwork as a torso which is precisely the form Benjamin had called upon in his dissertation on the Romantics to define the artwork within Goethe's theory of art. On this occasion, and in distinction to Goethe, Benjamin would now think the artwork in terms of a torso that remains a 'fragment of the true world' rather than a mere prototype whose significance depends on what is more complete than itself. In this respect, it is important to underline that the work is not completed in the expressionless but by the shattering (*zerschlagen*) wrought by the expressionless. This shattering accounts, on the one hand, for the individuality of the work of art, and, on the other, it grants a meaningful content to that work: a content that remains a sign of its individuality, its status as a torso.

The distinction of such a torso from the torso of Goethe depends for Benjamin on the shattering of what he refers to as the 'beautiful semblance' or the 'false, errant totality – the absolute totality' (ibid.). It is just such a semblance that characterizes the ideal of Goethe to the extent that every individual work of art is reduced to a semblance of that ideal. Earlier, in the same paragraph that describes the effect of the expressionless on such 'beautiful semblance', Benjamin speaks more directly of precisely what is interrupted. In these sentences, he describes the emergence of form out of chaos as well as the moment in which this emergence becomes appearance:

> Form ... enchants chaos momentarily [*auf einen Augenblick*] into the world. Therefore, no work of art may seem wholly alive, in a manner free of spell-like enchantment, without becoming mere semblance and ceasing to be a work of art. The life undulating in it must appear petrified [*muss erstarrt ... erscheinen*] and as if spellbound in a single moment [*in einem Augenblick*] ... What arrests this semblance, banishes the movement, and interrupts the harmony is the expressionless. (Ibid.)

In this role, the expressionless enacts what Benjamin calls a 'critical violence' that 'shatters whatever still survives as the legacy of chaos in all beautiful semblance' (ibid.). By shattering what occurs in a moment – in this sense, *Augenblick*, the distraction or looking away of the eye – the work of art is rescued from mere, beautiful semblance, that is, it is rescued from its petrification as form or semblance. Yet, what marks the occurrence of this rescue (and with it the completion of the work of art by the expressionless) is itself constituted as a moment, a pause that, through its interruptive character, maintains a relation between the ideal and appearance. This relation, rather than owe its existence to the positive representation of an ideal, now owes its existence to a problem whose lawfulness (*Gesetzlichkeit*) is 'grounded in the essence of the ideal' (*GS* 1.1: 172–3/*SW* 1: 334) rather than in its mere existence as an ideal. This problem – indicated by Benjamin through its sibling, philosophy, to be the problem of formulating the unity of philosophy – marks the means by which Benjamin will seek to preserve the possibility of a concept of criticism from within the relation of Goethe and the Romantics and their respective theories of art.

Foremost in this preservation (and distinctive in relation to Goethe and the Romantics) is the extent to which Benjamin will make this criticism rely on a moment of pausing or interruption through which the expressionless can produce its effect. Criticism, after Goethe and the Romantics becomes the uncovering of the work of the expressionless in art. As supplemental authority for this understanding of criticism, Benjamin will cite Hölderlin on the significance of the caesura while claiming for Hölderlin the rigour that the Romantics failed to exhibit: 'As a category of language and art and not of the work or of the genres, the expressionless can be no more rigorously defined than through a passage in Hölderlin's *Anmerkungen zum Ödipus*, whose fundamental significance for the theory of art in general, beyond serving as the basis for a theory of tragedy, seems not yet to have been recognized' (*GS* 1.1: 181/*SW* 1: 340). Benjamin's claim is more general than Hölderlin's and it is through this generalization of Hölderlin that Benjamin will justify his theory of art as appearance. For this justification, Benjamin offers the following passage from Hölderlin's 'Remarks on Oedipus': 'For the tragic transport is actually empty, and the most unrestrained. – Thereby in the rhythmic sequence of the representations wherein the transport presents itself, there becomes what in poetic meter is called caesura, the pure word, the necessary counter-rhythmic rupture' (ibid.). Although Benjamin will not emphasize Hölderlin's phrase 'pure word' in this context, the effect of the caesura indicating the operation of this word is described by Benjamin as that in which 'every expression simultaneously ceases [*sich ... legt*], in order to give free rein to an expressionless power [*Gewalt*] inside all artistic media'. And then continues: 'one could not characterize this rhythm any more aptly than by asserting that something beyond the poet interrupts the language of the poetry [*der Dichtung ins Wort fällt*]' (*GS* 1.1: 182/*SW* 1: 341).

What Benjamin enlists from Hölderlin is the designation of a place in which an expressionless power occurs. Hölderlin's indication of a moment of rupture within the representations that form an artwork is taken by Benjamin as strictly synonymous with the expressionless power he identifies as the element before which all understanding of the artwork comes to a halt. For Benjamin, this coming to a halt marks the point at which criticism finds its most philosophical justification, since this point also mirrors the highest problem of philosophy: the ideal of the problem. Accordingly, this rupture, this caesura in which the power of the expressionless is expressed, is fundamental to a project whose goal is to authorize criticism in the name of its sibling, philosophy. Hölderlin's ability to affirm this authorization of the concept of criticism Benjamin develops in the wake of Goethe and the Romantics rests upon an affinity between two moments whose only characterization is their expressionlessness. Two moments of silence that would always be the same. In Benjamin's case, such a silence marks the place of a problem in which the truth-content of the artwork (in other words the ideal of the problem) and its sibling, philosophy, are to be recognized. Such recognition is the task of criticism for Benjamin. But, given the affinity, through which this notion of criticism is developed, it is a criticism that strives to preserve philosophy as the authority of criticism. It is the ideal of the problem of philosophy that provides the truth-content to be revealed in the work of art.

In this respect, Benjamin formulates criticism as the pre-eminent mode of thinking such a truth-content. That this critical project should be undertaken in the name of truth raises considerably the stakes of the critical practice of Benjamin's day, while clearly distinguishing Benjamin from that practice – as his essay on Goethe's *Wahlverwandtschaften* also devotes considerable space to achieving. But, what Benjamin uses as the means to establish this affinity between criticism and philosophy – the rupture or coming to a halt that validates criticism – would also retain the greatest ambiguity with respect to the systematic, rigorous thought in which the resolution to the question of criticism introduced to 'historical thought' by Goethe and the Romantics is sought by Benjamin. As Philippe Lacoue-Labarthe has argued in remarks that echo Benjamin's own turn to Hölderlin, such a caesura cannot be disassociated from the modern formulation of criticism. In his essay, 'The Caesura of the Speculative', Lacoue-Labarthe observes that the caesura indicates 'a place so singular ... that it most probably marks the limit of *critical* power as such'.[13] The hesitancy of 'probably' reiterates the ambiguity of such a place (even to the extent of questioning its status as a place or a moment). But what Benjamin, Hölderlin and, after them, Lacoue-Labarthe, would insist upon here is a certain experience of the limit of criticism. That Benjamin would transform such a limit into criticism's most powerful insight into the work of art is a sign of the strength of his commitment to a Romantic project that continues to persist in the form of literary theory today. Indeed, to the extent that Romanticism announces the advent of criticism as the theory of art it announces the modern necessity of criticism for art. Benjamin responds to this necessity as he tries to establish a content for such a necessity and, in so doing, rescue criticism from its own most essential tendency, its own absolution as pure form or pure content. To stage this rescue in terms of a pure problem to which pure form and pure content are incomplete responses, and in terms of a history in which this pure problem persists, is to reveal the limit to which the theory of art must go in order to preserve a critical force. It is in the possibility of such a force that criticism would arrive at a content for itself. This is, in the end, not only the legacy of the theoretical project initiated by Romanticism but also, it leads directly to the systematic and rigorous delineation of the history in which the pure problem of criticism finds its significance for Benjamin.

THE ARTWORK AS BREACH OF A BEYOND

ON THE DIALECTIC OF DIVINE AND HUMAN ORDER IN WALTER BENJAMIN'S 'GOETHE'S *ELECTIVE AFFINITIES*'*

Sigrid Weigel

I THE BEYOND THAT INTERRUPTS THE LANGUAGE OF POETRY

[Not] this Nazarene character but rather the symbol of the star falling down over the lovers is the form of expression appropriate to whatever of mystery in the exact sense of the term indwells the work. (*SW* 1: 355, translation modified)[1]

By opposing the Nazarene character at the end of Goethe's novel to the falling star, Walter Benjamin in the final passage of his essay on *Elective Affinities* articulates his only significant objection to the novel, which, incidentally, provides the example for developing his philosophy and critique of art. Although his text on the whole refrains from evaluating the novel, since the critique of art is more concerned with a philosophical contemplation (*Anschauung*) of the work's completeness, Benjamin – with this one objection – immediately dismisses the entire ending of the novel. In particular, he targets 'those Christian-mystical moments' that, 'at the end', arise 'from the striving to ennoble everything mythic at ground level' (*SW* 1: 355). These elements are, according to Benjamin's description, 'out of place' (*fehl am Ort*). His observation refers not merely to the final sentence of *Elective Affinities*, in which the *topos* of a 'union of the lovers in death' flows into the image of a 'future resurrection': 'and what an amiable moment it will be when they some day will awake together' (*SW* 1: 355, transl. mod.). Rather, Benjamin's judgement of the narrator's Nazarene lapse

---

* Translated by Geraldine Grimm.

(*Verfehlung*) – which is 'out of place' (*fehl am Platz*) – as much pertains to the previous scene in the novel, in which Eduard praises Ottilie's death for amounting to an incomparable martyrdom and describes the dead beloved as a 'saint', thereby framing her death as if it were the imitation of Christ.

However, Benjamin's concern pertains less to the profaning of Christian martyrs through a human *imitatio Christi*, more to the way in which the novel's ending devalues a different kind of hope: the sort of hope that the narrator had cherished for the lovers six chapters earlier, i.e. in the thirteenth chapter of the second part, and had represented in the symbol of the falling star above them. Mostly 'due to this hope', the Christian-mystical moments of the novel's ending are qualified as 'out of place'; for the mystery that 'indwells' the work – at once the *caesura* of the work – is thereby sublated (*aufgehoben*) into the design of an ennobled Christian myth of resurrection (i.e. the union in death).

> That sentence, which to speak with Hölderlin contains the caesura of the work and in which, while the embracing lovers seal their fate, everything pauses, reads: 'Hope shot across the sky above their heads like a falling star.' They are unaware of it, of course, and it could not be said any more clearly that the last hope is never such to him who cherishes it but is the last only to those for whom it is cherished. With this comes to light the innermost basis for the 'narrator's stance'. (*SW* 1: 354–5)

When regarded as the 'narrator's stance', this hope refers not to the event itself but to the manner or way in which the 'meaning of the event' can be fulfilled. In this respect, then, this hope is not part of what is presented (*des Dargestellten*), but constitutes a moment of representation (*Darstellung*) itself, indeed, of the artwork itself. Such 'last hope', whose emergence is coeval with 'sealed fate', cannot be contained or set still in one image – for example, the image of the future resurrection from the dead. As 'that most paradoxical, most fleeting hope', this hope closes itself off from a translation into words, resists being rendered into a positive notion (*Vorstellung*), or into the language of rhetorical convention. Such hope has much more to do with what Benjamin calls 'something beyond the poet', which 'interrupts the language of the poetry' (*SW* 1: 341) (*das der Dichtung ins Wort fällt*).

The symbol of 'what juts into' (*das Hereinragende*)
Yet, this 'beyond' (*das Jenseits*) can only be expressed in the form of a symbol. Where the author of the novel introduces the falling star as a simile ('Hope shot across ... *like* a [falling] star'), Benjamin regards the star as a symbol marking the moment of mystery in the artwork. By way of a comparison to the mystery in drama – 'that moment, in which it juts out (*hineinragen*) of the domain of language proper to it into a higher one, unattainable for it', and which therefore 'can never be expressed in words but is expressible solely in representation' – Benjamin interprets the 'falling star' as 'an analogous moment of representation' (*SW* 1: 355). This means, consequently, that the star *is* not but also does not

signify the mystery; instead, it can be read as a symbol that alludes to a domain situated beyond the work of art – or to another language. Benjamin thus redefines the relationship of the mystery to the work, or the relation of the beyond to literature, via the figures of jutting into (*Hereinragen*), indwelling (*Einwohnen*), and falling into (*Einfallen*). As a 'form of expression appropriate to whatever of mystery in the exact sense of the term indwells the work', the symbol of the star signifies both an acknowledgement of the beyond as well as a reference to it, which is not expressed in the presented event but rather in the stance (*Haltung*) of narration.

The theory of the artwork here formulated implies that, on the one hand, the poet has to limit himself to his (human) power; yet, on the other hand, in representation and the narrative stance he is to mark and rupture the limit of his own language, by using it as a symbol of a different realm that lies beyond, thus allowing a 'mystery in the exact sense' (*SW* 1: 355) to 'indwell' his work. And the exact sense of mystery originates from antique Greek where *mysterion* means secret knowledge. Where Benjamin's theory of art – in the sense of the mystery's right to dwell in the work – originates from a strict delineation between human and divine orders, the Nazarene at the end of Goethe's novel by contrast presents the human imitation of a divine power (martyrdom and resurrection), thus levelling the distinction between human and divine orders. While in Goethe's novel the human characters assume a divine position, in Benjamin's essay the divine is admitted a place within the language of the artwork, or, better, assigned a breach through which what lies beyond the work juts into its language.

About the forgetting of the 'divine' in the reception of Benjamin's essay
As such, however, there emerges at the end of Benjamin's essay yet again a condensation (*Verdichtung*) of a motif that runs through the entire text as a compositional and structure-building moment – not in the thematic sense but rather as a 'moment of presentation (*Darstellung*)'. The motif in question concerns the drawing of boundaries between human capacity and the beyond bearing the name of the divine. Remarkably, this moment of presentation in 'Goethe's Elective Affinities' constitutes somewhat of a forgotten and silenced motif in the reception of Benjamin's essay. For at the centre of the text's afterlife stand those passages in which Benjamin casts the figure of Ottilie as an allegory of the artwork, out of which he develops his theory of 'unrevealability' as the essence of beauty. In addition, other elements such as the differentiation between commentary and criticism, between the material and the truth contents, have received due attention, no less so than Benjamin's exposition of the novel's mythical content and of the 'expressionless'. The latter is understood in contradistinction to 'semblance', or *Schein,* in the artwork, which functions as the point of junction between 'Goethe's Elective Affinities' and the history of aesthetic theory, especially the aesthetics of the sublime.[2]

The philosophical experience of divine imprint (Prägung): virtual formulatability
The trace of the 'beyond' and of the 'divine order' that traverses the essay has,

however, widely been forgotten, glossed over or ignored in the reception. And this, in spite of the fact that the central meaning of the 'divine imprint' for Benjamin's theory already gained expression in the essay's first part, which casts the relation between the artwork's content and matter in the famous image of the seal[3] (the content being the seal presenting matter). Subsequently, Benjamin adds that the content of matter is 'graspable only in the philosophical experience of its divine imprint, evident only to the blissful vision of the divine name' (*SW* 1: 300). However, the theory of art articulated at the end of the essay, gained from a dialectic between the human and divine orders, does not run counter to the one captured in the Ottilie allegory. For even when Benjamin speaks of the viewing of beauty as a secret, he brings the 'divine' into play by calling the secret the 'divine ground of the being of beauty'. The appearance of beauty as art would therefore have the ground of its 'being' in the divine, in the secret, 'since only the beautiful and outside it nothing can be essential (veiling or being veiled)' (*SW* 1: 351). It is true, according to Benjamin, that 'the task of art criticism is not to lift the veil but rather, through the most precise knowledge of it as a veil, to raise itself for the first time to the true view of the beautiful'. Therefore this concept originates in the philosophical acknowledgement that 'truth is not in itself visible and its becoming visible could rest only on traits not its own' (*SW* 1: 351). Instead, truth depends on the artwork's own 'virtual formulation' (*virtueller Formulierbarkeit*), so that the respect for work *and* truth commands restraint in view of this 'possibility of formulation' (*SW* 1: 334). For Benjamin, this restraint in view of the 'possibility of formulation' corresponds to an acknowledgment of the secret as a 'divine ground of the being of beauty'. This divine ground provides a sort of matrix for Benjamin's art theory and can only be ignored at the cost of a gross distortion of his philosophy of art.

Correspondences to the philosophy of language
By now, it should have become clear just how precisely this theory of art, published in 1924–25, corresponds to the essay on language Benjamin wrote almost a decade earlier. In that essay, the history of (human) language has its premise in a caesura – 'the spirit of language to be sought in the Fall' (*SW* 1: 72) – in which paradisiac language loses its magical moments and language turns into a sign system instead, meaning that language is 'not only communication of the communicable but also, at the same time, a symbol of the noncommunicable' (*SW* 1: 74). This function of language as a symbol of something verbally ungraspable is described very vividly in 'Goethe's Elective Affinities' as an event that concerns words themselves. For one must read Benjamin's phrase '*ins Wort fallen*' as a very literal event, when he says 'that something beyond the poet interrupts the language of the poetry' (*SW* 1: 341). If this 'beyond' in 'Goethe's Elective Affinities' predominantly carries the name of the divine, then the literalness of this event simultaneously also represents a possible condition for the fact that Benjamin in his later works will connect this breach of another knowledge to Freud's psychoanalytic definition of the language of the unconscious[4] – provided, however, that the latter is interpreted to mean that psychoanalysis, too,

is not concerned with the 'possibility of formulating' truth *itself* (*Formulierbar-keit*),[5] but rather with the specific forms in which truth becomes apparent differently – a truth nonetheless that must reside in the language of the unconscious as a virtual possibility of formulation.

2   THE BORDER OF DEMARCATION BETWEEN ART AND REDEMPTION

In 'Goethe's Elective Affinities', the theory of art derived from a dialectic between human and divine orders offers a countermodel to George and Gundolf's concept of art, according to which poetry itself is adorned with divine attributes, and art is construed as a pseudo- or quasi-religion. Since the separation of art and philosophy in antiquity is a result of the decline of myth (and its indifference to the category of truth), the construal of poetry as a quasi-religion merely performs a remythologization, which Benjamin counteracts by drawing a strict border of demarcation between the discourse of art and a 'speech *vis-à-vis* God'. Precisely by doing so, his essay touches upon a contemporary phenomenon, namely the reestablishing of art *as* cult or *as* mystery, which takes place not least in the aesthetic of the sublime:[6] art as a type of religion in a post-secularized age.[7]

A strict border line is drawn through Benjamin's essay, starting at the beginning of the second part with the sharp dissociation from Gundolf's mixing of art and religion in his *Goethe*, and, above all, his construction of the author as mythical hero, as a 'mongrel of hero and creator' (*SW* 1: 324), that is, as a suprahuman type of the Redeemer, who 'represents mankind through his work in the starry skies' (*SW* 1: 322). In what follows, I will cover some of the constellations that mark this drawing of a border, through which the concepts of the discourse of art are differentiated from those belonging to a different, divine system of meaning.

Task versus exactions
For Benjamin, 'the literary work of art in the true sense arises only where the word liberates itself from the spell of even the greatest task' (*SW* 1: 323). His critique of any confusion between literary works of art and a divine mission, or a divine mandate, targets the image of the poet in the George circle:

> This school assigns to the poet, like the hero, his work as a task; hence, his mandate is considered divine. From God, however, man receives not *tasks* but only exactions (*Forderungen*), and therefore before God no privileged value can be ascribed to the poetic life. Moreover, the notion of the task is also inappropriate from the standpoint of the poet. (*SW* 1: 323)

This radical rejection of any 'task' seeks to prevent the legitimization of the literary artwork on the basis of an authority alien to it, whatever its nature and description. Only when language is liberated from a determination of tasks can the 'true work of art' spring forth.

Creature versus produced form (Geschöpf vs. Gebilde)

The fact that Benjamin sees in the contemporary 'heroizing attitude' of the poet a continuation of the hubris already connected to the old genius concept is evident in his reflections on the metaphorical discourse of art that describes the production of art as creation: 'And indeed the artist is less the primal ground or creator than the origin or form giver [*Bildner*], and certainly his work is not at any price his creature but rather his form [*Gebilde*]' (*SW* 1: 323–4). However, this difference between creature and created form does not resolve itself in the simple differentiation between culture and nature. This is apparent in the following passage, which brings the concept of redemption into play: 'To be sure, the form, too, and not only the creature, has life. But the crucial difference between the two is this: only the life of the creature, never that of a formed structure [*des Gebildeten*], partakes, unreservedly, of the intention of redemption' (*SW* 1: 324, trans. mod.). While Benjamin alludes here by means of the life of created form (*Gebilde*) to the 'afterlife' (*Nachleben*) of works – about which he has more to say elsewhere, especially in 'The Task of Translator' – in the end the exclusiveness with which he ascribes redemption to the life of the creature implies the exclusion of the artwork from the sphere of the messianic. Thus, Benjamin's theory of art does not attribute a messianic quality to the literary work of art as such. Only in the author's or artist's stance can the hope of redemption be expressed. Yet, such hope does not apply to the author but to his characters, for Benjamin thinks that Goethe, through Ottilie's name, truly tried to 'rescue someone perishing, to redeem a loved one in her' (*SW* 1: 354, trans. mod.).

Love: sacrament and freedom versus decision

Even in the discussion of the concepts of love and marriage the above-mentioned line of demarcation plays a significant role. While Benjamin qualifies Gundolf's description of marriage as mystery and sacrament as mysticism, he discusses marriage as the interplay between its 'natural' moments – sexuality – and its 'divine component' – fidelity (*SW* 1: 326). Since 'the dark conclusion of love, whose daemon is Eros' implies a natural incompleteness of love, in so far as Eros is 'the true ransoming of the deepest imperfection which belongs to the nature of man himself' (*SW* 1: 345), and in so far as marriage is the expression for the endurance of love (i.e. for its supranatural endurance), marriage as the endeavour to attain its fulfilment and perfection entails a transcendent moment: the decision (*Entscheidung*). 'This annihilates choice in order to establish fidelity: only the decision, not the choice, is inscribed in the book of life. For choice is natural and can even belong to the elements: decision is transcendent' (*SW* 1: 346). If this decision is validated by a legal act, then in the 'divine moment' of matrimony theology juts into civilian life. 'For what is proper to the truly divine is logos: the divine does not ground life without truth, nor does it ground the rite without theology' (*SW* 1: 326). Benjamin's interpretation sees in Goethe's novel not the representation of competing laws but of the powers that emanate from the collapse of marriage: 'Yet these are surely the mythic powers of the law' (*SW* 1: 301). In his view, the characters of Goethe's novel exemplify how an underestimation of the 'divine moment' in marriage leads to a return of the mythic. The inability to decide, the relapse into a sacrificial myth, and the beseeching of 'fate', which characterizes the actions of the two couples – all of this Benjamin explains on the basis of their 'chimerical striving for freedom' (*SW* 1: 332). As educated, enlightened people, superior to the order of nature, they believe they have outgrown the need for the ritual, as is most evident in the scene where the headstones have been displaced:

> One cannot imagine a more conclusive detachment from tradition than that from the graves of the ancestors, which, in the sense not only of myth but of religion, provide the ground under the feet of the living. Where does their freedom lead those who act thus? Far from opening up new perspectives for them, it blinds them to the reality that inhabits what they fear. (*SW* 1: 302–3, trans. mod.)

Likewise, Benjamin's rejection of how Ottilie is described as a 'saint' (both in the novel and by Gundolf) is linked to the moment of her indecisiveness: 'Ottilie's existence, which Gundolf calls sacred, is an unhallowed one, not so much because she trespassed against a marriage in dissolution as because in her seeming and her becoming, subjected until her death to a fateful power, she vegetates without decision' (*SW* 1: 336–7).

Reconciliation: conciliation (Aussöhnung) versus absolution (Entsühnung)
Wherever the Goethe cult praises the 'suprahuman' (*Übermenschlich*), Benjamin counterposes a subject position, developed by a dual reference to 'natural' *and* 'supernatural' moments in life. The fateful nature of existence, in which Goethe's characters remain entangled, appears to him as a 'nexus of guilt and expiation' (*SW* 1: 307), which coincides with the representation of Ottilie's death as mythic sacrifice. The denial of the bond of 'natural life' to a higher, supernatural life consequently leads to a development of a 'culpable life' (*SW* 1: 307), in so far as precisely 'mere life' (*SW* 1: 308), stripped of any 'supernatural' demands, manifests itself as guilt, which Benjamin shows by commenting on the episode of Charlotte and Eduard's child and the interpretation of its death as expiation.

Benjamin's critique of Ottilie's so-called 'sacred death' also applies to the interpretation of her death as expiation, which likewise bases itself upon the model of fate as *Schuldzusammenhang*. Thus, Ottilie's death is at best 'atonement, in the sense of fate but not *holy absolution* – which voluntary death can never be for human beings but only the *divine death imposed* on them can become' (*SW* 1: 336). With this, the concept of absolution is linked back to the notion of a punishing God. For even the idea of a possible absolution from human guilt through self-sacrifice (which is, after all, the basis of martyrdom) is entangled in the confusion of human and divine concepts: 'For *reconciliation*, which is entirely supermundane and hardly an object for concrete depiction in a novel, has its worldly reflection in the *conciliation* of one's fellow man' (*SW* 1: 343).

Conciliation here has nothing in common with either clemency or toleration but instead coincides with a decision.

Benjamin discovers another form of 'false' reconciliation in sentimentality, which he describes as 'the semblance of reconciliation' (*SW* 1: 348–9). The blurring of recognition through sentimentality once more refers to the lack of differentiation: 'Neither guilt nor innocence, neither nature nor the beyond can be strictly differentiated for sentimentality' (*SW* 1: 348, transl. mod.). In this sense, sentimentality lies like a veil over Ottilie's beauty. 'For the tears of sentimentality, in which the gaze grows veiled, are at the same time the most proper veil of beauty itself. But sentimentality is only the semblance of reconciliation' (*SW* 1: 348–9). Only where through a moment of violent commotion sentimentality reaches the threshold of the sublime can semblance be represented as perishing. 'Any semblance which is represented in Ottilie's beauty is the one in decline.' And only there where the expressionless opposes semblance can one speak of a 'true work of art' in the sense of Benjamin's theory of art, so that the expressionless attains as it were the position of a placeholder for the secret – the divine ground of existence of beauty. 'Like revelation, all beauty holds in itself the orders of the history of philosophy. For beauty makes visible not the idea but rather the latter's secret' (*SW* 1: 351). The expressionless appears in the work of art as a guarantee against false mixtures or as 'critical force' that exposes the necessary differentiations. When Benjamin states that the expressionless interrupts (*ins Wort fallen*) harmony, then this is the name in the realm of art for what, coming from another place, beyond art, interrupts poetry.

3   THE RELATIONSHIP OF THE WORK OF ART TO THE TRAGIC

In order to grasp this category of the expressionless in more concrete terms, Benjamin undertakes some digressions into the realm of the tragic. Thus, the drawing of a strict border between the discourse of art and a 'speech before God' is corroborated by yet a different trace that carries the name of the tragic.

The tragic versus mourning

This course, too, starts out by delimiting itself from a myth typical of the Goethe cult, namely, the phrase that speaks of the 'tragic dimension in the life of the Olympian' (*SW* 1: 320). Even in this phrase confusion abounds; yet, this time the confusion does not pertain to the demarcation of the human from the divine but to that of the human from the tragic order: 'The tragic exists only in the being of the dramatic persona – that is to say, the person enacting or representing himself – never in the existence of the human being' (ibid.). This concept of the tragic, too, dates back to work from a decade before, to Benjamin's early work on language. One of the preliminary studies to the essay on language, 'The Role of Language in *Trauerspiel* and Tragedy', focused, among other things, on the difference between mourning – as a feeling whose transformation into words as phenomenon lies at the root of the *Trauerspiel* – and the tragic: 'It is the pure word itself that has an immediate tragic force' (*SW* 1: 59).

Given this definition of the tragic, Benjamin must also reject interpretations that lend a 'tragic quality' to Ottilie, whose 'lingering, at once guilty and guiltless, in the precincts of fate' gives her, 'for the fleeting glance' (that is, Gundolf's and François-Poncet's) 'a tragic quality' (*SW* 1: 337). 'Yet this is the falsest of judgments' (ibid.). Since the tragic is always linked to the word, it alone belongs to the tragic personae, to the tragic hero, whose place likewise is defined by means of a beyond, albeit, in this case, through the negation of a beyond that constitutes a specific 'here-and-now' (*Diesseits*). 'Beyond Guilt and Innocence is grounded the here-and-now of Good and Evil, attainable by the hero alone.' This is why Benjamin rejects the notion of Ottilie's 'tragic purification' as follows: 'Nothing more untragic can be conceived than this mournful end' (ibid.).

The expressionless as caesura in the tragic

In 'Goethe's Elective Affinities', the category of the expressionless constitutes the interface between the 'true work of art' and the tragic. For, in order to demonstrate that the expressionless is 'a category of language and art, not of the work or of the genres' (*SW* 1: 340), Benjamin takes a detour through Hölderlin's concept of caesura, through his 'Annotations to Oedipus', 'whose fundamental significance for the theory of art in general beyond serving as the basis of tragedy seems not to have been recognized' (*SW* 1: 340); Benjamin quotes Hölderlin's description of the caesura as mere word, i.e. as a 'counterrhythmic rupture' (*SW* 1: 340–41) in a rhythmic continuity, as which the tragic transport represents itself.[8] It is 'that caesura, in which, along with harmony, every expression simultaneously comes to a standstill, in order to give free reign to an expressionless power inside all artistic media' (*SW* 1: 341). The caesura therefore appears either as silencing, as objection, or also as 'something beyond the poet [that] interrupts the language of the poetry' (*SW* 1: 341).

Mysterium: the accord of hope and caesura

Following Hölderlin, the caesura is interpreted as an inherently, tragic constellation that signifies the site for a breach of a 'beyond' in the tragic order. In the final passages of Benjamin's essay this caesura is brought into accord with the star of hope. For the phrase about hope, which like a star falling from the sky shot across Eduard and Ottilie's heads, entails for Benjamin – 'to speak with Hölderlin' – the 'caesura of the work' (*SW* 1: 354). Thus the symbol of the star of hope does not only occupy in the novel the place of the expressionless, counteracting semblance *in* the work of art (and therewith the mythology of victim and martyr, attributed to the characters); rather, the function of the expressionless now explicitly fuses with that which interrupts the language of art from beyond, and thus acquires the meaning of 'the mystery in the exact sense of the term' (*SW* 1: 355).

In Benjamin's theory of art, figures of the tragic are being written about for a linguistic order, in which myth and tragedy have disappeared, and in which the subject finds itself instead positioned opposite a different kind of 'beyond'. In other words, Benjamin's star of hope is, therefore, placed exactly at the point where the acknowledgement of the secret (as a divine imprint of beauty) and the acknowledgment of a different language (of the expressionless or non-communicable) merge in the figure of the caesura, which is the condition of possibility for their breach, their falling or jutting into, coming from a beyond.[9]

NOTES

INTRODUCTION

1   The term *Frühromantik* (also 'Jena Romanticism') is used to refer to the first period (1790–1801) of the Romantic movement in Germany, in contradistinction to High and Late Romanticism. Its principal members consisted of the contributors to the movement's programmatic journal *Athenaeum* (1789–1800): the brothers August Wilhelm and Friedrich Schlegel, Novalis (Friedrich von Hardenberg), and the philosopher-theologian Friedrich Schleiermacher. The philosophies of Kant, Fichte and Schelling provided the main intellectual impetus to the Early Romantics' aesthetic and critical theories. Other literary authors associated with Early Romanticism include Caroline Schlegel-Schelling, Dorothea Veit-Schlegel, Ludwig Tieck and W. H. Wackenroder.

2   As fragment 116 of the *Athenaeum* fragments puts it: 'Romantic poetry is a progressive, universal poetry'. Friedrich Schlegel, *Philosophical Fragments*, trans. Peter Firchow (Minneapolis and London: University of Minnesota Press, 1991), p. 31. On the status of the project as a 'fragment of the future', see *Athenaeum*, fragment 22. (All subsequent references to 'fragments' from the *Athenaeum* will appear in the text as *Ath*. fgm., followed by the fragment's number.) For a discussion of the fragment and other definitions of the Romantic artwork, see also the chapter 'The Fragment' in Philippe Lacoue-Labarthe and Jean-Luc Nancy, *The Literary Absolute: The Theory of Literature in German Romanticism*, trans. Philip Barnard and Cheryl Lester (Albany, NY: State University of New York Press, 1988), pp. 39ff.

3   Benjamin, 'Announcement of the Journal *Angelus Novus*', in Walter Benjamin, *Selected Writings* (Cambridge, MA, and London: Harvard University Press, 1996), vol. 1: 292. All further references to this edition will appear parenthentically in the text as *SW*, followed by volume and page numbers.

4   For an analysis of the term *Kunstkritik* and critique/criticism, see also ' "Dichtermut" and "Blödigkeit": Two Poems by Friedrich Hölderlin, Interpreted by Walter Benjamin', Chapter 9, note 19, this volume.

5   Walter Benjamin, *The Correspondence of Walter Benjamin, 1910–1940*, trans. Manfred R. Jacobsen and Evelyn M. Jacobsen (Chicago, IL: University of Chicago Press, 1994), p. 119.

6   Within the context of this introduction the philosophical consequences of these issues cannot fully be explored. For a more extensive interpretation of Benjamin's conception of the Early Romantics' 'linguistic mysticism', 'mediate immediacy' (concept vs. intuition), positive vs. negative critique, Kant's esoteric side, Novalis's philosophy of nature and the Romantic symbol vs. dialectical allegory, see Beatrice Hanssen, 'Language and Mimesis in the Work of Walter Benjamin', in David Ferris (ed.), *The Cambridge Companion to Walter Benjamin* (Cambridge: Cambridge University Press, 2003).

7   Lacoue-Labarthe and Nancy, *The Literary Absolute*, pp. 11–12.

8   Benjamin, *Correspondence*, pp. 79–81.

9   Benjamin's negative appraisal of modern criticism also is voiced in *The Concept of Criticism*, pp. 154–5.

10 See Benjamin's essay 'The Task of the Translator', in Benjamin, *Selected Writings*, 1: 253–63. Benjamin's qualifying pronouncement about Romantic criticism comes somewhat as a surprise considering his avowed admiration of Romantic criticism, expressed in the 1922 announcement of *Angelus Novus*, cited earlier. Moreover, he fails to consider the intimate relation between the Romantics' practice of critique and their theory of translation, addressed in the *Athenaeum* fragments. For an analysis of the Romantic philosophy of translation, see also Antoine Berman, *The Experience of the Foreign: Culture and Translation in Romantic Germany*, trans. S. Heyvaert (Albany, NY: SUNY Press, 1992).

11 Schlegel, *Philosophical Fragments*, p. 45.

12 Walter Benjamin, *The Origin of German Tragic Drama*, trans. John Osborne (London: Verso, 1985), pp. 187–9.

CHAPTER 1

1   Compare the *Editorische Notiz* by Herman Schweppenhäuser, editor of the dissertation for the *Gesammelte Schriften*, published by Suhrkamp starting in 1974.

2   One could also refer to the biographical account, in French, by Friedrich Podkus, trans. by Maurice de Gandillac (in *Mythe et violence* [Denoël/Lettres nouvelles, 1971]) or to the chronology established by Guy Petitdemange at the beginning of the French translation of Benjamin's letters (*Correspondance* [Paris: Aubier Montaigne, 1979]).

3   Walter Benjamin, *Briefe*, ed. Gershom Scholem and Theodor Adorno, 2 vols (Frankfurt a. M.: Suhrkamp, 1978), 1: 201. Subsequent citations to this work appear in the text.

4   'Das Leben der Studenten', *Gesammelte Schriften*, ed. Rolf Tiedemann and Hermann Schweppenhäuser (Frankfurt a. M.: Suhrkamp, 1974–), 2.1: 75–87.

5   'The Task of the Translator', trans. Harry Zohn, in *Illuminations*, ed. Hannah Arendt (New York: Schocken, 1969), pp. 69–82.

6   'On Language as Such and on the Language of Man', trans. Edmund Jephcott, in *Reflections*, ed. Peter Demetz (New York: Harcourt, 1978), pp. 314–32.

7   On this subject, see Irving Wohlfarth, 'Sur quelques motifs juifs chez Benjamin', *Revue d'esthétique*, nouvelle séries, no. 1 (Privat, 1981).

8   Here, 'aesthetic [art] criticism' (*Kunstkritik*) signifies essentially 'literary criticism'.

9   Compare 'The Idea of Art', Part Two, Section 3 of *The Concept of Criticism SW*, 1: 165ff.

10 *Briefe* 1: 150. It is necessary to relate this motif to what is said about Kantian terminology in the letter to Scholem of 7 December 1917 (Benjamin is, besides, very attentive in the dissertation to the 'mystical terminology' of the Romantics). On this subject, Benjamin outlined a thesis project which would not be pursued:

> The study, of Kant's terminology, without doubt the only one in philosophy which not only arose completed but was created so, reveals its extraordinary power over

knowledge and however it may be, one learns a great deal from its immanent development and definition. In this sense, I have recently come across a topic which could eventually be agreeable to me for the doctorate: the concept of the 'infinite task' in Kant. (*Briefe* 1: 159).

11 Compare the letter to Scholem of 1 February 1918. Benjamin reaffirms the same impossibility.

From Kant's writings on history it is absolutely impossible to gain access to the philosophy of history. An alternative would be to have begun with the ethical; however, that is only possible within limits and Kant himself did not take this path. To convince yourself, read the 'Idea for a Universal History from a Cosmopolitan Point of View'. (*Briefe* 1: 176)

12 On this point, attention can only be drawn to the admirable essay by Hannah Arendt published in French in *Vies politiques* (Paris: Gallimard, 1974), pp. 244ff.

CHAPTER 2

1 Walter Benjamin, 'Selbstanzeige der Dissertation', in *Walter Benjamin: Gesammelte Schriften*, ed. Rolf Tiedemann and Hermann Schweppenhäuser (Frankfurt a. M.: Suhrkamp, 1974–), 1: 707–8.

2 *SW* refers throughout to: Walter Benjamin, *Selected Writings* (2 vols), ed. Marcus Bullock and Michael W. Jennings (Cambridge, MA/London: Belknap Press/Harvard University Press, 1996–7).

3 J. G. Fichte, *Versuch einer neuen Darstellung der Wissenschaftslehre*, in *Sämmtliche Werke* (9 vols), ed. I. H. Fichte (Berlin, 1845–6; repr. Berlin: de Gruyter, 1971), quotations from 1: 521ff.

4 J. G. Fichte, *Über den Begriff der Wissenschaftslehre*, in *Sämmtliche Werke* 1: 67.

5 Ibid., pp. 51ff., 71.

6 Ibid., p. 72.

7 Ibid., pp. 47ff.

8 J. G. Fichte, *Grundlage der gesamten Wissenschaftslehre*, in *Sämmtliche Werke* 1: 91.

9 Ibid., p. 123.

10 Novalis, *Schriften* (4 vols), ed. Paul Kluckhohn (Stuttgart: Kohlhammer, 1968–81), 2: 206.

11 Ibid., 1: 127.

12 Ibid., 2: 127, 131.

13 Friedrich Schlegel, *Kritische Friedrich-Schlegel-Ausgabe* (19 vols), ed. Hans Eichner (Paderborn/Munich/Vienna: Schöningh, 1958 onwards), 19: 25.

14 Novalis, *Schriften* 2: 131.

15   J. G. Fichte, *Die Wissenschaftslehre (1812)*, in *Nachgelassene Werke* (3 vols), ed. I. H. Fichte (Bonn, 1834–5; repr. Berlin: de Gruyter, 1962), quotations in 2: 325; and *Bericht über den Begriff der Wissenschaftslehre und die bisherigen Schicksale derselben (1806)*, in *Nachgelassene Werke* 2: 364.

16   Cf. Wolfgang Janke, *Fichte. Sein und Reflexion – Grundlagen der kritischen Vernunft* (Berlin: de Gruyter, 1970), p. 36.

17   Cf. the following two pieces of writing that appeared shortly after one another: *Zweite Einleitung in die Wissenschaftslehre* and *Versuch einer neuen Darstellung der Wissenschaftslehre*, in Fichte, *Sämmtliche Werke* 1, esp. pp. 459ff.; 521ff., 530.

18   Idem, *Grundlage*, p. 295.

19   Novalis, *Schriften*, 2: 113–25.

20   Ibid., 2: 113–17.

21   Schlegel, *Kritische Ausgabe* 18: 250.

22   Ibid., 2: 115.

23   Ibid., 18: 374.

24   Fichte, *Versuch einer neuen Darstellung der Wissenschaftslehre*, p. 526. In a strict sense, Fichte's immediate self-consciousness within intellectual intuition is 'not consciousness at all, not even a self-consciousness' (*Zweite Einleitung in die Wissenschaftslehre*, p. 459) – since speaking of a consciousness implies, within its traditional grammar, an '*of*' (i.e. consciousness '*of*' something) and thereby also precisely that subject–object division of (reflective) consciousness which Fichte's formulation of 'real self-consciousness' *qua* intellectual intuition seeks to overcome.

25   Idem, *Grundlage*, pp. 243–4.

26   Ibid., p. 217.

27   Ibid., p. 91.

28   This is demonstrated in the subsequent chapters of Winfried Menninghaus, *Unendliche Verdopplung: Die frühromantische Grundlegung der Kunsttheorie im Begriff absoluter Selbstreflexion* (Frankfurt a. M.: Suhrkamp, 1987).

29   Walter Benjamin, *Briefe*, ed. Gershom Scholem and Theodor W. Adorno (Frankfurt a. M.: Suhrkamp, 1966), p. 188.

30   Schlegel, *Kritische Ausgabe*, 12: 355, 357.

31   Paul Lerch, *Friedrich Schlegels philosophische Anschauungen in ihrer Entwicklung und systematischer Ausgestaltung* (Berlin: Germania, 1905), pp. 41ff.

32   Schlegel, *Kritische Ausgabe*, 12: 329.

33   Ibid., 12: 329, 335.

34   Ibid., 12: 332.

35 Ibid., 12: 325.

36 Ibid., 12: 326.

37 Ibid., 12: 329.

38 Ibid., 12: 340.

39 Fichte, *Grundlage*, p. 225.

40 Ibid., pp. 232–3ff.

41 Schlegel, *Kritische Ausgabe*, 2: 176.

42 Cf. Manfred Frank, 'Die Philosophie des sogenannten "magischen Idealismus"', *Euphorion* 63 (1969): 95.

43 Cf. the relevant points of clarification in Fichte, *Zweite Einleitung in die Wissenschaftslehre*, pp. 459–65 and 471–7, esp. p. 472.

44 Schlegel, *Kritische Ausgabe*, 18: 111, 208, 280, 281, 284.

45 Ibid., 18: 70, 40; 19: 57.

46 Ibid., 12: 355.

47 Novalis, *Schriften*, 2: 232.

48 Schlegel, *Kritische Ausgabe*, 18: 476.

49 Ibid., 18: 405.

50 Ibid., 18: 31, 3.

51 Ibid., 19: 129, and cf. p. 161, where Schlegel expressly demands of any 'critical' philosophy 'the destruction of the concept of substance'. Since Schlegel implicatively correlates the concept of positing with that of substance, one can also read this statement as a verdict on positing.

52 Fichte, *Grundlage*, pp. 273ff.

53 This entire study aims to put this footnote also – which on account of its significance by no means belongs in the small print – to the test.

54 Theodor Haering, *Novalis als Philosoph* (Stuttgart: Kohlhammer, 1954); and Manfred Dick, *Die Entwicklung des Gedankens der Poesie in den Fragmenten des Novalis* (Bonn: Bouvier, 1967).

55 Novalis, *Schriften*, 2: 107.

56 Cf. Dick, *Novalis*, pp. 23–7, 122–4.

57 Schlegel, *Kritische Ausgabe*, 18: 271.

58 Ibid., 18: 32.

59 Benjamin too, in an earlier passage in his exposition, refers to this 'dialectic': abso-
    lute reflection, as he puts it there, is nothing but an unfolding of 'original reflection'
    (*SW* 1: 130) – only at this point he has not yet implied that this 'first level of reflec-
    tion', for its part, arises 'from nothing'.

60 Fichte, *Grundlage*, p. 301.

61 Ibid.

62 Novalis, *Schriften*, 2: 114.

63 Cf. Menninghaus, *Unendliche Verdopplung*, p. 86.

64 It is indeed 'feeling' that Fichte defines as an action in which 'the "I" ... does not
    become conscious of itself' (Fichte, *Grundlage*, p. 297).

65 Schlegel, *Kritische Ausgabe*, 18: 309; and *Literary Notebooks 1797–1801*, ed. Hans
    Eichner (London: Athlone, 1957), n. 1990.

66 Ricarda Huch, *Blütezeit der Romantik*, 6th edn (Leipzig: Haessel, 1916), p. 107: 'The
    word "romanticize" ... can sometimes be translated as "becoming conscious" or "making
    conscious", and sometimes as "becoming unconscious" or "making unconscious".'

67 Schlegel, *Kritische Ausgabe*, 19: 164.

68 Menninghaus, *Unendliche Verdopplung*, pp. 200–5, esp. p. 203.

69 Fichte, *Grundlage*, pp. 225, 230.

70 Benjamin, *Briefe*, pp. 166, 171.

71 F. W. J. Schelling, *System des transzendentalen Idealismus*, in *Schriften von 1799–1801*
    (Darmstadt: Wissenschaftliche Buchgesellschaft, 1975), p. 600.

72 Cf. ibid., pp. 610ff..

73 F. W. J. Schelling, *Ideen zu einer Philosophie der Natur*, in *Schriften von 1794–1798*
    (Darmstadt: Wissenschaftliche Buchgesellschaft, 1980), p. 337.

74 Ibid., p. 338.

75 In this regard, I am contradicting Klaus Peter, who on the basis of certain scarcely
    plausible reasons has formulated a diametrically opposed line of argumentation.
    According to Peter 'it is rather Schelling than Schlegel [whom Benjamin describes] in
    his interpretations of Schlegel'. In *Idealismus als Kritik: Friedrich Schlegels Philosophie
    der unvollendeten Welt* (Stuttgart/Berlin/Cologne/Mainz: Kohlhammer, 1973), p. 26.
    Cf. also the similar line of argumentation in Klaus Peter, 'Friedrich Schlegels ästhe-
    tischer Intellektualismus: Studien über die paradoxe Einheit von Philosophie und Kunst
    in den Jahren vor 1800' (PhD dissertation, Frankfurt a. M., 1966), p. 27.

76 Cf. Haering, *Novalis als Philosoph*, pp. 610ff.

77 Cf. Dick, Novalis, pp. 328–30, 400–3.

78 Schlegel, *Kritische Ausgabe* 18: 518.

79 That the 'medium of reflection' concept pertains only to the interpretative language, but not to the interpreted one, is a point that Benjamin himself stresses clearly enough (*SW* 1: 132).

80 Fichte, *Grundlage*, pp. 199, 204.

81 In this reading of Fichte, I am following a rather customary tradition that is also widely attested in the research into Novalis. Alexis Philonenko, in his book *La Liberté humaine dans la philosophie de Fichte* (Paris: Vrin, 1966), has however put forward numerous arguments for a revision of this interpretation. According to Philonenko, the absolute 'I' is a *transcendental illusion* (in Kant's sense) which Fichte constitutes (or seizes on as an implication of formal logic) only in order to destroy it (and with it, formal logic) *as a sham* – through reference, specifically, to the conceptualization of imagination which would not in this regard be transcended by the absolute 'I', but by contrast would situate this within its boundaries. From this viewpoint, Fichte's and Novalis's systematic relation of the *absolute* and (hovering) *reciprocity* within *imagination* is an analogous one – in which regard it must remain mysterious as to why Fichte focuses on the sham character of an absolute 'I' *beyond* reciprocity only relatively little, and puts forward the opposite line of interpretation so powerfully.

82 Menninghaus, *Unendliche Verdopplung*, pp. 89ff.

83 Schlegel, *Kritische Ausgabe*, 18: 403.

84 Menninghaus, *Unendliche Verdopplung*, pp. 115ff.

85 Novalis, *Schriften*, 2: 296.

86 Ibid., 2: 238.

87 This re-evaluation by Benjamin, which neglects the activity of the cognitive subject in favour of the object's self-recognition (and which Benjamin himself contradicts at numerous points in his text) is also countered by various of the objections raised in Peter Gebhardt's essay 'Über einige Voraussetzungen der Literaturkritik Benjamins', in *Walter Benjamin – Zeitgenosse der Moderne*, ed. Gebhardt et al. (Kronberg: Scriptor, 1976), pp. 72–4.

88 Cf. Schlegel, *Literary Notebooks*, n. 1586; and *FS* 19: 164.

89 Idem, *Kritische Ausgabe*, 2: 182ff.

90 Cf. Götz Braun, *Norm und Geschichtlichkeit der Dichtung. Klassisch-romantische Ästhetik und moderne Literatur* (Berlin/New York: de Gruyter, 1983), p. 139.

91 Novalis, *Schriften*, 2: 108ff.

92 Ibid., 3: 253.

93 Fichte, *Grundlage*, pp. 219–22.

94 Novalis, *Schriften*, 3: 388.

95 Ibid., 2: 253.

96 Roman Jakobson, 'Linguistics and Poetics', in *Style in Language*, ed. Thomas A. Seboek (Cambridge/New York/London: MIT Press, 1960), pp. 370–71ff.

97   Ibid., p. 356.

98   Ibid., p. 371.

99   Heinz-Dieter Weber, *Friedrich Schlegels 'Transzendentalpoesie'. Untersuchungen zum Funktionswandel der Literaturkritik im 18. Jahrhundert* (Munich: Fink, 1973), p. 13.

100   Schlegel, *Kritische Ausgabe* 2: 208.

101   Idem, *Von der Schönheit in der Dichtkunst*, in *Neue philosophische Schriften*, with a commentary and introduction by Josef Körner (Frankfurt: a. M.: Schulte-Bulmke, 1935), p. 379.

102   Idem, *Kritische Ausgabe*, 1: 358.

103   Ibid., 2: 14.

104   Idem, *Literary Notebooks*, n. 1733.

105   Idem, *Kritische Ausgabe*, 2: 133.

106   Novalis, *Schriften*, 2: 470; and cf. *SW* 1: 153.

107   Schlegel, *Kritische Ausgabe*, 18: 106.

108   Cf. ibid., 2: 103, 169, 201; and 18: 20, 49, 114, 169.

109   Benjamin distinguishes characterization in Schlegel's sense from critique in that it lacks raising the work to a higher degree of its own being; as non-potentiating criticism, characterization is regarded by Benjamin as 'on the one hand, adapted to mediocre work and, on the other hand, according to the review of *Wilhelm Meister*, the business generally of unpoetic critics' (*SW* 1: 193, n. 183). Only a very small number of statements by Schlegel can be furnished that support this conception, which is presumably drawn from Rudolf Haym (cf. *Die Romantische Schule. Ein Beitrag zur Geschichte des deutschen Geistes*, 3rd edn [Berlin: Weidmann, 1914], p. 261); however, one of these statements *is* a celebrated one from the review of *Wilhelm Meister* (Schlegel, *Kritische Ausgabe* 2: 140). Generally, though, and quite contrarily, it is a high estimation of characterization that predominates: 'A characterization is a work of art of critique' (ibid., 2: 253) and therefore its highest form which, rather than being adapted only to mediocre work, indeed first grounds 'the selection of classics', and which, rather than being only the business of unpoetic critics, actually fulfils the demand for a critique that is itself poetic. Accordingly, René Wellek has previously challenged Benjamin's distinction of characterization and criticism ('The Early Literary Criticism of Walter Benjamin', in *Rice University Studies* 57.4 (1971): 127).

CHAPTER 3

1   Philippe Lacoue-Labarthe and Jean-Luc Nancy, *L'Absolu littéraire. Théorie de la littérature du romantisme allemand* (Paris: Seuil, 1978), p. 30. In a passage not taken up into the English translation (*The Literary Absolute*, trans. P. Barnard and C. Lester [Albany: SUNY Press, 1988]), the authors describe Benjamin's thesis, and note that 'it did not fail to create a "revolutionary" effect in traditional Romantic studies'. Winfried Menninghaus, *Unendliche Verdopplung. Die frühromantische Grundlegung der Kunsttheorie im Begriff absoluter Selbstreflexion* (Frankfurt a. M.: Suhrkamp, 1987).

2   Walter Benjamin, 'Der Begriff der Kunstkritik in der deutschen Romantik', in
    Gesammelte Schriften (Frankfurt a. M.: Suhrkamp, 1974–), 1.1: 9–122. All quotes
    within the text refer to this edition. The English translation used of Benjamin's doctoral
    dissertation is by David R. Lachterman, and has been revised by Piotr Parlej. This
    translation is unpublished.

3   In a letter of 8 November 1918, to Ernst Schoen, Benjamin writes that the work involved
    in writing his dissertation is not lost time: 'However, what I gain from it, namely an
    insight into the relation of a truth to history, will barely become articulated in it, but
    noticeable for intelligent readers I hope.' In another letter to Schoen of 7 April 1919, he
    remarks:

> A couple of days ago I finished the draft of my dissertation. It has become what it was
> supposed to become: an indication of the true nature of Romanticism totally
> unknown in the literature [on this subject] – yet only indirectly, because I could not
> deal with the centre of Romanticism, namely messianism (I have treated only its
> conception of art), and with something else that is very much upon my mind,
> without jeopardizing the required complex and conventional scientific attitude which
> I distinguish from the authentic one. Yet, I hope to have made it possible to become
> aware of this state of affairs from within this work. (Walter Benjamin, *Briefe*, ed.
> G. Scholem and T. W. Adorno [Frankfurt a. M.: Suhrkamp, 1966], 1: 202–3, 208.)

4   Since Benjamin does not let up on his criticism of the Romantic concept of art criticism
    in the second part of the dissertation – quite the opposite is true – it would seem that the
    peculiar fruitfulness that some Romantic propositions have gained in the theory of art,
    and to which Benjamin alludes, presupposes a critical dismantling of their specifically
    Romantic underpinnings.

5   Friedrich Schlegel, *Kritische Schriften* (Munich: Hanser Verlag, 1970), p. 424.

6   Indeed, it is highly doubtful whether the Romantic 'idea', or Absolute is an idea in the
    Platonic sense. See my 'Ideality in Fragmentation', in Friedrich Schlegel, *Philosophical
    Fragments*, trans. P. Firchow (Minneapolis, MN: University of Minnesota Press, 1991),
    xxviii–xxx.

CHAPTER 4

1   See the letter to Gershom Scholem, dated as June 1917, in which Benjamin returns to
    thoughts of a study of the Romantics, *The Correspondence of Walter Benjamin*, ed. and
    ann. Gershom Scholem and Theodor W. Adorno, trans. Manfred R. Jacobson and Evelyn
    M. Jacobson (Chicago, IL, and London: University of Chicago Press, 1994), p. 88.

2   Marcus Paul Bullock, *Romanticism and Marxism* (Frankfurt a. M., Bern, New York: Peter
    Lang, 1987), gives the most thorough and in some respects damaging account of
    Benjamin's faulty grasp of the differences between Friedrich Schlegel and Novalis, as well
    as of the unavoidable lacunae in Benjamin's knowledge of Schlegel on the basis of the
    texts available to him. See, in Chapter 2, 'Schlegel and Novalis', pp. 85–97. While
    recognizing the feints and deficits of Benjamin's exposition and argument, Winfried
    Menninghaus convincingly demonstrates the extent to which Benjamin's intuitive
    grasp of Romantic theory nevertheless deduces an authentic interpretation of reflexivity.
    See Winfried Menninghaus, 'Walter Benjamin's Exposition of the Romantic Theory of
    Reflection', in this volume. The German original can be found in Winfried Men-
    ninghaus, *Unendliche Verdopplung. Die frühromantische Grundlegung der Kunst im Begriff
    absoluter Selbstreflexion* (Frankfurt a. M., Suhrkamp, 1987), Chapter 2, pp. 30–71.

3   See Menninghaus, *Unendliche Verdopplung*, pp. 41–2.

4   Friedrich Schlegel, *Kritische Friedrich-Schlegel-Ausgabe*, ed. Ernst Behler with Jean-Jacques Anstett and Hans Eichner, Erste Abteilung (Kritische Neuausgabe), (Munich, Paderborn, Vienna: Schöningh, 1958ff.), 1.2: 336.

5   Walter Benjamin, *The Concept of Criticism in German Romanticism*, trans. David Lachtermann, Howard Eiland and Ian Balfour, in Walter Benjamin, *Selected Writings*, vol. 1, 1913–26, ed. Marcus Bullock and Michael W. Jennings (Cambridge, MA, and London: Harvard University Press, 1996), p. 173. Further quotations in English, identified by *SW*, volume and page number, are from this translation. Where I have modified or provided an alternative to the existing translation, this is indicated. I refer to the German text, Walter Benjamin, *Der Begriff der Kunstkritik in der deutschen Romantik*, in *Gesammelte Schriften*, ed. Rolf Tiedemann and Hermann Schweppenhäuser (Frankfurt a. M.: Suhrkamp, 1974), vol. 1.1, cited in the text as *GS*, followed by volume and page number.

6   The view of art outlined in the afterword to the dissertation under the rubric of 'das Musische' and attributed to Goethe is the very tactful *point de départ* for Andrew Benjamin's reading of Goethe's poem 'Immer und überall', 'Poetry and the Returns of Time: Goethe's "immer and überall" and "Wachstum" ', in Andrew Benjamin, *Philosophy's Literature* (London: Clinamen Press, 2001), pp. 135–45. This study, and particularly its accounts of Kant's view of the Absolute in the *Critique of Judgement* and of Walter Benjamin's understanding of critique (pp. 5–21) is the most sustained recent engagement with *Der Begriff der Kunstkritik*, and the present chapter benefits from its insights.

7   Friedrich Schlegel, *Kritische Friedrich-Schlegel-Ausgabe*, 1.5: 72. The Harvard edition rarely gives accessible references to recent editions of the Romantic authors Benjamin quotes, unless a numbered series of fragments (such as the *Athenäumsfragmente* or 'Lyceumsfragmente') are in question. And in this particular case, it is striking that Benjamin does not bother to refer to the title of the chapter from which he quotes – 'Eine Reflexion'. Menninghaus mercilessly unmasks the inadequacies of Benjamin's exposition here. See Menninghaus, *Unendliche Verdopplung*, pp. 31–2.

8   Johann Gottlieb Fichte, *Schriften zur Wissenschaftslehre*, ed. Wilhelm G. Jacobs (Frankfurt a. M.: Deutscher Klassiker Verlag, 1997), pp. 99–131; *Introductions to the Wissenschaftslehre and other writings*, trans. David Breazeale (Cambridge, IN: Hackett, 1994).

9   Walter Benjamin, *Illuminations*, trans. Harry Zohn (London: Collins/Fontana, 1973), pp. 255–66 ('Über den Begriff der Geschichte', *GS* 1.2: 691–704). Michael Löwy notes the similarity in 'Benjamin and Romanticism', *global benjamin* 1 (Internationaler Walter-Benjamin-Kongress, 1992), ed. Klaus Garber and Ludwig Rehm (Munich: Wilhelm Fink Verlag, n.d.), pp. 681–7, 683.

10   Menninghaus's structural account of Romantic theories of reflection identifies them, in their turn, as ' "reflect[ing]" the self-referential, differential system-character of language'. See Menninghaus, *Unendliche Verdopplung*, p. 58. Menninghaus comments that Benjamin follows Novalis and Schlegel in his emphatic use of the apparently 'inconspicuous term', but pursues it only intermittently. See particularly Menninghaus, *Unendliche Verdopplung*, pp. 92–4.

11   Friedrich Hölderlin, *Sämtliche Werke*. Kleine Stuttgarter Ausgabe, Lerausgegeben von Friedrich Beissner (Stuttgart: Cotta, 1946–62), 5: 311.

12 My reading departs from the *Selected Writings*: the quantifier of '*in* einigen *ihrer Ideenzusammenhänge*' cannot be read with the absolute '*ohne Fühlung*'. See *GS* 1.1: 26. The translation of '*Ideenzusammenhänge*' as 'the various ideas' fails to register the extra-ordinary insistence of Benjamin's vocabulary in this passage.

13 Rodolphe Gasché's exposition of Derrida's notion of 'the general text' in *The Tain of the Mirror* (London: Harvard University Press, 1986), pp. 278–93, can be read as a critique of the textuality implied here. See particularly p. 279, on text as dialectical sublation, p. 291, on 'the illusion of self-reflection of a text'.

14 See the passage in *The Concept of Criticism*, pp. 122–3, to which Benjamin's footnote (32) refers (*GS* 1.1: 30 referring to *GS* 1.1: 120).

15 Leibniz is of course an appropriate source for this modelling of Romantic notions of reflexivity, particularly as they are effected in Friedrich Schlegel's theorization of the fragment in the *Athenäumsfragmente*. Where the monads reflect the totality of their system more or less perfectly, the fragments are conceived as mirroring both the historical and cultural world which is their prismatic 'content' and their proper generic self-conception. See, for example, *Athenäumsfragmente* 121, 220, *Kritische Friedrich-Schlegel-Ausgabe*, 1.2: 184–5, 199–200.

16 For a brief account, see Philippe Lacoue-Labarthe, 'Introduction to Walter Benjamin's *The Concept of Art Criticism in the German Romantics*', *Studies in Romanticism* 31 (1992): 421–32 (Chapter 1 in this volume); Rodolphe Gasché in 'The Sober Absolute: On Benjamin and the Early Romantics', *Studies in Romanticism* 31 (1992): 433–53 (Chapter 3 this volume) identifies the esoteric dimension of the dissertation as 'Benjamin's massive and intransigent criticism of the romantic conception of art' (p. 452), disclosed in the final section on 'The Early Romantic Theory of Art and Goethe' which was not submitted for examination. Margarete Kohlenbach in 'The Desire for Objectivity: Walter Benjamin and Early Romanticism', *GLL* 48 (1995): 25–38, situates the dissertation in Benjamin's earlier work and identifies a recurrent concern in his repeated attempts to construct a religious position in a world of disenchantment.

17 See Maurice Merleau-Ponty, *L'Oeil et l'esprit* (Paris: Gallimard, 1964), and *The Merleau-Ponty Aesthetics Reader*, ed. Galen A. Johnson (Evanston, IL: Northwestern University Press, 1993).

18 Benjamin's letter to Scholem of June 1917 indicates as much: 'I will proceed by arranging some Friedrich Schlegel-like fragments, according to their *systematic* basic ideas …' See *The Correspondence of Walter Benjamin*, 88.

19 A similar series of manoeuvres can be found in Friedrich Schlegel's 'Gespräch über die Poesie' (Dialogue on Poetry), where Schlegel's introductory remarks locate a kind of *Ur*-poetry in the being of the earth. See *Kritische Friedrich-Schlegel-Ausgabe*, 1.2: 284.

20 Critique here is understood as the determination of the conditions of possibility of the work, in contrast to the evaluation of a work – by whatever standards of connoisseur-ship or tradition – in literary criticism.

21 The case Benjamin is making for the significance of the novel is taken up by Lacoue-Labarthe and Nancy in *L'Absolu littéraire* (Paris: du Seuil, 1978), with reference to the more extreme 'non-genre' of the fragment: a further determination of the absolute reflexivity of art as *prose*.

22 Lachtermann, Eiland and Balfour are misleading when they render this, presumably for reasons of euphony, as '*an* expression': epic retardation is central to the understanding of reflexivity Benjamin has developed.

23 On flamboyance in Schlegel's theory of the novel, see Marshall Brown, 'Theory of the Novel', in *Romanticism* (*Cambridge History of Literary Criticism*, Vol. 5), ed. Marshall Brown (Cambridge: Cambridge University Press, 2000), pp. 256–9. The classic case of the cult of the book is Chapter 5 of Part I of Novalis's *Heinrich von Ofterdingen*.

24 Benjamin takes the Romantics to task for confusing the categories of profane form, symbolic form and of criticism – and Gasché reinforces the case. See *GS* 1.1: 96–8; Gasché, 'The Sober Absolute', pp. 448–9: the translation of 'Tragweite der Reflexion', given here as 'the bearing of reflexion for the artwork' and reprinted unchanged in *Walter Benjamin. Theoretical Questions*, ed. David Ferris (Stanford: Stanford University Press, 1996), is certainly unclear and possibly misleading. Benjamin's reliance here and at a number of other points on the secondary literature current at the time is some indication of his difficulty in fabricating an argument and deserves examination.

25 My translation: the standard version wrongly translates '*der ausgehenden französischen Romantik*' as 'French Romanticism (which succeeded it)': this would require '*der von ihr ausgehenden*', and anyway it is a point Benjamin has just made.

26 Novalis's testimony here certainly confirms the confusions diagnosed by Marcus Paul Bullock as an effect of Benjamin's conceptual sleight of hand. See Bullock, *Romanticism and Marxism*, p. 90.

27 Andrew Benjamin, *Philosophy's Literature*, p. 111.

CHAPTER 5

1 A different German version of this chapter from 1993 can be found in C. Hart-Nibbrig (ed.), *Übersetzen: Benjamin* (Frankfurt a. M.: Suhrkamp, 2001). Benjamin's model of translation is also addressed in the contributions by Hans Jost Frey and Rainer Nägele in this volume and in Rainer Nägele, *Echoes of Translation: Reading Between Texts* (Baltimore, MD: Johns Hopkins University Press, 1997). On the model of the 'echo' and its Baroque and Romantic properties, cf. Bettine Menke, *Prosopopoiia. Stimme und Text* (Munich: Fink, 2000).

2 Cf. the English-language translation of these lines in Nägele, *Echoes of Translation*, p. 36, 33; and also Walter Benjamin, 'The Task of the Translator', trans. Harry Zohn, in *Walter Benjamin: Selected Writings Volume 1: 1913–1926*, ed. Marcus Bullock and Michael W. Jennings (Cambridge, MA/London: Belknap Press/Harvard University Press, 1996), pp. 258–9 (hereafter *SW*). This and other subsequent quotations from existing English-language translations of Benjamin have been lightly modified here with reference to the original German texts.

3 Walter Benjamin, 'One-Way Street', trans. Edmund Jephcott, in *SW* 1: 445.

4 The Task of the Translator', p. 258.

5 '. . . it is an age-old saying that however one calls into the forest, just so does it echo back' (Jakob Grimm, 'Über das Echo. Gelesen in der Akademie der Wissenschaften am 25. Juni 1863', in idem, *Kleinere Schriften 7. Bd. Recensionen und vermischte Aufsätze 4. Teil* (Berlin: Dümmler, 1884), pp. 499–512, quotation on p. 503). Carol Jacobs also

refers to this proverb – 'a German saying' that is echoed by Benjamin – in 'The Monstrosity of Translation'. However, Jacobs notes that: 'Translation's call into the forest of language is not a repetition of the original but the awakening of an echo of itself ... the sound that returns is its own tongue become foreign' (*MLN* 90 (1979): 755–66, quotation on p. 764).

6 Athanasius Kircher, *Neue Hall= und Thon=Kunst*, trans. Agatho Carione (Nördlingen: A. Kircher, 1684), p. 37.

7 See for example ibid., p. 30.

8 Echo poems found success in the Baroque period (cf. Johannes Bolte, 'Das Echo in Volksglaube und Dichtung', *Sitzungsberichte der Preussischen Akademie der Wissenschaften. Philosoph. Histor. Klasse* 1935: 262–98) and were subsequently taken up – backed up by the new literary theory of A. F. Bernhardi's *Sprachlehre* (1801–3) – within the lyric poetry of Romanticism (A. W. Schlegel, 'Waldgespräch', L. Tieck, C. Brentano; and cf. Menke *Prosopopoiia*, pp. 491–524).

9 G. P. Harsdörffer, *Der Mathematischen und Philosophischen Erquickstunden, 2. Teil* (1636; repr. Frankfurt a. M.: Keips 1990), p. 158.

10 As should be apparent, it is a problem of translation here. Publius Ovidius Naso, *Metamorphosen* [Latin/German] (Zürich/Düsseldorf: Artemis & Winkler, 1996), Vol. 3, v. 356–401, quotation from v. 391. Since Echo 'only repeats the final clause, she destroys his rejection and draws out of it desire ... Changing is Echo's lot.' (Peter Bexte, 'OH CET ECHO' in *Emile 2* (1989), 2: pp. 4–16, quotation on p. 8).

11 Walter Benjamin, 'The Role of Language in *Trauerspiel* and Tragedy', trans. Rodney Livingstone, in *SW* 1: 60.

12 Walter Benjamin, *The Origin of German Tragic Drama*, trans. John Osborne (London/New York: Verso, 1977), pp. 209–210; and Nägele, *Echoes of Translation*, p. 45.

13 J. A. Stranitzky, *Die Glorreiche Marter des Heyligen Joannes Von Nepomuckh unter Wenzeslao dem faulen König der Böhhmen und die Politischen Staats-Streiche, und verstelten einfalth des Doctor Babra eines grossen Fovirten des Königs gibt denen Staatsscenen eine Modeste Unterhaltung*, V. 849–68, in Fritz Homeyer, *Stranitzkys Drama vom 'Heiligen Nepomuck'. Mit einem Neudruck des Textes* (Berlin: Mayer & Müller, 1907), p. 170. Obviously, the 'echo play' of this extract is effective only in the original German. However, Quido's statements and Zytho's ominous echoic responses to them translate as follows: 'QUIDO: I mean the place where my soul lies safely. / ZYTHO: succumbs – / QUIDO: Will Augusta show me her heart, and also a favour? / ZYTHO: iron – / QUIDO: and will she come yet before the evening's radiance has faded. / ZYTHO: wounds – / QUIDO: I tend a chaste flame tinged not by crimson. / ZYTHO: stabbed to death.'

14 In the game with the discrepancy of sound and meaning, just as meaning in its return is startling, so too the appearance of cognition whence there is no sense seems eerie. The echo's Satanic traits reveal themselves in and through the figure of the intriguer, that 'master of meanings', and in the combination of infernal merriment and melancholic devotion (to the requisites) that is unique to him.

15 See A. Haverkamp, 'Milton's Counterplot. Dekonstruktion und *Trauerarbeit* 1637: "Lycidas"', *DVjs* 63 (1989): 608–27, esp. pp. 619–23; and on puns, etymology and echoes, cf. J. Culler, 'The Call of the Phoneme', in idem (ed.), *On Puns: The Foundation*

of Letters (Oxford: Basil Blackwell, 1988), pp. 1–16, esp. pp. 2–5. On the irony of translation, cf. 'The Task of the Translator', loc. cit. The confusion of homonym and synonym implies a connection between the echo and metalepsis; this is referred to as 'echo metaleptic' in John Hollander, *The Figure of Echo: A Mode of Allusion in Milton and After* (Berkeley, CA/London: University of California Press, 1981), pp. 113–32. Metalepsis is a cryptic 'echo': conversely, the realization of an echo trope, i.e. of meaning through confusion based on acoustic deception, requires the (double) operation of metalepsis – to hear something 'different' in the same sound, and to 'understand' a 'different' meaning in this. Metalepsis implies (in signifying) the synonymic replacement of a homonym.

16   This concept is borrowed from Renate Lachmann, 'Die "problematische Ähnlichkeit". Sarbiewskis Traktat *De acuto et arguto* im Kontext concettistischer Theorie des 17. Jahrhunderts', in idem (ed.), *Slawische Barockliteratur II* (Munich: Fink, 1983). The *concetto* or *acumen* is intent on soliciting astonishment, amazement and admiration on account of its own ingenious method. 'In the Baroque poetology of the *concetti*, the crisis of similarity appears in hypertrophy and the reversal of similarity ... The aesthetic and intellectual fascination of the tracts is dependent on similarity borne of dissimilarity and dissimilarity borne in similarity' (Lachmann, pp. 87–8).

17   Cf. ibid., pp. 109, 111; and on the typology of the *arguto* form of the *concetto*, see pp. 110–12.

18   Cf. *The Origin of German Tragic Drama*, p. 208, and see p. 198.

19   Ibid. p. 207.

20   Walter Benjamin, *Understanding Brecht*, trans. Anna Bostock (London: NLB, 1973), p. 52.

21   This illustration is well-known and was cited in the contemporary period; cf. for example Harsdörffer, 'Ein Gegenhall etwas anderes sagen machen / als man ihm zurufft', in *Mathematische und philosophische Ezquickstunden*, p. 161.

22   Kircher, *Neue Hall= und Thon=Kunst*, p. 38.

23   Harsdörffer cites a series of German-language examples of self-reflexive echoes, cf. 'Wer ist hier der *Wie der laut?* E. je / der / Laut', in *Mathematische und philosophische Ezquickstunden*, p. 162.

24   Reverberation – that which echoes enact upon understanding and authoritative communication – and its mastery were significant acoustic–architectural considerations with regard to places of worship, and remained so in the nineteenth century with regard to concert halls. Cf. Bexte, 'OH CET ECHO', pp. 10–11; and Wolfgang Scherer, 'Klaviaturen, Visible Speech und Phonographie: Marginalien zur technischen Entstellung der Sinne im 19. Jahrhundert', in *Diskursanalysen 1: Medien*, ed. F. A. Kittler et al. (Opladen: Westdeutscher Verlag, 1987), pp. 37–54, esp. pp. 42–3.

25   *The Origin of German Tragic Drama*, p. 213; and cf. Johann Wilhelm Ritter, *Fragmente aus dem Nachlass eines jungen Physikers: Ein Taschenbuch für Freunde der Natur* (Heidelberg, 1810; repr. Leipzig/Weimar: Kiepenheuer, 1984), pp. 268–9. *Written language* 'grows up' out of music, 'not directly from the sounds of the spoken word' (*The Origin of German Tragic Drama*, p. 214). As the word's counterpart, written language is –according to one of Ritter's allusions – 'a figure of the sound that is secreted from spoken language' (cf. Ritter, p. 268ff., 275, 277). Meanwhile, the allegorical 'written

language' is forever that which does not emerge 'into sound', but 'remains confined to silence' (*The Origin of German Tragic Drama*, pp. 201–2). In so far as this language approaches music, the 'self-indulgent delight in sheer sound played its part in the decline of the *Trauerspiel*', because its mechanism of expression, the 'obstacle of meaning and intrigue', lost 'its weight', (ibid., pp. 212–13).

26   *The Origin of German Tragic Drama*, p. 210, and cf. p. 209. 'The essence of the mourning play has already been established, then, in the old saying that "all in nature would begin to lament if it were bestowed a voice".' All in nature would lament over language – and the lament is the most impotent expression in language. (Cf. Walter Benjamin, 'On Language as Such and on the Language of Man', trans. Edmund Jephcott, in *SW* 1: 73–4.) The mourning play, and expression within it, occurs as an 'obstacle' that alludes to (and in this respect is also a manifestation of) lament as the (distorted) 'language' of nature.

27   Cf. Immanuel Kant, *Kritik der Urteilskraft, Werkausgabe*, ed. Wilhelm Weischedel, 2nd edn (Darmstadt: Wissenschaftliche Buchgesellschaft, 1975), 10: 142; and repeated almost identically on p. 165.

28   'The Role of Language in *Trauerspiel* and Tragedy', loc. cit.

29   'Nature, according to the mourning play, and the nature of the mourning play [*die Natur des Trauerspiels*] ... is obsessed by language, the victim of an endless feeling' (ibid). This is true *in that* the nature of the mourning play is (at one and the same time) 'represented' *as* natural language in the sound of those words whose resonance is collected and allowed to magnify by the language of the mourning play – as the sphere of the mourning play's pathos, turbulence and tension.

30   *The Origin of German Tragic Drama*, pp. 201ff.

31   Ibid., p. 201, modified translation; and Nägele, *Echoes of Translation*, p. 38.

32   Our translators, even the best ones, proceed from a mistaken premise. They want to turn Hindi, Greek, English into German instead of turning German into Hindi, Greek, English. Our translators have a far greater reverence for the usage of their own language than for the spirit of the foreign works ... The basic error of the translator is that he preserves the state in which his own language happens to be instead of allowing his language to be powerfully affected by the foreign tongue.' ('The Task of the Translator', *SW* 1: 261–2)

    This, as the following, is quoting Rudolf Pannwitz, *Die Krisis der Europäischen Kultur* [=*Die Freiheit des Menschen*, Vol. 1] (Munich–Feldafing: Verlag Hans Carl, 1921), pp. 240, 242–3.

33   'The Task of the Translator', loc. cit.

34   Pannwitz, *Die Krisis*, pp. 241–2; for Benjamin's stressing of this literalness, cf. 'The Task of the Translator', p. 262.

35   'The Task of the Translator', *SW* 1: 260.

36   Paul de Man, 'Conclusions', 'On Walter Benjamin's "The Task of the Translator"' (Messenger Lecture, Cornell University, 4 March 1983), in *Yale French Studies* 69 (1985): 25ff. ('The Lesson of Paul de Man'). Also in *The Resistance to Theory*, ed. Wlad Godzich (Minneapolis, MN: University of Minnesota Press, 1986); and cf. 'The Task of the Translator', *SW* 1: 260, 261.

37   Cf. 'The Task of the Translator', *SW* 1: 257.

38   Roman Jakobson observes in his 'Linguistische Aspekte der Übersetzung' that 'poetry is
     per definitionem untranslatable', because all 'grammatical categories' in it wear a
     'semantic face' (cf. 'The Task of the Translator', *SW* 1: 259), and all constituents of the
     linguistic code in it bear 'their own autonomous meanings', in that they stand in
     contiguous relation to one another. In *Übersetzungswissenschaften*, ed. Wolfram Wilss
     (Darmstadt: Wissenschaftliche Buchgesellschaft, 1981), pp. 195, 197.

39   Karl Maurer, 'Die literarische Übersetzung als Form fremdbestimmter Textkonstitu-
     tion', *Poetica* 8 (1976): 233ff, quotation on p. 235.

40   'The Task of the Translator', *SW* 1: 260.

41   De Man, 'Conclusions', p. 41.

42   Ibid., p. 30.

43   Kircher, *Neue Hall= und Thon=Kunst*, p. 39.

44   Harsdörffer, *Mathematische und philosophische Ezquickstunden*, p. 163; Harsdörffer also
     cites (p. 160) Greek words which ('from within themselves') 'echo in Latin'.

45   Kircher, *Neue Hall= und Thon=Kunst*.

46   Chladni subsequently argues in his works on acoustics that hearing and speaking tubes
     function no differently than echo effects. Cf. Ernst F. F. Chladni, *Entdeckungen über die
     Theorie des Klangs* (Leipzig: Weidman & Reich, 1787); and idem, *Die Akustik* (Leipzig:
     Breitkopf & Härtel, 1802).

47   'He who stands in position A. / will be of no other opinion / than that the echo or
     reverberating voice does come from position D. and is the voice / that he called out in
     the first instance; and the secret shall be concealed yet more deeply / the more similar
     that the voices are and the less that the one is aware of the other.' Kircher, *Neue Hall=
     und Thon=Kunst*.

48   Harsdörffer, *Mathematische und philosophische Ezquickstunden*, p. 158.

49   'The Task of the Translator', *SW* 1: 260; and Nägele, *Echoes of Translation*, p. 45.
     Cf. Carol Jacobs, *MLN*, 90 (1979): p. 764; and J. Hillis Miller, *Ethics of Reading. Kant,
     de Man, Eliot, Trollope, James, and Benjamin* (New York: Columbia University Press,
     1987), pp. 124–5.

50   'The Task of the Translator', *SW* 1: 262.

51   On '*Fortleben*', cf. ibid., pp. 254–8; and on this section and its imagery, cf. also de Man,
     'Conclusions', pp. 37–8, pp. 44–5.

52   Ovid, *Metamorphosen Buch III*, pp. 339–510.

53   Echo herself did not remain untouched by this: Herder rewrites the nymph's tale and
     removes every echo trope within the answer. Echo becomes (the figure of) nature's reply
     within 'sylvan conversations' and 'mountain voices' (see for example A. W. Schlegel,
     C. von Brentano, J. Grimm, Heine, etc.).

54   Ritter, *Fragmente*, p. 270.

55 'All *conveyed movement* (*mitgeteilte Bewegung*) by means of *oscillation* is made *effective* and into sounds, ... But all inner movement also is oscillatory, and no inner change occurs without outer change; thus there is sound here also' (ibid., p. 274). 'Every sound is a life of and *in* the resounding body that endures just so long as the sound itself, and with which it also expires. Every sound is an entire organism of oscillation, a figure and a form' (p. 270). For Ritter, every conveyance is a calling forth of this movement and oscillation: a self-conveyance that (instead of being static, self-identical and fixed in the present) is able only to become the 'object' of realization. 'At the same time, it becomes clear that speech and writing – in and off which we ourselves live in each present moment – are understood by us *least of all*: for that which is *called forth* is already *there*' (p. 279).

56 'Resonance' is the term given to this model of acoustical affection for magnetic influence by E. T. A. Hoffmann, who cites Ritter in his 'uncanny guest', in the short story of the *Serapion Brothers*, as well as in his 'Johannes Kreislers Lehrbrief' (the fourth piece from his so-called *Kreisleriana*).

57 Ritter, *Fragmente*, pp. 253, 269–70. Cf. also Benjamin's references to Ritter in *The Origin of German Tragic Drama*, pp. 213–14.

58 Cf. the entries in Grimm's *Deutsches Wörterbuch*: Echo (*das Echo*) – 'reverberation': 'and the echo, like speaking of bygone days, resounds again [Goethe]' (3: 19–20). 'Reverbera-tion' (*der Widerhall*) – ' "echo"; attested since the 14th Century': 'the sound that one hears, when the other has already passed, is named reverberation or echo [Harsdörffer, among others]' (29: 1024–5). The meaning of 'resonance' (*der Nachhall*) is defined as 'lingering, re-bounding sound; also reverberation, echo', and cf. also its 'figurative' meanings (13: 67–8).

59 Edgar Wind, 'Two Notes on the Cult of Ruins, 1. Ruins and Echoes', *Journal of the Warburg Institute* 1 (1937): 259. In the second section, 'Utopian Ruins', Wind cites Friedrich Schlegel's 'The historian is the backward-looking prophet'.

60 'Translations that are more than transmission of subject matter come into being when a work, in the course of its survival, has reached the age of its fame' ('The Task of the Translator', *SW* 1: 255). Translations realize the translatability of works; as such, they are not forms of these works' 'life', but rather 'a translation issues from the original – not so much from its life as from its "afterlife" '. Translation marks '*their* [the works'] *stage of continued life*' (*SW* 1: 254). 'For in its afterlife – which could not be called that if it were not a transformation and a renewal of something living – the original undergoes a change. Even words with fixed meaning can undergo a maturing process' (*SW* 1: 256). This constitutes the works' *mortification*.

61 Cf. 'The Task of the Translator', *SW* 1: 258. Within his definition of criticism as the works' '*mortification*', Benjamin himself pointed to his 'The Task of the Translator': criticism is a 'confining' and 'lingering' of 'creaturely life' (*The Origin of German Tragic Drama*, pp. 181–2). This 'definition' connects with 'Romantic criticism' in order to accentuate differently its defining moment of 'critical' 'dissolution' ('not supporting "comprehension" but *transforming the work of art into a new philosophical territory*'), and in order to reveal the discontinuity and the break. The concept of artistic criticism in the Romantic meant (according to Benjamin) that 'By *limiting* itself in its own form, it makes itself transitory in a contingent figure, but in that fleeting figure it makes itself *eternal* through criticism' (Walter Benjamin, 'The Concept of Criticism in German Romanticism', trans. David Lachterman et al., in *SW* 1: 182) – a point that Benjamin could scarcely have put more propitiously with regard to Echo, and which the echo *allegorically* re-accentuates.

62   Cf. 'The Task of the Translator', *SW* 1: 260. The interruption and disturbance of
      formed content by translation and criticism alike serves to represent a 'developmental
      state', whether it be the 'becoming' of language or of 'ideas'. 'Art [as criticism evinces] is
      merely a transitional stage of great works. These works [in the process of their coming
      into being] were something else, and will now [within the process of criticism] become
      different again' (Walter Benjamin [fgm. 138], in *Walter Benjamin: Gesammelte Schriften*,
      ed. Rolf Tiedemann and Hermann Schweppenhäuser (Frankfurt a. M.: Suhrkamp,
      1985), 6: 172, and cf. pp. 174, 179.

63   See for example the recollection titled 'Two Puzzling Pictures' in *Berlin Childhood*
      (ibid., 4: 254–5). Like his topography of translation, Benjamin's model of remembrance
      conceptualizes a functioning from the far bank which, in calling forth and calling out, is
      both put in place and passed (cf. Walter Benjamin, *The Arcades Project*, trans. Howard
      Eiland and Kevin McLaughlin [Cambridge, MA/London: Belknap Press/Harvard
      University Press, 1999], p. 206 (entry H2, 3) and p. 846 (entry I°, 2); and B. Menke,
      'Das NachLeben im Zitat. Benjamins Gedächtnis der Texte', in *Gedächtniskunst. Raum
      und Schrift*, ed. A. Haverkamp and R. Lachmann [Frankfurt a.M.: Suhrkamp 1991]).

64   The 'empty mussel-shell' of the 'nineteenth century', 'I hold it to my ear. What do I
      hear?' Recollection entitled '*Die Mummerehlen*' in *Berlin Childhood*, GS 4: 261–2.

CHAPTER 6

Of the two sets of page references following citations from Benjamin, the first is to the
collected works in German, *Gesammelte Schriften*, ed. Rolf Tiedemann and Hermann
Schweppenhauser (Frankfurt a. M.: Suhrkamp, 1972) (hereafter *GS*, followed by volume
and book number). The second page reference is to English translations from the *Selected
Writings*, ed. M. Bullock and M. Jennings (Cambridge, MA: Harvard University Press, 1996;
Vol. 2, 1998) (hereafter *SW*, followed by volume number), with the exception of *The Origin
of German Tragic Drama*, which is not included in the *Selected Writings*.

1   Walter Benjamin, 'Franz Kafka: Zur zehnten Wiederkehr seines Todestages' (*GS* 2.2);
     'Franz Kafka: On the Tenth Anniversary of his Death' (*SW* 2: 794–818).

2   Walter Benjamin, *Der Begriff der Kunstkritik in der deutschen Romantik* (*GS* 1.1); *The
     Concept of Criticism in German Romanticism* (*SW* 1: 116ff.).

3   Friedrich Schlegel, 'Ideen' in *Athenaeum: Eine Zeitschrift von A. W. Schlegel und
     F. Schlegel* 3.1 (Berlin, 1800), p. 9; 'Ideas' in *Philosophical Fragments*, trans. Peter
     Firchow (Minneapolis and London: Minnesota University Press, 1991), p. 101.

4   Novalis writes in the 35th of his *Logological Fragments* that 'True criticism must possess
     the capacity to bring forth the product it would criticize.' *Schriften* 2.1, ed. Hans-
     Joachim Mahl and Gerhard Schulz (Stuttgart: W. Kohlhammer, 1960), p. 534; trans. in
     German Romantic Criticism, ed. A. Leslie Wilson (New York: Continuum, 1982), p. 69.

5   Benjamin's choice of image is not, of course, philosophically innocent. The unfolding
     blossom as figure for the truth alludes not only to Schlegel, but, perhaps more sig-
     nificantly, to Hegel, writing five years later. In the second paragraph of the Preface to the
     Phenomenology, Hegel castigates 'the antithesis of truth and falsity' upon which most
     systems are either 'accepted or contradicted'. Conventional opinion,

     does not comprehend the diversity of philosophical systems as the progressive
     unfolding of truth [*die fortschreitende Entwicklung der Wahrheit*] but rather sees in it

simple disagreements. The bud disappears in the bursting-forth of the blossom, and one might say, the former is refuted by the latter; similarly, when the fruit appears, the blossom is shown up in its turn as a false manifestation of the plant, and the fruit now emerges as the truth of it instead. These forms are not just distinguished from one another, they also supplant one another as mutually incompatible. Yet at the same time their fluid nature makes them moments of an organic unity in which they not only do not conflict, but in which each is as necessary as the other; and this mutual necessity alone constitutes the life of the whole.

Benjamin's paired image of paper and flower both repeats and refuses Hegel's conception of the life of the whole: repeats it, in so far as it contests the flattened antithetical conception of truth which characterizes the 'paper parable'; refuses it, in so far as the flower, for Benjamin is not an image of truth coming to consciousness of itself via the labour of the negative. On the contrary, as I shall go on to argue, in Baroque, Baudelairean and Kafkan allegory, resolution in the Absolute is defeated precisely by the *non-coincidence* of truth with self-knowledge. The difference in German terminology employed by Hegel and Benjamin is instructive in this regard. Hegel's '*Entwicklung*', rendered by the translator as 'unfolding', is more literally translated as 'unrolling', a term which connotes the linear progress of a teleology (the unrolling of, say, a carpet comes to rest in a final state of flatness). As we shall see, Benjamin's *Entfaltung* is distinguished by the refusal of just this finality. G. W. F. Hegel, *Phänemonologie des Geistes* (Frankfurt a. M.: Suhrkamp, 1987), p. 3; *Phenomenology of the Spirit*, trans. A. V. Miller (Oxford: Oxford University Press, 1983), p. 5.

6   Friedrich Schlegel, *Athenaeum* 1.2: 54; *Philosophical Fragments*, p. 45. (Note *Athenaeum* fragment = *Ath*. fgm. hereafter.)

7   Gilles Deleuze, *Le Pli: Leibniz et le baroque* (Paris: Minuit, 1988); *The Fold: Leibniz and the Baroque*, trans. Tom Conley (Minneapolis, MN: Minnesota University Press, 1993).

8   Deleuze, *Le Pli*, p. 7; *The Fold*, p. 6.

9   Ibid., p. 10; p. 9.

10   Within contemporary theory, however, it is Jacques Derrida who has refracted the question of the fold most explicitly through the lens of reading and criticism. In 'The Double Session' ('La Double séance' in *La Dissémination* [Paris: Seuil, 1972], hereafter *LD*; *Dissemination*, trans. Barbara Johnson [Chicago, IL: Chicago University Press, 1988] hereafter *D*), an extended reading of Mallarmé's prose poem 'Mimique', the fold is brought into play as that which marks the text's parting of/with reference, with any 'mimetological' or 'Platonico-Hegelian' conception of mimesis: 'The syntax of the fold makes it impossible for us to arrest its play or indecision' (*LD*, p. 261/*D*, p. 231). Mallarméan mimesis, that is, is 'mimicry imitating nothing . . . a double that doubles no simple' (*LD*, p. 234/*D*, p. 206). As such, it is characterized by an always-prior *foldedness* which criticism (exemplified for Derrida by Jean-Pierre Richard's *L'Univers imaginaire de Mallarmé*) has perpetually sought to arrest or render secondary. Criticism's conception of the fold as prior or secondary is the index of its self-understanding. The attempt finally to unfold the fold of signification − as if the fold were an accident, 'a flexing back up in itself of a surface that was at first smooth and flat' (*LD*, p. 259/*D*, p. 229) − puts literary criticism at the service of a 'metaphysical mimetologism' (*LD*, p. 276/*D*, p. 245) which would culminate in a 'sure revelation of meaning' (*LD*, p. 293/*D*, p. 261). This is the logical itinerary of any thematic criticism, any reading that reduces the dissemination of meaning effects to a set (even a polysemy) of determinate meanings. 'In this wrinkle-free felicity [*ce bonheur qui ne ferait pas un pli*]', Derrida demands, 'Could there be anything

beyond a simple *parousia* of meaning?' (*LD*, p. 293/*CD*, p. 261). Derrida's 'wrinkle-free felicity' returns us to Benjamin's paper parable: 'it is the reader's pleasure to smooth it out so that he has its meaning in the palm of his hand'. Benjamin's Kafkan blossom would thus be the figure of an always-prior foldedness whose unfolding results not in complacent freedom from wrinkles, but in the revelation of just this irreducible foldedness. We will have further occasion to return to the insistence of wrinkles in Benjamin's thought, notably in our discussion of 'The Image of Proust'.

11   Further affinities, beyond the scope of this chapter, which suggest themselves: the employment of the Leibnizian monad as a means of representing the origin of the Baroque, as well as the identification of Proust and Kafka as exemplars of the folded work. See *Ursprung des deutschen Trauerspiel* (*GS* 1.1: 227–8); Gilles Deleuze, *Proust et signes* (Paris: Presses Universitaires de France, 1970); *Proust and Signs*, trans. Richard Howard (London: Athlone, 1999); Gilles Deleuze and Felix Guattari, *Kafka: Pour une littérature mineure* (Paris: Minuit, 1975); *Kafka: Towards a Minor Literature*, trans. Dana Polan (Minneapolis, MN: Minnesota University Press, 1986).

12   Schlegel, *Athenaeum*, 1.2: p. 79; *Philosophical Fragments*, p. 58.

13   Philippe Lacoue-Labarthe and Jean-Luc Nancy, *L'Absolu littéraire: théorie de la littérature du romantisme allemand* (Paris: Seuil, 1978), p. 390; *The Literary Absolute*, trans. Philip Barnard and Cheryl Lester (Albany, NY: SUNY Press, 1988), p. 117.

14   Lacoue-Labarthe and Nancy, *L'Absolu littéraire*, p. 390; *The Literary Absolute*, p. 86.

15   Schlegel, *Athenaeum*, 1.2: p. 55; *Philosophical Fragments*, p. 45.

16   Howard Caygill, *Walter Benjamin: The Colour of Experience* (London: Routledge, 1998). See especially Chapter 1.

17   Schlegel, *Athenaeum*, 1.2: 29–30; *Philosophical Fragments*, p. 32.

18   Schlegel, *Athenaeum*, 3.1: 21; *Philosophical Fragments*, p. 103.

19   Lacoue-Labarthe and Nancy, *L'Absolu littéraire*, p. 274; *The Literary Absolute*, p. 90.

20   Walter Benjamin, '*Die Aufgabe des Übersetzers*' in *GS* 4: 1; 'The Task of the Translator (*SW* 1); '*Zum Bilde Prousts*' (*GS* 2.1), 'The Image of Proust (*SW* 2). Carol Jacobs's essay, 'Walter Benjamin: Image of Proust', makes much of the literal translation of '*Zum Bilde Prousts*' as 'Towards the Image of Proust', pointing to the essay's complex interweaving of textual and biographical concerns. See Jacobs, *In the Language of Walter Benjamin* (Baltimore, MD: Johns Hopkins University Press, 1999).

21   Cited in Maurice Blanchot, 'L'Athenaeum' in *L'Entretien infini* (Paris: Gallimard, 1969) (hereafter *EI*), p. 500; 'The Athenaeum' in *The Infinite Conversation*, trans. Susan Hanson (Minneapolis, MN: Minnesota University Press, 1993), p. 356.

22   Just as Novalis speaks of 'true' criticism as 'the capacity to bring forth the product it would criticize' (see above, note 3), so in fragment 69 of *Pollen* he characterizes the highest form of translations ('mythic' translation) thus: 'They set forth the pure, ultimate character of the work of art. They give us not the actual work but its ideal.' *Schriften* 2.1; translated in *German Romantic Criticism*, p. 65.

23 This 'abyssal infinite' is what Rodolphe Gasché terms 'difference'. It is what refuses phenomenalization, integration into 'mythical linguistic relations'. 'Translatability' is the name for this ungraspable Other of natural language, which is not so much 'at hand' or unveiled in Hölderlin's translations as anticipated, 'fleetingly touched': 'By fleetingly touching in a disrupting movement away the webs of language that allow for no difference, difference is produced in the first place, and with it, the empty space of the Other of myth.' See 'Saturnine Vision and the Question of Difference: Reflections on Walter Benjamin's Theory of Language', in Rainer Nägele (ed.), *Benjamin's Ground* (Detroit, MI: Wayne State University Press, 1988), p. 74.

24 Schlegel, *Athenaeum*, 1.2: 81; *Philosophical Fragments*, p. 59.

25 Carol Jacobs, 'Walter Benjamin: Image of Proust' in *In the Language of Walter Benjamin* (Baltimore, MD: Johns Hopkins University Press, 1999), pp. 39–58.

26 The elective affinity of this passage to the following one from Blanchot's essay, 'Dreaming, Writing' ('*Rêver, écrire*'), on Michel Leiris, is worth remarking:

> Far from being absent, resemblances abound in dreams ... A being who suddenly begins to 'resemble' moves away from real life, passes into another world, enters into the inaccessible proximity of the image, is present nonetheless, with a presence that is not his own or that of another, an apparition that transforms all other presents into appearances ... The dream is a temptation for writing perhaps because writing also has to do with this neutral vigilance, that the night of sleep tries to extinguish but that the night of dreams awakens and ceaselessly maintains.

See *L'Amitié* (Paris: Gallimard, 1971), pp. 167–9; *Friendship*, trans. Elizabeth Rottenberg (Stanford, CA: Stanford University Press, 1997), pp. 144–5.

27 Jacobs, *In the Language of Walter Benjamin*, p. 45.

28 Walter Benjamin, *Ursprung des deutschen Trauerspiels* (*GS* 1.1); *The Origin of German Tragic Drama*, trans. John Osborne (London: Verso, 1985; hereafter *OGTD*).

29 We should recall here that in Schlegel's 'Ideas', religion is the ultimate consummation of art.

30 Walter Benjamin, 'Goethes Wahlverwandschaften', *GS* 1.1: 195; 'Goethe's Elective Affinities', *SW* 1: 351.

31 Blanchot, *L'Entretien infini*, p. 504; *The Infinite Conversation*, p. 359.

32 Ibid.

33 Walter Benjamin, *Briefe* 1, ed. Gershom Scholem and Theodor W. Adorno (Frankfurt a. M.: Suhrkamp, 1966), p. 323; 'Letter to Florens Christian Rang', *SW* 1: 389.

34 Blanchot, *L'Entretien infini*, p. 505; *The Infinite Conversation*, p. 359.

35 The distinction between Romantic and allegorical fragmentation is succinctly identified by Gasché in his comparison of the former with contemporary literary fragmentation: 'without a radical recasting, the Romantic notion of the fragment would be reductionist when applied to contemporary texts. Its focus lies in an *essential* incompletion, an incompletion that is itself a mode of fulfilment ... The radicality of contemporary texts, more cautiously, of some of its forms is (perhaps) to be attributed to an inessential (but

not, for that matter arbitrary) incompletion.' The same inessential incompletion aptly characterizes Benjaminian allegory. See 'Ideality in Fragments', Foreword to Schlegel, *Philosophical Fragments*, p. xxviii.

Put another way, allegory can be seen as a non-reflexive mode of incompletion, if reflexivity is to be understood as the work's coming to self-consciousness. Thus Derrida: 'the fold is not a form of reflexivity. If by reflexivity one means the motion of consciousness of self-presence that plays such a determining role in Hegel's speculative logic and dialectic, in the movement of sublation ... and negativity ... then reflexivity is but an effect of the fold as text' (*LD*, p. 302/*D*, p. 270).

36   Rodolphe Gasché, 'The Sober Absolute: On Walter Benjamin and the Early Romantics' in *Studies in Romanticism* 3, (Winter 1992); see also Chapter 3, this volume.

CHAPTER 7

1   A version of this essay appeared in Andrew Benjamin, *Philosophy's Literature* (Manchester: Clinamen, 2001). All references to Benjamin's work are in the first instance to the English translation and then to the original German edition (*SW* and *GS* respectively).

2   It is vital to acknowledge some of the ground-breaking work that has been done on Benjamin's paper on language. Three of the most important are Alexander Garcia Düttman, *La Parole donnée* (Paris: Galilée, 1989), pp. 151–64; Peter Fenves, 'The Genesis of Judgment: Spatiality, Analogy, and Metaphor in Benjamin's *On Language as Such and On Human Language*', in David Ferris (ed.), *Walter Benjamin: Theoretical Questions* (Stanford, CA: Stanford University Press, 1996), pp. 75–93; Winfried Menninghaus, *Walter Benjamins Theorie der Sprachmagie* (Frankfurt a. M.: Suhrkamp, 1995), pp. 10–33.

The approach adopted in this chapter has a specific agenda. Rather than offering a straightforward commentary on the language paper, its task is to work though Benjamin's text presenting a reading that has a twofold orientation. On the one hand to present the text as struggling with the problem of the universal – presented here in terms of the linguistic Absolute – and on the other to argue that, even though the Absolute depends upon its necessary absence, it does not follow that Benjamin's own invocation of mourning and melancholia are essential to the overall force of his argument.

3   While it is not argued in these terms, for an important reworking of the role of theology in Benjamin's work, see Peter Osborne, *The Politics of Time* (London: Verso, 1995), pp. 144–50. I have also engaged with this problem in my book, *Present Hope: Philosophy, Architecture, Judaism* (London and New York: Routledge, 1997), Chapter 2.

4   This position accords with the conventions of Genesis interpretation. See, for example, Julian Morgenstern, *The Book of Genesis* (New York: Shoken, 1965), pp. 37–60. It is perhaps curious that Benjamin does not note that God made 'man' (*mdah*) from 'the dust' (*hmdah*) (Genesis 2 .7). In other words, that 'man' was already present in the 'word' out of which he was created.

5   The interpretive question – and it will be the question allowing for a more critical stance to be taken in relation to Benjamin's overall argument – concerns how that which remains is to be understood. Moreover, there is the question of what position 'we' have to this now absent remainder. The 'we' in question is of course the subject of modernity.

6   While this claim does no more than describe the structure of Platonism, it is, nonetheless, essential that an example be given. In the *Phaedo*, where Plato's concern is to establish

how it is that an instance of beauty warrants the designation beautiful, he argues the following: 'whatever else is beautiful except for Beauty, is beautiful for no other reason than because it partakes [*metecei*] of that Beauty' (100c, 4–6). Partaking, or participation, establishes beauty itself as the cause (*aitia*) of the instance, the particular, being beautiful. There can be no other cause. Once this distinction is allowed, then it is possible to argue that it generates and sustains the question of the nature of beauty itself. Clearly, it is possible to move through the corpus of the dialogues locating similar examples. In each instance the point would be to demonstrate that the causal relation – a relation giving identity – was between the particular and that which was necessarily external to it.

CHAPTER 8

Citation to Benjamin's works is to volume and page number in *Gesammelte Schriften* [*GS*], ed. R. Tiedemann and H. Schweppenhäuser (Frankfurt a. M.: Suhrkamp, 1991), followed by parallel citation to volume and page number in *Selected Writings* [*SW*], ed. M. Bullock and M. Jennings (Cambridge, MA: Harvard University Press, 1996–9). In the case of the *Trauerspiel* book, parallel citation is to *GS*, followed by citation to *Origin of the German Tragic Play* [*OT*], trans. John Osborne (London: Verso, 1997). Citation to Novalis is to volume and page number in *Novalis Schriften* [*NS*], ed. R. Samuel, H.-J. Mähl and G. Schutz (Stuttgart: Kohlhammer, 1960–88), with parallel citation to *Philosophical Writings* [*PW*], trans. M. M. Stoljar (Albany, NY: SUNY Press, 1997), where available. Citation to Friedrich Schlegel is to volume and page number in *Kritische Friedrich Schlegel Ausgabe* [*KFSA*], ed. E. Behler, J.-J. Anstett, H. Eichner et al. (Paderborn: Schöningh, 1958–), with parallel citation to *Philosophical Fragments* [*PF*], trans. P. Firchow (Minneapolis, MN: University of Minnesota Press, 1991).

I thank Beatrice Hanssen for helpful comments on this essay.

1 *Der Begriff des Unbewußten in der transcendentalen Seelenlehre* (1927). Horkheimer had habilitated under Cornelius two years previously (in the same year as Benjamin's failure), writing on the theme of the unity of reason in Kant. Adorno successfully reapplied for the degree in 1931 with a thesis on Kierkegaard, which Paul Tillich supervised. This work, *Kierkegaard: Konstruktion des Ästhetischen*, owes much to Benjamin and is extremely important for a broad range of Adorno's views, particularly on the cognitive role of art.

2 See Susan Buck-Morss, *The Origin of Negative Dialectics: Theodore W. Adorno, Walter Benjamin and the Frankfurt Institute* (New York: Macmillan Free Press, 1977), for an account of Benjamin's influence on Adorno.

3 Letter to Scholem, 31 January 1918, Walter Benjamin, *Briefe*, ed. G. Scholem and T. W. Adorno (Frankfurt a. M.: Suhrkamp, 1978), 1:169; *The Correspondence of Walter Benjamin 1910–1940*, trans. M. Jacobson and E. Jacobson (Chicago, IL: University of Chicago Press, 1994), pp. 112–13.

4 *Kritik der Urteilskraft* [*KU*], in *Kants gesammelte Schriften*, ed. Preussische Akademie der Wissenschaften (Berlin: de Gruyter, 1902–), 5: 313. The Akademie pagination is margin-ally noted in *Critique of the Power of Judgment*, trans. and ed. P. Guyer and E. Matthews (Cambridge and New York: Cambridge University Press, 2000).

5 Kant states that an aesthetic idea is an intuition for which no adequate concept can be found. *KU*, pp. 342–3 (Remark I). What Kant means by calling an aesthetic idea an intuition is to underline its sensuous character. The aesthetic idea is not a representation of the work, it is an idea *in* the work. Cf. *Critique of Pure Reason* A567-71/B596-9 where Kant discusses what he calls an 'ideal of imagination'. He glosses this as the representation of a totality in a particular and states that it gives no rule, merely an archetypal example.

6   'Those forms which do not constitute the representation of a given concept itself, but which, as secondary representations of the imagination, express (*ausdrücken*) the derivatives (*Folgen*) connected with it, and its kinship with other concepts, are called (aesthetic) attributes', *KU*, p. 3115.

7   See Fred Rush, 'Kant and Schlegel', *Kant und die Berliner Aufklärung: Akten des 9. Internationalen Kant-Kongresses*, ed. V. Gerhardt, R.-P. Horstmann and R. Schumacher (Berlin: de Gruyter, 2001), 3: 618–25 for a non-organic reading of the relationship between idea and attribute. I now think that this is mistaken.

8   An excellent survey of these views is Samuel Monk, *The Sublime: A Study of Critical Theories in XVIII-Century England* (Ann Arbor, MI: University of Michigan Press, 1962).

9   I shall concentrate solely on the importance of Friedrich Schlegel and Novalis for Benjamin. They are the primary protagonists in his dissertation and essential for his development. Benjamin also reflected deeply on Hölderlin during this period and, in some ways, Hölderlin's anti-subjectivism is better suited to Benjamin's own views. For the importance of Hölderlin for Benjamin, see Beatrice Hanssen, ' "Dichtermut" and "Blödigkeit": Two Poems by Hölderlin; Interpreted by Walter Benjamin', Chapter 9 this volume.

10 Manfred Frank has emphasized a sharp contrast between Romanticism and Idealism focusing, as I shall here, on the issue of the lack of reflective access to the Absolute. *Unendliche Annäherung: Die Anfänge der philosophischen Frühromantik* (Frankfurt a. M.: Suhrkamp, 1997), pp. 831–61; see also *Einführung in die frühromantische Ästhetik* (Frankfurt a. M.: Suhrkamp, 1989), pp. 222–3, 248–72. Dieter Henrich finds similar themes in Hölderlin: *Der Grund im Bewußtsein: Untersuchungen zu Hölderlins Denken (1794–1795)* (Stuttgart: Klett-Cotta, 1992). Karl Ameriks, *Kant and the Fate of Autonomy* (New York: Cambridge University Press, 2000) is a very astute account of the immediate reaction to Kant, concentrating in part on some of the figures important to the Jena Romantics, i.e. Jacobi and Reinhold.

11 *Fichte-Studien* 1: 16/*NS* 2: 114. There is no English translation of the *Fichte-Studien*, Novalis's most important philosophical text, though one is underway in the *Cambridge Texts in the History of Philosophy* series, ed. and trans. Jane Kneller.

12 The Romantic reply to the Hegelian claim that conceptual thought is not limited to representation (or reflection) would quite probably be that what Hegel calls 'speculation' is what Kant would call 'mere speculation' – in essence a form of special pleading designed specifically to surmount the difficulty without stopping to ask whether it might be possible that it is insurmountable.

13 *Blüthenstaub* 1, *NS* 2: 413/*PW*, p. 23: 'we seek everywhere the unconditioned, but only ever find things' ('*wir suchen überall das Unbedingte, und finden immer nur Dinge*'). Here Novalis is playing on the shared root 'Ding', thing. The unconditioned is no thing at all, it is 'un-thinged' – it cannot be individuated. All we ever encounter is the conditioned.

14 This is, for instance, Schelling's claim in the ultimate sections of his *System of Transcendental Idealism* (Tübingen: Cotta, 1800).

15 I discuss fragments in more detail *infra* Section 3. Karl Heinz Bohrer probably overstates the case when he claims that the connection between irony and fragmentary discourse in Romanticism is overlooked until Benjamin's dissertation. See 'Sprachen der Ironie – Sprachen des Ernstes: das Problem', in *Sprachen der Ironie – Sprachen des Ernstes*, ed. K. H. Bohrer (Frankfurt a. M.: Suhrkamp, 2000), pp. 11–12. Rudolf Haym

noted the connection as early as 1870. *Die romantische Schule* (Berlin, 1870; repr. Darmstadt: Wissenschaftliche Buchgesellschaft, 1961), p. 262. I would agree, however, that Benjamin first put the proper emphasis on the connection.

16 Schlegel tends to express the tension inherent in irony in at least three different ways. Perhaps the most famous characterization involves the idea that the ironist oscillates between self-creation (*Selbstschöpfung*) and self-annihilation (*Selbstvernichtung*) (*Ath.* fgm. 51, *KFSA* 2: 172/*PF*, p. 24; cf. *Krit.* fgm. 48, *KFSA* 2: 153/*PF*, p. 6 (irony as paradox)). A slight variant (more explicitly Fichtean) identifies three elements, adding self-limitation (*Selbstbeschränkung*) as a median term (*Krit.* fgm. 28, *KFSA* 2: 150/ *PF*, p. 3). A second way Schlegel expresses the point, and one that brings the metaphysics of it to the foreground, is that irony allows an intimation, or even a 'clear consciousness' (*klares Bewusstsein*) of the Absolute (*Ideen* 69, *KFSA* 2: 263/*PF*, p. 100). Yet a third way of stating the contrast is in terms of the relationship of ancient to modern poetry that so concerned Schlegel.

17 *Ath.* fgm. 238, *KFSA* 2: 204/*PF*, pp. 50–1; *Krit.* fgm. 117, *KFSA* 2: 162/*PF*, pp. 14–15.

18 Cf. Benjamin's close connection of Romantic irony with the essentially interpretive task of translation. 'The Task of the Translator', *GS* 4: 15/*SW* 1: 258.

19 Schlegel often compares fragments to monads. See, e.g. *Philosophische Lehrjahre* (1798), *KFSA* 18: 42–53.

20 But whereas Leibniz allows for the being of one monad (God) with infinite depth of apperception (and therefore, knowledge of all past, present and future states of the world and of the inherent interconnection of all monads), this idea has no affirmative metaphysical place in Jena Romanticism. For to say that a fragment could attain this sort of inclusiveness is just to say that there could be a fragment that adequately represents or reflects the Absolute and that is, in turn, just to say that such a fragment would not be a fragment at all.

21 The concept of the *ordo inversus* is found throughout Novalis's writings. See, e.g. *Fichte-Studien* 1: 32, *NS* 2: 127; 1: 36, *NS* 2: 128; 1: 41, *NS* 1: 131; and 1: 44, *NS* 2: 133. The best analysis of this doctrine is Manfred Frank, *Einführung in die frühromantische Ästhetik* (Frankfurt a. M.: Suhrkamp, 1989), Vorlesung (lecture) 15.

22 Julian Roberts, *Walter Benjamin* (London: Macmillan, 1982), pp. 111–15 contains a particularly clear account of Benjamin's theory of language.

23 Many of Hamann's thoughts on language are contained in his response to Herder's 'Über den Ursprung der Sprache' (1772), J. G. Herder, *Sämtliche Werk*, ed. B. Suphan (Berlin, 1891), 5: 1–148, 'Des Ritters von Rosencreuz letzte Willensmeinung über den göttlichen und menschlichen Ursprung der Sprache' (1772), J. G. Hamann, *Sämtliche Werke*, ed. J. Nadler (Vienna: Herder Verlag, 1949), 3: 25–33. They also occur in his esoteric writings of the mid 1770s to mid 1780s, but the biblical background for the account under consideration was laid as early as his *Biblische Betrachtungen eines Christen* (1758), in *Samtliche Werke* 1: 7–249. Hamann was not a direct influence on the Jena circle, though they knew him well through Jacobi, with whom Hamann shared an extensive correspondence and an interest in Hume.

24 *Ideen*, 95; *KFSA* 2: 265/*PF*, pp. 102–3.

25 On this point see Winfried Menninghaus, *Walter Benjamins Theorie der Sprachmagie* (Frankfurt a. M.: Suhrkamp, 1980), pp. 16–17.

26   It should be clear that the conception of particularity central to Benjamin's view of language has nothing to do with the atomistic idea of a 'bare' particular native to a broad spectrum of modern philosophy. For Benjamin, particularity has nothing to do with a thing considered how it is apart from any human experience of it. Quite the opposite: that conception of particularity is based on a false view that 'experience' is to be understood as limited to expressly categorical thought, such as science. Rather, Benjamin holds that particularity must be understood within the ambit of human experience as a thing's inherent significance – it is the riot of ways that a thing is already significant, prior to attempts to control and categorize this significance. Such higher order thought is, among other things, a reaction to the fecundity and onrush of meaning, not a bestowing of meaning on an inert natural item.

27   Compare *GS* 2.1: 210–13/*SW* 2: 720–2 with *GS* 2: 204–9. Benjamin explicitly connects the ability to register similarity without collapsing difference and astrological concepts *GS* 2.1: 207, 209, and *GS* 2.1: 211/*SW* 2: 721. Cf. the notes from the period 1919–21 on the concepts of analogy and relationship. *GS* 6: 43–53.

28   The idea stems from Goethe. Benjamin is very concerned to distinguish this sort of 'seeing' from Kantian and Husserlian theories of perception, which he thinks are vitiated by their reliance on the concept of synthesis. As we shall see, in some of his moments, Benjamin rather hastily assimilates synthetic thought to discursivity and discursivity to conceptual reduction. Given this, he quite probably means this perception to be entirely synoptic (see *GS* 1.1: 216–17/*OT*, pp. 36–7). Further evidence of this is his claim that this perception is 'non-intentional' (*GS* 1.1: 217/*OT*, p. 37). By this, Benjamin may mean merely that mimetic thought is subconscious, tacit or otherwise without (conscious) purpose. But he may also be claiming that such perception does not take an intentional object (i.e. 'intentional' in Brentano's sense).

29   Benjamin's acceptance of non-'auratic' art also points in this direction. 'The Work of Art in the Age of Mechanical Reproduction', *GS* 1.2: 714–36 (French version), cf. ibid., pp. 470–508. Aura decreases in proportion to Weberian disenchantment and increased instrumentalization of thought. While it is true that Benjamin in places expresses reservations about loss of aura (his writings on surrealism, for instance *GS* 2.1: 295–310), his view was generally positive – the thought being that demystification of the artwork allows it a new, expressly political (i.e. Brechtian) role.

30   '*Erkenntniskritisch*' is not a term unique to Benjamin. It figures in three traditions of which he was very much aware. The first is the biblical hermeneutic line we have considered. The second is early positivism in the philosophy of science, for instance, Ernst Mach. The Marburg Kantians (Cohen, Natorp, Cassirer) also deployed the word. I thank Don Howard for making me aware of the use of the term in the second of these traditions.

31   For purposes of discussion, I treat as equivalent (a) conceptual thought, (b) propositional thought, and (c) conceptual judgement. Benjamin does not make distinctions between having a concept and deploying it in judgement. Nor does he speak explicitly of propositional attitudes, though I take it that his criticisms would apply here as well.

32   One might want to argue that Benjamin's form of anti-essentialism is more palatable if restricted to terms or concepts that refer to 'non-natural' objects where it makes sense to attend to the open extension of the concept that may be sensitive to the role it plays in changing historically situated ways of life. On this understanding, one could give a definition of 'calcium', and the definiteness of concept would not raise any problem, yet terms like 'pity' or 'private' would be subject to anti-essentialist caveats. I take this to be one of the main ways that Nietzsche, Wittgenstein and Foucault can be considered 'anti-essentialists'. Benjamin never makes this qualification.

33 See *Negative Dialektik* (Frankfurt a. M.: Suhrkamp, 1970), passim.

34 Adorno urges that this is just the sort of connection between elements that parataxis allows. For an especially clear statement, see 'Parataxis. Zur späten Lyrik Hölderlins', in *Noten zur Literatur* (Frankfurt a. M., 1974), pp. 447–91. See 'Parataxis: On Hölderlin's Late Poetry', in Adorno, *Notes to Literature*, trans. S. W. Nicholson (New York: Columbia University Press, 1992), 2: 109–49.

CHAPTER 9

1 This essay from 1989 first appeared in a slightly different version in *Modern Language Notes* (Comparative Literature Issue) 112 (1997): 786–816.

2 Manfred Frank and Gerhard Kurz, 'Ordo inversus. Zu einer Reflexionsfigur bei Novalis, Hölderlin, Kleist und Kafka', in Herbert Anton, Bernhard Gajek, and Peter Pfaff (eds), *Geist und Zeichen Festschrift für Arthur Henkel zu seinem sechzigsten Geburtstag* (Heidelberg: Carl Winter Verlag, 1977), pp. 75–97.

3 Ibid., p. 75.

4 Ibid.

5 Theodor W. Adorno, 'Parataxis. Zur späten Lyrik Hölderlins', in Adorno, *Noten zur Literatur* (Frankfurt a. M.: Suhrkamp, 1974), pp. 447–91. All further references are to the English translation: Theodor W. Adorno, 'Parataxis: On Hölderlin's Late Poetry', in Adorno, *Notes to Literature*, ed. Rolf Tiedemann, trans. Shierry Weber Nicholson (New York: Columbia University Press, 1992), 2: 109–49.

6 Friedrich Hölderlin, 'Reflexion', in *Sämtliche Werke* (Stuttgart: W. Kohlhammer Verlag, 1961), 4.1: 233–6. How subversive parataxis truly was, becomes evident in the post-Idealistic, materialistic drama of Georg Büchner, specifically the play *Dantons Tod*, whose paratactical constructions run counter to the violence of the hierarchical *Satz*, imposed by Robespierre's tyranny of virtue and voiced in St Just's famous speech. See also Volker Klotz, *Geschlossene und offene Form im Drama* (Munich: C. Hanser, 1960), pp. 233ff.

7 Friedrich Hölderlin, *Essays and Letters on Theory*, trans. and ed. Thomas Pfau (Albany, NY: SUNY Press, 1988), p. 45.

8 Adorno, 'Parataxis', p. 112.

9 Ibid., p. 145.

10 Ibid., pp. 147, 149.

11 Ibid., pp. 134–5; see German original, p. 475.

12 As in *Wort an Wort fügen*: to string words together.

13 For a more extensive discussion of Benjamin's influence on Adorno's thought, see Beatrice Hanssen, *Walter Benjamin's Other History: Of Stones, Animals, Human Beings, and Angels* (Berkeley, CA: University of California Press, 1998, 2000), passim.

14   See the introduction to this volume, as well as the third section of this chapter below.

15   Walter Benjamin, *The Correspondence of Walter Benjamin, 1910–1940*, ed. Gershom Scholem and Theodor W. Adorno, trans. Manfred R. Jacobson and Evelyn M. Jacobson (Chicago, IL, and London: University of Chicago Press, 1994), p. 146.

16   Ibid., p. 85.

17   In his monograph on Benjamin, Scholem recounted the following:

> On October 1 [Benjamin] spoke about Hölderlin and gave me a typewritten copy of his essay 'Zwei Gedichte von Friedrich Hölderlin' ['Two Poems of Friedrich Hölderlin'], which contained a profoundly metaphysical analysis, written in the first winter of the war, 1914–15, of the two poems 'Dichtermut' ['Poet's Courage'] and 'Blödigkeit' ['Timidity']. Only later did I realize that this gift was a sign of his great trust in me. Hölderlin, who had been rediscovered by Stefan George and his group, was regarded by the circles in which Benjamin moved between 1911 and 1914 as one of the supreme figures in poetry. Benjamin perceived his deceased friend Heinle, whom Ludwig Strauss later described to me as 'a wholly pure lyric poet', as a figure akin to Hölderlin. As was evident from Benjamin's every reference to Heinle, death had moved his friend to the realm of the sacrosanct. Yet Benjamin's notes in his *Berliner Chronik* clearly reveal that there had been no dearth of major tensions between the two friends in Heinle's lifetime, even during the period immediately preceding Heinle's death. In the course of the above-mentioned conversation about Hölderlin I first heard Benjamin refer to Norbert von Hellingrath's edition of Hölderlin as well as to von Hellingrath's study of Hölderlin's Pindar translations, which had made a great impression upon Benjamin. But at the time I knew very little about such things.

See Gershom Scholem, *Walter Benjamin: The Story of a Friendship* (New York: Schocken, 1981), p. 17.

18   Walter Benjamin, 'The Task of the Translator', in Benjamin, *Selected Writings 1913–1926*, volume 1, ed. Marcus Bullock and Michael W. Jennings (Cambridge, MA, and London: Harvard University Press, 1996), p. 262. (All further references to this edition will appear parenthetically in the text as *SW*, followed by volume and page references.)

19   The English term 'criticism', as used for Benjamin's *Kunstkritik*, does not wholly render the original term, which literally means art criticism. Granted in his 'Introduction' to *The Concept of Criticism in German Romanticism* Benjamin addressed the equivocation that adhered to Friedrich Schlegel's concept of *Kunstwerk*; while the latter covered both *Poesie* (literature) and art, more often than not it was used by Schlegel to refer to literature. This is the result, Benjamin added, of the fact that Schlegel omitted to provide a theory that clearly delimited poetic (or literary) expression from the other art forms (*SW* 1: 118). Yet, the English 'criticism' does not do justice to the *object* of Romantic art criticism (which could include paintings, as Novalis's notes on the Sistine Madonna, cited in the dissertation, indicate). In addition, the German *Kunstkritik* also resonates with Kant's *Kritik* (critique, critical philosophy). Though Benjamin meant to distinguish the Early Romantics' theory of objective reflection and their turn to the autonomy of art from Kant's subject-centred faculty of judgement, he sometimes played on the Kantian resonances of the term. See, for example, his analysis of the Early Romantics' indebtedness to the positive, but in end also negative, force of Kantian critique (*SW* 1: 142–3). I analyse the dialectics of critique (*Kritik*) in more detail in the introduction to *Critique of Violence: Between Poststructuralism and Critical Theory* (London and New York: Routledge, 2000), pp. 1–15.

20   Benjamin, *Correspondence*, p. 88.

21   See also Walter Benjamin, *Gesammelte Schriften*, ed. Rolf Tiedemann and Hermann Schweppenhäuser (Frankfurt a. M.: Suhrkamp, 1974–), 1.1: 86, and Michael Jennings, 'Benjamin as a Reader of Hölderlin: The Origins of Benjamin's Theory of Literary Criticism', *German Quarterly* 56 (1983): 544–62. Further references to the Suhrkamp edition of Benjamin's collected writings are cited in the text as *GS*, followed by volume and page numbers.

22   Benjamin's conception of a '*verkleinerte Welt*' may be related to Hölderlin's '*Welt im verringerten Maaßstab*'. See also Gerhard Kurz's notes on this Hölderlinian figure in 'Ordo inversus', p. 86.

23   See a letter Benjamin sent to Ernst Schoen, in Benjamin, *Correspondence*, p. 139.

24   For a quite different interpretation of Benjamin's understanding of sobriety and the Absolute, see Rodolphe Gasché, 'The Sober Absolute: On Benjamin and the Early Romantics', in this volume. Gasché proposes an interesting new reading of Benjamin's dissertation that goes against its standard reception, when he notes that it provides 'repeated, if not systematic criticism of Romantic philosophy'; furthermore, '[its] presentation of the main axioms of Romantic thought is not without ambivalence. At times Benjamin shows little sympathy, or even direct hostility toward the Romantics' insight.' Centring on the term 'sobriety', whose ambiguous sense – 'prosaic, plain, ordinary, sober' – is underscored, Gasché concludes that the study ends up rebuking the Early Romantics' so-called profanation (de-sacralization, de-divinizing) of the Absolute: 'Presented in the individualizing mode of prose, the sober Absolute appears as something absolutely prosaic – itself a fact, only the potentiation of the transitory contingency of the singular work.' While it is true that Benjamin's dissertation tendered occasional criticism of the Early Romantics, the study enthusiastically embraced the Romantic critical project, including Friedrich Schlegel's non-eidetic, 'mystical terminology' (*SW* 1: 139) – much as (in his early period, at least) Benjamin extolled Kant's mysticism (*SW* 1: 142; see also *GS* 6: 39). A different interpretation emerges from Benjamin's gloss of the 'prosaic' and 'sobriety', if, rather than reducing the 'sober' to the colloquial 'plain' and 'ordinary', one follows the genealogy of sobriety (*Nüchternheit*) back to its Platonic and Hölderlinian roots – meanings that Benjamin detected in the Early Romantics' theory of prose and in the 'prosaic'. Lauding the extraordinary richness of the Early Romantics' belief that the idea of poetry is prose, he linked it to Hölderlin's principle of the sobriety of art. 'This principle is the essentially quite new and still incalculably influential leading idea of the Romantic philosophy of art; what is perhaps the greatest epoch in the West's philosophy of art is distinguished by this basic notion. Its connection with the methodological procedure of that philosophy – namely, reflection – is obvious. In ordinary usage, the prosaic – that in which reflection as the principle of art appears uppermost – is, to be sure, a familiar metaphorical designation of the sober. As a thoughtful and collected posture, reflection is the antithesis of ecstasy, the mania of Plato. Just as, for the Early Romantics, light occasionally operates as a symbol of the medium of reflection, of infinite mindfulness, so Hölderlin, too, says: "Where are you, thoughtful one, who must always / Turn aside at times? Where are you, Light?" ' (*SW* 1: 175). As I suggest, Benjamin's investigation of sobriety – the necessary (ethical) limit to mere nebulous, unbounded ecstasy – already emerged in the early Hölderlin essay, where it culminates in an evocation of the Hölderlinian caesura (see the analysis below).

25   Hölderlin, *Essays and Letters on Theory*, pp. 45–6; for the German original, see Hölderlin, 'Reflexion', in Hölderlin, *Sämtliche Werke* 4.1: 233. Hölderlin's discussion of ecstasy, it has been argued, needs to be related to Plato's *Phaidrus*, as well as to Longinus's treatise

on the sublime. Wolfgang Binder first established this connection to Longinus (see his editorial comments in Hölderlin, *Sämtliche Werke*, 4.1: 233). Both the words 'temperance' (in Hölderlin's *Essays and Letters on Theory*, cited above) and 'sobriety' capture some of the multiple connotations associated with the Greek *sophrosune*, whose assets Socrates lauds in *Cratylus*.

26   Peter Szondi, 'Überwindung des Klassizismus: Der Brief an Böhlendorff vom 4. Dezember 1801', in *Schriften* (Frankfurt a. M.: Suhrkamp, 1978), 1: 346, 364. See also Lawrence J. Ryan, *Hölderlins Lehre vom Wechsel der Töne* (Stuttgart: W. Kohlhammer, 1960), p. 356.

27   Szondi, 'Überwindung', p. 366.

28   See Hölderlin, *Sämtliche Werke*, 2.2: 527. Benjamin's analysis focused on the first version of 'Dichtermut'. As he observed, 'a version that belongs between the earliest and the latest ("The Poet's Courage", second version) will not be discussed here, since it is less essential' (*SW* 1: 21).

29   In what follows, I cite from Stanley Corngold's expert translation, 'Two Poems by Friedrich Hölderlin – "The Poet's Courage" and "Timidity"' (*SW* 1: 18–36).

30   Johann Wolfgang von Goethe, 'Brief Goethes and K. F. v. Reinhard vom 31.12.1809', cited in Hans Gerhard Gräf, *Goethe über seine Dichtungen. Versuch einer Sammlung aller Äusserungen, des Dichters über seine poetischen Werke* (Frankfurt a. M.: Literarische Anstalt, 1901–14), 1: 862.

31   See, for example, E. Schwinger, 'Form und Inhalt', in *Historisches Wörterbuch der Philosophie*, ed. Joachim Ritter (Darmstadt: Wissenschaftliche Buchgesellschaft, 1971); Norbert von Hellingrath, *Pindarübertragungen von Hölderlin. Prolegomena zu einer Erstausgabe* (Leipzig: Breitkopf and Härtel, 1910); Elisabeth Rotten, *Goethes Urphänomen und die platonische Idee* (Marburg: (Hof-Buchdr.-Weimar), 1910); Reinhold Schwinger, *Innere Form. Ein Beitrag zur Definition des Begriffes auf Grund seiner Geschichte von Shaftesbury bis W. v. Humboldt* (Munich: C. H. Beck, 1934); Oskar Walzel, introduction to the *Goethe-Jubiläums-Ausgabe*, and Walzel, *Gehalt and Gestalt im Kunstwerk des Dichters* (Berlin: Athenaion, 1923). For a more recent use of the term, see Fredric Jameson, *Marxism and Form: Twentieth-Century Dialectical Theories of Literature* (Princeton, NJ: Princeton University Press, 1971), pp. 401–4, 409.

32   Goethe, 'Aus Goethes Brieftasche', *Weimarer Ausgabe* 1: 37, 313; cited in Rotten, *Goethes Urphänomen*, p. 84.

33   Paul Natorp, *Kant and die Marburger Schule. Vortrag gehalten in der Sitzung der Kunstgesellschaft zu Halle a.S. am 27 April 1912* (Berlin: Verlag von Reuther & Reichard, 1912), p. 7.

34   See also Benjamin's 'Theses on the Problem of Identity' (*SW* 1: 75–7) ['Identitätsthesen' *GS* 6: 27–9], as well as his letter to Scholem of 23 December 1917 (Benjamin, *Correspondence*, pp. 105–7).

35   On the place of this figure in Benjamin's work and on Hölderlin more specifically, see also Rainer Nägele, *Theater, Theory, Speculation: Walter Benjamin and the Scenes of Modernity* (Baltimore and London: Johns Hopkins University Press, 1991), and 'Benjamin's Ground', *Studies in Twentieth-Century Literature* 11.1 (Fall 1986): 5–24.

36   Hölderlin, *Sämtliche Werke*, 4: 241–65.

37 See also Adorno's discussion of this point in his essay 'Parataxis'.

38 Here one finds possibly a reference to Shaftesbury's *The Moralists*, in which the order of 'Dead Forms' stood for the first and lowest degree of beauty.

39 On this point, see also Dieter Henrich, 'Hölderlin über Urteil and Sein. Eine Studie zur Entstehungsgeschichte des Idealismus', *Hölderlin-Jahrbuch* 14 (1965–6): 88.

40 On the notion of death as *Grenzsituation*, see Karl Jaspers, 'Tod', cited in Hans Eberling (ed.), *Der Tod in der Moderne* (Frankfurt a. M.: Syndikat, 1984), pp. 63–70.

41 See Adorno, 'Parataxis'; Philippe Lacoue-Labarthe, 'Die Zäsur des Spekulativen', trans. Werner Hamacher and Peter Krumme, *Hölderlin-Jahrbuch* 22 (1980–1): 203–31; Peter Szondi, 'Versuch über das Tragische', in Szondi, *Schriften*, 2.

42 Translated by Michael Hamburger.

43 Hölderlin, *Sämtliche Werke*, 2: 90.

44 For a more elaborate interpretation of the Goethe essay, see Beatrice Hanssen, *Walter Benjamin's Other History*, Chapter 5.

45 For a critical account of Gundolf's Goethe monograph, see also Benjamin's unpublished fragment, 'Comments on Gundolf's *Goethe*' (*SW* 1: 97–9).

CHAPTER 10

1 Martin Heidegger, *Hölderlins Hymnen 'Germanien' und 'Der Rhein', Gesamtausgabe* (Frankfurt a. M.: Klostermann, 1980), 39: 213–14. Henceforth cited in the text as *GA* 39. All translations in this essay have been prepared for this volume, and all references and notes have been added by the translator.

2 The reference is to the French translation of 'Hölderlin und das Wesen der Dichtung', 'Hölderlin et l'essence de la poésie', in Heidegger, *Qu'est ce que la Métaphysique* (Paris: Gallimard, 1937). As Michel Deguy and François Fédier noted upon its re-edition, this translation 'magisterially inaugurated the epoch of Heidegger translation in France, and truly initiated a first public to his readings'. See their comments in the French translation of *Erläuterungen zu Hölderlins Dichtung, Approche der Hölderlin* (Paris: Gallimard, 1973), p. 39.

3 Heidegger, *Hölderlins Hymnen 'Germanien' und 'Der Rhein', Gesamtausgabe* 39: 1.

4 Heidegger, ' "Nur noch ein Gott kann uns retten." *Spiegel*-Gespräch mit Martin Heidegger am 23 September 1966', in *Der Spiegel* (31 May 1976): 20.

5 Heidegger, 'Brief über den "Humanismus" ', in *Wegmarken, Gesamtausgabe*, 9: 338–9.

6 See Heidegger, *Einführung in die Metaphysik* (Tübingen: Niemeyer, 1987), p. 131.

7 See the letter to Casimir Ulrich Böhlendorff of 4 December 1801, in *SA* 1: 425.

8 Heidegger, 'Brief über den "Humanismus" ', 9: 338.

9   Heidegger, *Hölderlins Hymnen*, 39: 290, for example.

10   See, for example, Lacoue-Labarthe, *Le Mythe nazi* (La Tour d'Aigues: Editions de l'Aube, 1991), esp. pp. 32–50; trans. Brian Holmes as 'The Nazi Myth' in *Critical Inquiry* 16: 2 (1990): esp. pp. 296–303; 'The Essence of National Socialism and Its Destiny', trans. Simon Sparks, in Philippe Lacoue-Labarthe and Jean-Luc Nancy, *Retreating the Political*, ed. Simon Sparks (London: Routledge, 1996), 148–56.

11   See Heidegger, 'Der Weg zur Sprache', in *Unterwegs zur Sprache, Gesamtausgabe* (Frankfurt a. M.: Klostermann, 1985), 12: 234–8.

12   Pierre Klossowski, 'Entre Marx et Fourier', *Le Monde*, 31 May 1969, supplement: special page devoted to Walter Benjamin.

13   Martin Heidegger, *Erläuterungen zu Hölderlins Dichtung, Gesamtausgabe* (Frankfurt a. M.: Klostermann, 1988), 4: 36–7.

14   Ibid., 4: 37.

15   Ibid.

16   Walter Benjamin, 'Zwei Gedichte von Friedrich Hölderlin', in *Gesammelte Schriften*, ed. Rolf Tiedemann and Hermann Schweppenhäuser (Frankfurt a. M.: Suhrkamp, 1977), 2.1: 105–26. (Hereafter *GS*.)

17   '*Timidité ou "gaucherie".*' Lacoue-Labarthe's point of reference here is the French translation of the essay by Maurice de Gondillac, who chooses *timidité*. See 'Deux poèmes de Friedrich Hölderlin', in *Mythe et violence* (Paris: Denoël, 1971), pp. 51–78.

18   *GS* 2.1: 105.

19   Since, for reasons he outlines, Lacoue-Labarthe maintains de Gondillac's translation of *das Gedichtete* by *le dictamen*, a word as 'foreign' to French ears as to English, the term 'dictamen', rather than 'poetized', has been retained throughout.

20   *GS* 2.1: 105–6.

21   *GS* 1.1: 125.

22   *GS* 2.1: 105.

23   *GS* 2.1: 105–6.

24   Immanuel Kant, *Kritik der reinen Vernunft*, ed. Raymund Schmidt (Hamburg: Felix Meiner, 1956), A 141; B 181.

25   *GS* 2.1: 106–7.

26   See Heidegger, 'dichterisch wohnet der Mensch …', in *Vorträge und Aufsätze* (Pfullingen: Neske, 1954), pp. 181–98.

27   *GS* 2.1: 107.

28   Thomas Mann, 'Freud and the Future', in *Essays of Three Decades* (New York: Philosophy Library, 1947), 425.

29   *GS* 2.1:107.

30   *GS* 2.1:108.

31   Ibid., 2.1:109–10.

32   *GS* 2.1:114.

33   See Theodor W. Adorno, 'Parataxis', in *Noten zur Literatur III, Gesammelte Schriften* (Frankfurt a. M.: Suhrkamp, 1971), 9:447–91.

34   *GS* 2.1:123.

35   *GS* 2.1:124.

36   Ibid.

37   *GS* 2.1:125.

38   *GS* 2.1:125–6.

39   *GS* 2.1:126.

40   *GS* 1.1:100–1.

41   See Jean-Christophe Bailly, *Le Fin de l'hymne* (Paris: Bourgeois, 1991).

42   Jacques Lacan, *L'Ethique de la psychanalyse: Le séminaire de Jacques Lacan*, Vol. 7 (Paris: Seuil, 1986).

CHAPTER 11

1   Walter Benjamin, 'Selbstanzeige der Dissertation', *Gesammelte Schriften* (Frankfurt a. M.: Suhrkamp), 1.2:707–8 (translation mine). Throughout this essay, and unless otherwise noted, the term 'Romantics' refers specifically to the group of German writers who collectively inaugurated the era of Romanticism at Jena during the late 1780s and early 1790s, foremost amongst this group being Friedrich and August Wilhelm Schlegel, Novalis and Ludwig Tieck.

2   *Der Begriff der Kunstkritik in der deutschen Romantik, Gesammelte Schriften, GS* 1.1:11. Subsequent references to Benjamin's writings will be to this edition. Translations used in this essay, unless otherwise indicated, are from the first volume of the *Selected Writings*, ed. Michael Jennings et al. (Cambridge: Harvard University Press, 1996). References to this edition and volume of the Harvard translations (*SW* 1) will follow the parenthetical references to the German edition.

3   To Ernst Schoen, 8 November 1918:

> From the Romantic concept of criticism, the modern concept of criticism has arisen; however, for the Romantics, 'criticism' was a quite esoteric concept (of which they had several but none as secret) which based on mystical presuppositions whatever concerned knowledge and which in whatever concerns art includes the best insights of contemporary and later poets in a new concept of art which is in many respects *our* concept of art.

Walter Benjamin, *Briefe*, ed. Theodor Adorno and Gershom Scholem (Frankfurt a. M.: Suhrkamp, 1978), 1: 203/ *The Correspondence of Walter Benjamin* (Chicago, IL: University of Chicago Press, 1994), p. 136.

4   This criticism by Benjamin is accompanied by the following statement: '[Schlegel] wanted to define this concept [of the idea of art] as an idea in the Platonic sense, as a *proteron te phusei*, as the real ground of all empirical works, and he committed the old error of confounding "abstract" and "universal" when he believed he had to make that ground into an individual' (*GS* 1.1: 90/*SW* 1: 167). As Rodolphe Gasché has pointed out, Benjamin's critique of Schlegel's error may also be in error to the extent that Benjamin confuses the Platonic idea with the Romantic Idea. See, 'The Sober Absolute', Chapter 3, this volume.

5   Benjamin's account of this problem occurs in an argument that identifies Goethe's ideal of art as nature and distinguishes between the presentation of nature in the artwork and the presentation of the truth of nature. The passage is as follows:

> It is not in eternal becoming, in creative movement within the medium of forms [of the Romantics], that the primal source of art, according to Goethe's understanding, resides. Art itself does not create its archetypes, they rest, prior to all created work, in that sphere of art where art is not creation but nature. To grasp the idea of nature and make it serviceable for the archetype of art (for pure content) was, in the end, Goethe's mission ... the proposition that the artwork imitates nature can be correct, if, as the content of the artwork, only nature itself and not the truth of nature is understood. It follows from this that the correlate of the content, what is presented (hence nature), cannot be compared with the content. (*GS* 1.1: 112/*SW* 1: 180)

6   See, Benjamin, *Der Begriff der Kunstkritik*, pp. 159–61, and Philippe Lacoue-Labarthe and Jean-Luc Nancy, *The Literary Absolute* (Albany: SUNY Press, 1988), pp. 101–19.

7   Although in this early essay some of the topics that guide the later discussion of Goethe and the Romantics already emerge, most notably, the question of poetic form and Benjamin's reference to the *Gedichtete* (the 'poetized') by which Benjamin refers to what can be analysed in the work of art. On this early writing on Hölderlin, see the essays by Tom McCall, 'Plastic Time and Poetic Middles: Benjamin's Hölderlin', in *Walter Benjamin on Romanticism*, ed. David Ferris, *Studies in Romanticism* 31: 4 (Winter 1992), and David Wellbery, 'Benjamin's Theory of the Lyric', in *Benjamin's Ground*, ed. Rainer Nägele (Detroit, MI: Wayne State University Press, 1988).

8   That Goethe should be chosen ground for Benjamin's examination of the concept of criticism opened by the dissertation is already signalled within the dissertation when Benjamin cites Friedrich Schlegel's remark on Goethe's *Wilhelm Meister*: 'no other is to the same degree a work' (*GS* 1.1: 75/157).

9   This same passage also exists as an earlier draft of an unpublished fragment written under the title, 'The Theory of Criticism' (*GS* 1.3: 833–5/*SW* 1: 217–19). This fragment dates from 1919–20, precisely the time when Benjamin writes the dissertation on the Romantics. In some respects this fragment is more explicit than the expression of the same ideas in the published version of the essay on Goethe's *Wahlverwandtschaften* and will be referred to where appropriate.

10 The use of the word 'affinity' to describe this relation is also Benjamin's as a later part of the passage under discussion here confirms: 'the work of art ... enters into the most precise relation to philosophy through its affinity (*Verwandtschaft*) with the ideal of the problem' (*GS* 1.1: 172/*SW* 1: 334). Immediately prior to describing this relation,

Benjamin had also spoken of the affinity between certain 'constructions' and the ideal of the problem. On this occasion 'affinität' is used (*GS* 1.1: 172/*SW* 1: 334).

11 Only in the fragment known as 'Theorie der Kunstkritik' does Benjamin explicitly describe 'the ideal of the problem' in philosophy. This description is as follows: 'The ideal of the problem is an idea which is referred to as an ideal because it refers not to the immanent form of the problem but rather to the transcendent content of its answer, even though [it refers to this content] only through the concept of the problem itself, in the concept of the unity of its answer' (*GS* 1.3: 833–4/*SW* 1: 218; translation modified). As this passage still shows, what remains at stake is the knowledge and recognition of this reference, this indicating (*bezeichnen*), if the critical task Benjamin seeks to preserve after the Romantics is to be authorized.

12 It is beyond the scope of the present chapter to develop fully the interplay between the *Verwandtschaft* of Goethe's text and Benjamin's critical position.

13 Philippe Lacoue-Labarthe, 'The Caesura of the Speculative' in *Typography* (Cambridge: Harvard University Press, 1989), p. 212. The relation of Hölderlin to Benjamin would be given a different twist by Lacoue-Labarthe's argument in this essay since, in distinction to what Benjamin seeks to establish for criticism through the notion of a 'pure problem' of criticism and the ideal of the problem in philosophy, Lacoue-Labarthe emphasizes the singularity of Hölderlin within a history 'not solely empirical, but not ideal or pure either' (p. 212). For Lacoue-Labarthe, the history to which Hölderlin belongs is the 'history of the completion of philosophy' (p. 212). It is in turning away from, that is, by systematically and rigorously evading such completion, that Benjamin preserves criticism. As Benjamin and Hölderlin would then be witness to, the limit of criticism makes no judgement about the authority of criticism, thereby assuring both its preservation and deconstruction.

CHAPTER 12

1 Walter Benjamin, *Selected Writings, Volume 1*, ed. Marcus Bullock and Michael Jennings (Cambridge, MA: Harvard University Press, 1996), p. 355. All further page references appear parenthetically in the text.

2 See, for example, Winfried Menninghaus, 'Das Ausdruckslose. Walter Benjamins Kritik des Schönen durch das Erhabene', in *Walter Benjamin (1892–1940) zum 100. Geburtstag*, ed. Uwe Steiner (Bern/New York: P. Lang, 1992), pp. 33–76.

3 See, in this respect, Fritz Gutbrodt, 'Wahl: Verwandschaft. Benjamins Siegel', in *Modern Languages Notes* 106 (1991): 555–88.

4 For a discussion of this reading of Freud and the psychoanalytic reformualtion of the 'Messianic' in Benjamin's late work, see Sigrid Weigel, *Entstellte Ähnlichkeit. Zur theoretischen Schreibweise in Walter Benjamins Schriften* (Frankfurt a. M.: Fischer, 1997), translated as *Body- and Image-Space: Re-Reading Walter Benjamin* (London: Routledge, 1996).

5 Compare Stéphane Mosès, 'Über die erkenntnistheoretischen Voraussetzungen der Psychoanalyse', in Sigmund Freud, *Einführung in die Psychoanalyse* (Hamburg: Europäische Verlagsanstalt, 1994), pp. 23–58.

6 As a prototype for this phenomenon one might name Barnett Newman, who, with his programmatic text; 'The Sublime is Now' (1948), introduced a renaissance of the sublime, and who integrates in his own work Christian, Jewish and Native-American motifs

without differentiation. See Barnett Newman, *Schriften und Interviews 1925–1970* (Bern/Berlin: Grachnang & Springer, 1990).

7   For the contemporary debate, see *Die Gegenwart der Kunst. Ästhetische und religiöse Erfahrung heute*, ed. Jörg Hermann, Andreas Mertin and Eveline Valtink (Munich: Fink, 1998).

8   Friedrich Hölderlin, 'Anmerkungen zum Oedipus', in Hölderlin, *Sämtliche Werke und Briefe*, ed. Michael Knaupp (Munich: C. Hanser, 1992) 2: 309–16.

9   One could also say that this is the place where his Hölderlin studies and his conversations with Scholem cross each other.

CONTRIBUTORS

ANDREW BENJAMIN is Professor of Critical Theory at Monash University in Melbourne, Australia. His most recent publications include *Present Hope: Philosophy, Architecture, Judaism* (London: Routledge, 1997), *Architectural Philosophy* (London: Athlone, 2000) and *Philosophy's Literature* (Manchester: Clinamen, 2001).

JOSH COHEN is Lecturer in English at Goldsmiths College, University of London. He is the author of *Spectacular Allegories: Postmodern American Writing and the Politics of Seeing* (London: Pluto Press, 1998), and essays on modern philosophy, literature, and cultural theory. His *Interrupting Auschwitz: Art, Religion, Philosophy* (London: Continuum, 2003) is forthcoming.

DAVID S. FERRIS is Professor of Comparative Literature and Humanities at the University of Colorado, Boulder. He is the author of *Theory and the Evasion of History* (Baltimore, MD: Johns Hopkins University Press, 1993) and *Silent Urns: Romanticism, Hellenism, Modernity* (Stanford, CA: Stanford University Press, 2000). He is also the editor of *Walter Benjamin: Theoretical Questions* (Stanford, CA: Stanford University Press, 1996) and *The Cambridge Companion to Walter Benjamin* (Cambridge: Cambridge University Press, forthcoming).

RODOLPHE GASCHÉ is Eugenio Donato Professor of Comparative Literature at the State University of New York, Buffalo. In 1994, his *Inventions of Difference: On Jacques Derrida* (Cambridge, MA: Harvard University Press) appeared. He is also the author of *The Tain of the Mirror: Derrida and the Philosophy of Reflection* (Cambridge, MA: Harvard University Press, 1986), *The Wild Card of Reading: On Paul de Man* (Cambridge, MA: Harvard University Press, 1998), and, most recently, published *Of Minimal Things: Studies on the Notion of Relation* (Stanford, CA: Stanford University Press, 1999).

BEATRICE HANSSEN is Professor of German at the University of Georgia, Athens. She is the author of *Walter Benjamin's Other History: Of Stones, Animals, Human Beings, and Angels* (Berkeley, CA: University of California Press, 1998, 2000), *Critique of Violence: Between Poststructuralism and Critical Theory* (London: Routledge, 2000), and co-editor of *The Turn to Ethics* (London: Routledge, 2000).

PHILIPPE LACOUE-LABARTHE is Professor of Philosophy and Aesthetics at the University of Strasbourg. His publications in English include *Typography: Mimesis, Philosophy, Politics* (Cambridge, MA: Harvard University Press, 1989),

Heidegger, Art and Politics: The Fiction of the Political (Oxford: Blackwell, 1990), and *Musica Ficta: Figures of Wagner* (Stanford, CA: Stanford University Press, 1994). He translated Hölderlin's own translation of Sophocles's *Antigone* into French.

BETTINE MENKE is Professor of Comparative Literature at the University of Erfurt, Germany. Her many publications include *Sprachfiguren. Name–Allegorie– Bild nach Walter Benjamin* (Munich: Fink, 1991), and, most recently, *Prosopopoiia. Stimme und Text bei Brentano, Hoffmann, Kleist und Kafka* (Munich: Fink, 2000).

WINFRIED MENNINGHAUS is Professor of General and Comparative Literature at the Free University, Berlin. His many publications include: *Walter Benjamins Theorie der Sprachmagie* (Frankfurt a. M.: Suhrkamp, 1980); *Schwellenkunde, Walter Benjamins Passage des Mythos* (Frankfurt a. M.: Suhrkamp, 1986); *Unendliche Verdopplung. Die frühromantische Grundlegung der Kunsttheorie im Begriff absoluter Selbstreflexion* (Frankfurt a. M.: Suhrkamp, 1987); and *Ekel. Theorie und Geschichte einer starken Empfindung* (Frankfurt a. M.: Suhrkamp, 1999).

ANTHONY PHELAN is Fellow of Keble College and Faculty Lecturer in German at Oxford University, England. He is the author of *Rilke: Neue Gedichte* (London: Grant & Cutler, 1992) and editor of *The Weimar Dilemma: Intellectuals in the Weimar Republic* (Manchester: Manchester University Press, 1985). The present essay on Benjamin's dissertation is part of a larger project on the Romantic novel and its successors.

FRED RUSH is Assistant Professor of Philosophy at the University of Notre Dame. He has published on Kant, Hegel, Heidegger, critical theory, German Romanticism, and contemporary aesthetics, and is the editor of the forthcoming *Cambridge Companion to Critical Theory* (Cambridge: Cambridge University Press). At present, he is completing a book entitled *Irony and Idealism*, on the philosophical significance of the concept of irony, from Early Romanticism to Kierkegaard.

SIGRID WEIGEL is Professor of Comparative Literature at the Technical University, Berlin, and Director of the *Zentrum für Literaturforschung*, Berlin. Among her books are *Body- and Image-Space: Re-Reading Walter Benjamin* (London: Routledge, 1996); *Entstellte Ähnlichkeit. Walter Benjamins theoretische Schreibweise* (Frankfurt a. M.: Fischer, 1997); and, most recently, *Ingeborg Bachmann. Hinterlassenschaften unter Wahrung des Briefgeheimnisses* (Vienna: Zsolnay, 1999). She is also co-editor of *Trauma. Zwischen Psychoanalyse und kulturellem Deutungsmuster* (Cologne: Böhlau, 1999); *Lesbarkeit der Kultur. Literaturwissenschaft zwischen Kulturtechnik und Ethnographie* (Munich: Fink, 2000); and *Gershom Scholem. Literatur und Rhetorik* (Cologne: Böhlau, 2000).

INDEX

Adorno, Theodor Wiesengrund 18, 123, 134, 139–42, 157, 169, 175, 229n., 233n.
Allemann, Beda 170
Apollo 147, 153, 158
Aristotle 150

Bataille, Georges 167
Baudelaire, Charles 11, 102, 105, 108, 110
Benjamin, Walter
  'Announcement of the Journal *Angelus Novus*' 4, 207n.
  'Der Begriff der Kunstkritik in der deutschen Romantik' ('The Concept of Criticism in German Romanticism') 1–6, 9–18, 19–50, 52–68, 69–82, 99–102, 124, 142–8, 158, 161, 181–8, 235n.
  'Comment's on Gundolf's *Goethe*' 237n.
  'Commentaries on Poems by Brecht' ('Kommentare zu Gedichten von Brecht') 88
  'Fate and Character' 159
  'Goethe's Elective Affinities' 5, 6, 107, 141, 143, 144, 151, 158–62, 170, 183–94, 197–206
  'On the Image of Proust' 102, 104–6
  'Franz Kafka' 102, 103
  'On Language as Such and on the Language of Man' 28, 111–22, 124
  'The Life of Students' 10
  'On the Middle Ages' 146
  Das Passagen-Werk (*The Arcades Project*) 3
  'The Role of Language in Trauerspiel and Tragedy' 85, 204
  'The Task of the Translator' 4, 83, 102, 103, 104, 110, 143, 202, 208n.
  'Two Poems by Friedrich Hölderlin' 5, 139–62, 169–79, 188, 234n., 235n.
  Ursprung des deutschen Trauerspiels (Origin of the German *Trauerspiel*) 4, 83, 85, 86, 87, 89, 90, 132, 133, 134, 135, 142, 145, 146, 150, 158, 159, 161, 162

Blanchot, Maurice 107, 227n.
Böhlendorff, Casimir Ulrich 147
Buber, Martin 4, 12, 13
Büchner, Georg 233n.

Cassirer, Ernst 232n.
Chladni, Ernst Florens Friedrich 95
Cohen, Hermann 17, 232n.
Corbin, Henry 164
Cornelius, Hans 123, 229n.

de Man, Paul 90, 91, 145
Deleuze, Gilles 99,
Derrida, Jacques 225n., 226n., 228n.
Dilthey, Wilhelm 2, 154, 160
Dionysus 158

Eichendorff, Joseph von 75, 80

Fichte, Johann Gottlieb 1–3, 19–49, 55, 56, 57, 70, 71, 73, 77, 81, 99, 125, 126, 128, 139, 144–6, 155, 207n., 210n., 213n.
Flaubert, Gustave 81
Foucault, Michel 232n.
Frank, Manfred 139
Freud, Sigmund 123

Gandillac, Maurice de 170
Gautier, Théophile 81,
George, Stefan 2, 81, 143, 160, 201
Goethe, Johann Wolfgang von 3, 5, 18, 54, 55, 60, 70, 76, 79, 80, 149–150, 153, 158–162, 181, 182, 183–94, 197–206, 240n.
Gundolf, Friedrich 2, 160, 201, 202, 203, 205

Hamann, Johann Georg 116, 130, 131, 231n.
Harsdörffer, Georg Philipp 85, 92, 93, 94
Hegel, Georg Wilhelm Friedrich 21, 124, 127, 170, 173, 224n., 225n., 230n.
Herder, Johann Gottfried 130, 145, 149
Herbertz, Richard 144

Heidegger, Martin   10, 11, 14, 139, 142, 163–79
Heinle, Friedrich C.   143
Hellingrath, Norbert von   143
Hölderlin, Friedrich   5, 6, 11, 13, 18, 65, 69, 72, 73, 90, 104, 139–58, 163, 164, 165, 166, 167, 168, 169–79, 194, 195, 198, 205, 241n.
Homer   166
Huch, Ricarda   36
Husserl, Edmund   232n.

Jakobson, Roman   46, 47, 91, 222n.
Jean Paul   4, 159
Jünger, Ernst   169

Kafka, Franz   98, 108, 123, 139
Kant, Immanuel   1, 2, 5, 14, 15, 16, 17, 30, 49, 50, 54, 78, 89, 111, 123, 124, 125, 126, 127, 132, 136, 149, 166, 170, 171, 172, 207n., 208n., 209n., 213n., 229n., 230n., 232n., 234n., 235n.
Kierkegaard, Søren   229n.
Kircher, Athanasius   84, 92, 93, 94
Klages, Ludwig   136
Kleist, Heinrich von   139
Klossowski, Pierre   167
Kurz, Gerhard   139

Lacan, Jacques   178
Lacoue-Labarthe, Philippe   4, 51, 100, 102, 104, 106, 145, 195, 217n.
Leibniz, Gottfried Wilhelm   74, 99, 127, 128, 132, 135, 217n.
Lessing, Gotthold Ephraim   79
Longinus, 1st cent.   235n., 236n.

Mach, Ernst   232n.
Mallarmé, Stéphane   81, 103
Mann, Thomas   173
Marx, Karl   124, 166
Merleau-Ponty, Jacques   75

Nancy, Jean-Luc   4, 51, 100, 102, 104, 106, 145
Natorp, Paul   150–1, 232n.
Nietzsche, Friedrich   10, 158, 165, 166, 168, 169, 232n.

Novalis (von Hardenberg, Friedrich)   1–6, 16, 19–49, 51–68, 69–82, 98, 99–102, 103, 106, 125, 126, 128, 129, 139, 143, 207n., 232n.

Ovid   85, 88, 94

Pannwitz, Rudolf   90
Pindar   72, 146, 174, 234n.
Plato   14, 62, 65, 120, 132, 136, 148, 151, 228n., 235n., 240n.
Plotinus   149
Proust, Marcel   102, 104, 105, 106

Rang, Florens Christian   107
Rilke, Rainer Maria   169
Ritter, Johann Wilhelm   89, 95, 96, 223n.
Rotten, Elisabeth   149
Rousseau, Jean-Jacques   170

Schelling, Friedrich Wilhelm   21, 29, 30, 33, 37, 38, 41, 45, 157, 167, 207n.
Schiller, Friedrich von   153, 156
Schlegel, August Wilhelm von   11, 16, 82, 99, 167
Schlegel, Friedrich von   1-6, 11, 14, 16, 19–49, 51–68, 69–82, 99–102, 125, 126, 128, 129, 143, 146, 167, 183, 184, 192, 207n, 211n., 214n., 231n.
Schlegel-Schelling, Caroline   207n.
Schleiermacher, Friedrich Daniel Ernst   16, 60, 207n.
Schoen, Ernst   10, 13, 17, 18, 180, 239n.
Scholem, Gershom   14, 15, 16, 17, 144, 169, 234n.
Shaftesbury, Anthony Ashley Cooper, Earl of   149
Shakespeare, William   78
Socrates   236n.
Sophocles   90, 143, 154, 157, 158, 177
Szondi, Peter   147, 148, 157

Tieck, Ludwig   16, 70, 207n.

Veit-Schlegel, Dorothea   207n.

Wackenroder, Wilhelm Heinrich   207n.
Wellek, René   214n.
Wittgenstein, Ludwig   232n.